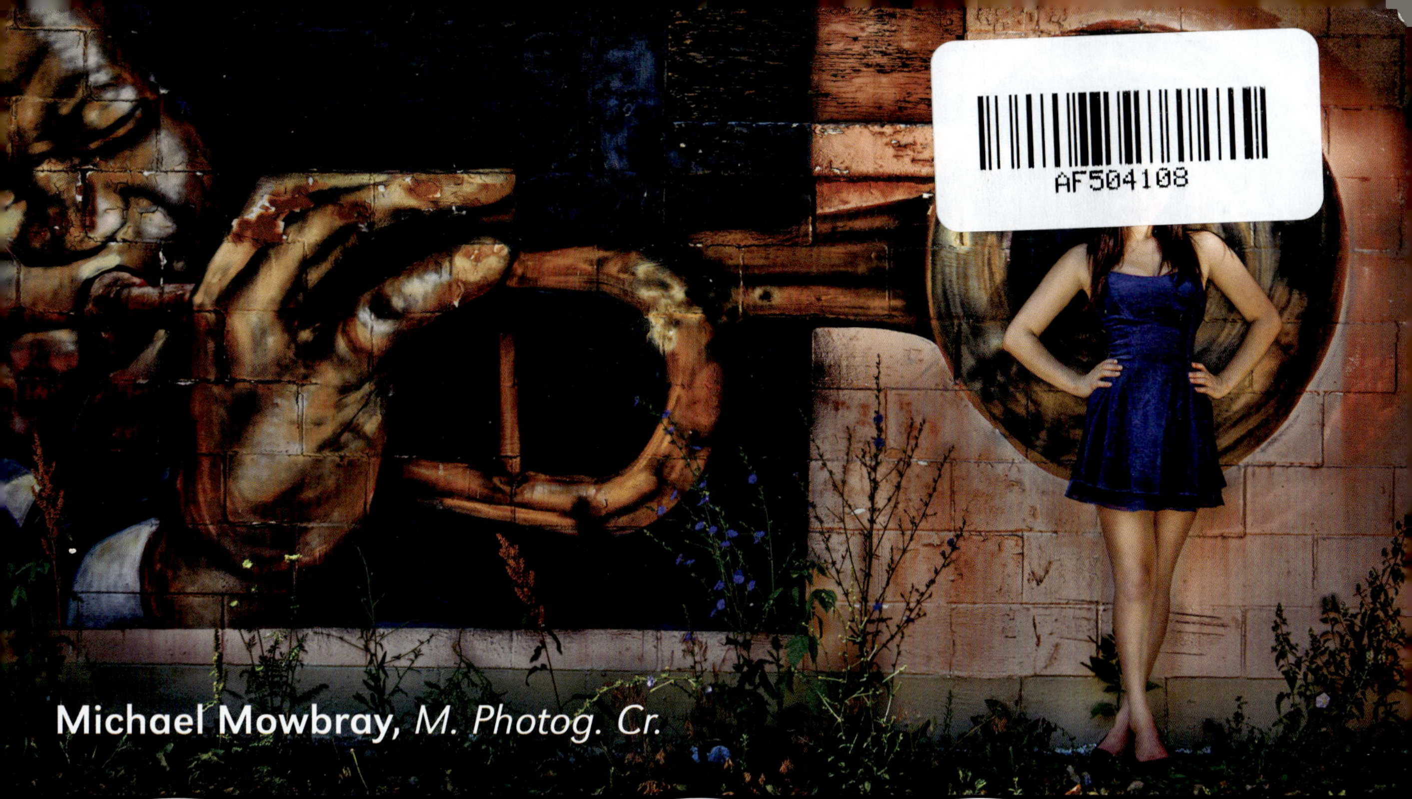

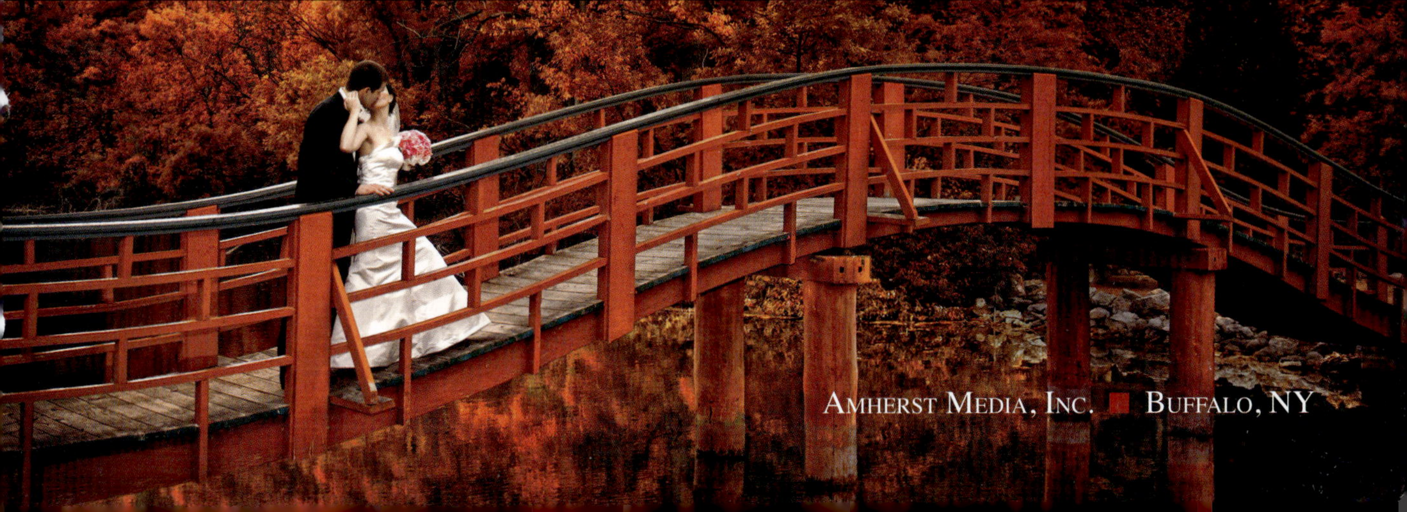

Michael Mowbray, *M. Photog. Cr.*

SHOOT
TO THRILL

Speedlight flash techniques for photographers

AMHERST MEDIA, INC. ■ BUFFALO, NY

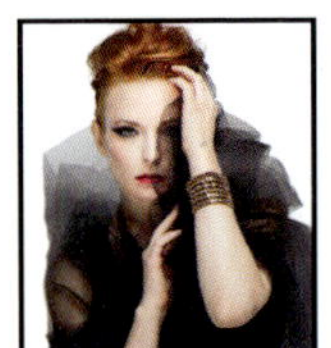

On the Front Cover:
Model: Erin Thomson
Hair/Makeup: Vanexa Yang
For more on this shoot, see pages 38–39.

Acknowledgments:
Contributing Hair/Makeup Artists: Vanexa Yang, Katrina King, Christy Grace
Assistants: Krystal Lamberty, Olivia Linden, Rachel Waldmer, Callie Strouf, Allison Halkey, Brianna Mowbray, James Stepp, David Grupa

Published by:
Amherst Media, Inc.
P.O. Box 586
Buffalo, N.Y. 14226
Fax: 716-874-4508
www.AmherstMedia.com

Publisher: Craig Alesse
Senior Editor/Production Manager: Michelle Perkins
Associate Editor: Barbara A. Lynch-Johnt
Associate Publisher: Kate Neaverth
Editorial Assistance from: Carey A. Miller, Sally Jarzab, John S. Loder
Business Manager: Adam Richards
Warehouse and Fulfillment Manager: Roger Singo

ISBN-13: 978-1-60895-691-3
Library of Congress Control Number: 2013952500
10 9 8 7 6 5 4 3 2 1

Check out Amherst Media's blogs at: http://portrait-photographer.blogspot.com/
http://weddingphotographer-amherstmedia.blogspot.com/

Contents

About the Author 8
Foreword 9

Section 1

Core Concepts

1. TTL Speedlight Exposure 12
Trying to Turn It Gray 12
Bend Exposure to Your Will. 12
Why Add Flash? 13
How Flash Interacts with TTL 15

2. High-Speed Sync (HSS/FP) 18
Maximum Flash-Sync Speed. 18
Deep Depth of Field 19

3. Flash Communication 20
Infrared Communication 20
Radio Communication. 20
Adjustments from the Camera Position 21

4. Hard Light or Soft Light 23
What It Means. 23
Controlling the Light Quality 23
Two Approaches 23

5. Lighting Kits and Setups 26
Studio Portrait Kit. 26
Location Corporate Headshot Kit 27

Environmental Portrait Kit. 28
Location Senior Portrait Kit. 28
Wedding Kit 29

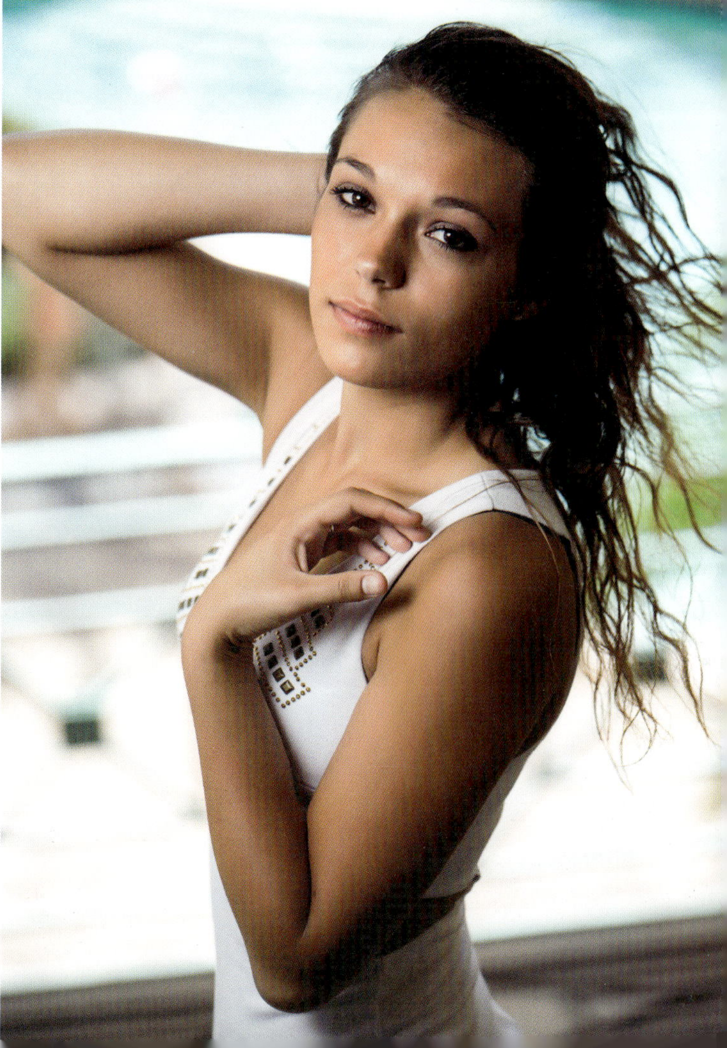

Speedlights in Action

1. In the Spotlight 32
Open doors to find inspiration

2. Madonna of the Rocks 35
Work with what nature gives you

3. Temptress 38
Find a muse to help you explore creatively

**4. When It's Art,
It's Not Cheating** 40
Go the extra distance to complete your vision

5. Bridge Players 42
Speedlighting in the rain

6. Arising 44
Create your own sunrise

7. Luminous 46
A play of light and dark

8. A Dip in the Sun 48
A new view on an old pose

9. Bench Pressing 50
Get low, get wide, shoot big

**10. Boldly Light Where
None Has Gone Before** 52
Create light to make any location fit your vision

11. Going Parasoling 54
Dramatic profile lighting in the midday sun

12. Rusty 56
Big softboxes can work outside

13. The Spiky Sun 58
Shoot deep and get a spiky sun

14. Katie 60
An alternate take on a classic studio portrait

**15. Making Light
Where There's Nothing at All** 62
Shoot at night

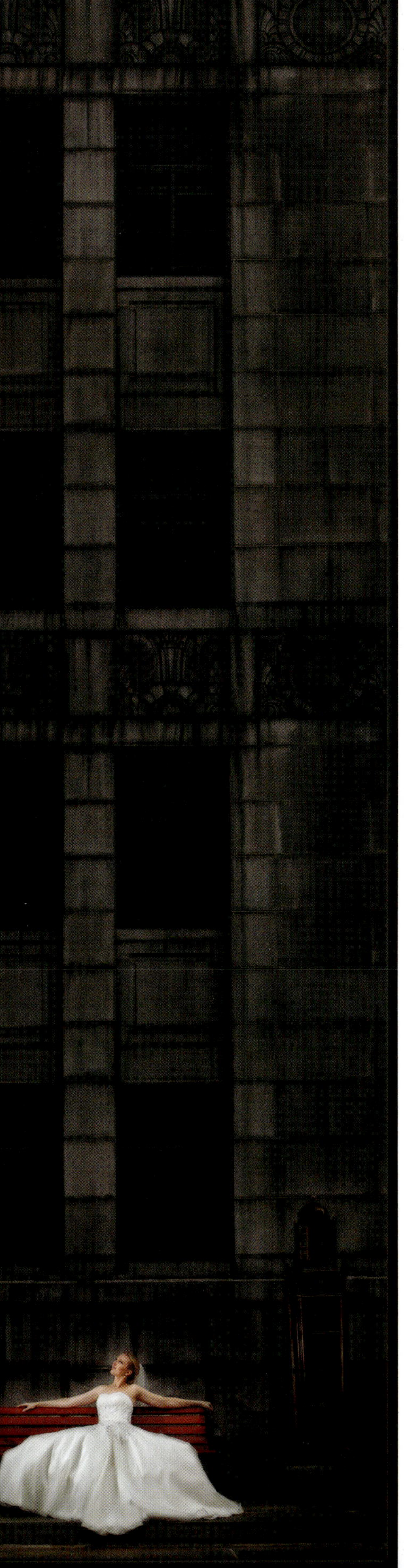

16. Is this Iowa? No, It's Phoenix 64
Fight the strong desert sun and win

17. Going Out on a Limb ... or Tree 66
Where studio strobes are not practical

18. Night and Day 68
Daytime for night in a noir concept

19. Sunset 70
The classic sunset portrait request

20. A Little Flare 72
Put the sun in your background

21. Black Swan 74
Uplight for drama

22. Raising the Level of Difficulty 76
Understand what TTL "sees"

23. Clean and Simple 78
Speedlights for classic studio portraiture

24. Bending the Light 80
The Lightbender softbox for a beauty portrait

25. Have Light, Will Travel 82
Beauty lighting in unusual locations

26. A Bounce and a Kiss 84
Bounced flash portraits on location

27. Getting a Little Punchy 86
Punch up boring, soft light outside

28. Wandering Eye 89
Nissin alternatives to Canon and Nikon flashes

29. Here, Kitty Kitty 92
TTL model images outside in the brutal cold

30. Many Ways to Soften 94
Simple diffusion panels, instant softboxes

31. Lighting with an Accent 96
Your speedlight as an accent light

32. Isolating the Subject 98
Using framing and light to pull attention

33. Zooming Is Far Out 100
Extra power and distance from your flash

34. A Kiss of Light 102
Cut the green color cast

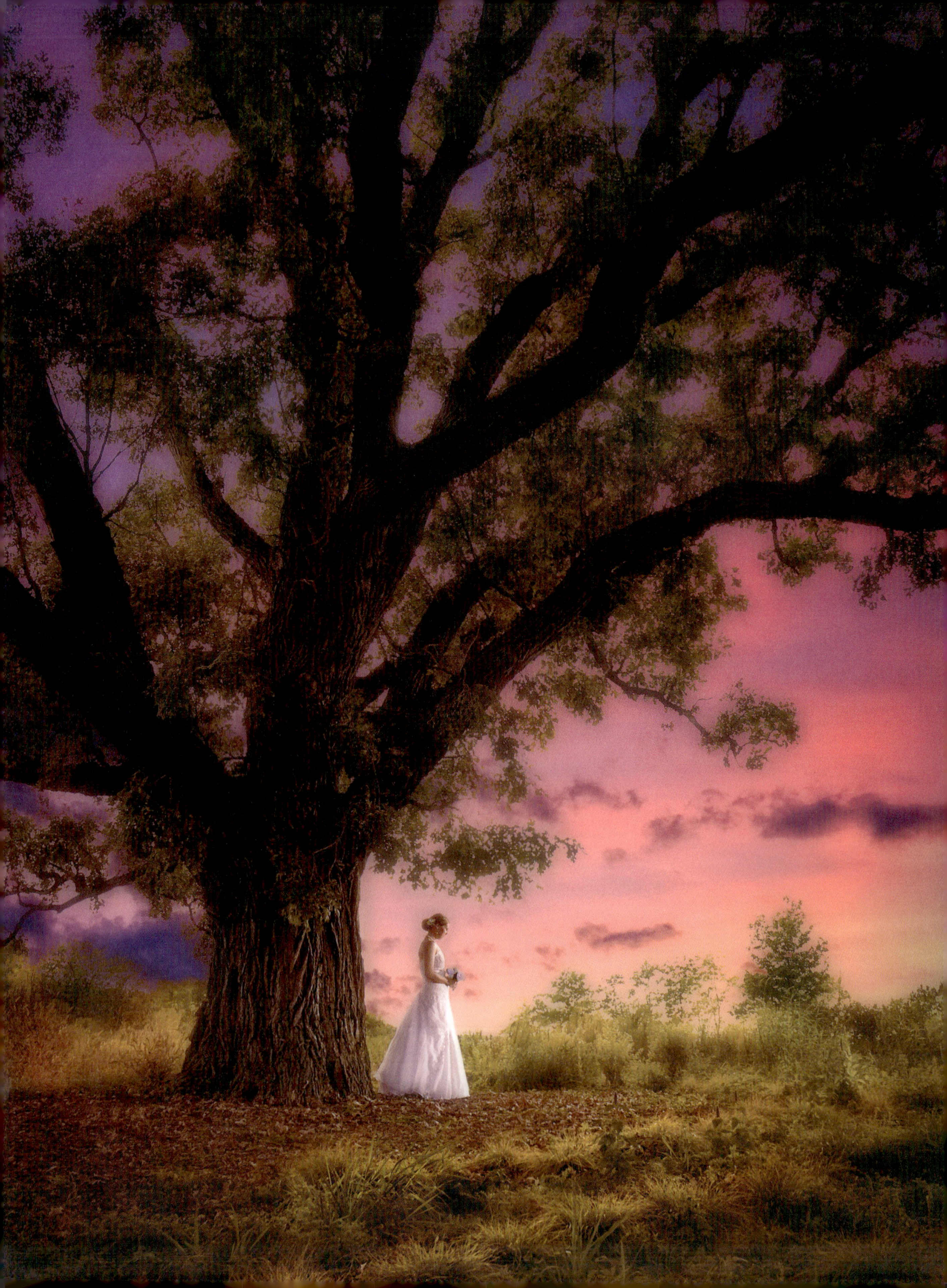

35. Theatrical Performance 104
Creative light in a historic theater

36. Brassy and Sassy 106
Cool and unusual places for portraiture

37. Quiet Beauty 109
Adding drama to a classic bridal portrait

38. Glam Black & White 110
A high-contrast black & white beauty portrait

39. Empire of the Sunset 112
Working with TTL to create a powerful portrait

40. Let There Be a Light 114
Speedlights and a little Photoshop magic

41. Doing Double Duty 116
Controlling the direction and spread of light

42. Joan of Arch 118
Lighting a dramatic bridal pose on location

43. Take the Dress for a Walk 120
The visual contrast of pretty versus gritty

44. Lighting Naturally 122
Soft speedlight to blend with outdoor light

45. Spice It Up with a Little Color 124
Using colored gels on location

46. Temperature, Temperature 126
Cool blue tones in tungsten light

47. Getting Soft on Location 128
Creating an instant softbox on location

48. Vintage Studio 130
Studio light modifiers with speedlights

49. Slash of Light 132
A simple spotlight effect with the Snootzie

50. Environmental Portraits 134
Executive portraits, quickly and efficiently

51. In Depth Lighting 136
Switch the depth of field with TTL speedlights

52. Spring Out of the Blossoms 138
Separate subjects from a busy background

53. Blue Sky at Night 140
Lighting a nighttime portrait

54. Building Family Connections 142
A new way to create winning family portraits

55. Xtreme Portraits for Athletes 144
Compositing leads to big sales

56. Filling the Blues 146
More than half the battle outdoors

57. TTL Studio Portraits 148
Know TTL better by using it for everything

58. Smoking Hot Bass Riff 150
Creating a cool look for an aging rocker

59. Going Commercial, Part 1 152
Complex lighting for a commercial project

60. Going Commercial, Part 2 154
Green screening for maximum flexibility

Conclusion 156
References 157
Index 158

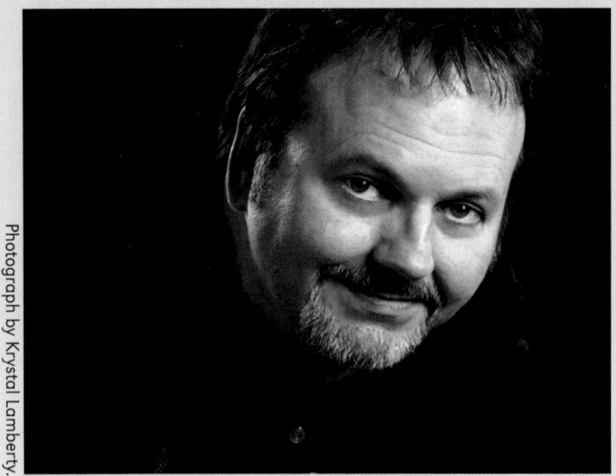

About the Author

Since opening Beautiful Portraits by Michael in 2001, Michael Mowbray (M. Photog, Cr.) has gone on to win many awards for his portraiture and was named International PPA Photographer of the Year Gold Medalist in 2011 and Bronze Medalist in 2012 and 2013. He has had the highest scoring wedding portrait in Wisconsin six out of the past seven years. He has won the prestigious Kodak Gallery Award five times and the Fuji Masterpiece Award for Outstanding Wedding Portraiture three times. Michael has also been named one of the Top 10 photographers in Wisconsin multiple times. He has earned both his Master Photographer and Photographic Craftsman degrees from Professional Photographers of America (PPA), and speaks around the country on the topics of weddings, seniors, and speedlights. See more of Michael's work at his consumer web site: www.beautifulportraits .com. His web site dedicated to photographer education can be found at: www.michael mowbray.com.

Foreword

Ever wonder if speedlights could work for lighting everything at your studio? I asked myself that very question several years ago. As a creative and technical challenge, I was determined to find the answer. And the answer? It was a resounding "Yes!" I now use speedlights for 99.9 percent of my lighting work. I use them in the studio and on location, on camera or off camera—everywhere.

Benefits

As primarily a senior and wedding photographer, I have found that speedlights fit my working style to a T. The funny thing is, I own a complete set of studio lights that are now sitting in the closet gathering dust. I've found that as I've built my lighting style around the mastery of speedlights, my work has gotten better. I've crafted a unique style, my sales have increased, and my workflow has become simpler. Plus, I've gotten my evenings back in the summer. I now schedule my senior sessions between 10AM and 6PM. I no longer chase light, I create it. And I no longer fear the sun, I embrace it.

What You'll Learn

In this book, I will show you how I use speedlights to create my portraiture, from dramatic award-winning imagery to bread-and-butter everyday work. After covering the basics, I will take you through the creation of sixty images.

I will break them down for you, showing you how the lighting was set up and sharing the creative and technical thoughts behind each portrait.

Gear

Throughout the book, I use the words "speedlights" and "flashes" interchangeably, and both terms refer to the common battery-powered flashgun that fits into the hot shoe on your camera (though I prefer to set mine free to roam the countryside). My cameras of choice are the Canon 5D MKIII and 5D MKII, and

"Ever wonder if speedlights could work for lighting everything at your studio?"

the primary flash model used to create the vast majority of images in the book is the Canon 580EX II. You do not need to exactly replicate the gear I used to create these images; Nikon gear works just as well, and other third-party brands of flashes (I'm partial to the Nissin di866 II) can give you a lot of the same features and some good bang for your buck.

Hopefully you can use this book as inspiration to jump-start your speedlight portraiture!

Core Concepts

It's important to understand several core concepts in order to best leverage the information in this book and maximize your speedlight photography. These concepts are:

1. TTL speedlight exposure control.
2. High-speed sync (HSS) for Canon cameras and focal plane (FP) for Nikon cameras.
3. How speedlights can communicate TTL information across distances.
4. The definitions of and differences between soft and hard light.

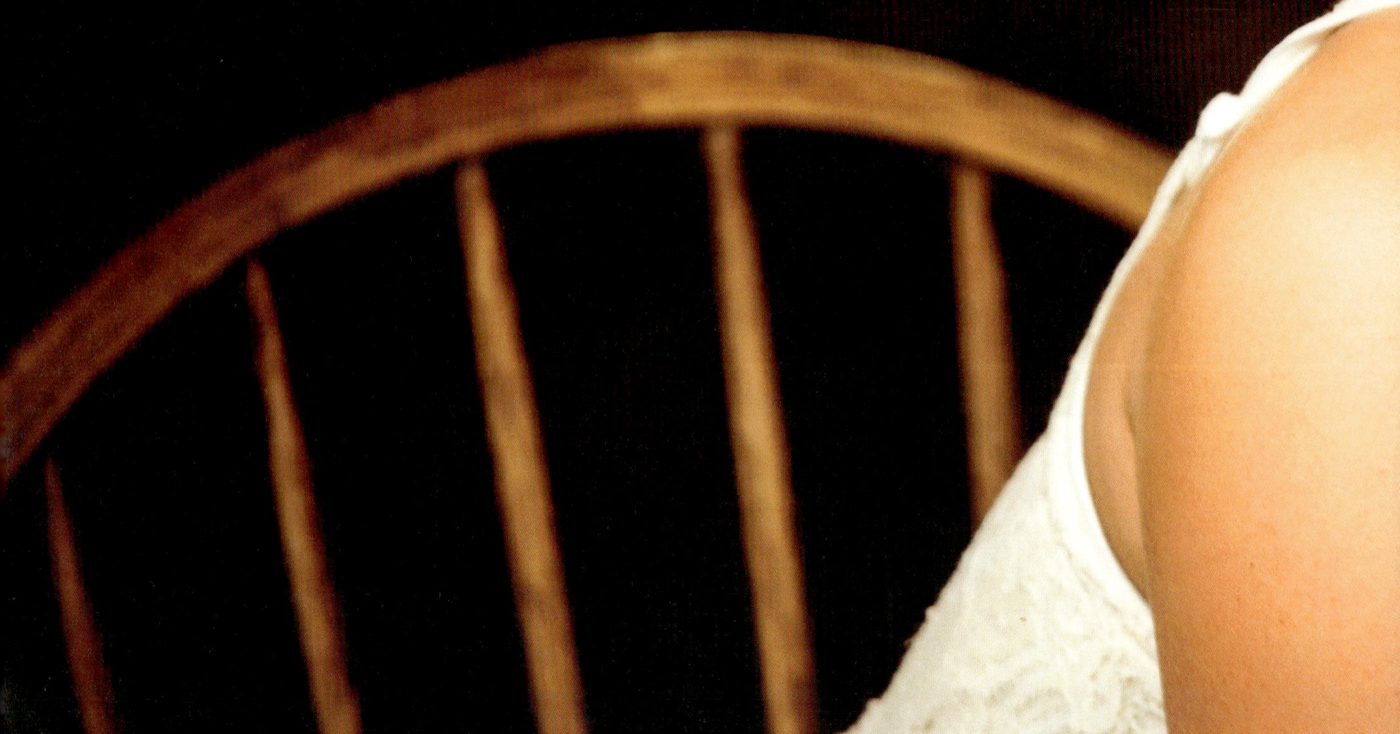

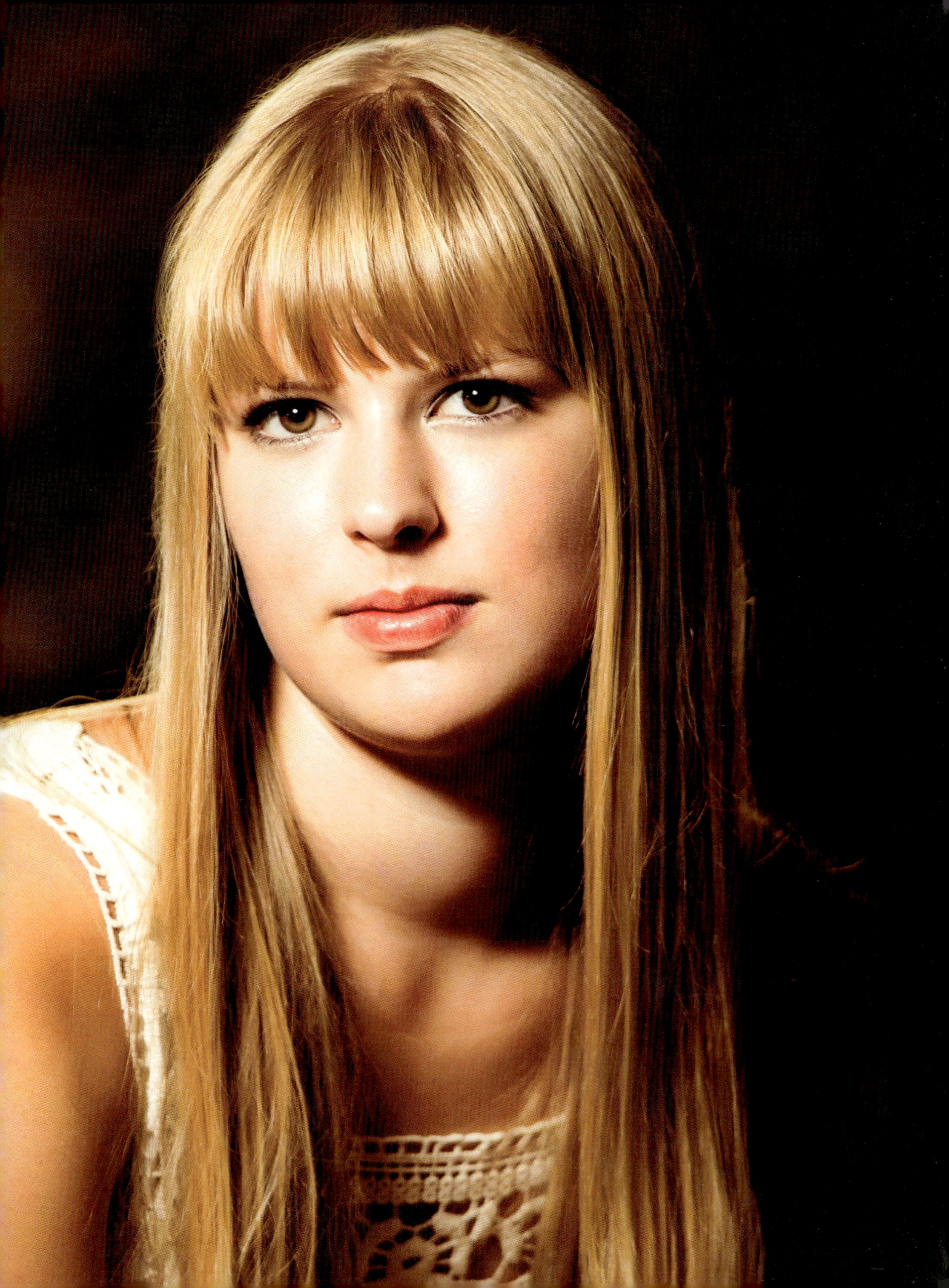

1. TTL Speedlight Exposure

At the center of my outdoor and location lighting technique with speedlights is an understanding of how the flash and the camera interact using the TTL (through the lens) metering system.

Trying to Turn It Gray

TTL hinges off the camera's built-in reflective metering system. A reflective metering system measures the light that bounces off the subject and comes back through the lens (hence "TTL"). Then, the reflective/TTL meter has one job and one job only: it has to make a recommended exposure setting that will balance out the scene to an average reading of 18 percent gray (or the mid-point on a histogram showing luminance; also called middle gray). Let me restate that in more simple terms: your camera's metering system wants to turn everything into middle gray. Taking a portrait of a

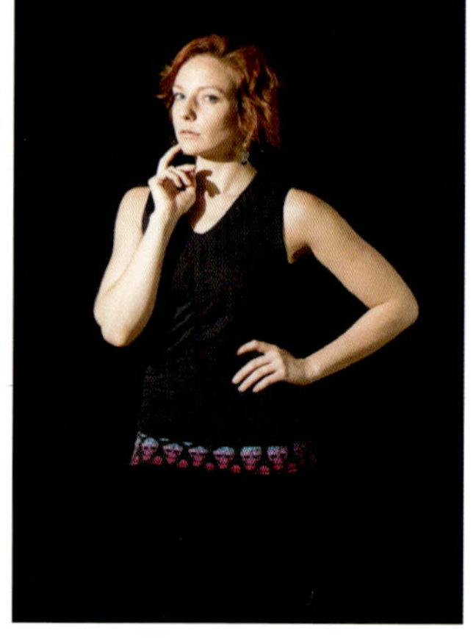

Reading the dark outfit and background, the camera's metering system overexposed the subject to achieve a "balanced" exposure. It is important to understand how the TTL metering system functions and how it "sees" any given scene.

polar bear on a snowy field? Your camera's metering system will want to turn it gray. Taking a portrait of a black panther on a black velvet rug? Your camera's metering system will want to turn it gray.

Bend Exposure to Your Will

Exposing images could be a troublesome process if one did not know this fact. However,

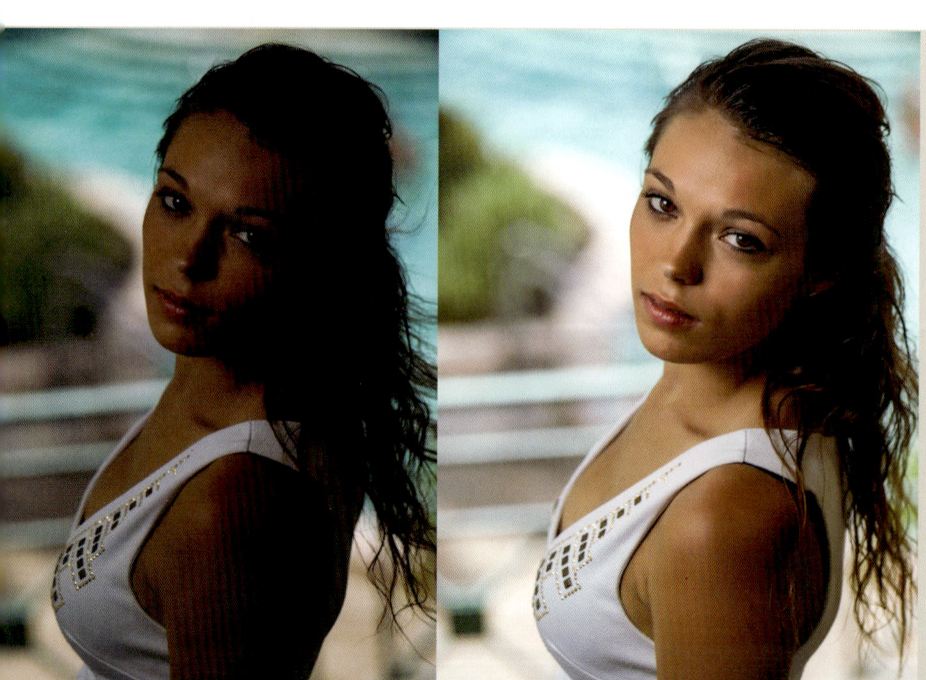

LEFT—The camera's reflective metering system read the model's background and averaged it for a "balanced" exposure. Unfortunately, it was incorrect for the subject.

RIGHT—By adjusting the exposure compensation—and, more importantly, by adding more flash exposure—we now have a properly exposed image.

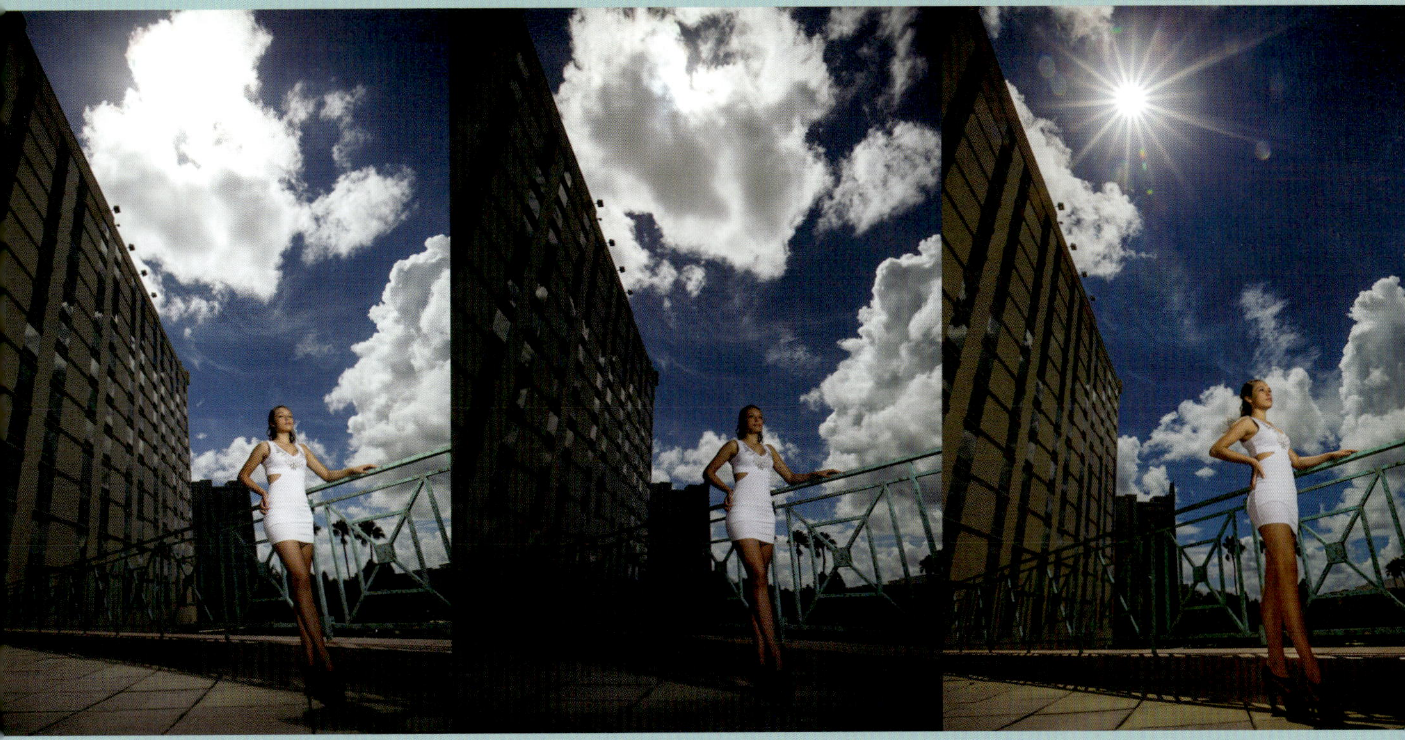

This image shows an adequate exposure for the ambient sky combined with the off-camera flash to light the subject. But creatively, I wanted more drama.

Here, I purposely underexposed the sky—but now the subject is also underexposed.

In the final image, I used my "spiky sun" technique and kept the sky dark and saturated while adding more flash exposure to draw attention to the primary subject.

now that we are armed with an understanding of how TTL works, we can use this constant to help us make our desired exposures. Notice I didn't say "accurate" exposures. While it is important to know how to record an accurate exposure showing the true tonality of a scene, it is even more important to know how to push exposures and bend them to our wills to produce what we want from a creative perspective.

For example, I often purposely underexpose midday blue skies in order to render a deeper blue (see the images above). In reality, the sky at that time—to the naked eye—was not as deep as I chose to render it, but I made a creative and technical decision to make the sky darker. I did that by understanding the camera's TTL meter reading and by knowing how to override my camera's automated exposure settings in order to achieve my desired result.

Why Add Flash?

Let me use a midday, full-sun, outdoor bridal portrait as an example and I will explain my core technique in full.

1. The Sun as Backlight. My first step is to use the sun as a backlight only. This means that the sun is serving as a hair and edge light, but more importantly, it is not on the subject's face, causing harsh shadows or a serious case of the squinties.

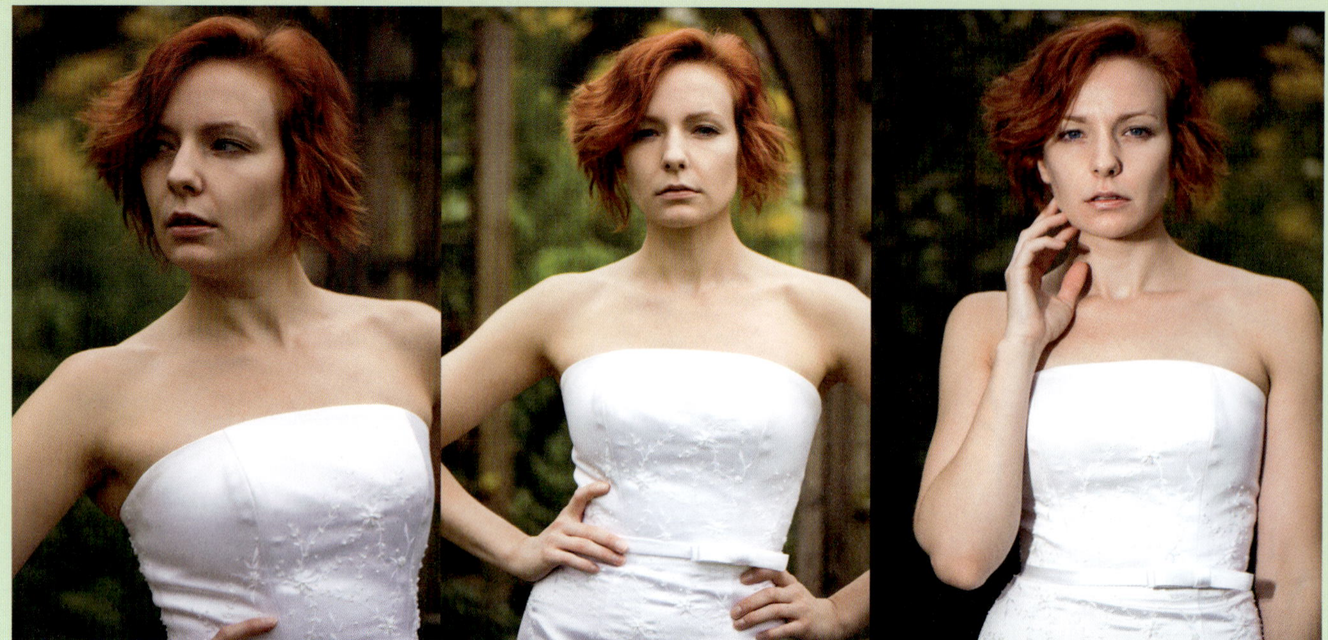

If we expose solely for the ambient light in the background, the backlit subject is underexposed and has a poor quality of light on her face.

Here, I exposed for the subject. It was an overcast day, so the background maintained an acceptable exposure value. However, the lighting on her face is still poor. Her eyes are going dark; it needs fill.

Finally, I added a bare speedlight for fill and more dimensional light. Notice the more natural skin tone; the color cast from the grass and foliage was neutralized by the speedlight.

The problem is that the bulk of the ambient light (from the sun) in the scene is coming from *behind* my subject. This would render her face dark (underexposed) if I were to create an accurate exposure for the scene around her. Alternately, I could choose to spot meter the

> *"The sharp, reflected light from a silver reflector is frequently too much for the subject to handle."*

bride's face and expose for that meter reading—but then the background and the sky behind my bride would be blown out (overexposed).

2. Add Fill. My other option is to add light in order to fill the shadow on the front of my bride and to help balance out the exposure.

I could use a reflector to accomplish this, but reflectors often cause a case of the squinties; the sharp, reflected light from a silver reflector is frequently too much for the subject to handle. I could try a softer white reflector, but that would not provide enough light to balance the exposure of the background sky in order to render it the deeper tone of blue I desire.

In this example, if I want to accomplish my creative goal, the only real lighting choice to is to use off-camera flash to create enough light to fill the shadow side of my bride and to give me the exposure I desire.

I choose speedlights as my lighting tool because they give me the option of using high-speed sync (HSS) in order to have shallow depth of field in my portrait, or I can choose to have a greater depth of field by choosing settings that do not need the HSS feature (more on HSS in the next chapter). The cool part is that I can make that decision at the camera position without running to reset my flash. Also, I can easily photograph the first frame with a wide aperture (like f/4) for a shallow depth of field, then make a quick setting change on the camera and shoot the next frame at a small aperture (like f/22) for a very deep depth of field.

I do this by leveraging the TTL system's ability to adjust exposure settings using my input.

How Flash Interacts with TTL

We'll talk about manual settings in a moment, but first let's cover how the flash interacts with the camera's TTL system. I already described how the TTL system reacts to the ambient light it "sees." But how does it account for and incorporate TTL flash? On Canon and Nikon cameras, the default system is as follows:

1. Read the Ambient Light. The meter first reads the ambient light in the scene and calculates an exposure balancing it to middle gray.

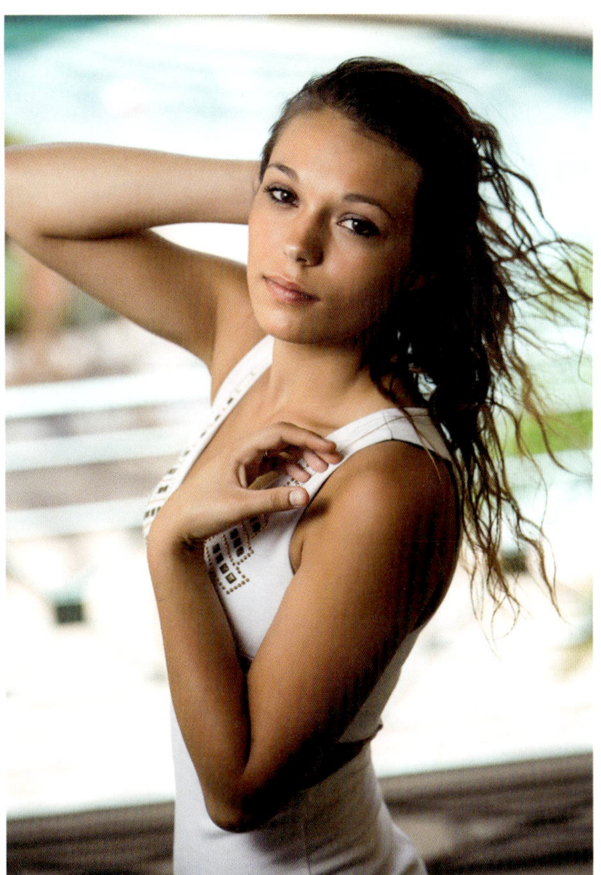

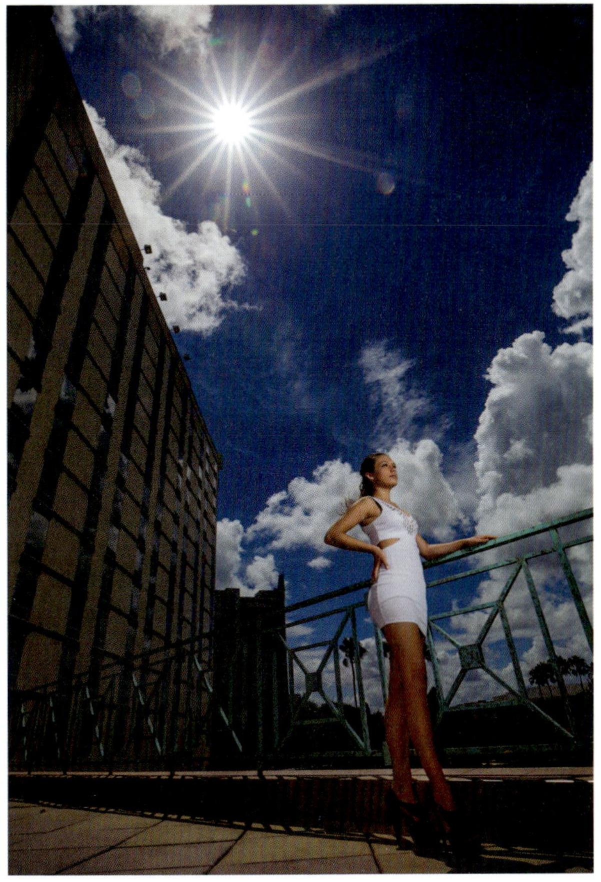

2. Check the Camera Settings. The camera then takes into account any settings you have made that affect the exposure. These include the ISO setting as well as the shooting mode— whether your camera is set to manual, aperture-priority (Av), shutter-priority (Tv), or program.

Manual Mode. If the manual mode is selected, the camera simply marks the point on your meter scale where you will achieve a "balanced" exposure based on averaging the scene to middle gray. It's up to you to manually change the settings from there.

Aperture-Priority (Av) Mode. If the aperture-priority mode is selected, the camera takes into account your hard-set aperture and adjusts your camera to the corresponding shutter speed in order to achieve a "balanced" exposure based on averaging the scene to middle gray.

Shutter-Priority (Tv) Mode. If the shutter-priority mode is selected, your camera takes into account your hard-set shutter speed and sets your camera to the corresponding aperture in order to achieve a "balanced" exposure based on averaging the scene to middle gray.

Program Mode. If you selected the program mode, go sit in the corner and ponder your poor life choices.

3. Checking the Exposure Compensation Setting. Next, if you are in aperture- or shutter-priority mode, the camera takes into account whether you have dialed in any exposure compensation. The exposure compensation setting allows you to override the camera's metering system to make desired exposure adjustments. Remember our polar bear on the snowfield example? If you dialed in an exposure compensation setting of $+1\frac{1}{3}$EV, the camera would record the white of the scene properly. You are essentially telling the system to ignore what it sees and not to underexpose to make the white subject gray. You are the master and know better.

4. Testing the Flash Output. Next, if you have a speedlight on-camera, turned on, and set to TTL, the camera senses that and will fire a preflash to illuminate the scene at $\frac{1}{32}$ power. It reads the reflection of this flash, mixes it in with the exposure already determined for the ambient-light scene, and then sends a command to the flash to fire it at the power level appropriate for achieving and maintaining a balanced exposure according to all of the settings and adjustments above in point #2.

Flash Exposure Compensation. One side-track to this combined exposure is if you have separately set any flash exposure compensation (FEC) on your flash or in your camera. If this is the case, the camera then adds to or subtracts from the flash exposure based on this override.

5. Making the Exposure. Finally, the shutter opens and your camera records the exposure.

What have I described here is a pretty complex scenario that all happens in a fraction of a second as you start to depress your shutter button. This, my friends, is why cameras and dedicated TTL speedlights cost so much; they

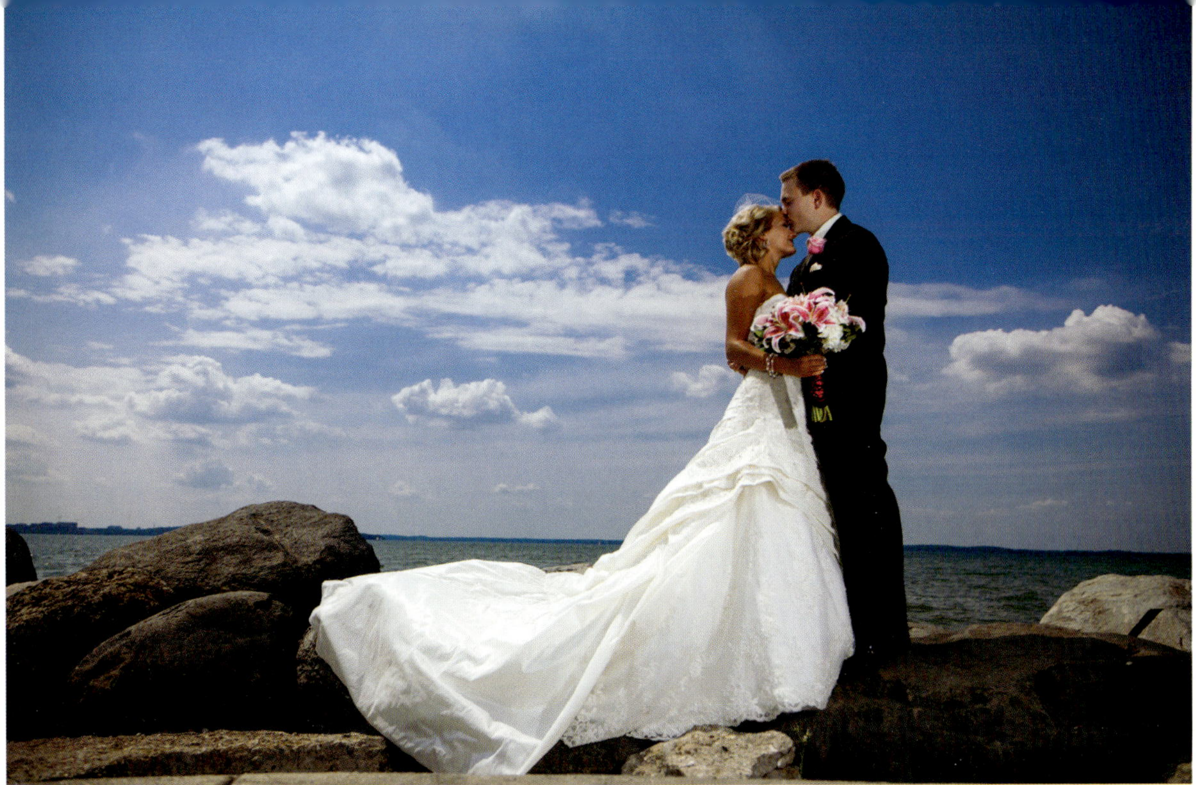

I shot this in aperture-priority mode at $^1\!/_{3200}$ second and f/4 at ISO 100 with $-^1\!/_3$EV exposure compensation.

have these complex brains inside to help you get the right exposure. We just need to be smart enough to understand what the camera is "seeing" and know when to override and adjust the flash/camera settings based on what we want the camera to record from our own creative and technical point of view. Professional photography is not for dummies.

Practical Example. Now, let's apply this knowledge to the example we already looked at: a bride out in the midday sun. For a shallow depth of field portrait, my preferred camera settings are aperture-priority mode, ISO 100, and f/4.

As my camera reads the ambient light in the scene, it sees a lot of bright, blue sky and a white dress. Because its job is to achieve a balanced exposure and to render everything to 18 percent gray, it will automatically underexpose

the scene slightly. Still, I will typically dial in $-^1\!/_3$ EV exposure compensation to further underexpose the ambient light and deepen the sky.

The camera will provide the appropriate corresponding shutter speed—which, in this case, is $^1\!/_{3200}$ second. Holy cats! That's a fast shutter speed, right? This is a major reason I default to the aperture-priority mode for this type of portrait; once the shutter speed climbs above $^1\!/_{500}$ second, I really no longer care how high it goes. It won't affect my ability to hand-hold the camera or to stop average motion. I let the camera worry about it and figure out the proper setting.

But wait a minute. How can the flash handle a shutter speed that fast? Isn't the camera's maximum flash-sync speed around $^1\!/_{200}$ second? Yes, it is with normal settings. Read on to learn how we can resolve this issue.

2. High-Speed Sync (HSS/FP)

Maximum Flash-Sync Speed

The maximum flash-sync speed (sometimes called the X-sync speed) is around $\frac{1}{200}$ second, depending on the camera model. This is the shortest shutter speed at which both of the camera's shutter curtains are completely clear of the image sensor, allowing the instantaneous burst of flash to simultaneously expose the entire frame. If you exceed this shutter speed, one or both of the shutter curtains will block the flash's light from reaching the sensor, resulting in a dark bar or underexposed area at the edge of the frame.

So what are we to do in a situation like the one that concluded the previous section? Well, if

I used a dual off-camera flash setup with on-camera flash to add fill light and achieve the dramatic exposure on the facing page.

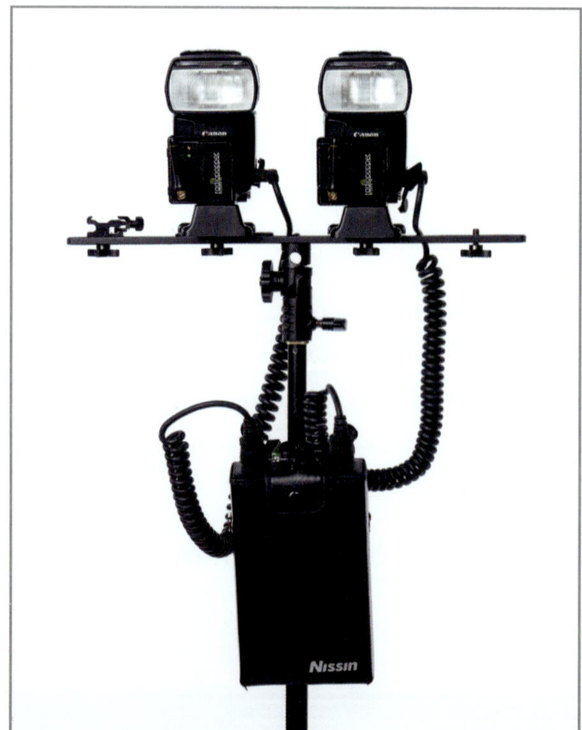

you set the flash to HSS (Canon) or the camera to FP (Nikon), something magical happens: the flash no longer fires *one* quick burst of light. Instead, it pulses to time the very narrow gap between the front and rear curtains of the shutter as it passes in front of the sensor. This creates an even flash exposure across the entire scene.

"So what are we to do in a situation like the one that concluded the previous section?"

Best of all, it allows you to use a wide-open aperture (and the very short shutter speeds that correspond) in order to achieve shallow depth of field. The trade-off is the HSS pulsing robs a lot of power from the flash, so you need to work with the flash very close to your subject (the closer the better), or you need to double up speedlights in order to compensate for the power loss. This is the option I typically choose.

In practice, I fire a quick test shot with an image like this and then adjust the exposure compensation and flash exposure compensation to taste. As a general rule, I try not to turn down the exposure compensation to more than $-1\frac{1}{3}$ EV. Once I go below that point, the ambient light seems just to "disappear." It could be a quirk in the system, but it is what I have found works for me.

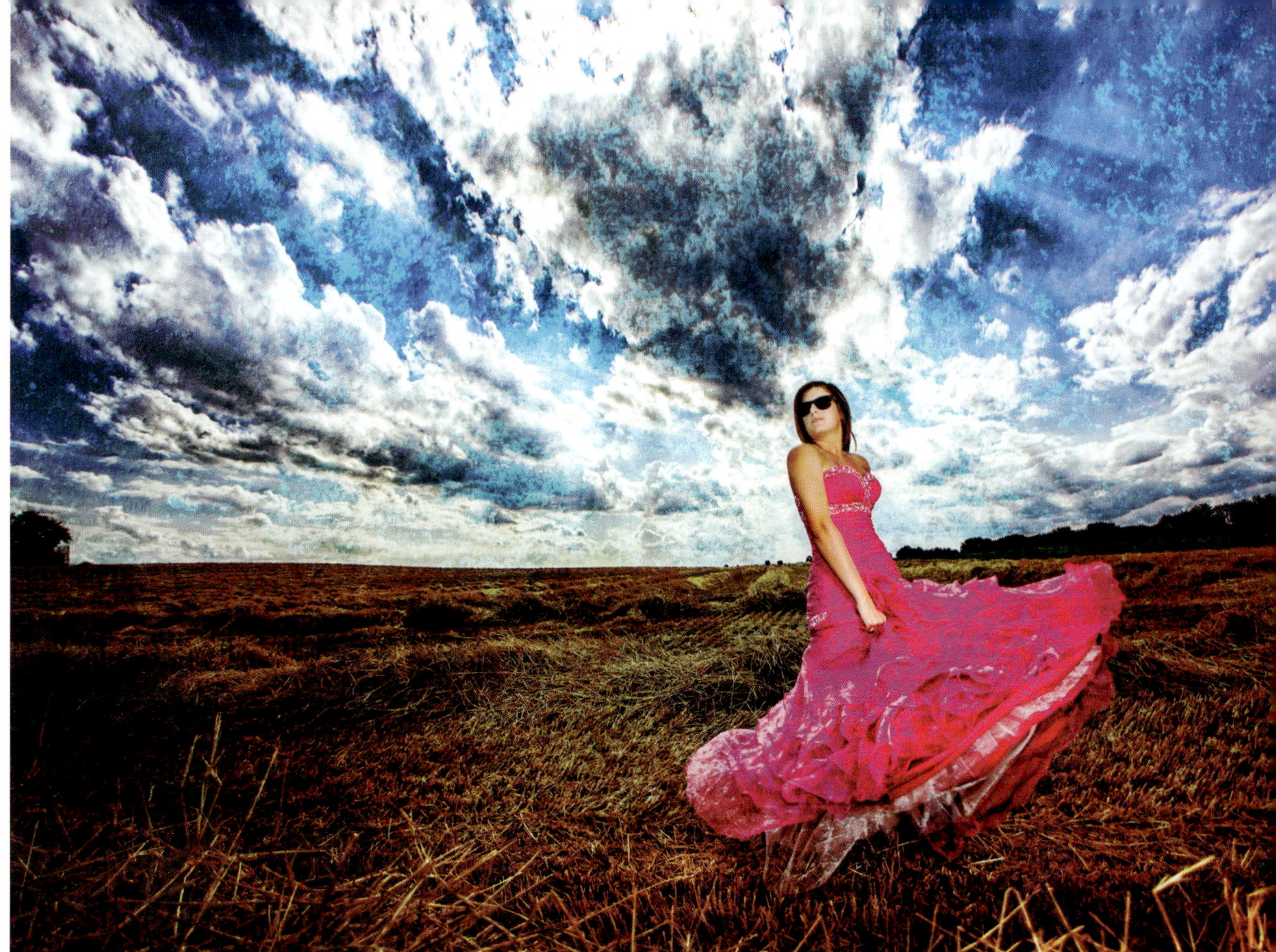

My preferred outdoor lighting setup consists of two Canon 580EX II flashes connected to RadioPopper PX receivers and powered by a Nissin P300 dual flash battery. I added a texture screen and an effect from Topaz Adjust to punch it up even more.

Deep Depth of Field

Another option when using TTL is to purposely *avoid* HSS and maximize the depth of field (with a small aperture setting). I use this technique when I want to place the sun in the shot. You will see several images in this book where I included a nice, spiky sun placed in my composition. That's this technique in action. I simply switch from aperture-priority to the manual mode, set my shutter speed to $\frac{1}{200}$ second, and set my f-stop to anywhere between f/16 and f/22. My goal is to use f/22 to get the best

"spiky sun" (caused by the aperture blades). If I cannot get my flash close enough to achieve this aperture, I open up my aperture until I can get the exposure I desire. By dropping the shutter speed to the camera's maximum X-sync speed (the fastest "normal" shutter speed that will sync with my flash), I am allowing the flash to fire at full output without having to go into the power-robbing HSS mode. (Remember: HSS is only necessary when you need a shutter speed faster than your maximum X-sync speed.)

3. Flash Communication

The last piece of the speedlight puzzle is the communication between your camera and your flash(es) when they are not physically connected to the camera.

Infrared Communication

Canon and Nikon each have a built-in, line-of-sight infrared communication system. This is controlled by a hot shoe–mounted flash set to "master" (Canon) or "commander" (Nikon), or by a dedicated proprietary transmitter (ST-E2 for Canon; SU-800 for Nikon) in the hot shoe. This device then communicates the TTL information back and forth to the other slave/remote off-camera flashes using infrared signals.

Potential Problems. This system works quite well when the master and slave flashes are close to one another. However, when you place the off-camera flash in a softbox, you can lose this communication ability. In addition, bright sunshine outside may interfere with these signals and can cause them to be inconsistent. Distance can also be a problem; the effective range is 25–30 feet outdoors in "favorable" conditions.

Radio Communication

Many photographers elect to add on a radio-based system to assist the infrared system and make it more reliable in unfavorable situations.

The two main aftermarket systems available to photographers are the RadioPopper PX and the PocketWizard TT Flex. I use the RadioPopper PX system and will feature that throughout the book; it is simply the gear that works best for me and with which I have the most expertise. Others certainly use the PocketWizard TT Flex system successfully.

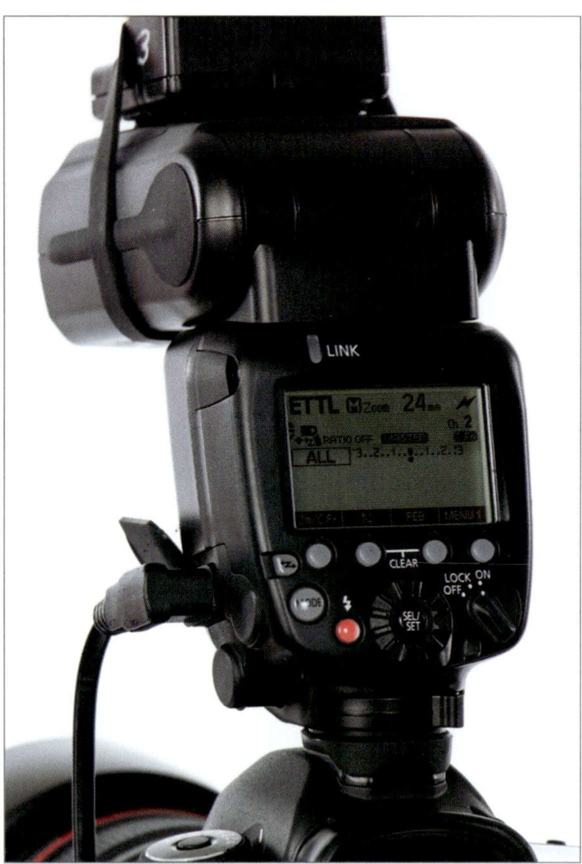

The new Canon 600EX-RT works well with the older 580EX II flash and the RadioPopper PX system—as long as the transmitter setting on the flash is set to "optical" (note the lightning bolt in the upper right-hand corner of the display).

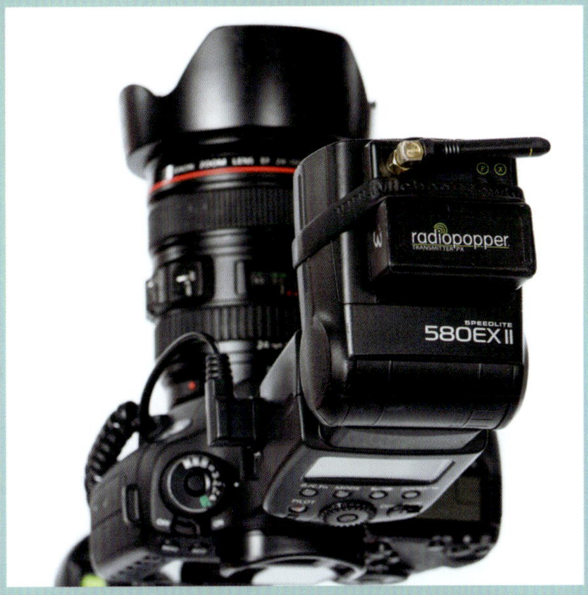

My RadioPopper PX transmitter attaches to the top of my master flash using Velcro and one of my branded silicone bands.

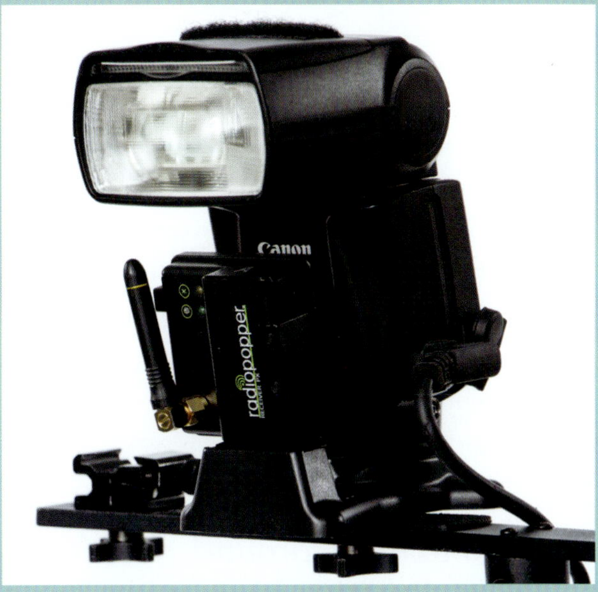

A RadioPopper PX receiver attached to a Canon 580EX II flash.

The RadioPopper PX is a simple but effective radio-based conduit for the built-in infrared system. A PX transmitter attaches with Velcro onto the top of your master flash head. This unit intercepts the signal from your flash head as the TTL information is sent. It then transmits this data packet via radio waves to the PX receiver connected to your off-camera flash. At that point, the PX receiver converts the radio signal back to infrared and feeds this information optically into the infrared port on the front of your off-camera flash.

It might seem a little clunky, but I have found the system to be supremely effective. It allows me to trigger off-camera flash units that are far away, tucked away into softboxes, hidden around corners—almost anywhere within a couple of hundred feet of my camera position.

It's not for everybody (the same way that TTL speedlight photography is not for every-body), but for those of us who can grasp it, this is a difference-maker and a significant competitive advantage.

Adjustments From the Camera Position

Since a studio lighting environment is a controlled environment by nature, I need the ability to consistently set and control my lights for repeatable results. This can be easily handled by setting each speedlight manually and meter-

More on Radio Communications

The newer Canon 600EX-RT has a built-in radio communication system, which I feature on several images in this book. However, since Nikon does not have an equivalent (at the writing of this book), and because a majority of photographers in the field are still using older systems, I will focus primarily on the pros and cons of the infrared system and its after-market helpers like the RadioPopper PX and PocketWizard TT Flex systems.

ing each for the desired results, much the same way as one would when using standard studio strobes. This method works great until I wish to move the subject or one of the lights. This change in the distance between the repositioned lights and the subject also changes the effective light output and meter reading. Quite simply, the light will look different from my original intention.

This can get tedious if you like to move around, redirect the subject, and tweak shots for different creative looks. You can't run over to your lights every couple of shots and manually make changes—that would greatly interrupt the flow of the portrait session. The alternative is that you just use the same lighting setup over and over again, which can kill your creativity and the ability to provide different looks for the client. I've always believed the more unique, quality looks you can provide, the better chance you have for selling more to each client.

Wouldn't it be great if you could dial your speedlights' power up and down right from the camera position? Guess what—you can! With the newer Canon 600EX-RT speedlights, you can manually adjust the power settings in up to five different groupings (such as main, fill, and accent lights) from the camera position using a master flash or the ST-E3-RT controller. These use radio frequencies to communicate power settings to each flash.

The only downside is that all of the speedlights used must be Canon 600EX-RTs. The built-in radio system will not work with other flashes, including other Canon flashes. If you are like me and use older Canon or Nikon flashes, you can use an ingenious device called a RadioPopper Cube as part of the RadioPopper JrX system. (*Note:* Canon 580EX II, 580EX, 430EX II, and 550EX flashes, as well as the Nikon SB800 and SB600 flashes, will work with the Cube; Nikon's SB910, 900, and 700 flashes cannot have their power controlled with the Cube.) The flashes I listed slide onto the RadioPopper Cube like a hotshoe. When a JrX receiver is connected to the Cube, you can use a JrX transmitter to dial the power up and down for three separate groups of flashes. This is ideal for my standard setup of main light (group 1), fill light (group 1 or 2), and edge lights (group 3).

With this setup, I can make technical and creative adjustments from the camera position, which allows me to work quickly and—more importantly—stay engaged with my subject. I can photograph one shot with standard portrait lighting, then tweak the power on group 2 to drop or turn off my fill for edgier, more shadow-intensive lighting. Then I can tweak the power up on group 3 for stronger accent lighting to make the look even edgier.

It really can be that quick and simple—and I never need to move or touch a flash.

4. Hard Light or Soft Light

The final core concept I wish to emphasize is the difference between hard and soft light, both in definition and in use.

What It Means

Soft light is defined by a gradual transition (across a broad area) from highlight to shadow. This tends to smooth fine detail and subdue contours.

Hard light is defined by a quick transition (across a narrow area) from highlight to shadow. This tends to emphasize fine detail and enhance contours.

Controlling the Light Quality

The hardness or softness of the light is directly related to the size of the light source relative to the subject. Soft light is produced by sources that are *large* relative to the subject; hard light is produced by sources that are *small* relative to the subject. The term "relative" is key here.

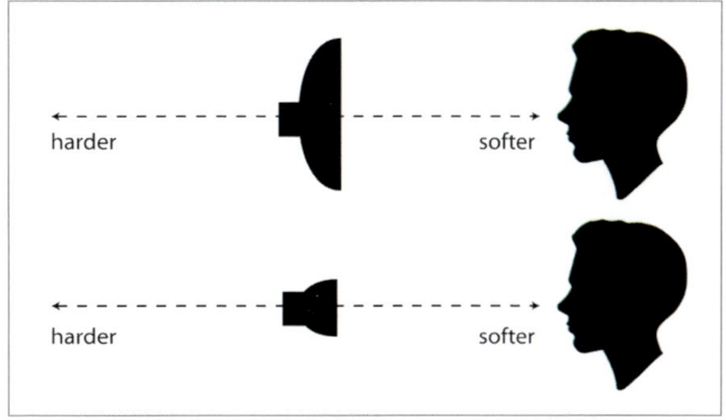

Regardless of its size, as the distance between the modifier and the subject grows, the light becomes progressively harder.

"The size of the sun relative to me as the subject is very small. It would provide very hard light."

The sun is a huge light source, the largest object in our galaxy. Yet, on a sunny day I can close one eye and hold up my thumb to block

the sun. Because it is so far away, the size of the sun relative to me as the subject is very small. This source would provide very hard light.

Conversely, a 60-inch octobox placed 2 feet from my face would be huge relative to me. If I looked directly at it, it would envelop my entire field of view. Accordingly, this source would provide very soft light.

With that knowledge, you can probably guess that a bare, unmodified speedlight is an inherently hard light source. In average use, it will always be small relative to the subject.

Two Approaches

Given that fact, I work with speedlights in two basic ways:

1. Work with the Hard Light. I use the hard nature of the bare speedlight to coordinate with the hard nature of the sun and other hard light sources to create dramatic portraits. In doing so, I use dramatic posing and storytelling to work hand-in-hand with the dramatic lighting so everything makes sense visually. To me, it does not make sense to use hard lighting for a standard smiley head shot. It's incongruent. The majority of my outdoor portraiture is based upon using bare speedlights.

"I modify the hard speedlight with softening devices such as softboxes and diffusion panels."

2. Soften the Light with a Modifier. I modify the hard nature of the speedlight with softening devices such as softboxes and diffusion panels (and to a lesser degree, umbrellas) to spread the light and to create a light source that is larger light relative to my subject. This type of lighting is more conducive to portraits where the subject is looking at the camera and/or smiling. Virtually all of my in-studio portraiture is based on using softening devices. It works well for romantic couple portraiture, as well.

There are always exceptions to these rules, but these are the core tenets of my speedlight portraiture.

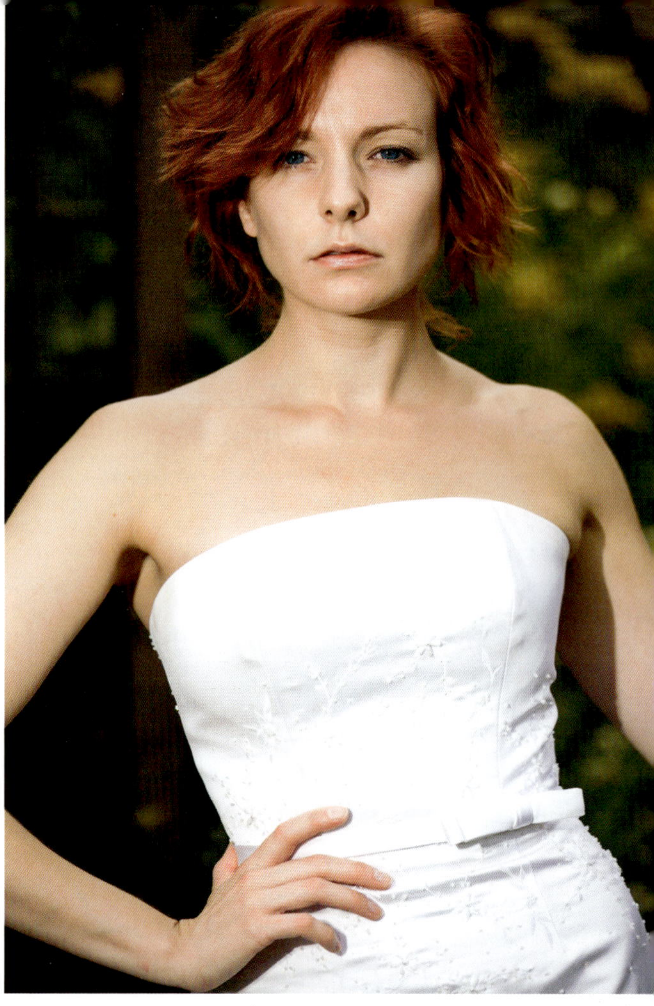

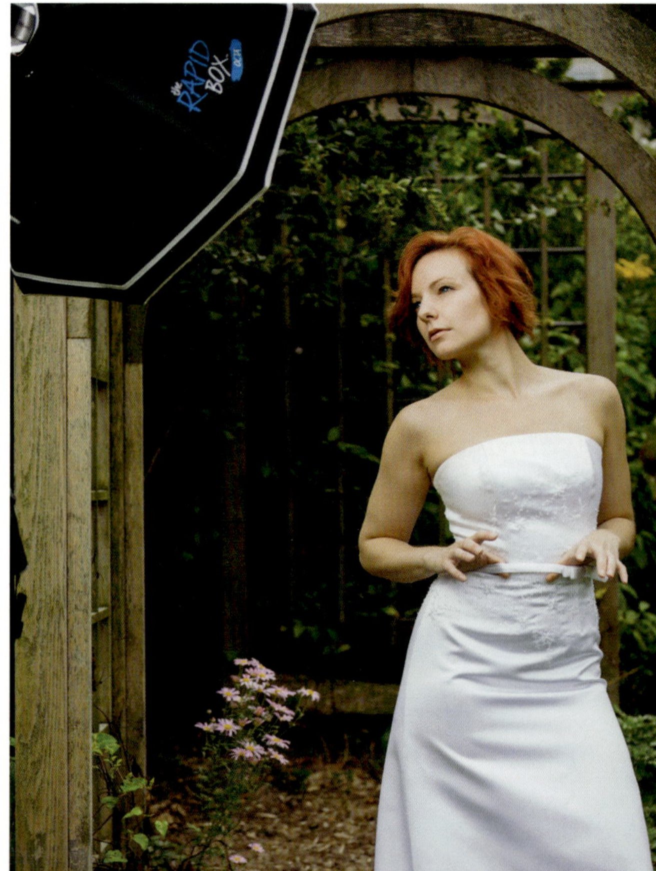

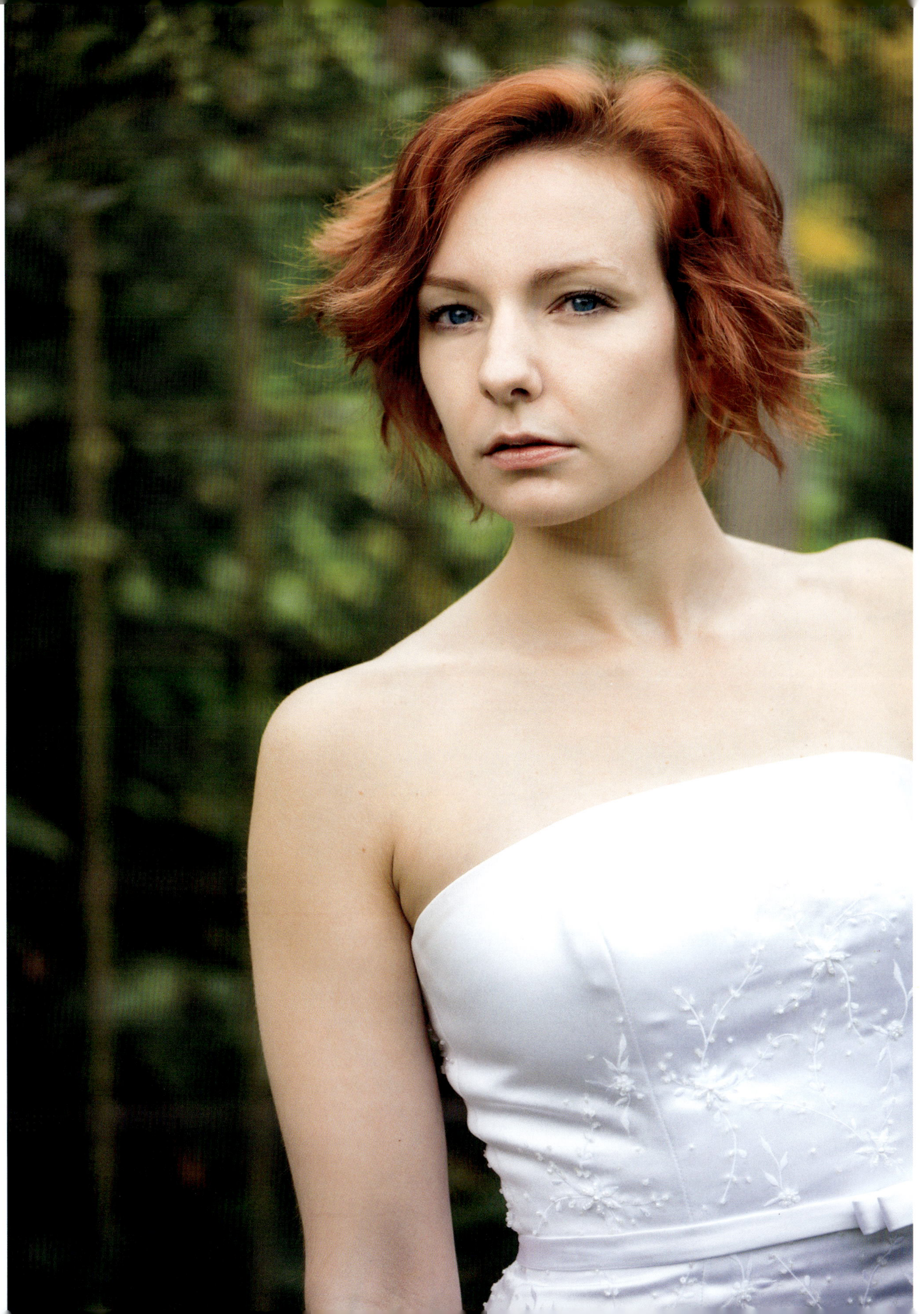

5. Lighting Kits and Setups

I use several different gear kits and setups for the different types of portraiture that I do. While there are some commonalities, each has its own unique qualities.

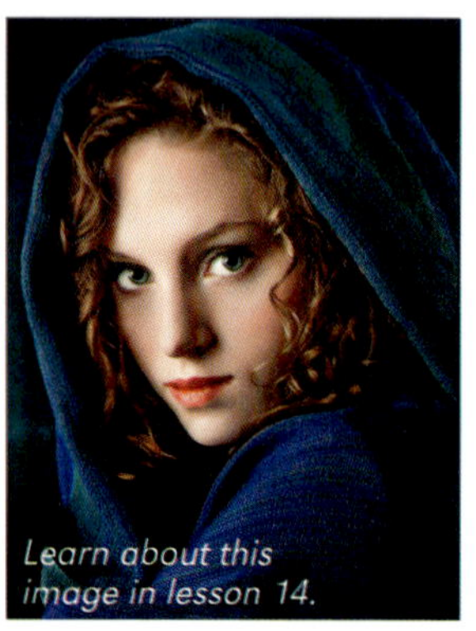

Studio Portrait Kit

I commonly use four or more speedlights for my studio portraiture: one main, one fill, and two edge lights (one on either side and behind the subject). Or, I will use one edge light and one up higher as a hair light. My go-to setup for studio portraits is:

Main Light. 60-inch Creative Light octobox with a Canon 580EX II fired and controlled using a RadioPopper JrX receiver with a RadioPopper Cube (set to group 1) connected to a Nissin PS300 power pack for fast recycle times.

"My fill light is typically at least two times as far from the subject as the main light."

Fill Light. Photek 60-inch Softlighter with a Canon 580EX II fired and controlled using a RadioPopper JrX receiver with a RadioPopper Cube (group 1 or group 2) connected to a Nissin PS300 power pack for fast recycle times.

I generally control the effect of the fill light and overall contrast ratio using the distance to the subject. My fill light is typically at least two times as far from from the subject as the main light. Alternately, when the fill is set to group 2, I can turn the power up and down separately from the main light in group 1. However, I often choose to leave group 2 open for a background light, an additional accent light, or for a Lightbender uplight (refer to some of my fashion headshots in this book) if so desired.

Diffuse the Light

Because speedlights are a hard light source (as previously detailed in chapter 4), it is important soften the light to meet accepted portrait lighting standards. While this is true for studio strobes as well, it seems to be a concept that many photographers cannot wrap their head around. "You can use a speedlight with a softbox?" Yes, of course. You can also use speedlights with umbrellas, parabolics, beauty dishes, etc. You just need the appropriate adapter (as you would with a studio strobe). For softboxes, this adapter is called a speed ring. Many softbox manufacturers offer speedrings for speedlights. My softbox of choice for studio use is the line from Creative Light. Creative Light offers a complete range of common softbox sizes, ranging from a large 4x6-foot box to a small 2x2-foot box. There are other softboxes that work well with speedlights, such as the Westcott Apollo umbrella-style boxes, the Photek Softlighter, and even the venerable Larson line of high-quality softboxes.

Edge/Accent/Hair Lights. Creative Light 1x4-foot stripboxes outfitted with egg-crate grids to narrow the light, with a Canon 580EX II fired and controlled using a RadioPopper JrX receiver with a RadioPopper Cube (set to group 3) connected to a Canon CPE3 power pack for fast recycle times.

Variations. In addition, I will mix these in the following variations from time to time:

22-Inch Beauty Dish. A beauty dish with diffusion sock can be ordered from Kacey Enterprises to fit one or two speedlights. I use this for fashion/model headshots and to replace my 60-inch octobox to mix up my lighting.

48-Inch Larson Lightbender. This unique softbox features a curved front face and can be used as the main light for beauty lighting, as an uplight, or as an edge light.

3.5x5.5-Foot Larson Softbox. I originally purchased this to work with my AlienBees strobes, but then had the box retrofitted to work with one or two speedlights. It works either as a main light or a fill light.

Location Corporate Headshot Kit

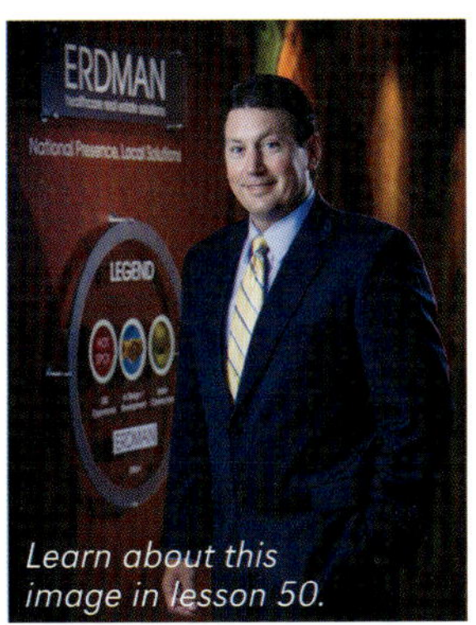

Learn about this image in lesson 50.

My location headshot kit is similar in setup to my studio kit with one notable exception: I swap out my studio softboxes for portable, quick-setup Westcott softboxes. The Westcott Apollo softboxes pop up and fold down like umbrellas, making them perfect for when you're transporting gear to locations by yourself. I have also added in several Westcott Rapid Boxes. These are unique beauty-dish style softboxes that also are based on a pop-up umbrella design.

I typically use a three-light setup consisting of a main, fill, and hair/edge light. Because these location sessions often consist of thirty or more headshots that must maintain exact lighting consistency, I set my main and fill lights manually on the flashes themselves. My hair light, however, is still controlled by a RadioPopper Cube, letting me adjust it lower for light-haired subjects or turn it off for bald guys (to avoid nasty specular highlights). For a subject with thick, lustrous brunette hair, I turn it up.

Main Light. A 50-inch Westcott Apollo with a Canon 580EX II set manually and fired using a RadioPopper JrX receiver (group does not matter) and connected to a Nissin PS300 power pack for fast recycle times.

Fill Light. 28-inch Westcott Apollo with a Canon 580EX II set manually and fired using a RadioPopper JrX receiver (group does not matter) and connected to a Nissin PS300 power pack for fast recycle times.

Hair Light. 26-inch Westcott Rapid Box with a Canon 580EX II fired and controlled with a RadioPopper JrX receiver with a Radio-Popper Cube (group 3) and connected to a Canon CPE3 power pack for fast recycle times.

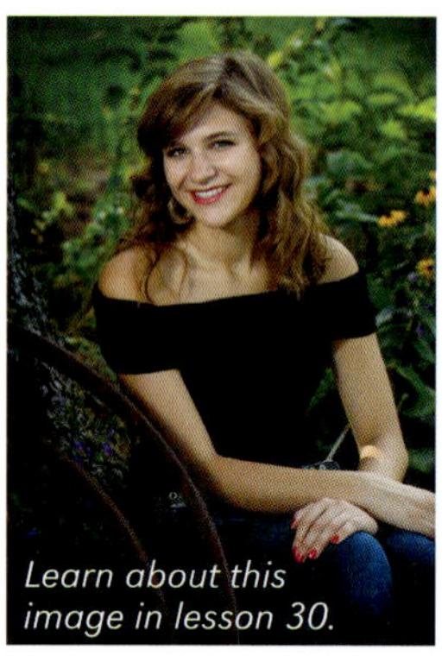

Learn about this image in lesson 30.

Environmental Portrait Kit

The kit and use stays much the same, but will vary depending on the space available and the quantity/variety of portraits I need to do. For a single portrait, I will keep the setup the same, but may or may not use the fill light depending on whether or not I have glass or windows in the background that may show reflections. If I need to do a variety of environmental portraits, or portraits for multiple people in different locations, I switch back to using RadioPopper Cubes with my flashes to give me the speed and flexibility I need to adjust my lighting on the fly.

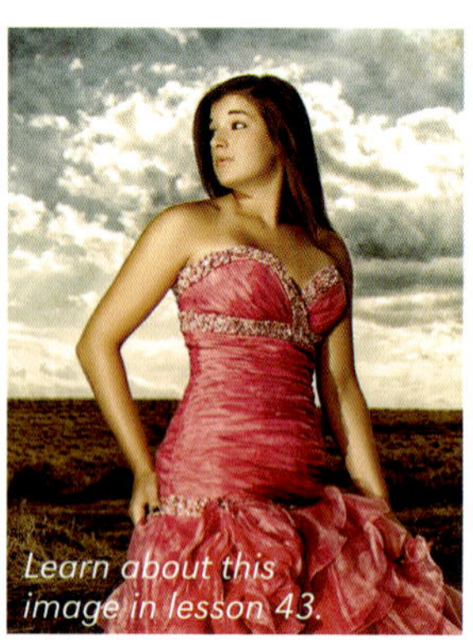

Learn about this image in lesson 43.

Location Senior Portrait Kit

Location senior portraits pose numerous challenges. Almost all non-studio senior portraits happen outside; seniors seem to crave these images. In my area they occur in the middle of the summer, and often in the middle of a bright, sunny day—not the ideal time for outdoor portraits by any means. This challenge is compounded by the need, in most cases, to create a shallow depth of field to blur distracting backgrounds. Lastly, we often have a time constraint; we are trying to get as many "looks" done as possible within their contracted ses-

sion time. My solution? I use the many benefits of eTTL speedlights: portability, power, intelligence, and—last but not least—the ability to shoot at wide apertures in bright sunlight with high-speed sync (detailed in chapter 2). For seniors, I keep my kit and lighting setups simple so that we can quickly and easily move to different locations.

Main Light. When working on location with seniors, I have two different main-light approaches, depending on the available light.

In Full Sun. In full sun, I use two Canon 580EX II flashes on an RPS Studio LightBar (which holds up to four speedlights) fired in remote eTTL using the RadioPopper PX System. The lights are connected to a Nissin PS300 power pack for fast recycle times. The PS300 (and the newer PS8) will power two speedlights simultaneously.

In Shade. In shade, I use a Canon 580EX II flash in a Westcott 26-inch Rapid Box fired in remote eTTL using the RadioPopper PX System. This is also connected to a Nissin PS300 power pack for fast recycle times.

Fill Light. I often have my on-camera flash work as both the master flash (controlling the off-camera flashes) and as a fill light from the camera position so I can choose whether or not to have it fire. Generally, I only have it fire when I am photographing in full sun and need the extra power to soften and fill the shadows on my subject.

For these shots, I prefer to use a 70–200mm IS f/4 Canon lens wide open at f/4 to create nice bokeh that helps separate my subject from the background.

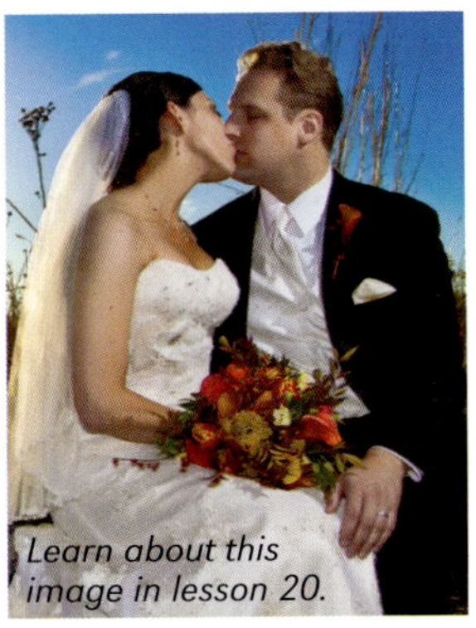
Learn about this image in lesson 20.

Wedding Kit

Weddings are an entirely different animal, but of all the kits I have described so far, the one I use for location senior portraits comes closest to matching. I use the same methodology for location bridal party portraits. Additionally, I often use a 24–105mm or 20mm lens to provide dramatic perspective for portraits.

Bounce Flash. In addition to the approaches described in the previous section, I use bounced on-camera flash throughout the day when photographing indoors. For these images, I leave my flash in eTTL mode and set my exposure manually in-camera based on how much ambient light I want to use in my shot.

On-Camera eTTL Plus Off-Camera Flash. I also use an interesting hybrid approach to lighting at receptions. I use on-camera flash in eTTL mode—but I use it *indirectly* (I do not point it directly at my subjects). Instead, I point it straight up and use a rectangular cap diffuser to scatter it and kick the light forward.

In these shots, my on-camera flash serves as a fill light and works in conjunction with two additional off-camera flashes that I set at separate corners of the dance floor. These off-camera flashes are adjusted manually, typically to $\frac{1}{16}$ power. I connect them to RadioPopper JrX receivers.

To fire them, it gets interesting. I use a RadioPopper PX transmitter attached to my on-camera flash, which is not only set to eTTL but also to master mode. In this mode, the flash emits a signal with all the eTTL information. The JrX receivers connected to the off-camera flashes cannot interpret all of the eTTL information, however. All they hear is "Fire!"—and they do, because they are set to the same radio frequency as the PX system.

I set my camera's exposure based on the off-camera flashes lighting the dance floor, knowing that the on-camera master flash will do a wonderful job of providing nice front fill light on whatever I see. Depending on my angle to the off-camera flashes, they can act as double edge lights, or as main and accent lights, or solely as the main lights. It's a great system and provides me with consistent, high-quality light on the dance floor.

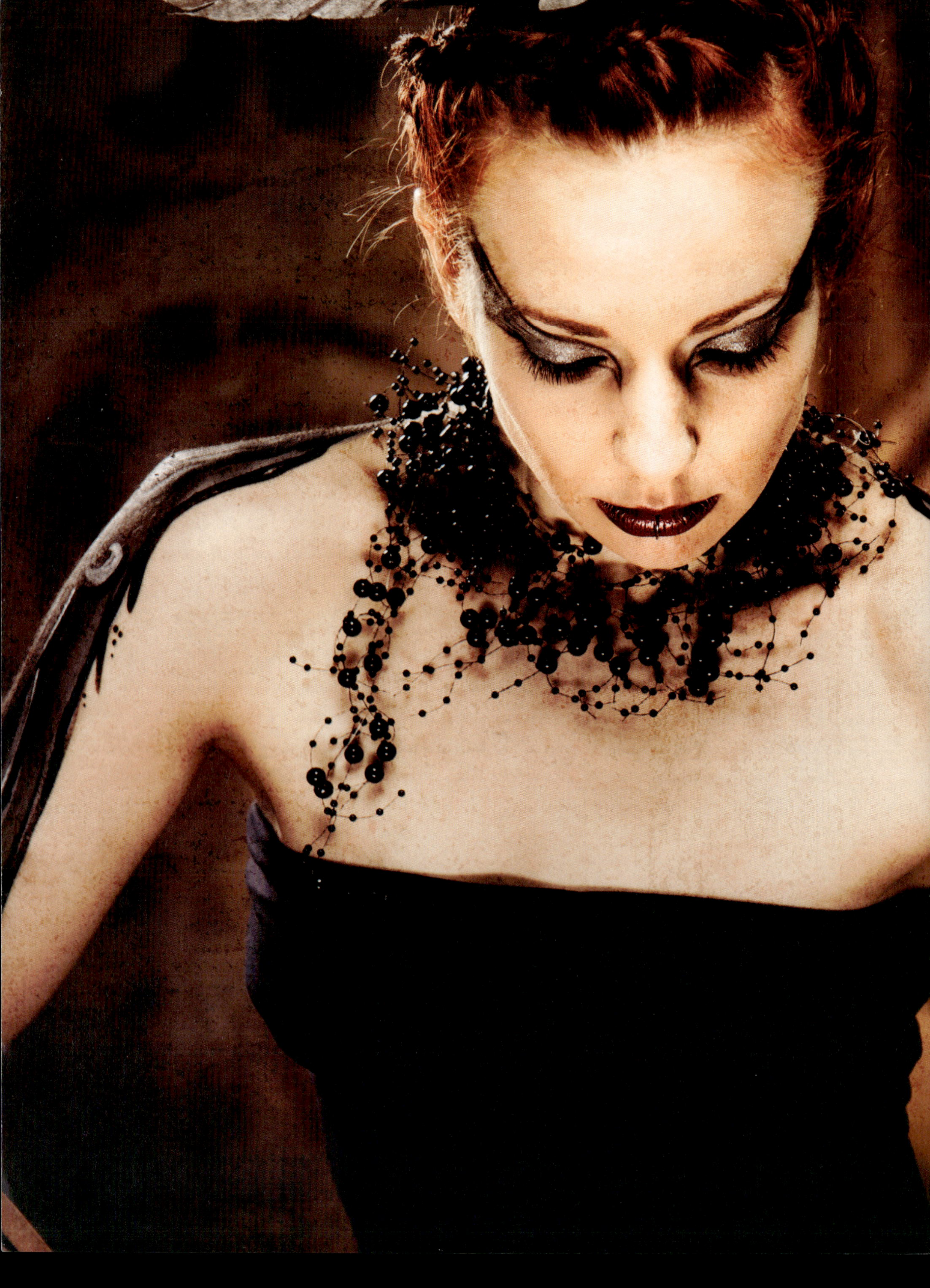

Speedlights in Action

Now that we've covered the basics, let's look at how speedlights can be implemented effectively in a wide variety of real situations. Among other things, we'll be looking at:

1. Balancing speedlights with ambient light throughout the day for controlled effects.
2. Implementing speedlights in complex (and simple) studio portrait lighting setups.
3. Adding modifiers to refine the effects you create.
4. Creating cohesive images through the careful integration of posing, lighting, and composition.

In the Spotlight

Open doors to find inspiration

Sometimes plan B can turn out better than plan A. This happens often on wedding days as I need to constantly change and adapt to the flow of events.

Rain Leads to Exploration

In this case, the heavens let loose with a soaking rain just as we were prepared to go outside and create outdoor bridal portraits. Okay, initiate plan B! In this case, that involved quickly scan-

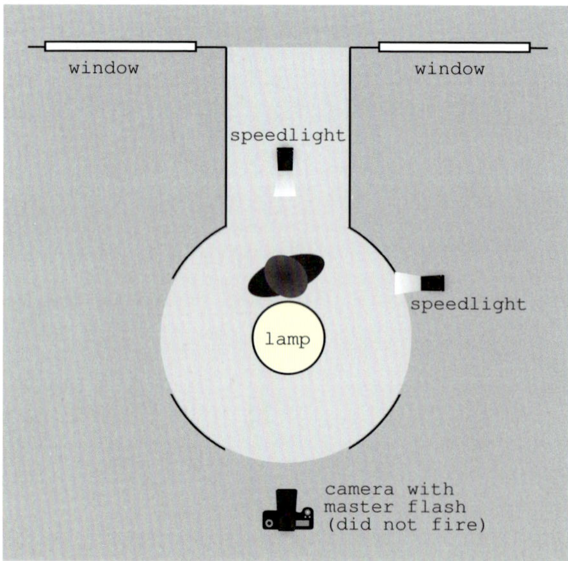

Camera: Canon 5D MKII with Canon 24–105L IS lens set to 24mm
Exposure: ¹/₅₀ second, f/4, ISO 800 (manual)
Lighting: Canon 580EX II speedlight on-camera set to master (did not fire) with RadioPopper PX transmitter. Two Canon 580EX II speed-lights off-camera set to slave and fired with RadioPopper PX receivers.

ning around to see what indoor backgrounds I could find to work with at the venue. On the hunt to discover appealing locations, I found myself peeking through closed doors to see what might lie on the other side. When I opened this door, I said, "Holy cow!" The banquet facility where the event was being held

"I found myself peeking through closed doors to see what might lie on the other side."

doubles as a restaurant the rest of the week, and I had just opened the door to the separate dining area. Talk about cool architectural and compositional elements! I knew that those two hallmarks of my style would be perfectly cap-tured in this setting.

Lighting Objectives

While the room was beautiful, it did present me with several light challenges:

1. **The Room.** I wanted to maintain the am-biance of the room, which meant exposing for enough of the ambient light to give a sense of space.
2. **The Windows.** I wanted to expose for the windows in the back and not allow them to

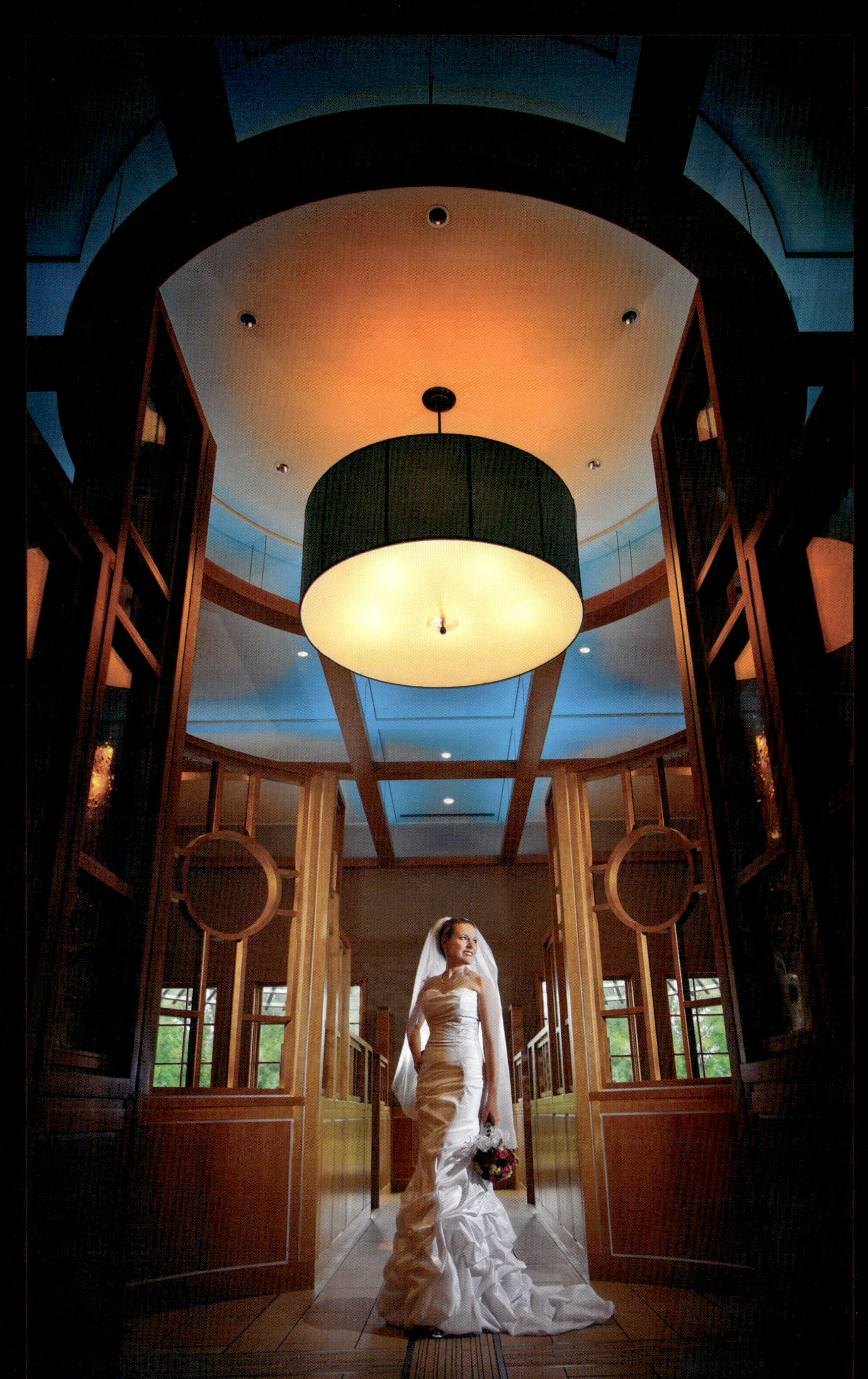

blow out completely to white. Fortunately, the overcast rainy day knocked down the outdoor light to a level I could work with.

3. **The Bride** I also needed to carve out my own dramatic lighting on the bride. I wanted to clearly separate her from the rest of the visual story so that she would become the focal point of the composition.

Good Light + "God" Light

I elected to go with a two-speedlight setup. The main light was on a stand held up and tipped down toward the subject by my assistant, Rachel. The backlight created what I call my "God light" setup because it has a halo effect. I placed a speedlight directly behind the subject and aimed at the small of her back. This created

excellent rim lighting. Both off-camera flashes were set to eTTL in slave mode and triggered using RadioPopper PX receivers. The main light was set to group A and the backlight to group B. A ratio of 8:1 (A:B) was used. To provide more of a spotlight effect and to eliminate flare, my assistant placed a Snootzie adapter on the main light.

In postproduction, the windows were burned down slightly.

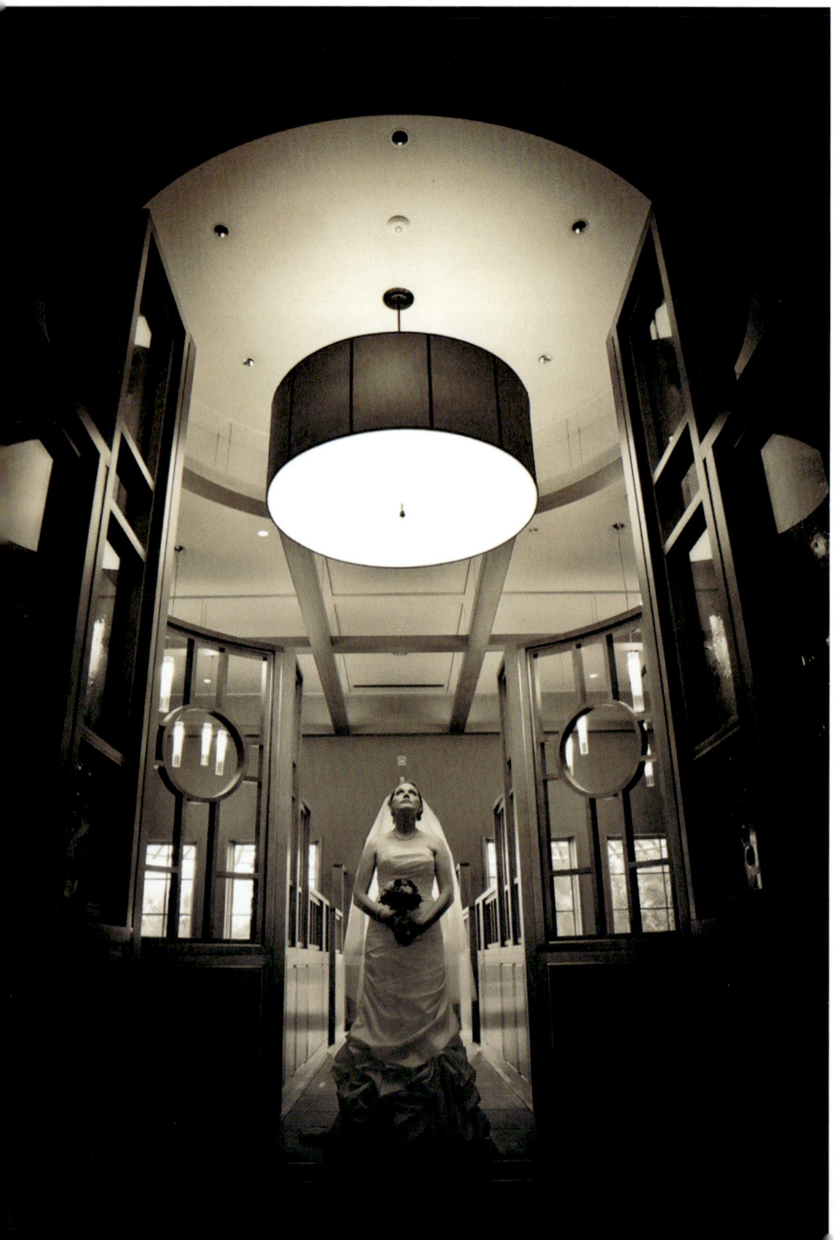

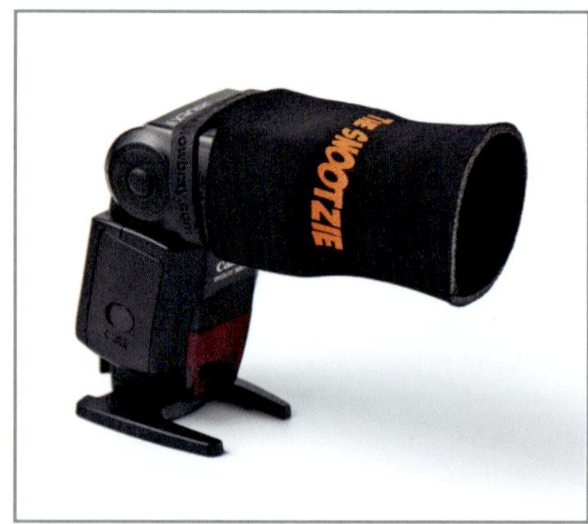

ABOVE—The Snootzie adapter narrows the light beam to eliminate flare.

LEFT—An alternate image with processing from my "Golden Crunch" Lightroom preset.

t some point, early in every photographer's career, one hears that the best outdoor light can be found on overcast days. Then, as we advance in our mastery of light and portraiture, we learn that this sentiment is basically just rubbish. True, the overcast skies do diffuse the harsh sun. Unfortunately, all of this diffuse light is coming *straight down* at our portrait subjects. Without any light augmentation, we are left with low contrast imagery and raccoon-eyed subjects. Yuck.

Unruffled

I was faced with the aforementioned lighting scenario on this wedding day. The bride really wanted portraits by the water, and we are blessed with beautiful lakes in my home base of Madison, Wisconsin.

"Unfortunately, all of this diffuse light is coming straight down at our portrait subjects."

If I were a so-called "natural light photographer" I would have needed to use a reflector to create some semblance of light direction and

Straight out of the camera, and a slightly different pose than the final image (turn the page to see that).

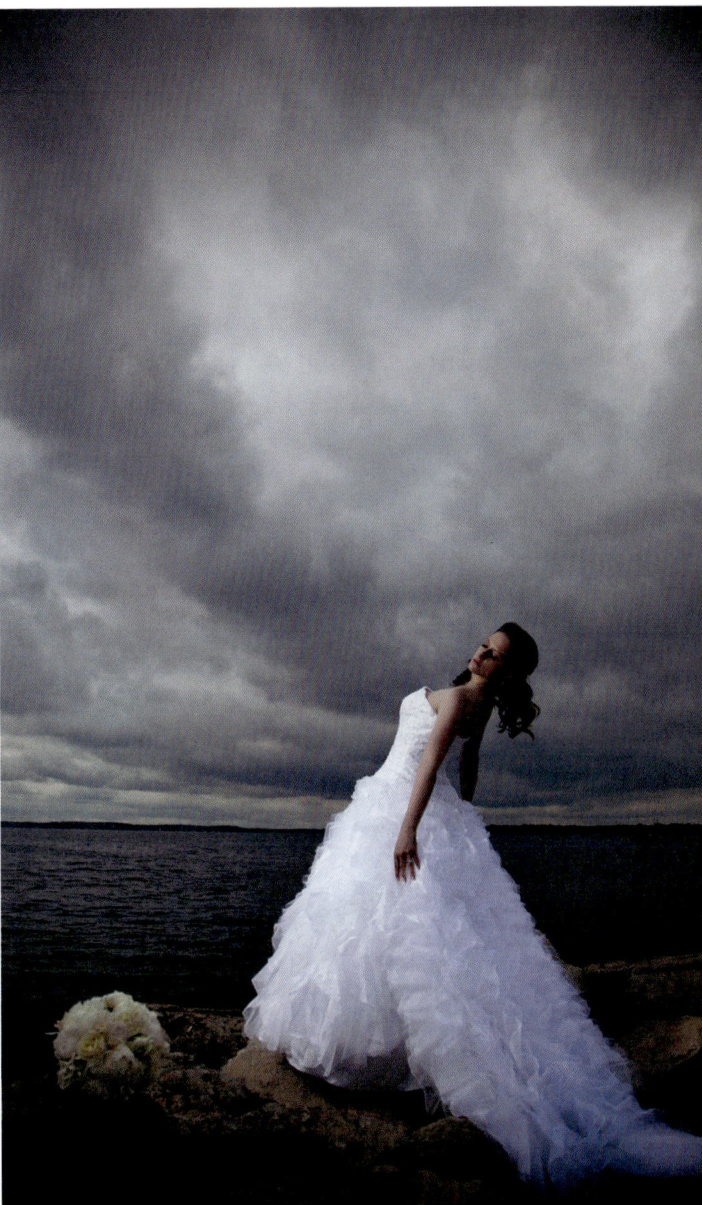

Camera:	Canon 5D MKII with Canon 24–105L IS lens set to 24mm
Exposure:	$^{1}/_{2000}$ second, f/4, ISO 100 (aperture priority)
Lighting:	Canon 580EX II speedlight on-camera set to master (fired as fill) with RadioPopper PX transmitter. Two Canon 580EX II speedlights off-camera set to slave (group A) and fired with RadioPopper PX receivers.

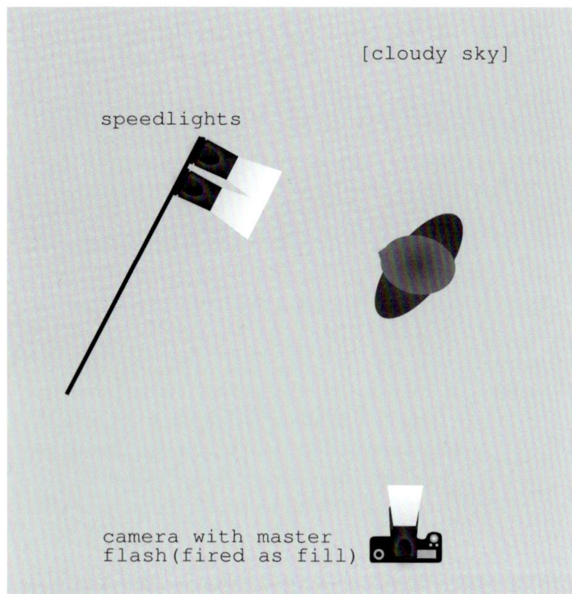

contrast in the portrait. Or, I could have just exposed for the face. However, this would still have left the sky brighter than the subject. It would have dwindled away in whitish nothingness, rather than being the dramatic background I envisioned. Fortunately, I am inclined to bend

Shapes and Textures

Look at that sky. While the day was overcast, the clouds also had an interesting shape and texture. Now, look at the bride's dress. In its skirt, you'll see similar shapes and textures. What a perfect opportunity to bring them together in the composition!

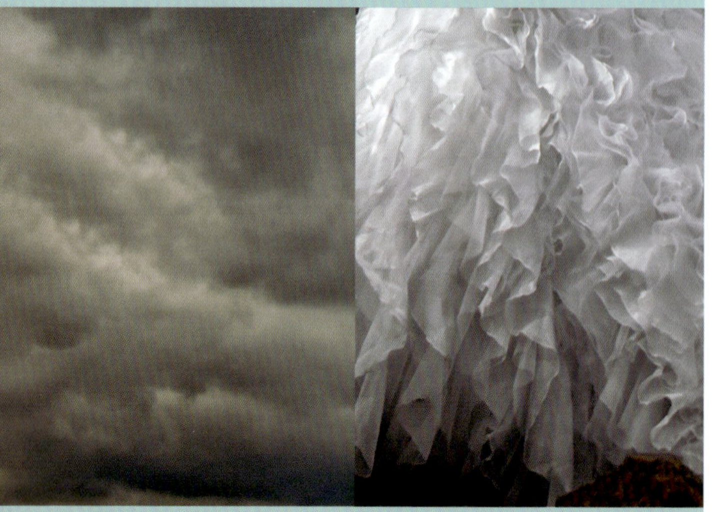

light to my will and to create light where it is needed—and it was definitely needed here.

Posing

Knowing that Adrienne, the bride, had a background in dance, I was able to coax her into a back-bend pose that was appropriate to the look I envisioned.

A Profile in Lighting

The next step was to light it in a way that would simulate a stray shaft of sunlight reaching down to embrace her.

In order to provide proper, classic profile lighting, I had my assistant, Olivia, hold two speedlights on a light stand out over the water and aimed back at Adrienne. I lay down on the sidewalk and shot back up toward Adrienne to accentuate the dramatic pose and to capture more of the sky.

"I laid down on the sidewalk and shot back up toward Adrienne to accentuate the dramatic pose."

Both of the off-camera speedlights were triggered using the RadioPopper PX system. My on-camera flash was set to master and fired in and HSS (high-speed sync) mode, adding some fill light to help open up the detail on the dress.

Postproduction

I used Nik Color Efex Pro's Tonal Contrast filter in postproduction to help pull out more detail in the dress and sky.

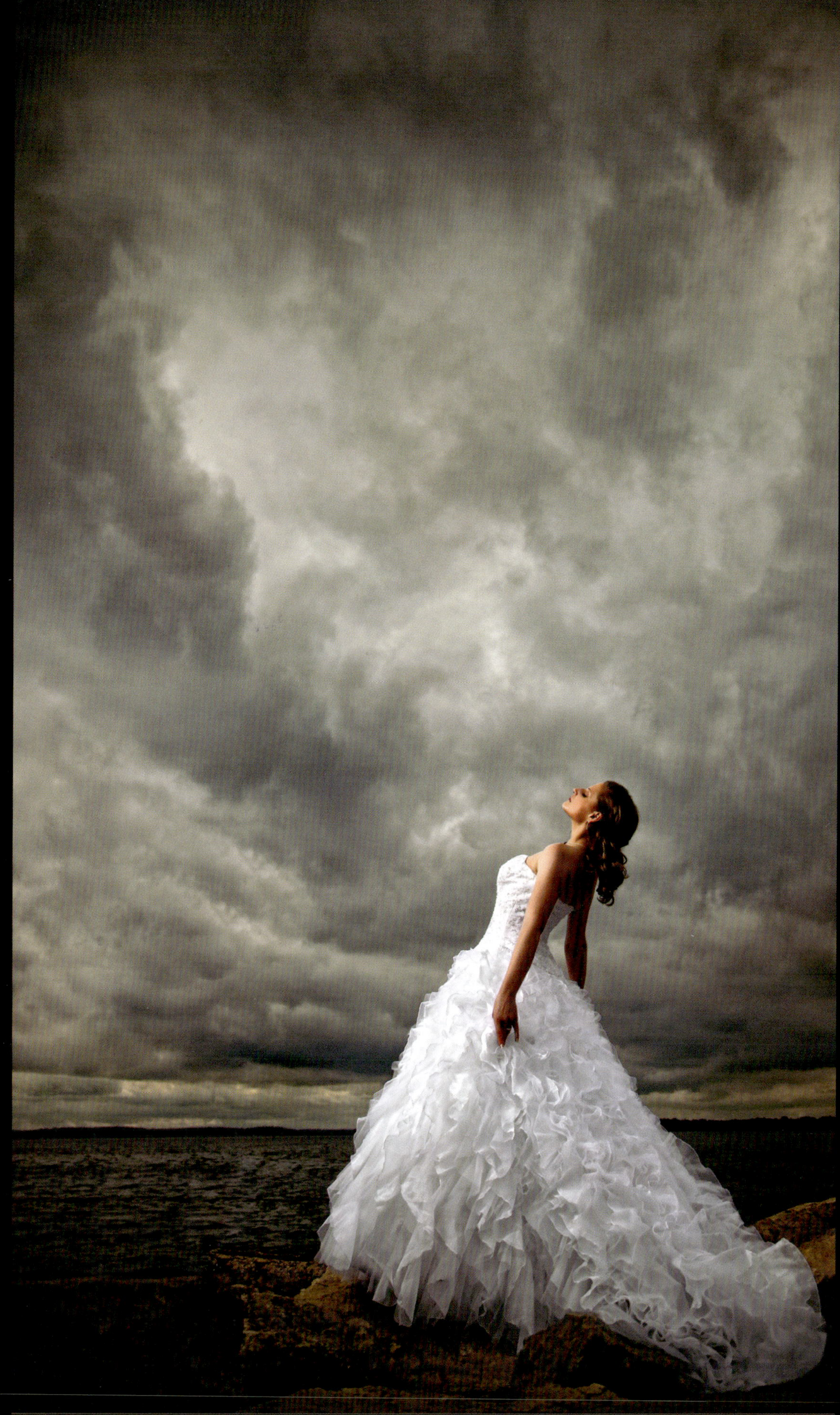

Temptress

Find a muse to help you explore creatively

Every artist needs a muse or two . . . or three. Earlier in my career, I resisted working with models. Maybe I was intimidated; perhaps I was too shy (yeah, right). Mostly I wasn't even sure how to contact one. Now, I regret the time I wasted when I could have been experimenting and growing as an artist. Take my advice, photographers young and old: find a muse. It could be a model. It could be a good friend, or just an acquaintance. Find someone who inspires you creatively and practice your art, then push it to the limits.

I'm Muse Using

I've been fortunate to find a handful of muses, and Erin Thomson is one of them. In addition to being a striking model, Erin is a bundle of ideas. I feed off of her outpouring of creativity and leverage it into my own vision.

The images here are from a session where we collaborated with makeup artist Vanexa Yang. The larger image is from near the end of our session, when we were all really hitting stride. It was shot on a green screen (we were experimenting and I wanted some options), but I found that the play of light and dark on a simple white background offered the most impact.

Camera: Canon 5D MKII, Canon 85mm f/1.8 lens
Exposure: $^1/_{125}$ second, f/9, ISO 400 (manual)
Lighting: Three Canon 580EX II speedlites manually controlled with RadioPopper JrX system and RadioPopper Cubes. *Main light:* 22-inch Kacey Enterprises beauty dish with a white diffusion sock. *Edge lights* (2): 1x4-foot Creative Light softboxes with speedlight speedrings and front egg crates.

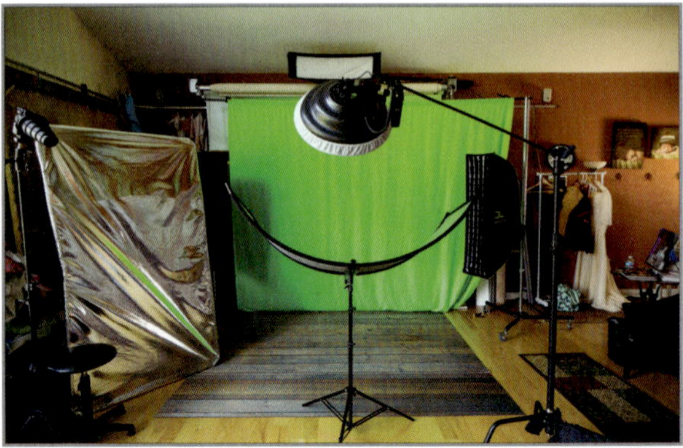

My standard beauty lighting setup, shown from the camera position.

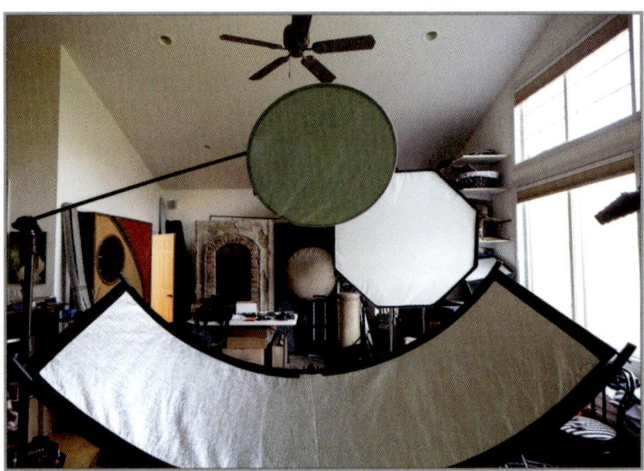

From subject side you can better see the Eyelighter reflector and the positioning of the beauty dish.

Lighting for Beauty

The lighting incorporated one of my favorite beauty setups. The main light was a 22-inch beauty dish, in front of and slightly tilted down toward Erin to light the mask of her face and to provide a catchlight. A curved Eyelighter reflector (manufactured by Larry Peters) bounced light back up into her face, softening shadows and providing a unique catchlight in the bottom of her iris. Dual edge lights set to approximately 45 degrees and behind her created separation. That's it—three lights and a reflector for beautiful lighting.

Speedlight Control

The speedlights were all Canon 580EX IIs. I used the RadioPopper JrX system coupled with their proprietary RadioPopper Cubes. The speedlights attach to this hotshoe-style adapter, allowing me to manually tweak the output up and down from the JrX transmitter at camera position. This is my standard in-studio setup.

The JrX system accommodates three separate control channels. The main light in the beauty dish was set to channel 1. The dual edge lights were both set to channel 3. I normally reserve

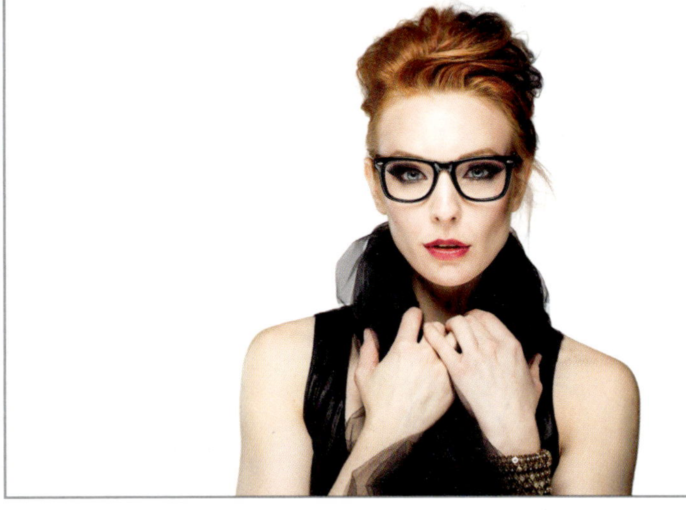

channel 2 as a fill light or a separate hair light, but neither was used in this case.

One non-intuitive aspect of the setup was that the speedlights were all set to eTTL, though not fired in eTTL. The eTTL setting allows the RadioPopper Cube to communicate with the speedlight and choke the power up and down by leveraging the TTL system. I told you, it's not intuitive—but it works beautifully.

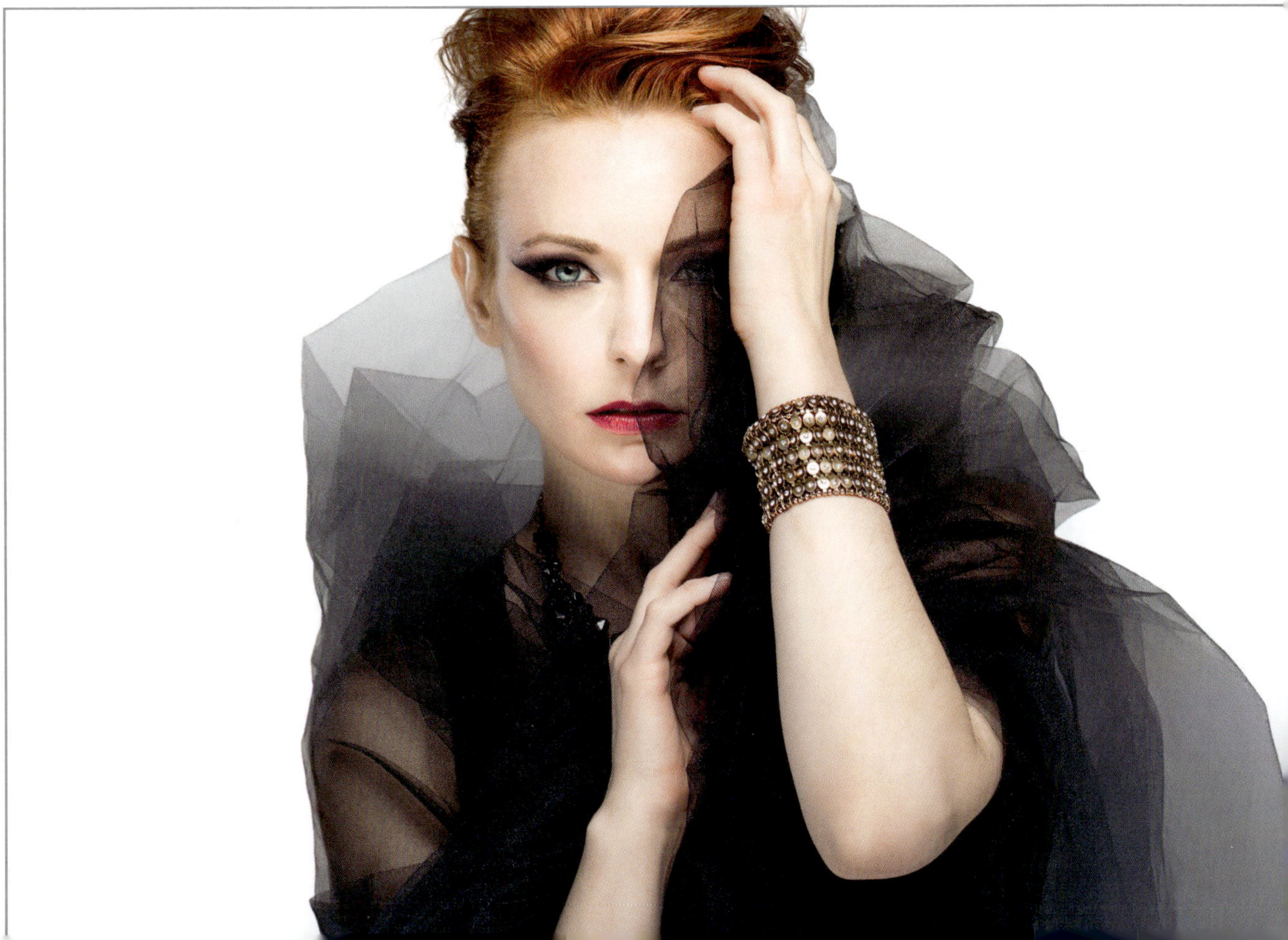

4 | When It's Art, It's Not Cheating

Go the extra distance to complete your vision

I began transitioning to a 99.99 percent speedlight studio in 2010. I was a heavy speedlight user prior to that but primarily used them on-camera for candid wedding work. I preferred AlienBees strobes in the studio and Quantum flashes on location. So let's set the wayback machine to 2009 to show an example of what I was doing back then.

Quantum Theory

Quantum flashes are, in my opinion, beefed up speedlights with an external power pack. They can be used as on-camera flashes but are most often used off-camera. That's how I used them during my two-year flirt with Quantums.

> *"At the time, I did not have the gaggle (swarm? herd?) of speed-lights that I currently possess."*

I worked with Quantum QFlash X2 and T2 flashes. The X2 is a revved-up version of the T2 that runs off 400ws Lumedyne power packs. These are handy when you need a lot of portable power, but heavy and not geared for a long day of shooting. Plus, the power difference isn't as great as I hoped. The X2 provided just over 1 stop more power than the 580EX II; the T2 output $\frac{1}{3}$ to $\frac{1}{2}$ stop more than the 580EX II.

So why did I even use them? Excellent question. At the time, I did not have the gaggle (pod? swarm? herd?) of speedlights that I currently possess. Used Quantums with battery packs could be found on eBay for less than the cost of new speedlights, so I opted to use them as my off-camera flashes for weddings and location work rather than investing in more speedlights. It was a worthy experiment, but it delayed my full conversion to speedlights.

Jalapeño Lighting

For wedding portraits, my methodology was simple but effective. My assistant would hold the Quantum up on a monopod (I called this combination the "jalapeño on a stick," in hom-

The original capture.

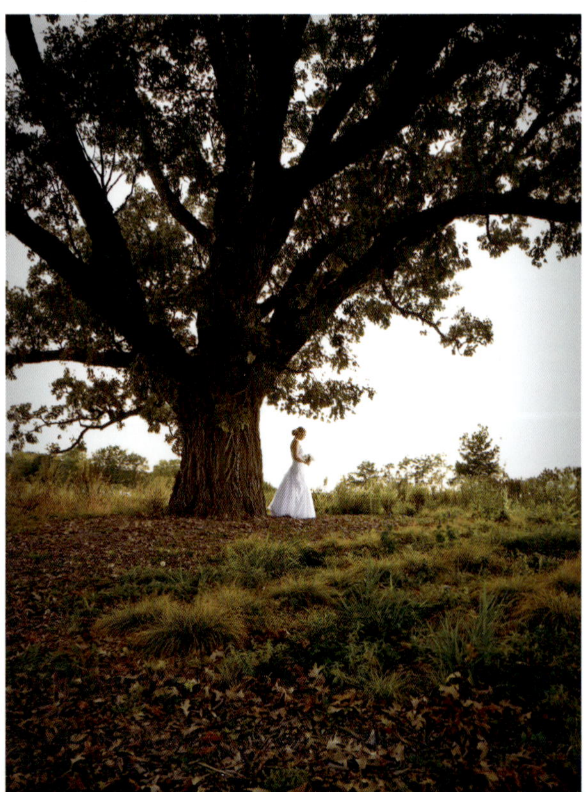

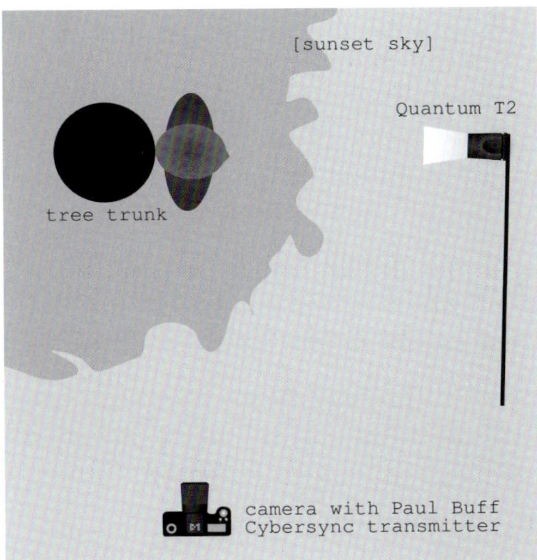

age to comedian Jeff Dunham). I would have her set the power anywhere from $\frac{1}{8}$ to full power, depending on the lighting situation, then I would walk her back and forth and in and out from the subject until I got the lighting pattern and volume that I wanted. It wasn't elegant, but it worked quickly on location.

For this shot my assistant, Alli, was perpendicular to the camera and facing directly toward the bride (just out of frame on the right). The Quantum T2 was set to $\frac{1}{2}$ power. The ambient light was primarily from behind my subject, so I needed to create direction and dimension with the off-camera lighting. I set my exposure to hold detail in the shadow parts of the tree and adjusted Alli's position with the lighting until I achieved the desired lighting look. The flash lit the bride, opened up detail on the tree trunk, and added interest on the grass.

Camera: Canon 5D MKII with Canon 24–105L lens at 24mm
Exposure: $\frac{1}{80}$ second, f/4, ISO 200 (manual)
Lighting: Quantum T2 at $\frac{1}{2}$ power triggered by Paul Buff Cybersync transmitter and receiver

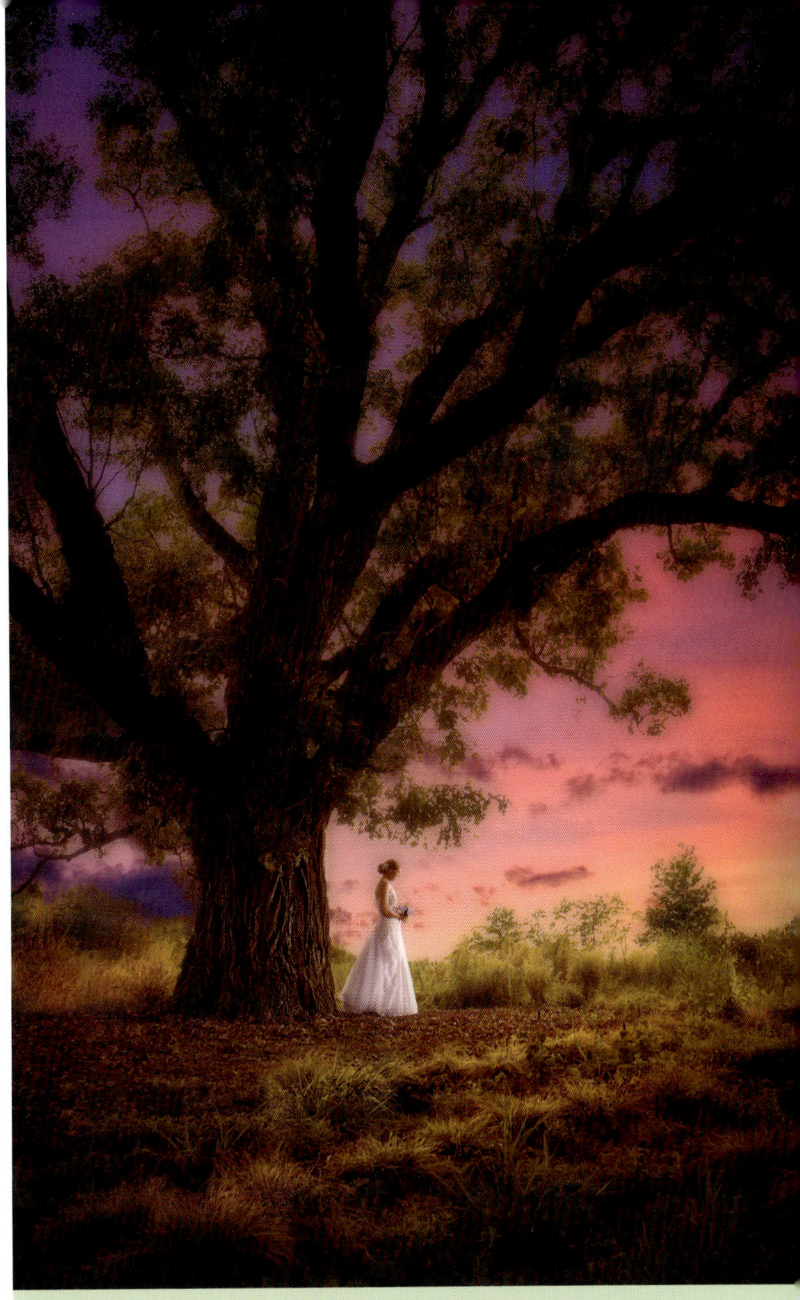

This image earned a Best of Show (Wedding) award in Wisconsin, as well as Kodak Gallery and Fuji Masterpiece awards. It has also become an iconic image in my portfolio, drawing brides to me for my artistic approach to wedding photography.

Not Cheating?

So what's the "art isn't cheating" part? I was shooting toward a dead, white sky—and it was 4:47PM, so I didn't have time to wait for a sunset. I let the sky go an even white, planning to add a beautiful sunset in postproduction. I dropped in the colorful sky as an overlying layer above the white sky and set the blend mode on the new layer to Multiply. Only minimal masking was needed along the horizon line and in a few spots on the tree and leaves to complete the look.

5

Bridge Players

Speedlighting in the rain

Into every life a little rain must fall. But what if it is on a wedding day? Do you stay inside? If so, that's fine with me. I'll be the one outside creating images like this.

A Bridge Not Too Far

The rain started moments after we arrived at the beautiful Rotary Gardens. Luckily, Dan and Catherine were game to keep going. I positioned the couple on the Japanese bridge, placing Dan on the down slope since he is much

The final result earned a Best of Show (Wedding) award in Wisconsin, as well as a Kodak Gallery Award.

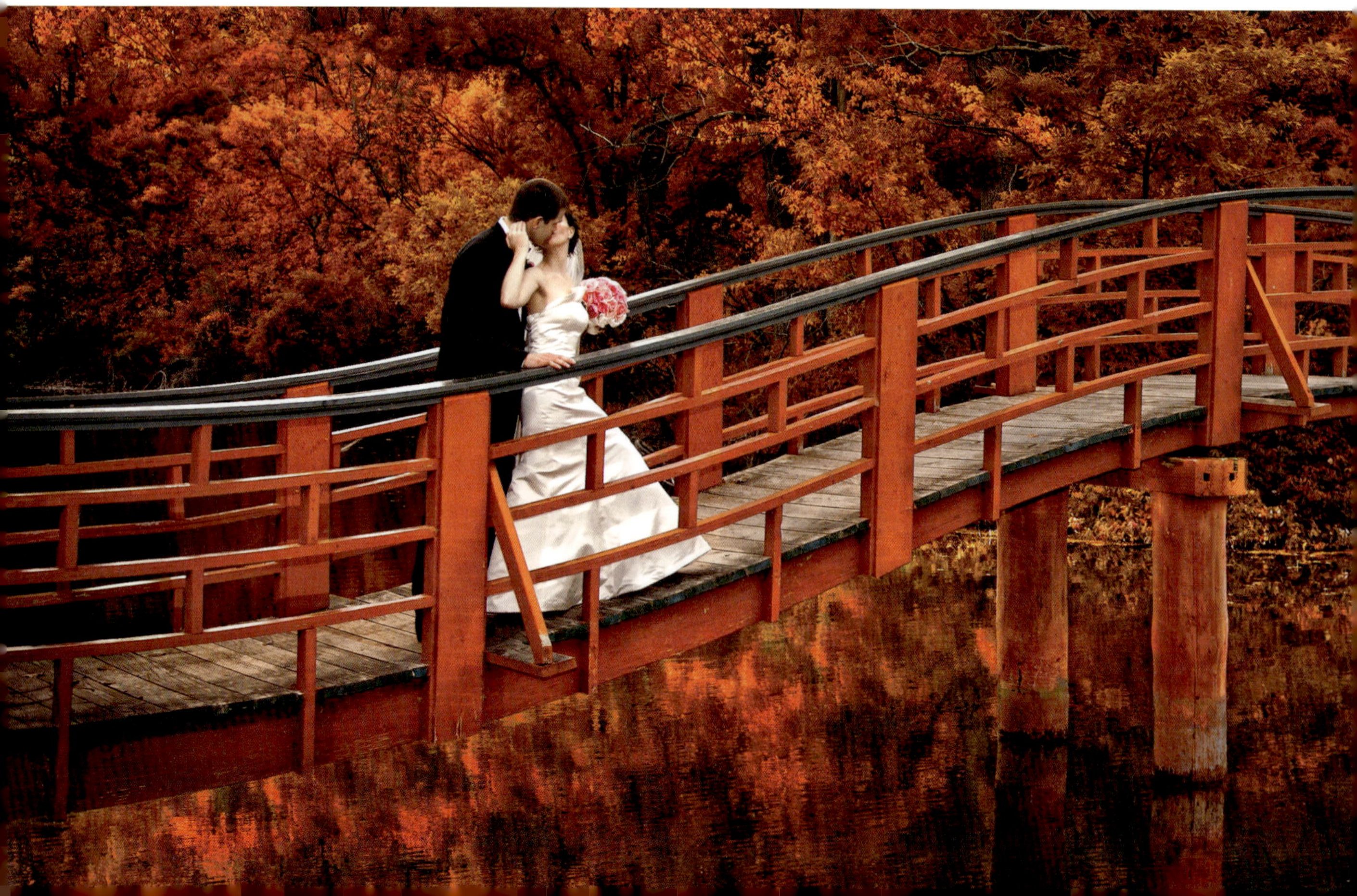

taller than Catherine. This evened their heights and allowed for the romantic pose I envisioned.

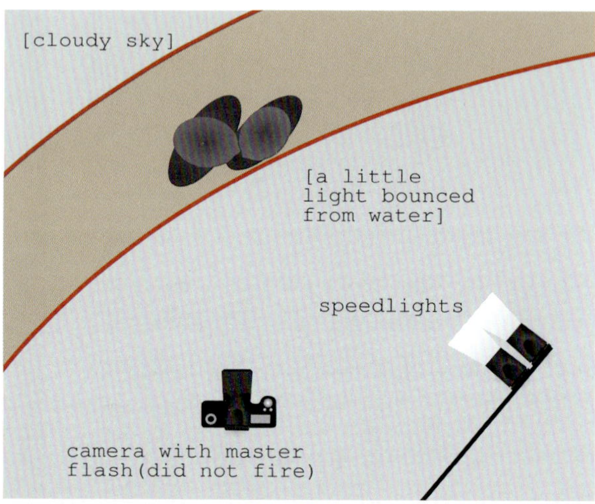

The light from the overcast sky was soft, but it was coming straight down, with just a little reflecting from the water. I needed some lateral direction for better dimension and separation. I positioned my assistant, Olivia, to camera right with a Canon 580EX II speedlight at the edge of the water, about 80 feet from the couple. The flash was set to eTTL in slave mode and fired via the RadioPopper PX. The subdued ambient light let me bump up to ISO 640 for more power from my off-camera flash.

An Extra Step

It is critical to get images right in the camera, but in this case I also envisioned something more: a picturesque fall background. Unfortunately, the wedding took place in September, long before the trees had the vibrant fall colors for which Wisconsin is known. This image needed an extra step to be "complete." It's this extra

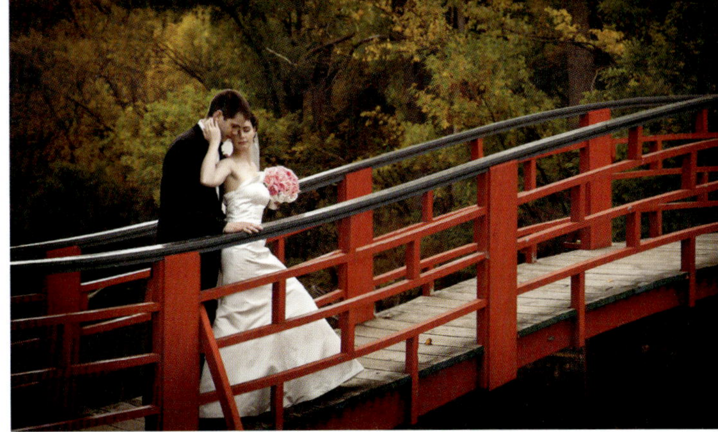

The original capture lacked the fall colors I envisioned.

step, taken when necessary, that helps differentiate me from other photographers. You need to be able to "see" the possibilities at the time of capture, then bring that potential to fruition.

In postproduction, I used filters from Nik Color Efex Pro 3.0: Indian Summer (turns green foliage into fall colors) and Tonal Contrast (pumps up contrast, detail, and saturation). I masked to constrain the Indian Summer treatment to the foliage and to remove the Tonal Contrast effect from the subjects' skin (where it can create an unpleasant look).

I also enhanced the reflection in the water by copying some of the trees and overlaying them at a low opacity. The original red of the bridge clashed slightly with the oranges of the foliage, so I color shifted it into the orange spectrum. Lastly, I cropped to a panoramic composition to heighten the overall impact of the image.

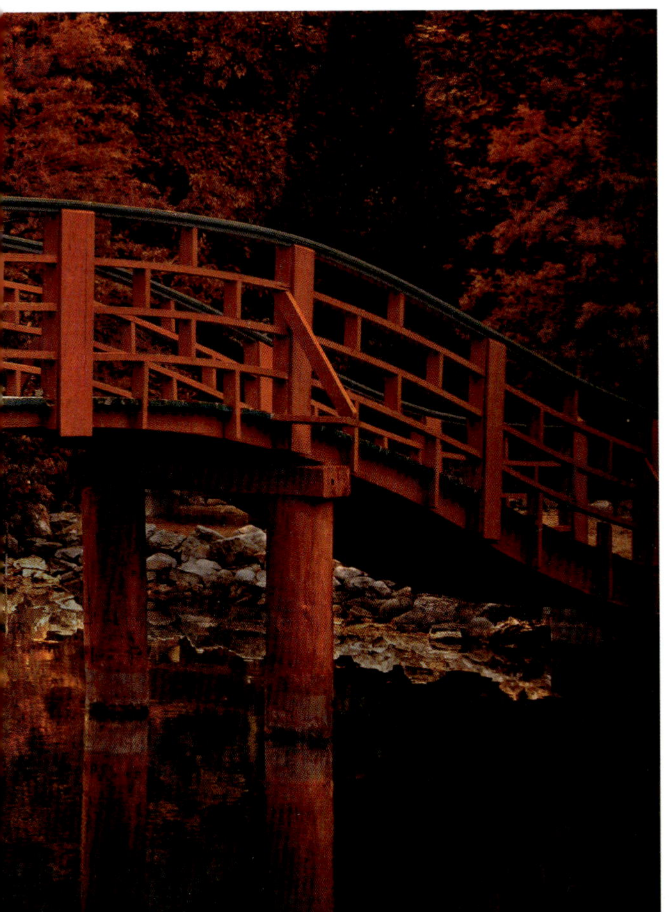

Keep Dry

To protect it from the rain, everything on the light stand was covered with a clear plastic bag—the type that I use to cover wall portraits when delivering them to my clients.

Camera: Canon 5D MKII with 24–105L lens at 40mm
Exposure: 1/200 second, f/6.3, ISO 640 (aperture priority)
Lighting: Canon 580EX II speedlight on-camera set to master (did not fire) with RadioPopper PX transmitter. Canon 580EX II off-camera set to eTTL and slave mode, fired with RadioPopper PX receiver.

6

Arising

Create your own sunrise

I often used speedlights to battle the sun in the middle of the day. But sometimes I also use them to create the sun. This wedding image is such an example.

Something to Crow About

Most of our wedding day coverage starts at noon or 1:00PM. Sometimes we start as early as 11:00AM. However, Bao and Daniel had a morning ceremony planned—and they also wanted to have the majority of their couple and wedding-party photographs created prior to the ceremony. So my primary associate, Krystal Lamberty, and I got up at 0-dark-30 in order to prepare for the day's coverage and arrive at a little country church by 7:00AM. As we opened the car doors, we literally heard a rooster crow. Yes, it was *that* early.

Here Comes the Sun

Our early-morning experience was what inspired my idea for this image. The concept was the bride greeting and embracing the sunrise on the morning of her wedding. As it turned out, by the time we finished with our images at the country church and traveled to our primary location (the state capitol building), it was

Camera: Canon 5D MKII with 24–105L lens at 24mm
Exposure: ¹/₂₅₀ second, f/5.6, ISO 200 (aperture priority)
Lighting: Canon 580EX II speedlight on-camera set to master (did not fire) with RadioPopper PX transmitter. Two Canon 580EX II speedlights off-camera set to eTTL and slave mode, fired with RadioPopper PX receivers. On the camera-right flash, a Snootzie was added to narrow the beam.

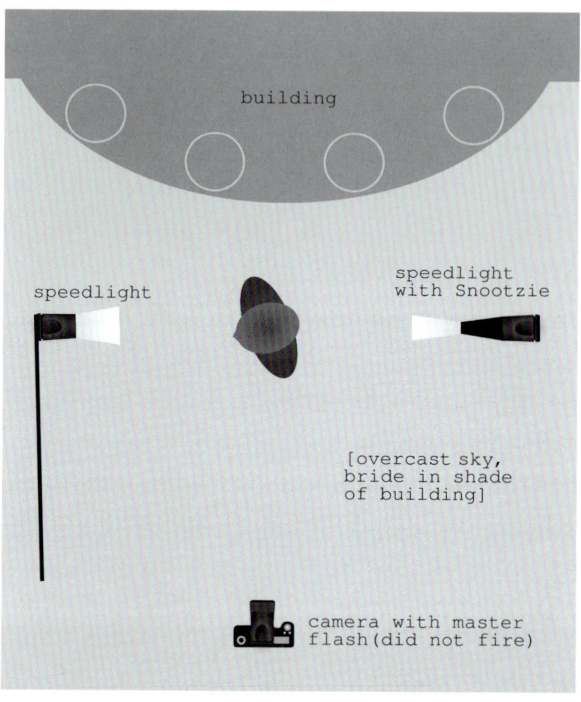

9:00AM—more than a little late for a real sunrise shot with natural light. Undaunted, I guided the clients to the shaded side of the capitol and

"The 'sun' was a bare speedlight held up high on an extended light stand."

used speedlights to create my desired lighting for the concept.

The "sun" was a bare speedlight held up high on an extended light stand. Additional

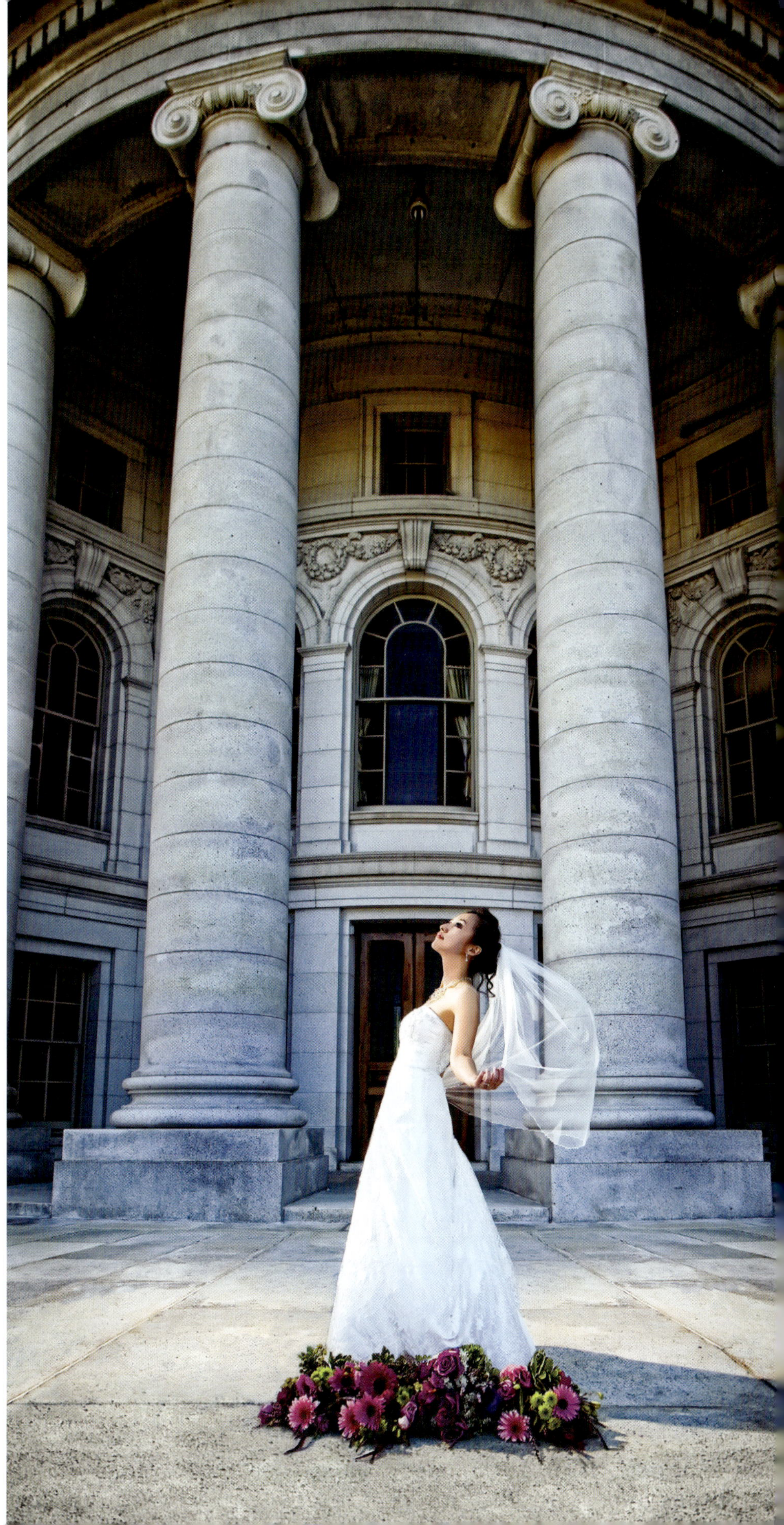

separation lighting was added to camera right, consisting of a speedlight with a Snootzie attachment to tighten the beam and prevent lens flare. This separation light was aimed at her veil.

Both speedlights were set to eTTL in slave mode with the main light set to group A and the edge light set to group B. This allowed me to create a ratio on my master flash. The radio was set to 8:1 (A:B).

Postproduction

The colors and detail in the image were enhanced with Nik Color Efex Pro's Tonal Contrast filter.

Surprise!

As my finger was literally on the shutter, we had a last-second creative addition. At the urging of one of the bridesmaids, the bouquets were placed at the bride's feet. I don't generally go for the "put the bouquets on the train" look or other hokey stuff like that . . . but for some odd reason, it kind of works here.

7 | Luminous

A play of light and dark

Acommon theme across much of my location work is the use of speedlights to create light and contrast where none currently exists in the scene.

On this particular day, we were working under overcast skies, and occasional light rain

"I spied the red bench in front of the brutish gray expanse of a state office building."

was moving into the area as we were wrapping up our location photography. In fact, we were actually done shooting on location and were walking back to the reception venue when I spied the red bench in front of the brutish gray expanse of a state office building.

With the bride Nicole's fair skin, blond hair, and white wedding dress, I felt it was a perfect opportunity to play with a variety of contrasts, working with light against dark, and pretty against dank.

> **Camera:** Canon 5D MKII with 24–105L lens at 24mm
> **Exposure:** $^1/_{400}$ second, f/5.6, ISO 400, $+^2/_3$EV exposure compensation (aperture priority)
> **Lighting:** Canon 580EX II speedlight on-camera, set to master (did not fire) with RadioPopper PX transmitter. Canon 580EX II speedlights off-camera set to eTTL and slave mode, fired with RadioPopper PX receiver.

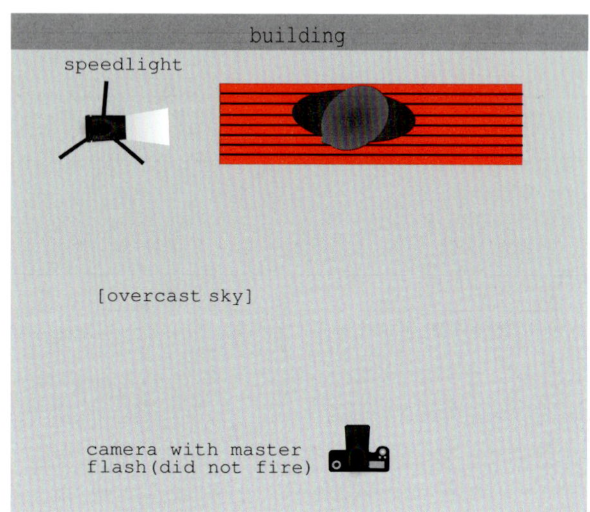

Getting Something Out of My Tax Dollars

With the gray dinginess of the government building serving as a frame, I wanted the bride to appear to be the only source of light in the composition.

One speedlight was set up on a light stand to camera left and placed just out of frame to light the bride, posed in profile. I lay down with my camera in the street in order to get the angle I needed and shot the image with my zoom lens adjusted to its widest setting: 24mm.

Postproduction

Knowing that the use of this lens would cause obvious distortion on the architecture, I planned to straighten the building in the postproduction process—and possibly to extend its

Distortion

This alternate version shows the build-ing distortion caused by the use of the wide-angle lens.

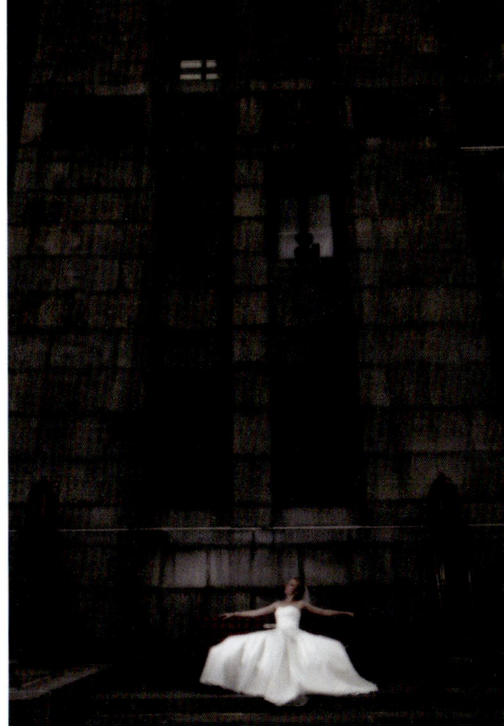

apparent height by adding another story or two.

In addition, the two lamp posts were originally off center and needed to be repositioned to enhance the symmetry of the composition.

Finally, I further darkened the back-ground and softened the shadow cast by the bride onto the face of the building. The resulting image draws focus and at-tention to the bride, even though she is quite small in the frame.

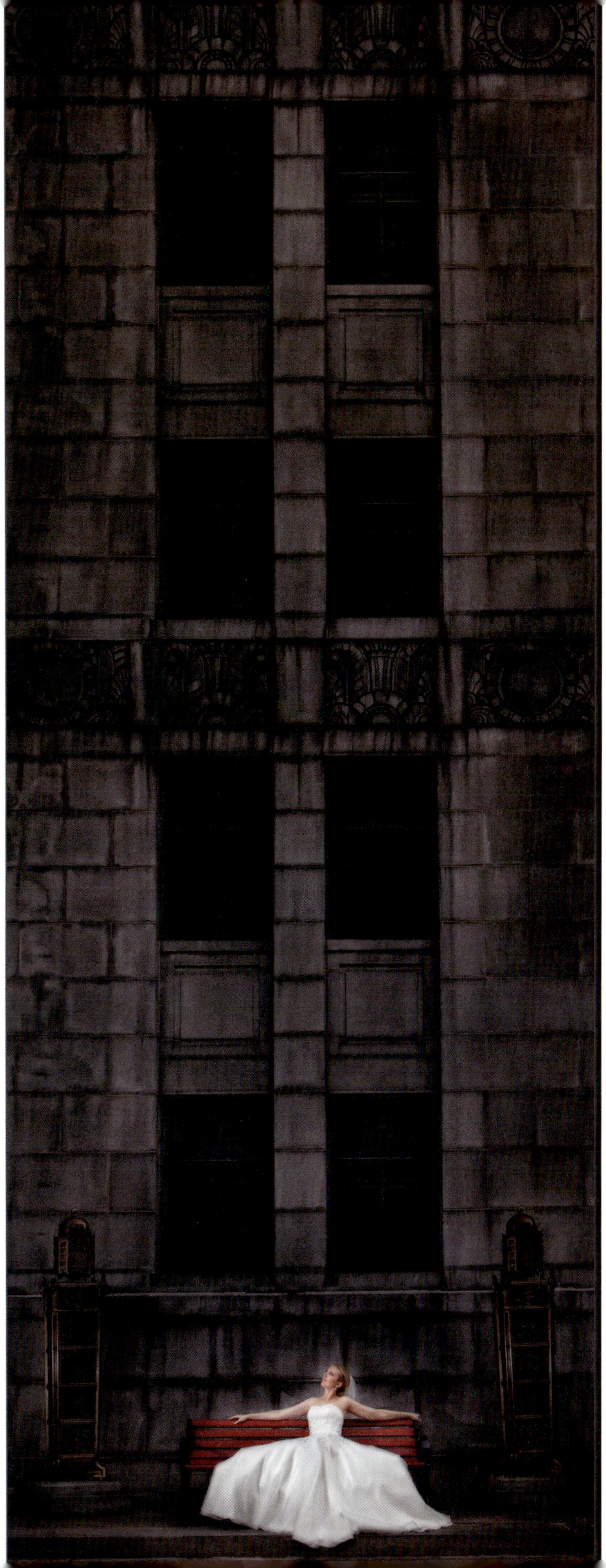

The final image earned a Best of Show (Wed-ding) award in Wisconsin.

A Dip in the Sun

A new view on an old pose

The dip is a classic yet somewhat cliché pose for wedding couples. Still, I see few that are executed well. The pose needs a semblance of spontaneity, even if the moment was constructed and directed.

"A lens of any focal length can be used for a portrait—if it is used correctly."

For this classic dip shot, I incorporated three additional levels of sophistication that help separate it from the average shot.

1. **Camera Angle.** I got low and shot back toward a vibrant blue sky with interesting puffy clouds.
2. **Lens Selection.** I used a 15mm fisheye lens as my portrait lens. (Purists may call "foul" at this, but I will explain my choice in a moment.)
3. **Flash Fill.** I mixed in high-speed flash to fill in unsightly shadows and to better match the sky in the background.

Camera: Canon 5D MKII with 15mm lens
Exposure: 1/640 second, f/6.3, ISO 160, +1/3EV exposure compensation (aperture priority)
Lighting: Canon 580EX II speedlight on-camera set to eTTL

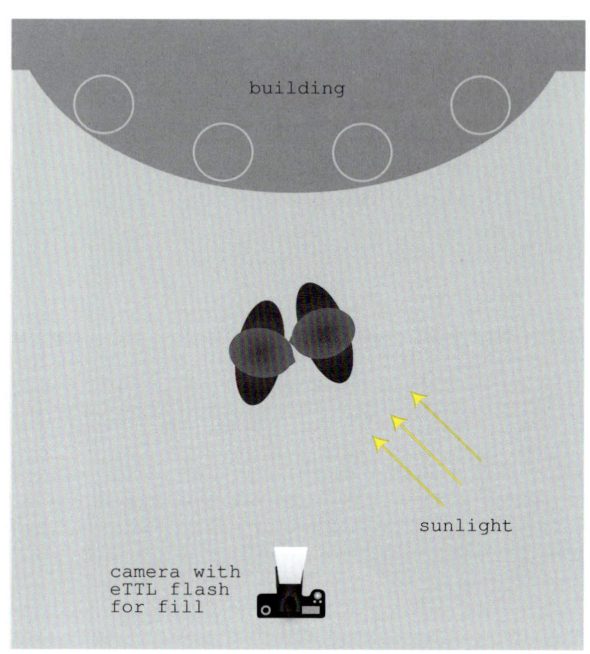

Something's Fishy Here

"A fisheye lens is *not* a portrait lens," thunders the rigid purist. While I agree that it is not a standard choice, I would argue that a lens of any focal length can be used for a portrait—if it is used correctly. In this image, I wanted the couple to be more dominant than the large capitol dome behind them. Using the fisheye made the building visually recede while placing the emphasis on the couple in the foreground. I was only a few feet away from the couple, but the fisheye makes them appear to be a "normal" distance away from me. I kept my subjects toward the center of the frame to minimize distortion, which increases toward the edges.

This image was selected for the PPA Loan Collection.

Fill Me In

The sky behind the dome was the last bit of open sky as heavy cloud cover was rolling in. The subjects were actually in the front edge of this cloud cover. I added fill flash from my on-camera speedlight to open up the shadows on them and to provide contrast that matched the background.

Postproduction

I adjusted for distortion using the excellent lens adjustment tools found in Lightroom and Photoshop. Finally, I cropped to a tall, narrow format to enhance the composition and eliminate any distortion at the edges of the original frame.

Getting Low

A low camera angle adds impact and drama to the image. If you shoot everything at eye level, mix it up a little! You're missing opportunities to gain interesting perspectives that the average person cannot already see in a scene. Here, the composition places the subjects' faces right on the power point of a one-third line (study the Rule of Thirds if you are not familiar with it).

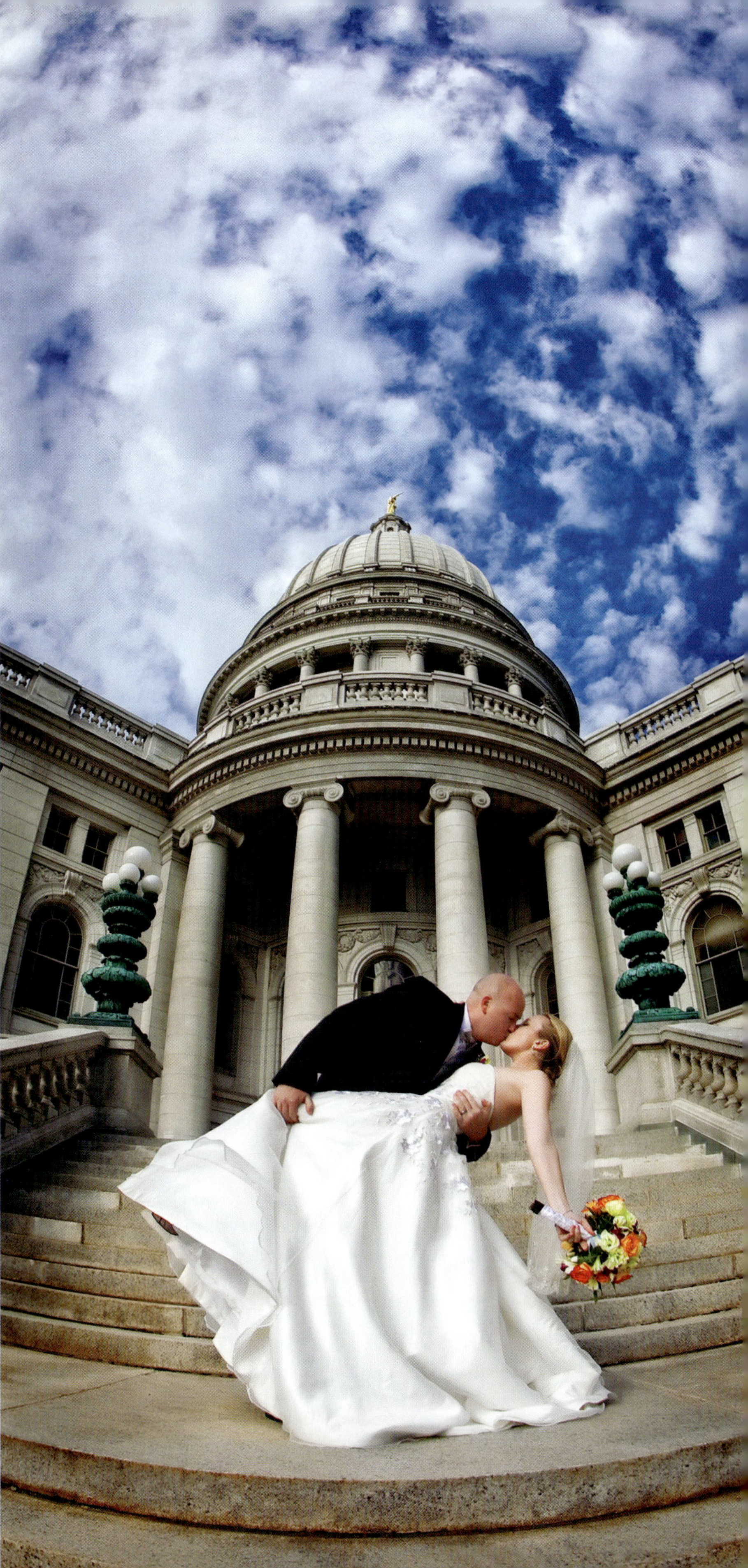

9 | Bench Pressing

Get low, get wide, shoot big

This is a second image from my wedding with Adrienne, the bride with the ruffled dress seen in section 2. Again, I was working with an overcast yet interesting sky, so I had most of the ambient light coming from behind the subjects. In this case, I used a combination of three speedlights as directional fill, combined with a 15mm fisheye lens in order to force the perspective and capture as much of the interesting sky as I could.

Dynamic Composition

I positioned Adrienne and her groom, Kerry, at the ends of the benches and had them lean across to meet in the middle with a kiss. This added a touch of romance as well as a more dynamic pose with the angles of their torsos. It also allowed the two benches to serve as leading lines and frames for the couple. Additionally, I swept the dress out to the front to provide another leading line and to also serve as a complement to the texture of the sky.

I lay on the concrete (I seem to do this a lot; it's tough staying clean at a wedding) to enhance the compositional angle.

Lighting

My on-camera flash fired low to fill the lower half of the scene. My two off-camera speedlights

> **Camera:** Canon 5D MKII with 15mm lens
> **Exposure:** $^1/_{2000}$ second, f/4.5, ISO 100, $-^1/_3$EV exposure compensation (aperture priority)
> **Lighting:** Canon 580EX II speedlight on camera set to master (fired) with RadioPopper PX transmitter. Two Canon 580EX II speedlights off camera set to eTTL and slave mode, fired with RadioPopper PX receivers.

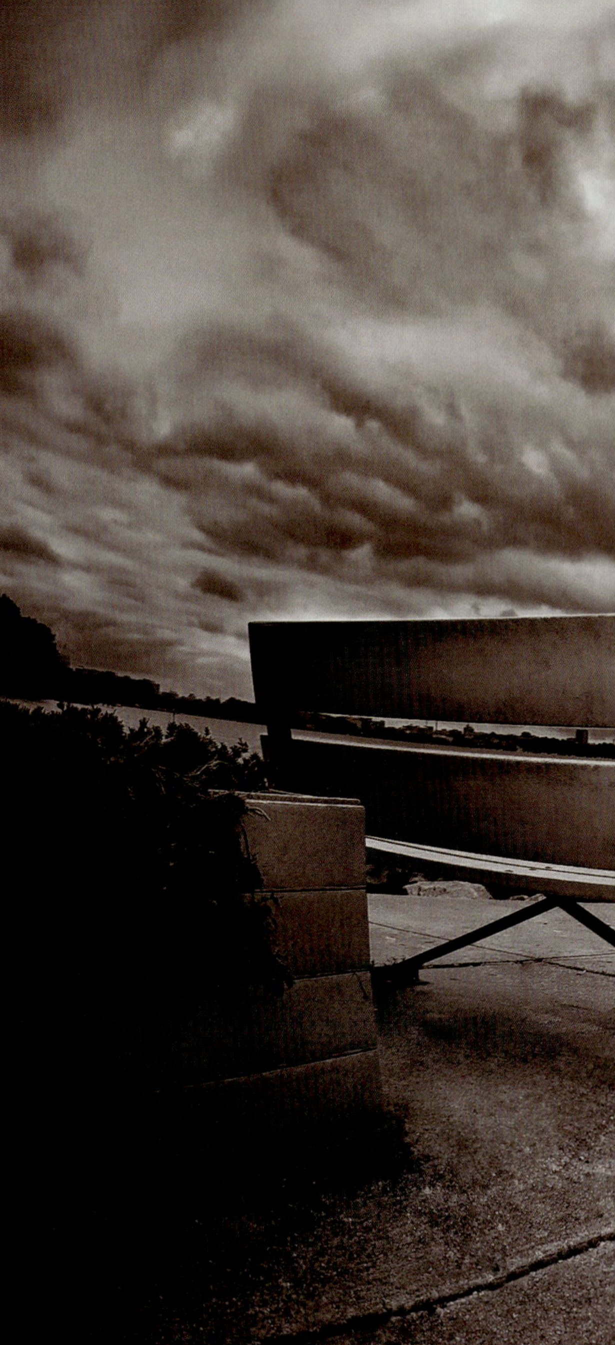

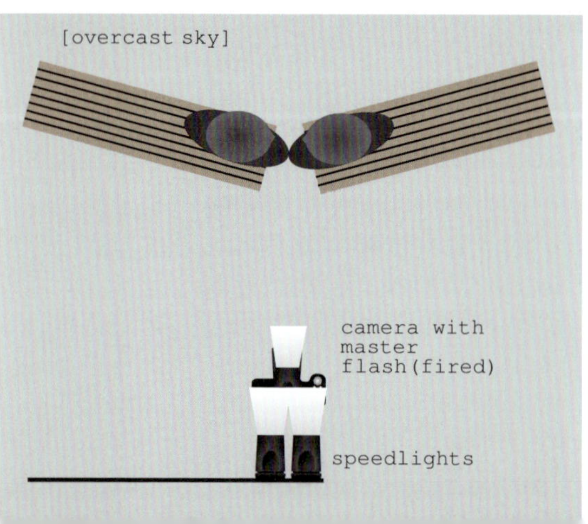

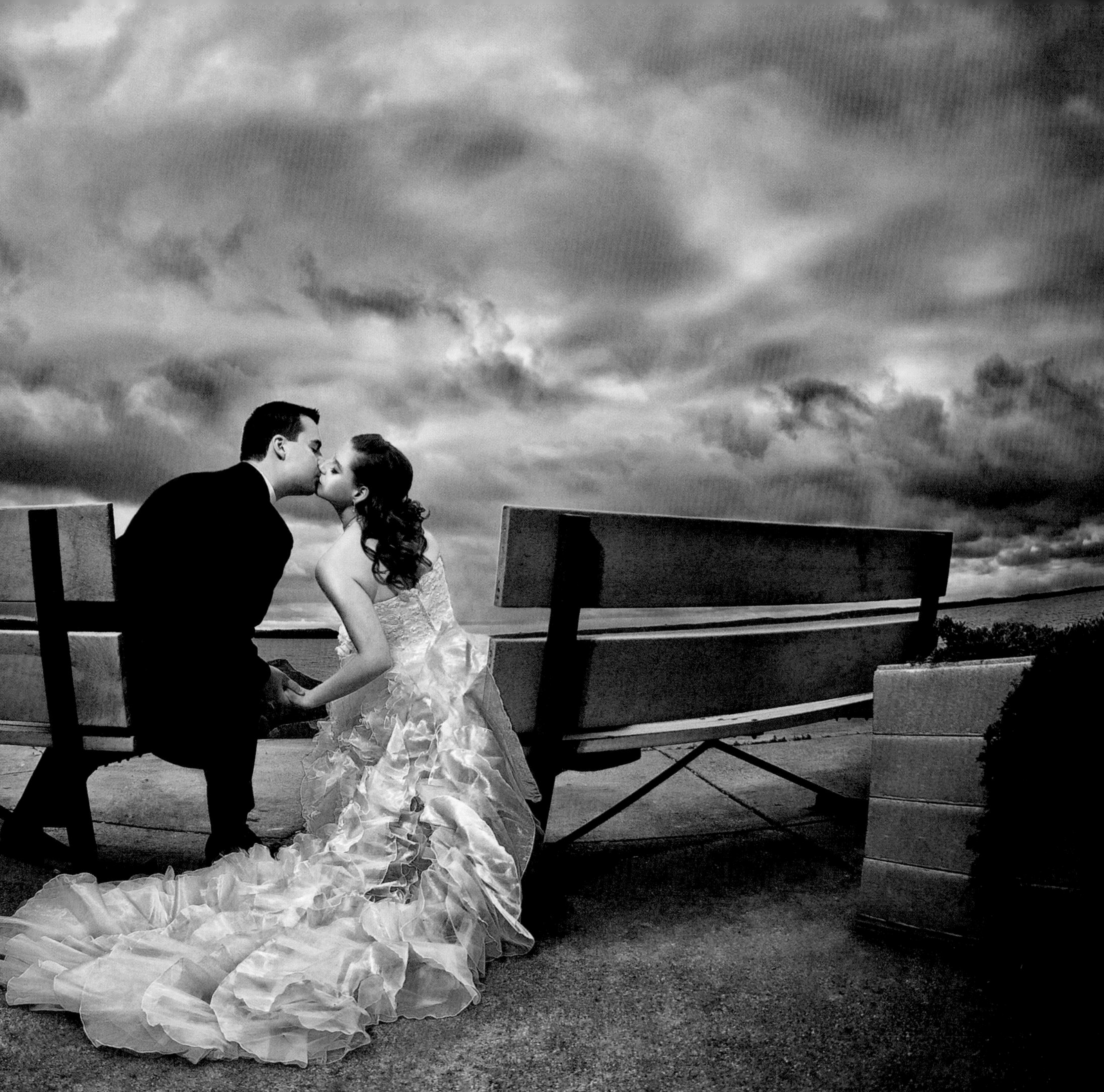

ganged together from above and tipped down to provide pleasing light on the couple's faces. All flashes were in high-speed sync (HSS) eTTL in order to maintain the exposure of the sky while keeping a more shallow depth of field.

Fixing the Fish

I fixed most of the fisheye distortion in Lightroom, then converted the image to a warm-tone monochrome using my Chocolate Thunder Lightroom preset. The texture in the scene was enhanced using Nik's Tonal Contrast filter.

10

Boldly Light Where None Has Gone Before

Create light to make any location fit your vision

One of the major advantages of a speed-light portrait system is that it allows me to create the light that I want virtually anywhere. That opens up so many possibilities. There's no more, "That would be an awesome spot, but the sun is too bright." I simply mix in some speedlights in high-speed sync (HSS) mode and tame the sun. Likewise, there's no more, "That

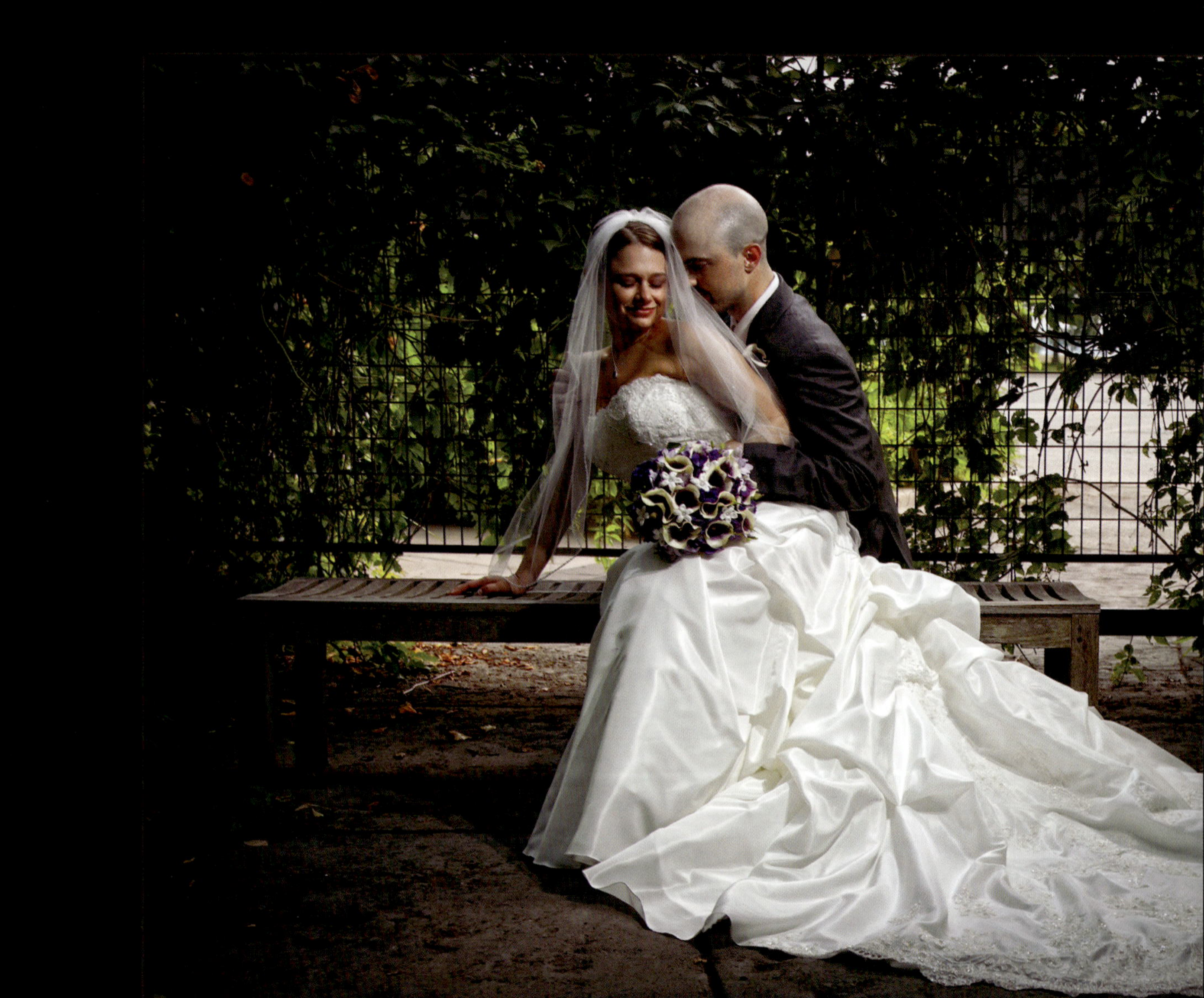

would be a great spot but the light is blah." I spice it up with some speedlights and create my own interesting light. That is exactly what I did for this portrait. By adding my own light, this interesting but underlit nook magically became a great photo setting.

Something Unexpected

I saw this alcove with a bench tucked away from the major attractions in the local botanical gardens where *everybody* shoots the same locations.

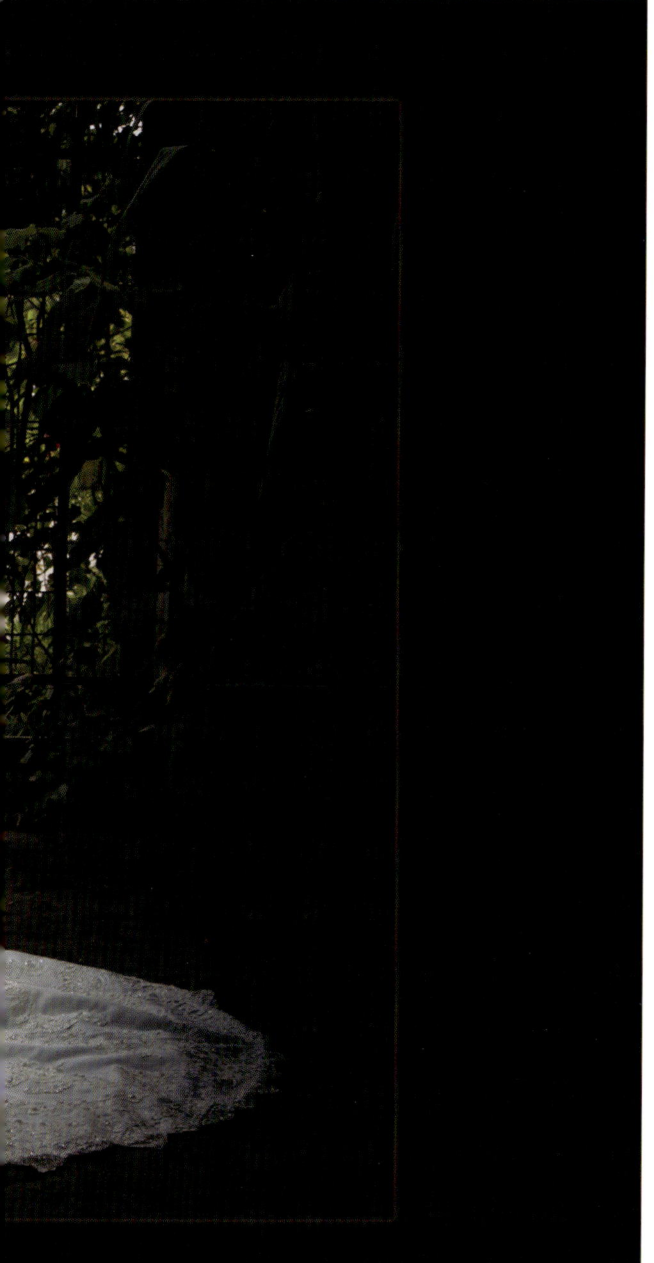

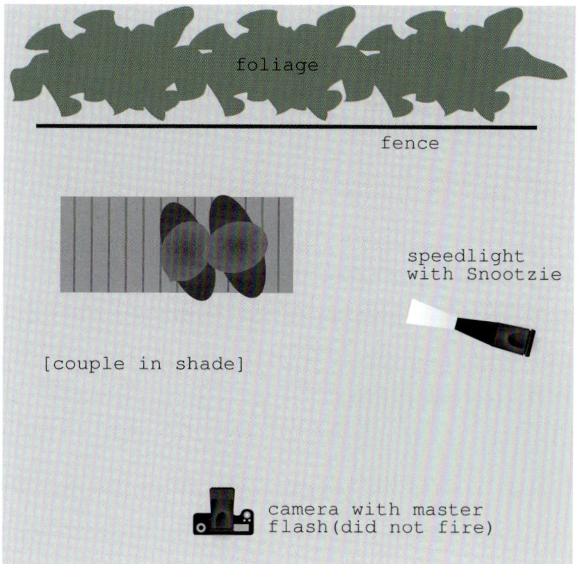

I was looking for something different, something intimate in this very public place. When I saw this little spot, I realized that a little bit of lighting would make it work quite nicely.

Lighting and Posing

While I am know for my dramatic and artistic work, I also like to create romantic portraiture of the wedding (and I shoot a lot of photojournalistic images, too!).

With this portrait, I wanted something showing the two of them in a moment alone, away from the throngs. I snuggled Chad in tightly to his bride and had them close their eyes and enjoy the moment. The lighting was simply one off-camera speedlight fitted with a Snootzie to give a spotlight effect.

It's a simple, but it's still well lit—and it has emotional meaning for the couple.

Camera: Canon 5D MKII with 24–105L lens at 45mm
Exposure: $^1/_{250}$ second, f/5.6, ISO 200 (aperture priority)
Lighting: Canon 580EX II speedlight on-camera set to master (did not fire) with Radio-Popper PX transmitter. Canon 580EX II speedlight off-camera set to eTTL and slave mode, fired with RadioPopper PX receiver.

11

Going Parasoling

Dramatic profile lighting in the midday sun

You will notice that most of the images shown in this book do not feature the subjects smiling and looking straight at the camera.

While images like that are a necessary element of any portrait and wedding photographer's portfolio, they are also fairly boring, cliché, and expected. I like to stretch to create the unexpected because it ensures that I stand out from other photographers. This helps me attract more business.

"I see it as a modern take on a turn-of the-century-portrait with a fashionable lady . . ."

Perhaps more importantly, however, is that this artistic type of imagery is also well-suited to being displayed by clients as wall art in their homes. If you think about it, which is more appropriate and easier to sell as a large wall portrait: a tightly cropped, smiling headshot, or a moodier, dramatic image with artistic and architectural elements? I rest my case.

Pretty Polly

The title I had in mind when I created this image was *Pretty Polly*. Essentially, I see it as a modern take on a turn-of the-century-portrait with a fashionable lady holding a parasol on a seaside boardwalk. In this case, Katherine's dress beautifully accentuated her curves, so I needed to show off both aspects of the concept. The parasol nicely finished off the image.

The Nitty Gritty

I positioned the bride on a stone pier near the student union at the University of Wisconsin. A double speedlight setup was extended on a stand and held out over the water (scary!) and aimed back at the bride. This created the beautiful short profile lighting.

My on-camera master flash fired as fill and I was able to create a nice ratio of main to fill light simply by positioning the camera (and, thereby, the on-camera fill light) farther away

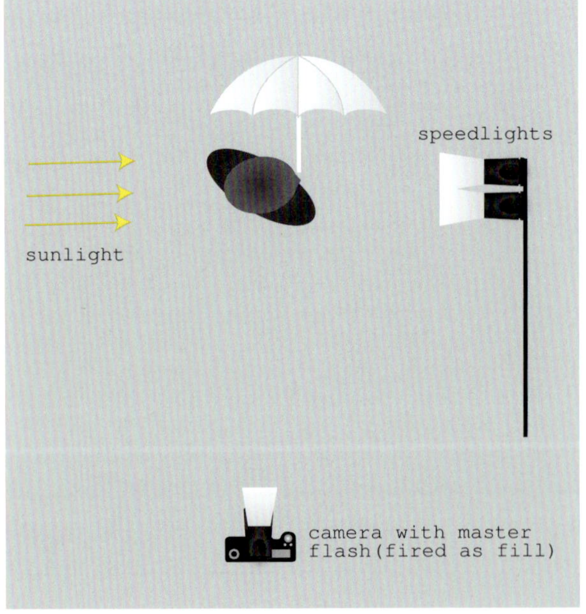

from the bride than the
main lights. The edge lighting on the left of the subject
was from the sun.

Postproduction

In postproduction, I
pumped up the sky using
my Gimme Sky Lite Light-
room preset and tweaked
the contrast and detail using
Nik's Tonal Contrast filter.
I added a texture overlay
from my Textureland col-
lection. Finally, I cropped to
a tall, narrow format for a
pleasing composition.

Camera: Canon 5D MKII
with Canon
24–105L lens
at 24mm

Exposure: $^1/_{2500}$ second, f/4.5,
ISO 100, $-^1/_3$EV
exposure
compensation
(aperture priority)

Lighting: Canon 580EX II
speedlight on-
camera set to
master (fired) with
RadioPopper PX
transmitter. Two
Canon 580EX II
speedlights off-
camera set to eTTL
and slave, fired
with RadioPopper
PX receivers.

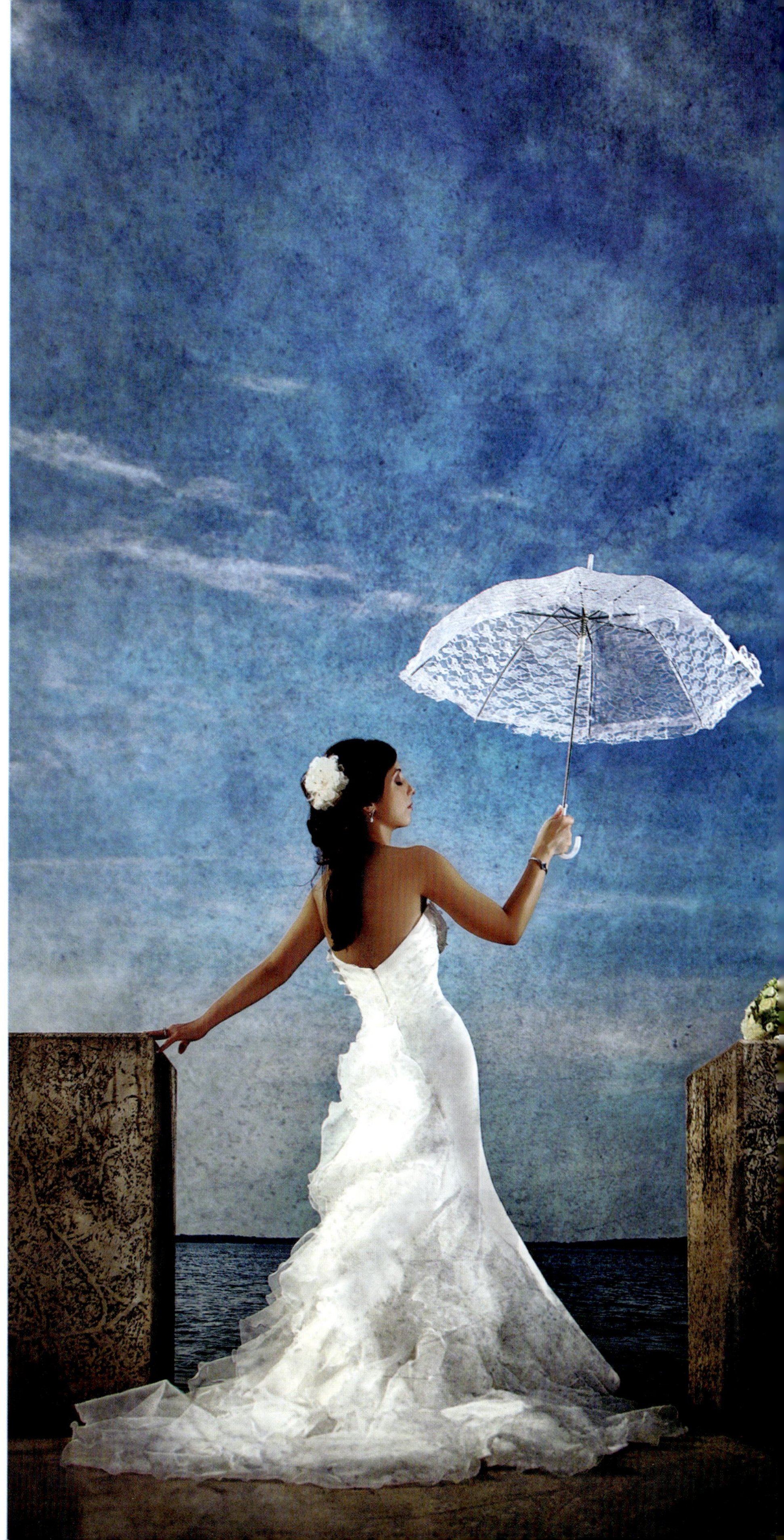

12

Rusty

Big softboxes can work outside

I don't often use large softboxes outside, but when I do, it's a Westcott model. My 50-inch Apollo softbox by Westcott collapses like an umbrella, making it very portable. Yet

"As soon as I saw the chains, I knew that McKenzie would totally rock them."

it delivers a very nice, soft look. It's my go-to modifier when very diffused light and portability are needed for an on-location shoot.

Working It at a Workshop

The image on the facing page is of McKenzie, one my favorite models (and another muse). I created it while teaching my "Flash Dancing" workshop at another photographer's studio.

As we were exploring outside, I saw a tool shed toward the back of the studio's grounds. Todd, the studio owner, thought I was nuts for wanting to shoot in there. As soon as I saw the chains, though, I knew that McKenzie would totally rock them. And she did—even though the rust gave her Cheetos® fingers.

Big Soft Light

My lighting setup here was pretty simple. I had one Canon 580EX II mounted on a RadioPopper Cube and triggered with a RadioPopper JrX receiver. Using the JrX transmitter in my hotshoe, I was able to remotely turn the power up and down on the speedlight from the camera position. This is my favored studio setup, and the one that I would recommend to anyone who wants to set up a true speedlight studio (see chapter 5 in section 1 for more on studio setups).

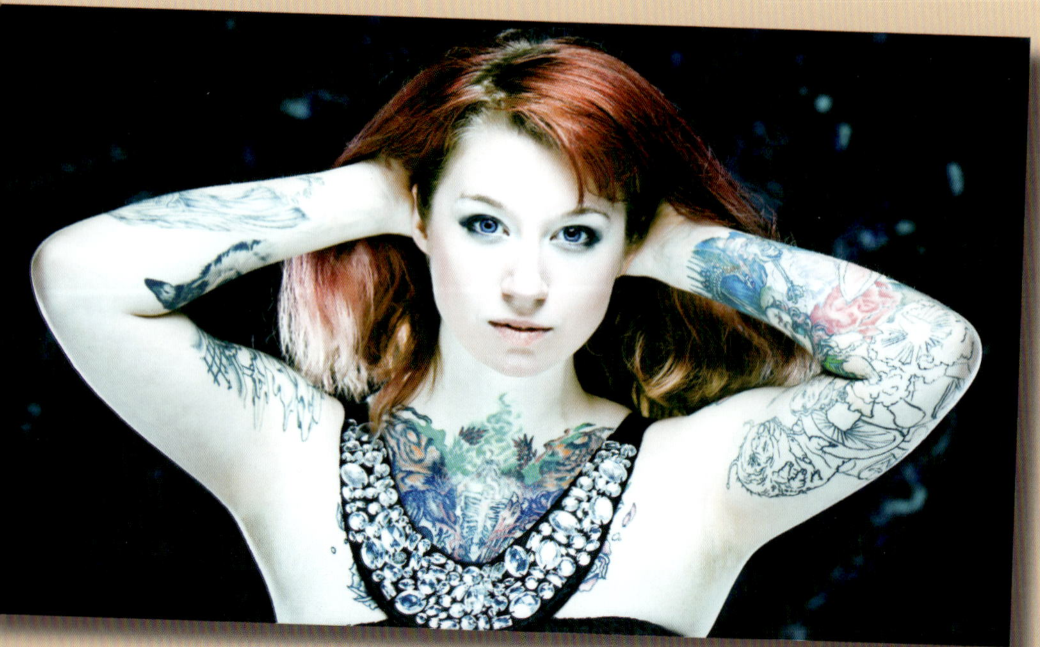

Beauty Lighting

During our session with McKenzie, I also ducked inside and demonstrated a classic beauty lighting setup. I just love McKenzie's ink! See lessons 24 and 25 for more on beauty lighting techniques.

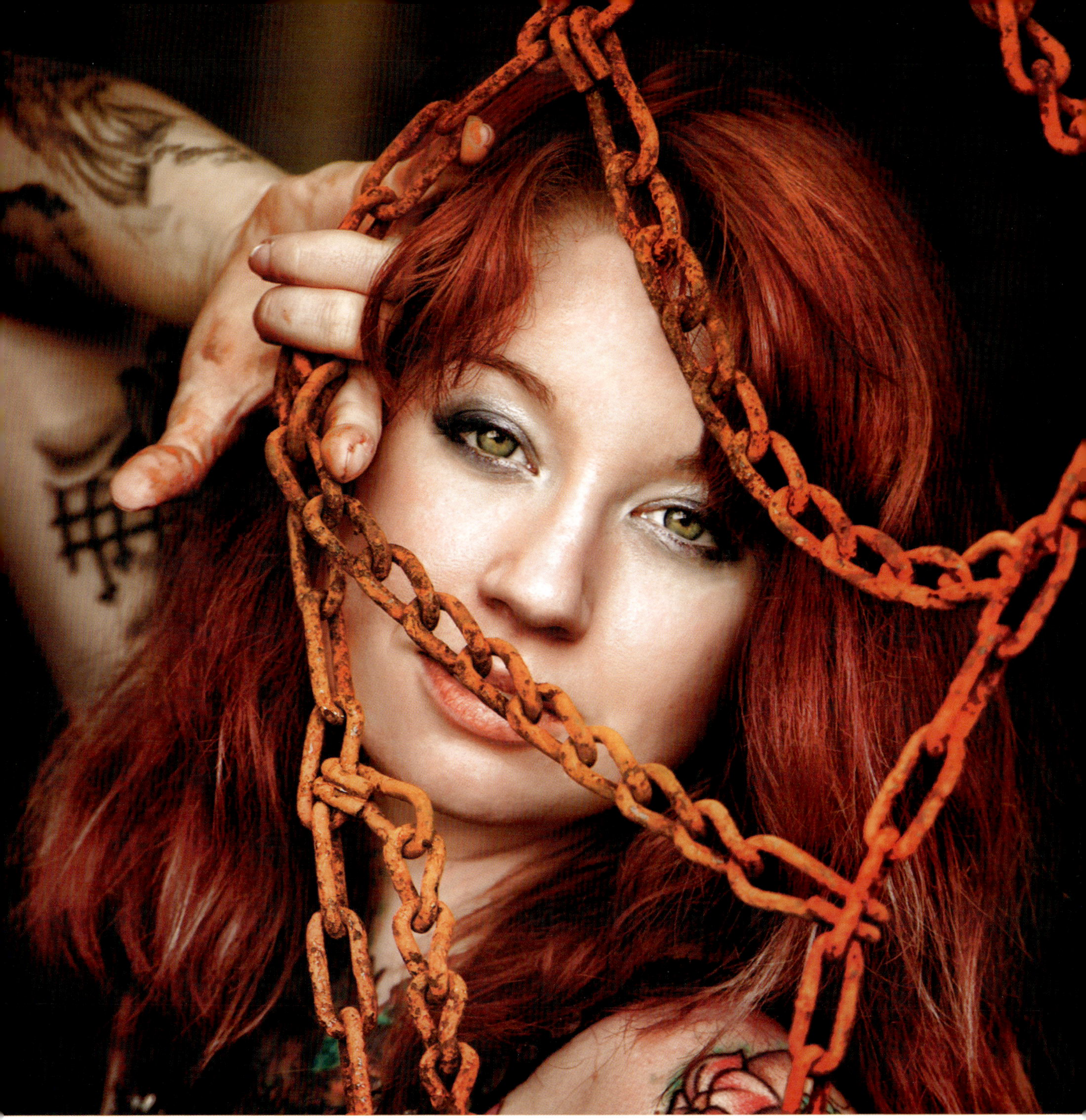

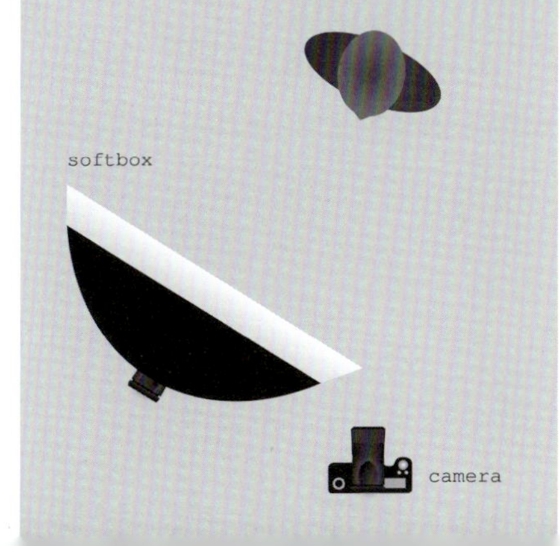

Camera: Canon 5D MKII with Canon 70–200mm lens at 173mm
Exposure: $1/160$ second, f/4.5, ISO 100 (manual)
Lighting: Canon 580EX II speedlight off-camera in a 50-inch Westcott Apollo softbox. Flash affixed to a RadioPopper Cube with a RadioPopper JrX receiver connected. Flash set to eTTL to allow the RadioPopper Cube to manually turn power up and down by leveraging the eTTL system. Trigged with the RadioPopper JrX transmitter.

13

The Spiky Sun

Shoot deep and get a spiky sun

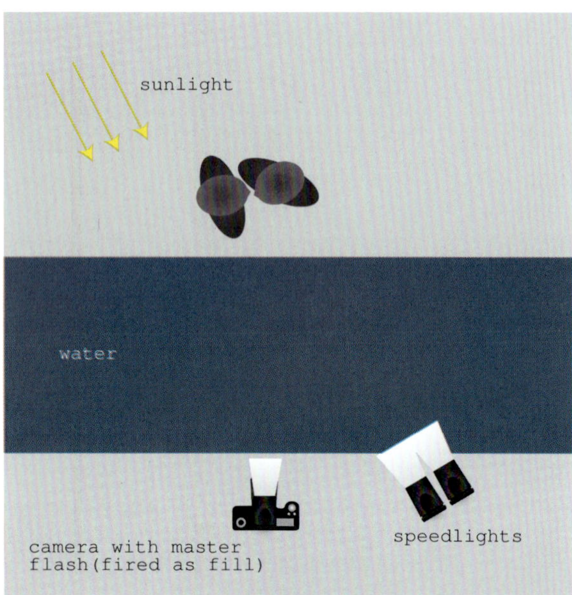

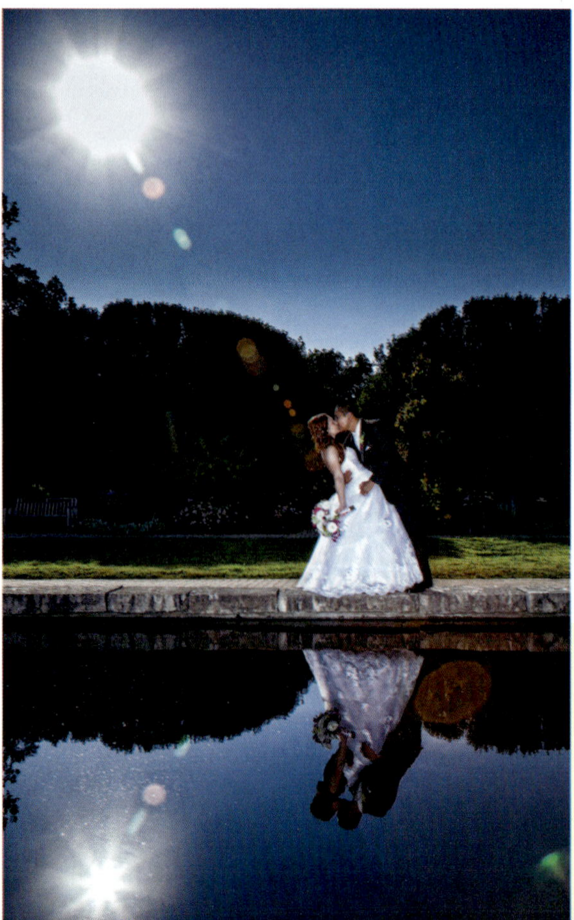

Much of the hubbub surrounding speed-lights the past few years has centered around their unique ability to achieve shutter sync speeds of $\frac{1}{1000}$ second and higher, allowing photographers to create portraits with shallow depths of field even in full sunlight.

Flash Power & Depth of Field

Of course, we shouldn't forget that extreme depth of field has its merits, too—especially when we can put a nice spiky sun into the composition. An added plus is that we can take advantage of the full power of our speedlights. (While I do think it is a fair trade-off when I want a shallow depth of field, the cool high-speed sync [HSS] technology definitely robs a *lot* of power from our speedlights.)

How much power is there? In the image to the left, I had enough to achieve f/13 even across the reflecting pool—roughly 30 to 40 feet. I fired three speedlights together, two off-camera and one on-camera. For a more fully-formed sun and the ultimate in spikiness, I recommend an aperture of f/16 to f/22.

The Shape of the Sun

The shape of your spiky sun depends on the blade configuration in your lens. The image on

Camera: Canon 5D MKII with Canon 24–105mm lens at 24mm
Exposure: $\frac{1}{200}$ second, f/13, ISO 100 (manual)
Lighting: Canon 580EX II speedlight on-camera set to master (fired) with RadioPopper PX transmitter. Two Canon 580EX II speed-lights off-camera set to eTTL and slave mode, fired with RadioPopper PX receivers.

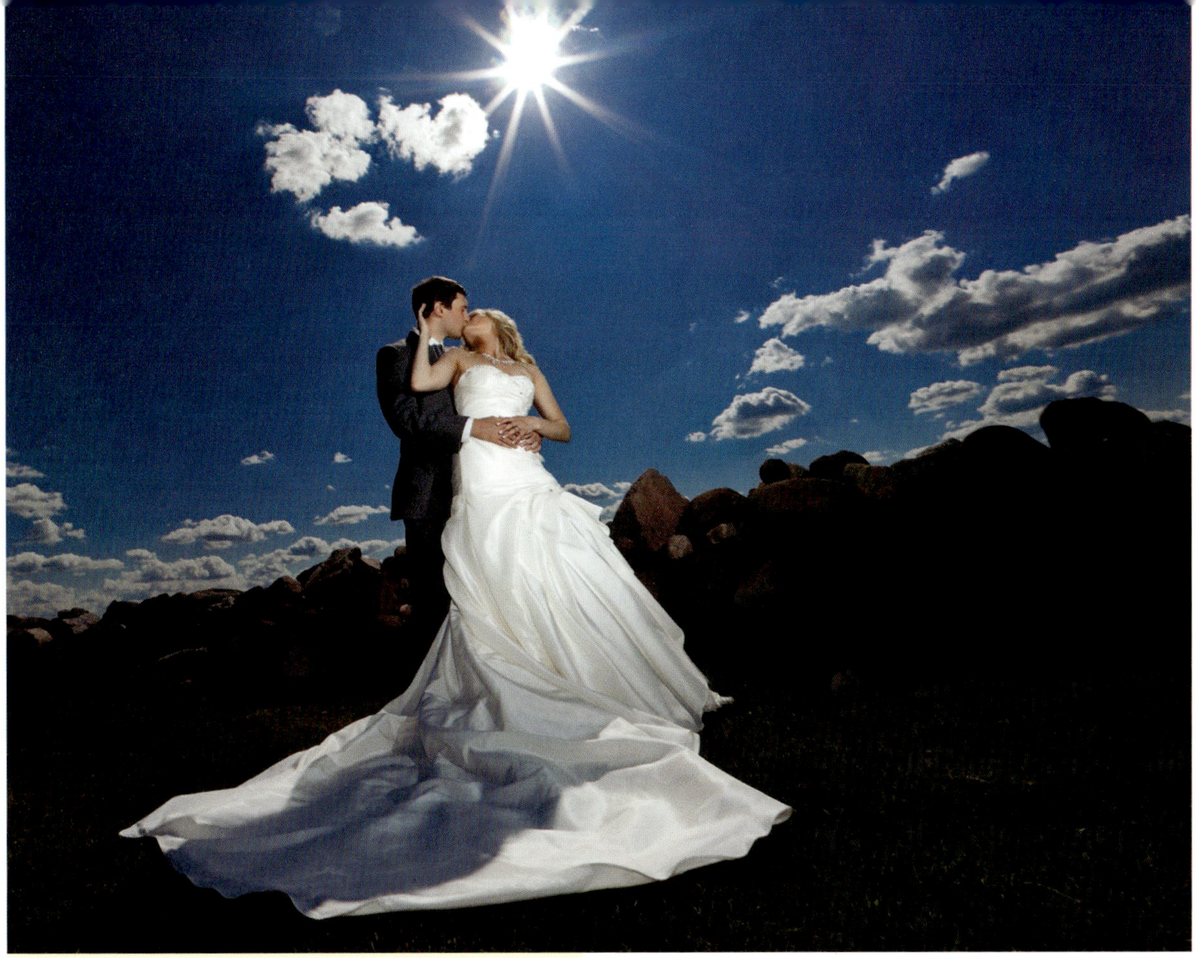

the left page was captured with a Canon 24–105mm lens, which has eight curved aperture blades. My favorite lens for the spike effect is my 15mm fisheye. It has only five blades but it delivers a nice shape to the spiked sun, as seen in the image above.

I'm currently field testing the Sigma 20mm f/1.8 lens and will be anxious to see how it handles the spike test with its nine aperture blades. Why a 20mm lens? It's the Goldilocks effect; sometimes 24mm isn't wide enough, and sometimes 15mm is too wide . . . so perhaps 20mm will be just right.

Available Light Only

This is an alternate shot by my assistant, Krystal Lamberty, showing how the scene appeared when photographed using just the available light (without the addition of flash). A big difference.

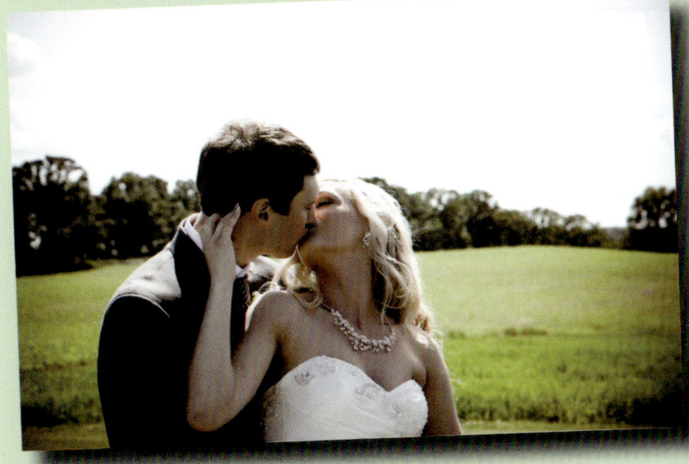

14

Katie

An alternate take on a classic studio portrait

This image was created toward the end of an already fabulous senior portrait session with Katie. I had already incorporated a number of different looks and styles in her session, so I was reaching deeper to find one more. Honestly, I didn't need to reach too deeply, though, because the answer was right in front of me: by mixing around the tools I was currently using, I could great a different look.

Don't Settle

In the studio, it is easy to get stuck in the habit of using the same modifiers and the same lighting setups over and over. If it's not broken, why fix it—right? Wrong! This mind-set robs you of many opportunities.

1. **More Choices.** Clients like choices, especially if they are investing a lot of money.
2. **More Sales.** Choices can often lead to bigger sales, as clients feel the need to order more of these varied looks and styles. This is especially true with the high-school senior market.
3. **Enhanced Mood.** Use the appropriate lighting style to fit the desired mood of the portrait. "Drama" typically equates to hard light; "pretty" equates to soft light.
4. **More Flattering Portraits.** Not everyone will look good with your "favored" lighting style. You need to be able to match the lighting to the subject's physical features.
5. **Personal Inspiration.** Using the same lighting for every session is boring. It fails to ignite the creative fires and imagination.

I could keep going, but these are the five big reasons to push yourself to develop new approaches.

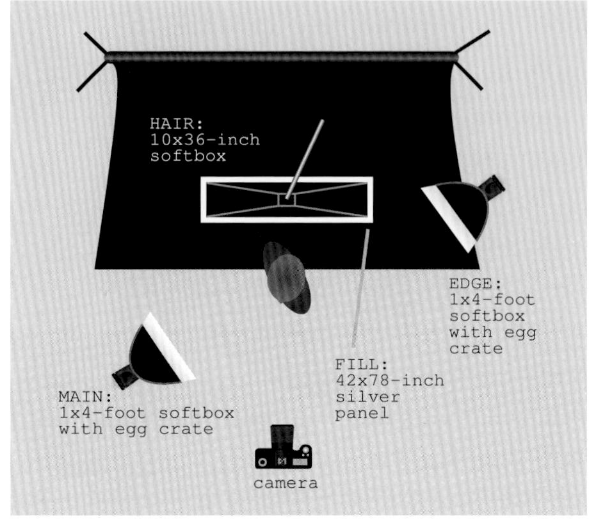

Getting Edgier

I often use a large softbox as my main light, a 4x6-foot silver reflector as fill, a 10x36-inch stripbox up high (9 feet) and directly behind the subject as a hair light, and 1x4-foot stripboxes on either side and behind the subject to create edge/rim lighting and separation from the background. I use variations of this setup as my primary base—my go-to lighting. It works for the vast majority of my subjects, and it worked well for Katie, too.

However, I wanted something more dramatic for this image featuring a handmade scarf that she and her mom had recently purchased. I had the perfect background to match the colors of the scarf (I pride myself on having a solution for virtually any color combination a client may bring to the studio). We played with the scarf for a couple of poses using my go-to lighting, draping the scarf as a quasi-shawl and such. Then, I thought the scarf would be dramatic framing her face and in contrast to her beautiful auburn hair.

To match the drama, I wanted a punchier, narrower beam of light. The solution? I dropped the large 60-inch octobox out as my key and swapped in the 1x4-foot stripbox that was to camera left behind Katie. All the other lighting positions stayed the same. I directed Katie towards a more neutral expression. The result is a striking, timeless image.

The Subconscious McCurry

I love the enigmatic, *Mona Lisa*-like partial smile, as well as how her eyes are emphasized by the punchier lighting. Afterwards, I was reminded of the famous Steve McCurry image of an Afghan girl. It was totally unintentional at the time, but one never knows where creative references lurk deep in the subconscious. I'll call it a happy accident—and, to this day, one of my favorite senior portraits.

This image was honored by being featured in the PPA Showcase Collection.

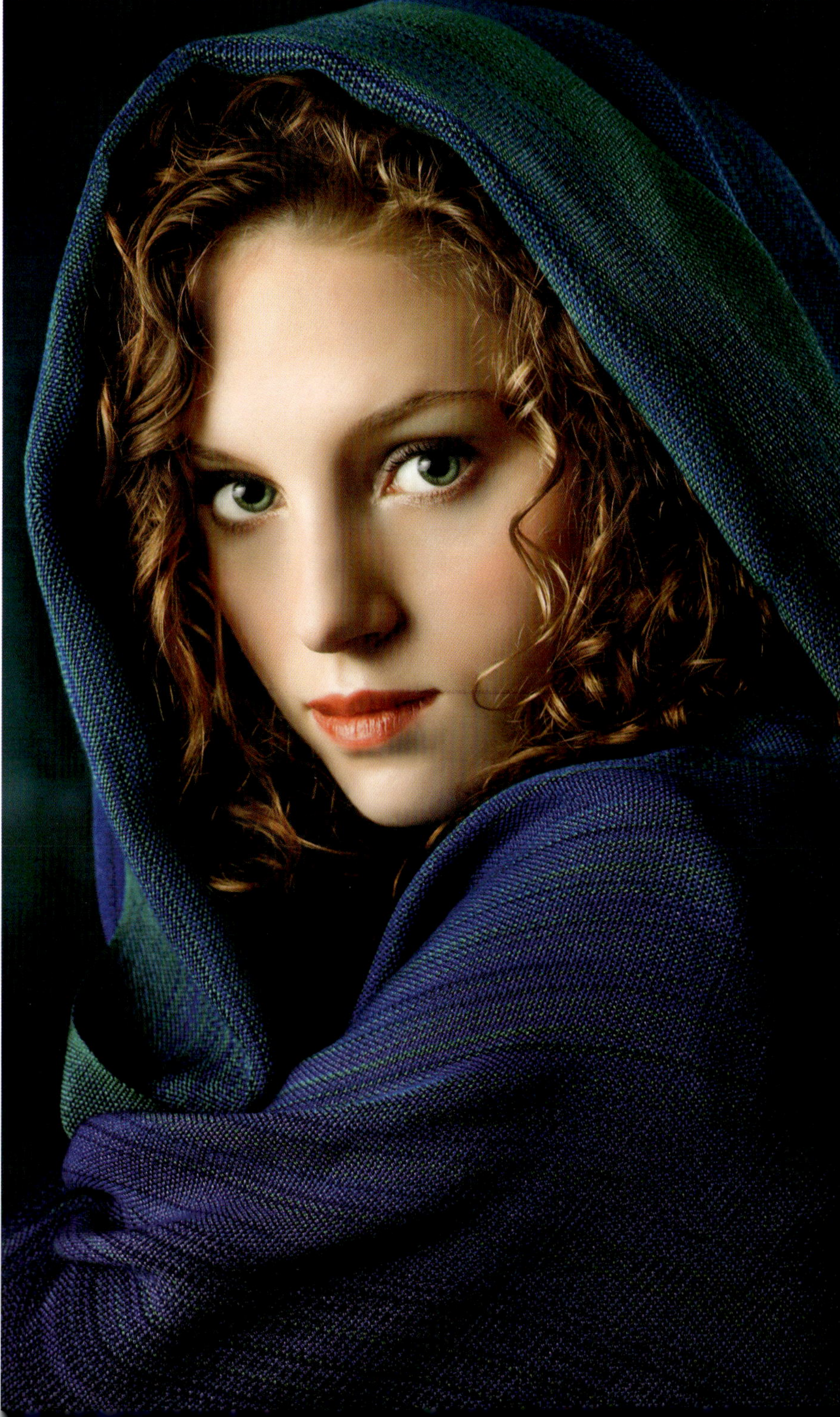

15

Making Light Where There's Nothing at All

Shoot at night

I find it interesting that a bride can plan her day down to the minute, with everything thought out to the tiniest detail—except for

TTL and Speed

Leveraging the TTL system in your speedlights can help you work quickly in adverse conditions or with tight schedules. In total, we spent seven minutes photographing the portraits at this location.

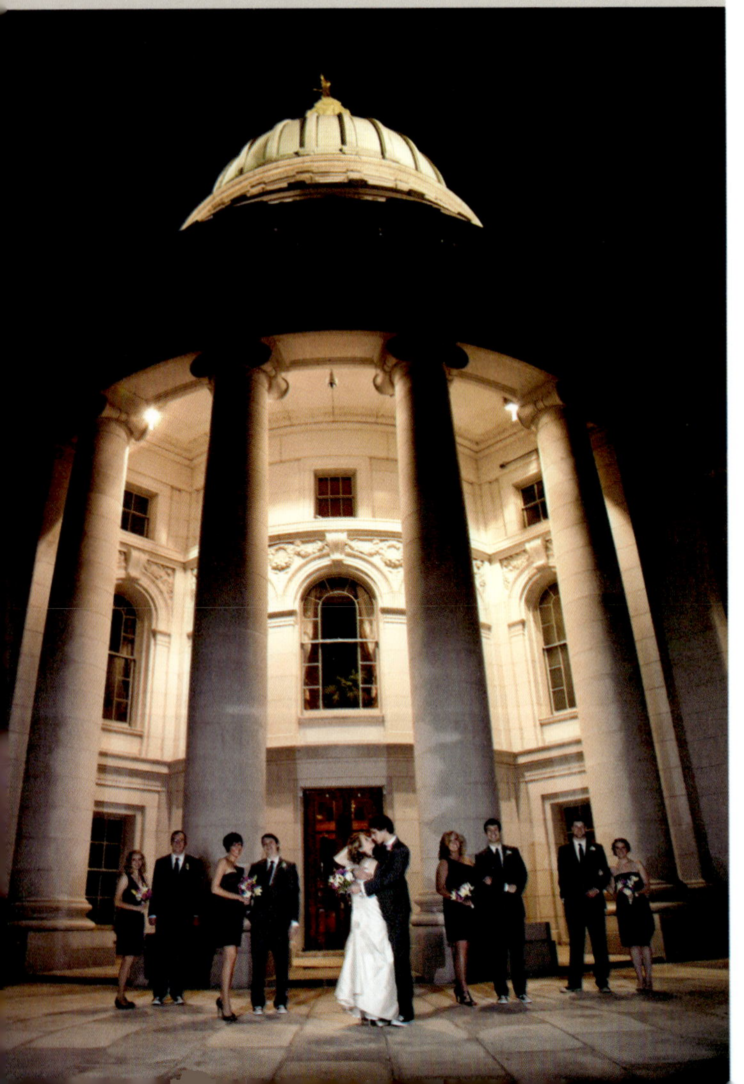

how the season will affect the photography. I have had outdoor weddings scheduled for months where we still get snow in Wisconsin. I have had brides request fall color portraits in September (um . . . the colors don't change around here until mid-*October*).

After Dark

Then, I get the occasional weddings where outdoor portraits are scheduled for after sunset. Such was the case here. It was a November wedding that happened after the daylight savings time change. The outdoor portraits were scheduled to start at 6:00PM. Unfortunately, the sun set at 4:45PM. Add in an hour's worth of delays (they were a great, fun couple, but also a bit loosey-goosey with the schedule) and we didn't get to our primary outdoor location until a little after 7:00PM. In other words, it was dark. Fortunately, since it was November in Wisconsin, it was also cold. (That was sarcasm.)

A Capital Idea

I am known for my location portraits for weddings, and my lovely couple really wanted awesome outdoor images. It was a major reason they hired me, so I couldn't disappoint. It was time to analyze the situation, dig deep, and create something cool—and do it before my bride became a bridesicle. TTL to the rescue.

Camera: Canon 5D MKII with Canon 15mm lens

Exposure: 1/30 second, f/5, ISO 1250 (manual)

Lighting: Canon 580EX II speedlight on-camera set to master (did not fire) with RadioPopper PX transmitter. Two Canon 580EX II speedlights off-camera set to eTTL and slave mode, fired with RadioPopper PX receivers.

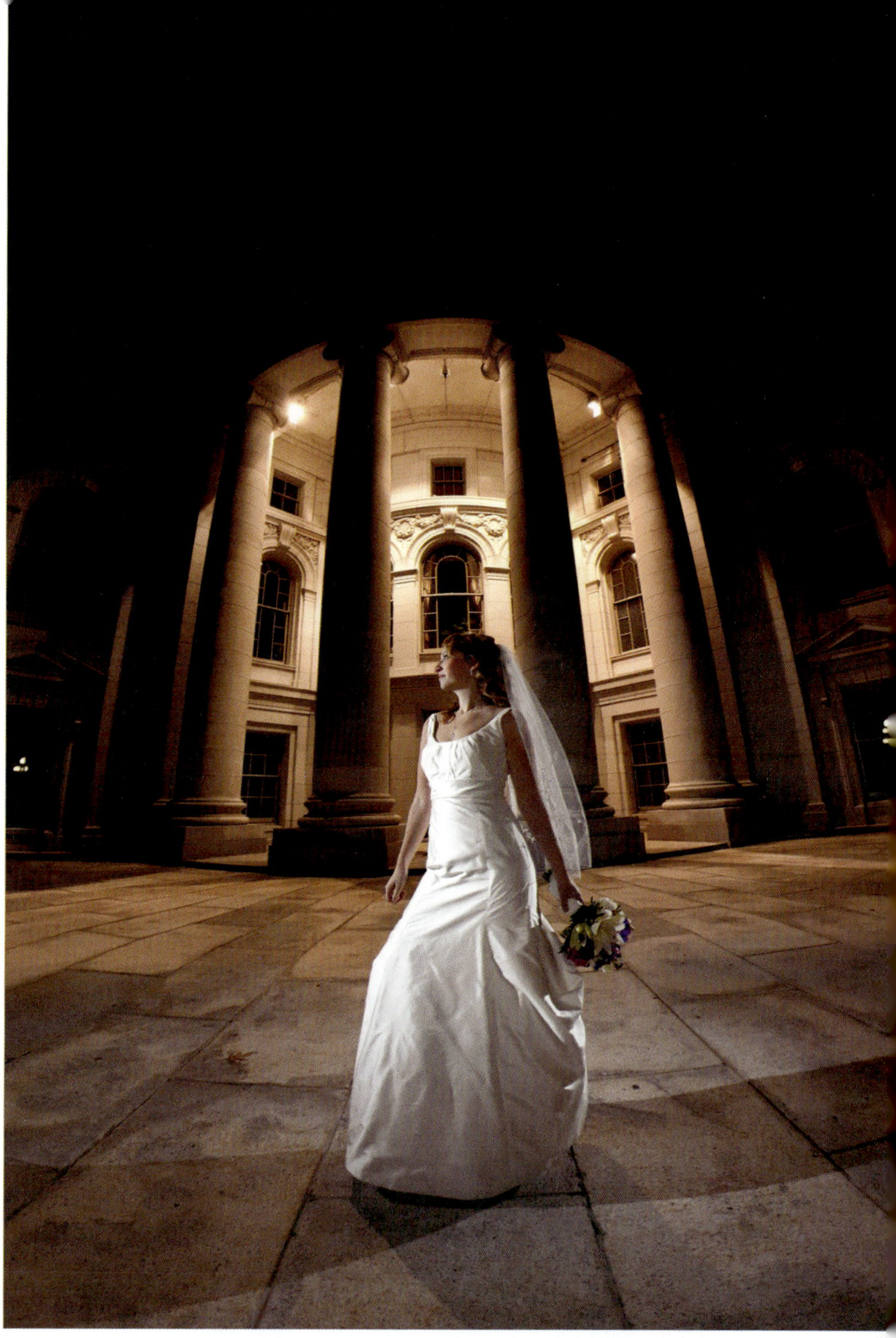

As there was no ambient light where I positioned the bride for the dramatic image seen to the right, I had to bring in my own light. This setup consisted of two off-camera speedlights. One served as the main light; this was positioned to camera left. The other speedlight added edge/separation lighting. To create a ratio between the main light and the edge light, I placed the main light closer to the subject.

Exposure and Composition

I had to bump my ISO up to 1250 to hold the ambient light in the background and use a shutter speed where I was comfortable hand-holding as I crouched for the shot. I selected a 15mm fisheye lens to enhance the drama by making the columns in the background lean away from the subject. This also helped me to include more of the scene and create a greater sense of depth.

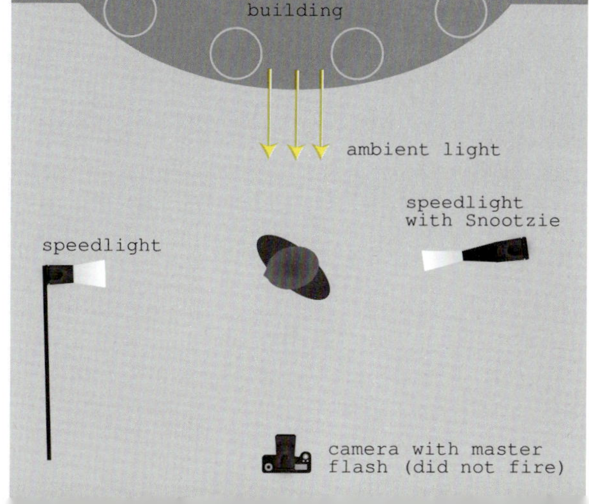

16

Is this Iowa? No, It's Phoenix.

Fight the strong desert sun and win

When folks view this image at a bridal show or during a consultation, I am often asked, "Where was this taken?" In a deadpan, I reply, "Iowa." Then I add, "Well, southern Iowa." They respond with a slightly puzzled look, then a knowing nod—as if it were an established fact that the southern part of Iowa is arid.

Destination USA

Newer photographers are often intoxicated by the glamour of jetting off to exotic locations to shoot on sandy beaches by day and sip mojitos by night. Most think it will be like a vacation. In reality, these endeavors are far from a vacation. The cost of flying with bags of gear, coupled with the anxiety of what you will do if something is lost, broken, or stolen in the process, makes for a stressful experience. For these reasons (and many more) I limit my "destination" weddings to the good old USA. No passport. No customs. No job visas. Far fewer headaches.

"An interesting thing happened on my way to creating glorious new imagery in this frontier . . ."

When my nephew asked if I would fly to Arizona to photograph his March wedding, it met all my criteria. First and foremost, it was my nephew and he was honoring me with the request; he and his bride-to-be had their hearts set on me. Plus, it was in the USA, and it was in a warm location during a month notorious for dismal weather in Wisconsin. Count me in!

Sand, Sand, and More Sand

Of course I was looking forward to the family wedding (honestly, I was), but also I was looking forward to the chance to photograph in a new location. However, an interesting thing happened on my way to creating glorious new imagery in this frontier. As I looked south, I saw brilliant blue sky, sand, cacti, and a mountain range in the distance. I thought, "Okay.

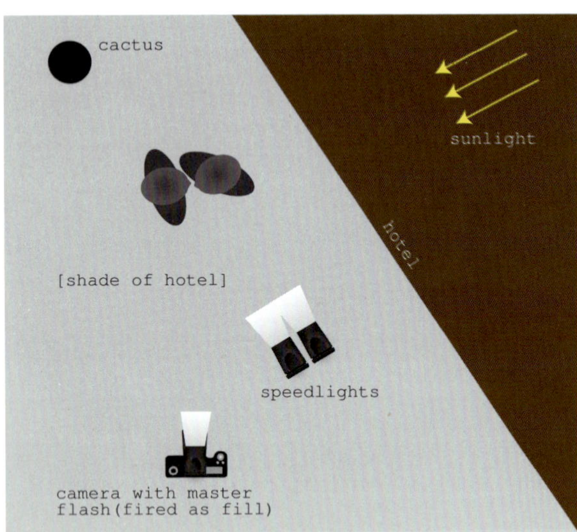

Camera: Canon 5D MKII with Canon 70–200mm lens at 173mm
Exposure: $1/500$ second, f/4.5, ISO 100 (aperture priority)
Lighting: Canon 580EX II speedlight on camera set to master (fired) with RadioPopper PX transmitter. Two Canon 580EX II speedlights off-camera set to eTTL and slave mode, fired with RadioPopper PX receivers.

Cool. I can work with that." As I turned and looked east, I saw . . . a brilliant blue sky, sand, cacti, and a mountain range in the distance. As I turned north, again I saw—well, you get the picture. Everything looked the same.

Now, in truth, it wasn't *quite* that bleak. I did have the adobe buildings at the Fort Mc-Dowell Resort where the ceremony and reception were being staged, and I was able to create some cool images using aspects of the architecture. But given the locale, I had to create a great sky-sand-cacti image as a center-piece to the collection.

Lighting

I placed my couple in the shade of the hotel, primarily to make it more comfortable for them. They could keep their eyes open with-out squinting from the strong sunlight. It also allowed me to tailor the light on them to what I wanted creatively. Because of the strong lighting in the back-ground and the framing of the shot, I added two off-camera speedlights to camera right to light

them properly, balancing the couple with the background and holding the tone in the sky. My on-camera flash also fired as a fill light.

I framed the couple with a scrub bush and one of the ubiquitous saguaro cacti found in the area. They finished it perfectly with a dynamic pose and beautiful, loving expressions.

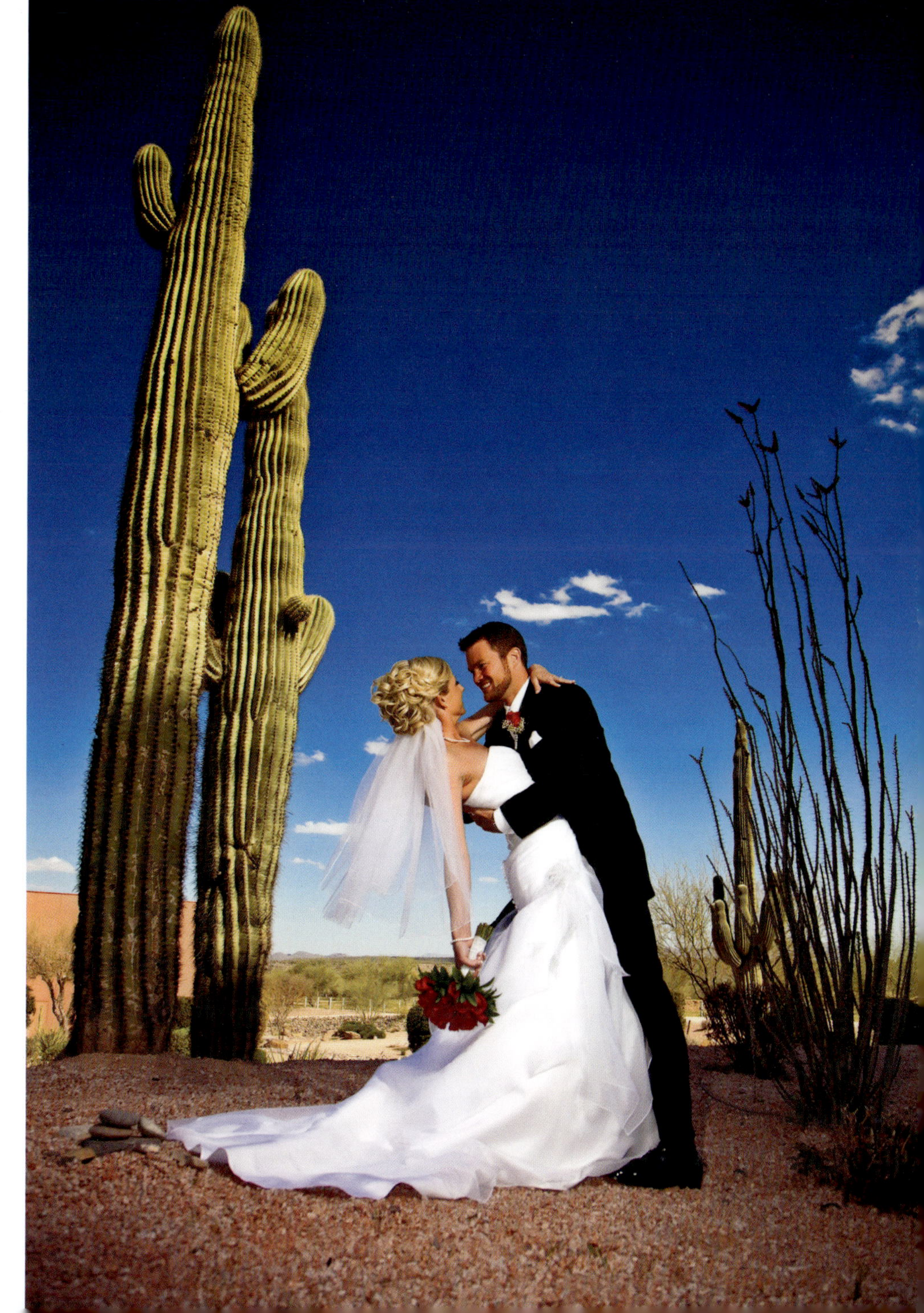

17

Going Out on a Limb . . . or Tree

Where studio strobes are not practical

I have done very few "trash the dress" sessions—and, admittedly, it is because I rarely float the suggestion. I would rather have them spend the extra money on upgrading the album or purchasing wall portraits. Additionally, most of my brides are too in love with their dresses to entertain the thought of running around in the woods or gritty urban alleys in ways that may get the dress hopelessly dirty.

Trash the Dress as Plan B

But then there was Daisy. After a lengthy tussle with the Chicago Parks police and a bout with rain, we were ultimately zeroed out from doing the fun location shots we had planned for her wedding day. Once again, it was time for plan B. This time, it involved meeting up again to do a "trash the dress" session several months after the wedding.

Camera: Canon 5D MKII with Canon 24–105mm lens at 24mm

Exposure: $^1/_{100}$ second, f/7.1, ISO 200, $-^1/_3$EV exposure compensation (aperture priority)

Lighting: Canon 580-EX II speedlight on-camera set to master (did not fire) with RadioPopper PX transmitter. Canon 580EX II speedlight off-camera set to eTTL and slave mode, fired with RadioPopper PX receiver.

Logging In a Cool Shot

I had spied this fallen tree in a park and cata-logued it as a possible shooting spot. It took a little maneuvering to get Daisy out there—and perhaps as much work for my assistant, Krys-tal, to climb out and hold a light stand with a speedlight over Daisy on the log. Of course, this is still much more easily done with a speedlight than with a studio strobe!

I wanted the scene to look like it was deep in a forest. It had to have that dark feeling of a densely wooded area. Unfortunately, this wooded patch with a stream wasn't as dense and dark as I wanted. In fact, it was pretty bright and a little sparse in areas. I needed to pull the ambient light way down to darken the base of the image. Then I added directional light on the bride using my speedlight.

Postproduction

I burned down some tones and patched up several sparse areas in postproduction.

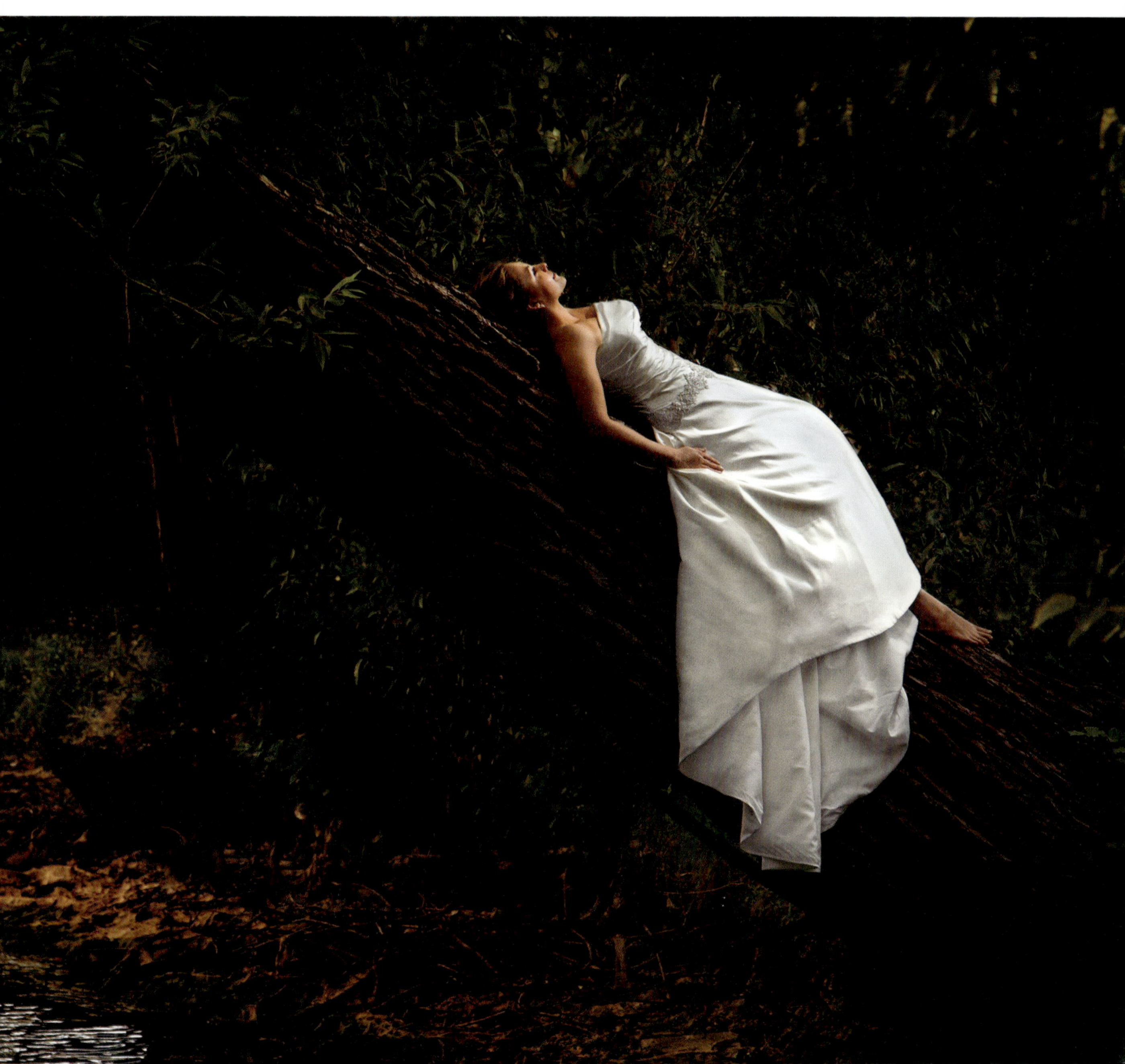

18

Night and Day

Daytime for night in a noir concept

Especially for weddings, the locations and light conditions I am handed often don't jibe with my "ideal" or the creative idea that I have in mind. These challenges have led me to a philosophy of being able to shoot anything, anywhere, anytime. Not only does this make me indispensable to clients (and different from my competitors), it meets my artistic needs. Of course, speedlights play an important role in this philosophy.

Nighty Night

The use of speedlights to battle the full sun is much ballyhooed by myself and other speedlight aficionados. But the same high-speed sync

An alternate that also clamped down on the ambient.

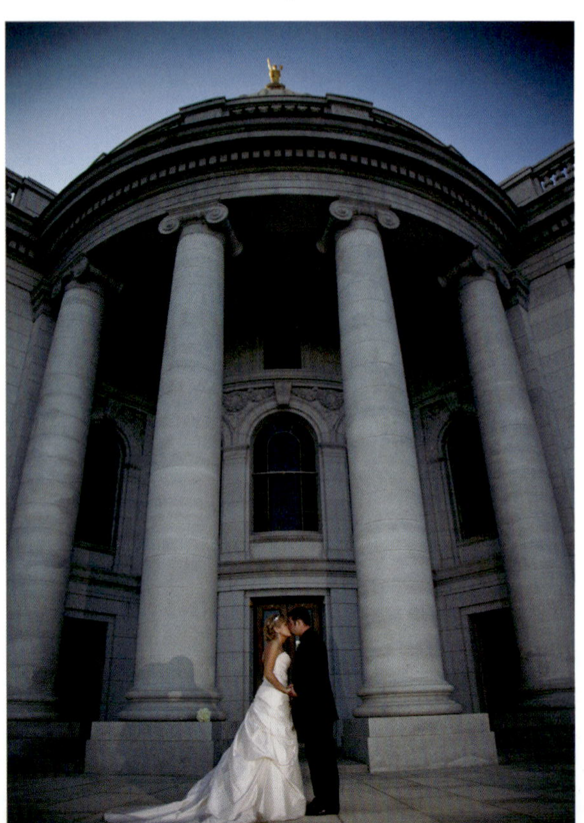

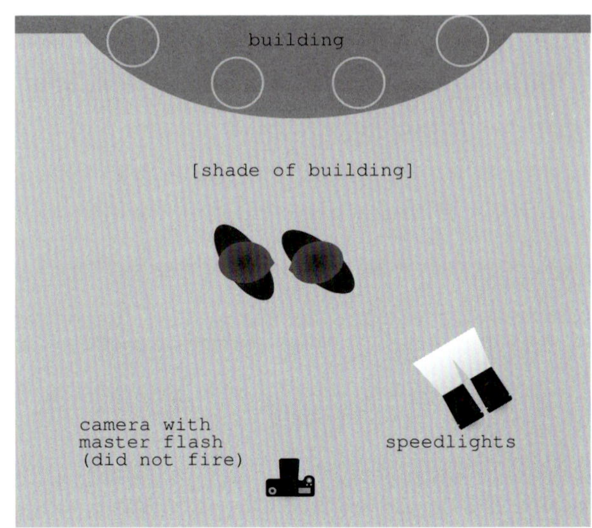

(HSS) feature we use for this technique can also be used in other creative ways. Here, I wanted a moodier image, one that gives the viewer a voyeuristic sense of catching the couple in a private moment. Even though we were in the shade of the capitol building, it was still broad daylight in a public place. In order to enhance this sense of intimacy, I choked down the ambient light to create the base mood of the image, and then used off-camera speedlights to carve out my desired mood lighting on the couple. This helped to minimize the public setting and to isolate the subjects so that the focus stayed on them.

Postproduction

The final piece of the puzzle was in post. I am a fan of postproduction efficiency and have created a number of Lightroom presets to accomplish editing effects that previously could only be done in Photoshop. This speeds up my processing workflow immensely. Time is money in this business. The Lightroom preset applied to the image below is Golden Crunch from my Preset-O-Rama collection, which yields a classic Hollywood-style black & white look.

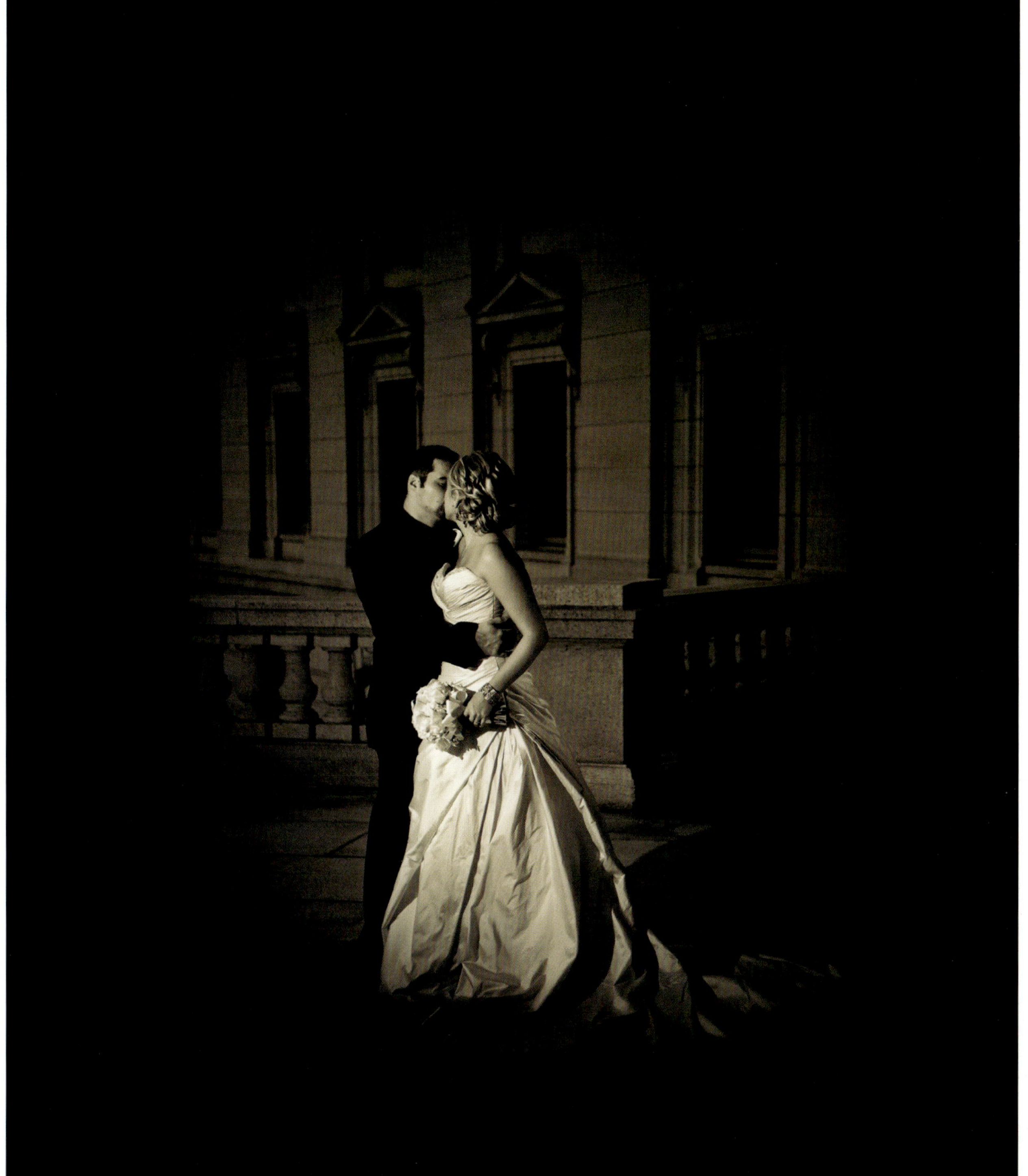

Sunset

The classic sunset portrait request

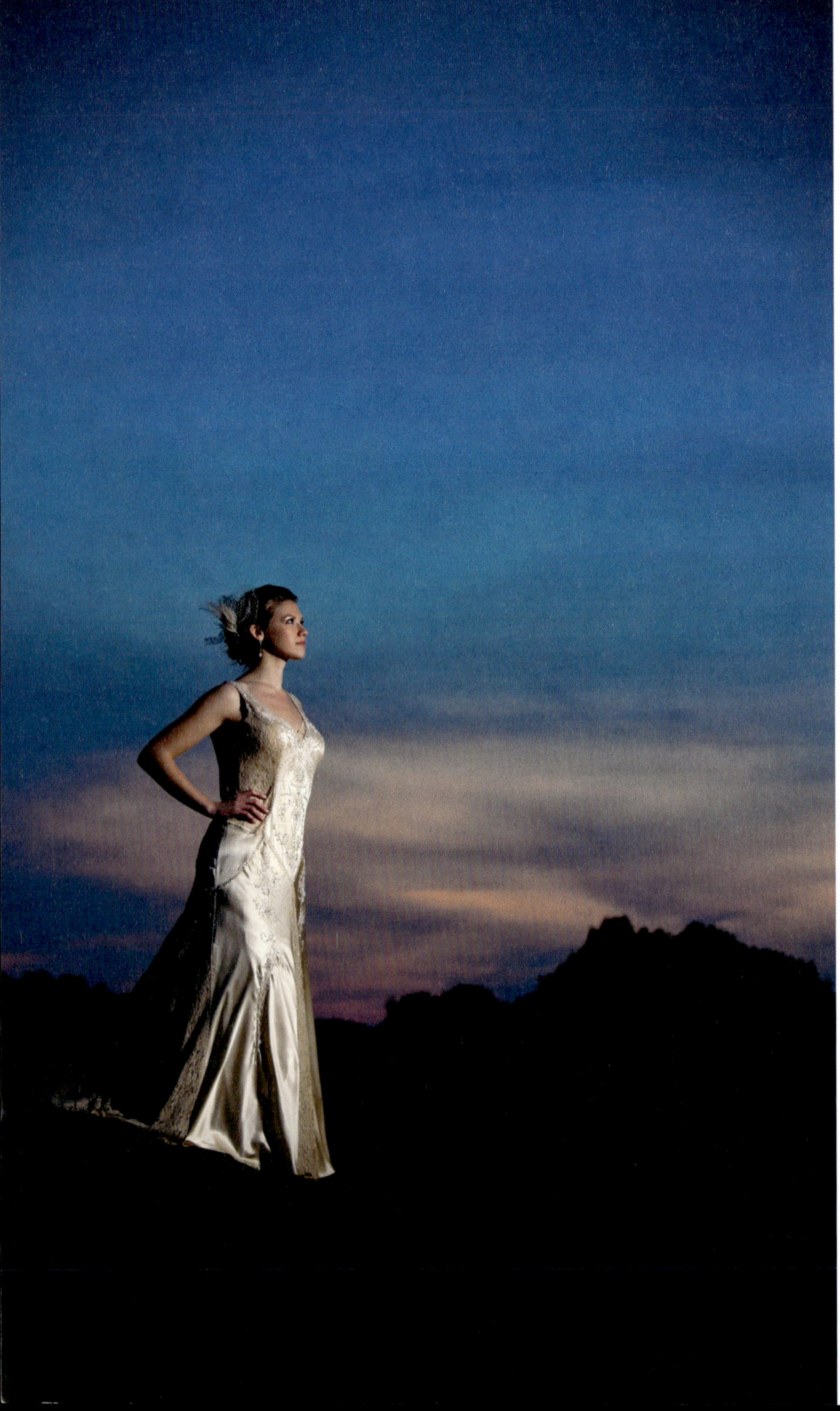

The classic sunset offers a beautiful landscape but a difficult portrait. If you expose for the subject, your sunset is lost. If you expose for the sunset, your subject is lost in the darkness. It makes for an obvious auxiliary lighting situation.

Lighting and Exposure

In this example, I had a beautiful bride and a beautiful sunset, so I needed to show off the beauty of both simultaneously.

Using aperture priority, I started my exposure based on the in-camera ambient reading of the scene. Then, I incorporated two off-camera speedlights on a stand to light the bride. One speedlight was attached to

Camera: Canon 5D MKII with Canon 24–105L lens at 24mm

Exposure: $^1/_{1000}$ second, f/4.5, ISO 800, $-1^2/_3$EV exposure compensation (aperture priority)

Lighting: Canon 580EX II speedlight on camera set to master (did not fire) with RadioPopper PX transmitter. Two Canon 580EX II speedlights off camera set to eTTL and slave mode, fired with RadioPopper PX receivers.

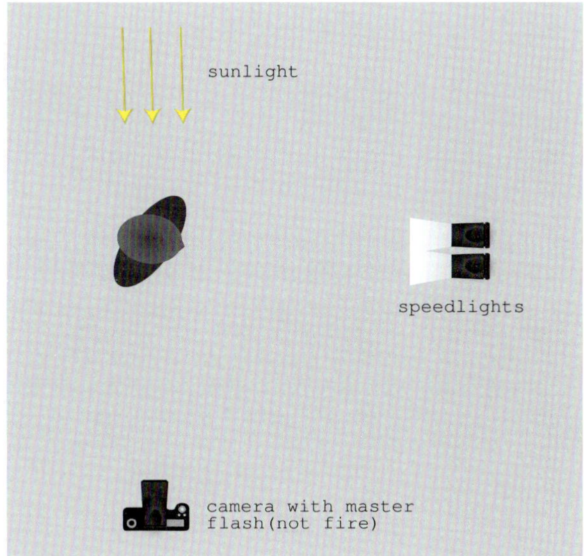

the top of the stand and set at eyebrow height to light the bride's face. The second speedlight was affixed to a studio clamp attached to the light stand and set at approximately waist level to light the lower half of the bride in order to have a pleasing profile from top to bottom without an excessive vignette.

> *"I started my exposure based on the in-camera ambient reading of the scene."*

The first image I shot was usable, but I felt that the sky needed to deepen more. I adjusted my in-camera exposure compensation to $-1\frac{2}{3}$EV. This darkened the sky appropriately and allowed my off-camera speedlight to carve out the desired lighting pattern in order to highlight the bride in the foreground while maintaining a rich and colorful sunset in the background.

TTL and Aperture Priority

You will notice in the technical specs throughout this book that I often use the aperture-priority mode when using TTL flash outside. Purists would certainly denounce any sort of automated feature, including TTL and aperture priority. I counter that purists probably cannot create what I do in the brief amount of time that I have when working on location with clients who have high expectations (and rightly so).

As a master photographer, I am fully capable of metering and using manual settings. In some cases, however, I choose to use a proven workflow that is expedient for achieving the desired results. That often includes the use of aperture priority and TTL flash—especially in sunny situations. We spend thousands of dollars on our advanced digital cameras, and hundreds of dollars apiece for TTL speedlights. Why not use this technology to our advantage?

I'm not advocating that we set the mode dial to "P" for program (or "pray" as we often derisively joke). However, in aperture priority I can choose my desired f-stop to control my depth of field. This is always my first technical decision in conjunction with my creative vision for the image.

In aperture priority, I pick my aperture and the camera chooses a shutter speed that will provide a "proper" exposure. Once the corresponding shutter speed is at $\frac{1}{500}$ second or faster, I no longer care how high it goes. It just doesn't matter to me for portraiture. I'm not trying to freeze Indy cars; I'm trying to create a portrait. The metering system in the camera is smart enough to get me close to where I want to be, if not dead-on.

I can fire a test shot and then quickly adjust my exposure compensation (EC) to darken down or brighten up the ambient light, and I can adjust my flash exposure compensation (FEC) to brighten or darken how my flash affects the scene. It is a very expedient and effective workflow for shooting at outdoor locations. In fact, this quick approach is vital in a situation like the one shown here; the sun was dropping rapidly and any amount of running back and forth to meter would have caused me to miss the shot entirely.

20

A Little Flare

Put the sun in your background

Yes, Virginia (or Steve, or whoever you are), you *can* battle the sun. You can use it as a backlight—heck, you can even put it right in the shot!

Hay, That's Rustic

The theme for this late October wedding in the Great Lakes region of Chicago was rustic/vintage. The reception was held in a beautiful old barn, converted to event use, that is situated on the edge of a nature preserve.

It was a must to incorporate the golden brown grasses covering the nature preserve's restored prairie. I chose a seated pose on a bench along a path through the grasses. This yielded a composition with the sun skimming across the grass and backlighting Ryan and Stacie.

Camera: Canon 5D MKII with Canon 24–105L lens at 24mm
Exposure: $1/2500$ second, f/4, ISO 100 (aperture priority)
Lighting: Canon 580EX II speedlight on-camera set to master (fired as fill) with RadioPopper PX transmitter. Canon 580EX II speedlight off-camera set to eTTL and slave mode, fired with RadioPopper PX receiver.

A Flair for Flare

Given the low angle of the sun in the autumn sky, I worked it right into the composition, add-

Breaking the Rules

One of my all-time favorite couples, Ryan and Stacie are creative, fun-loving actors who also love the great outdoors (beyond doing Shakespeare in the Park). As evidence, I refer you to the photo below, where we "stole" a canoe.

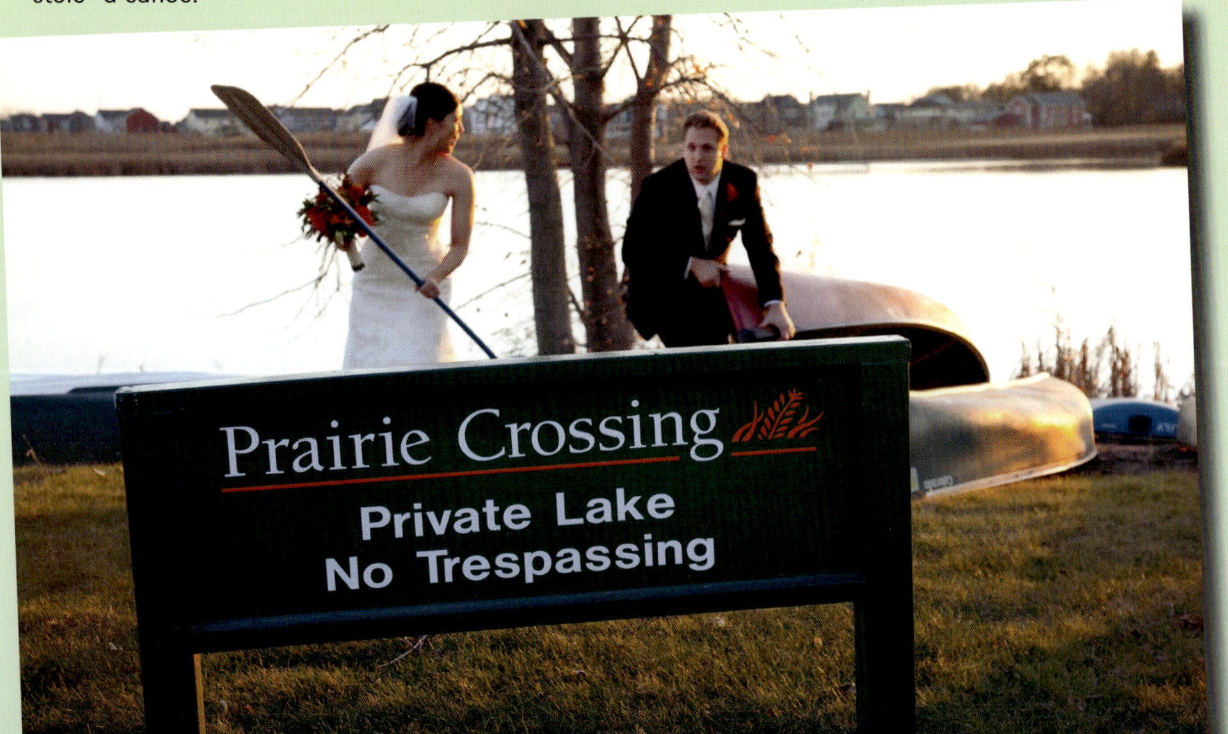

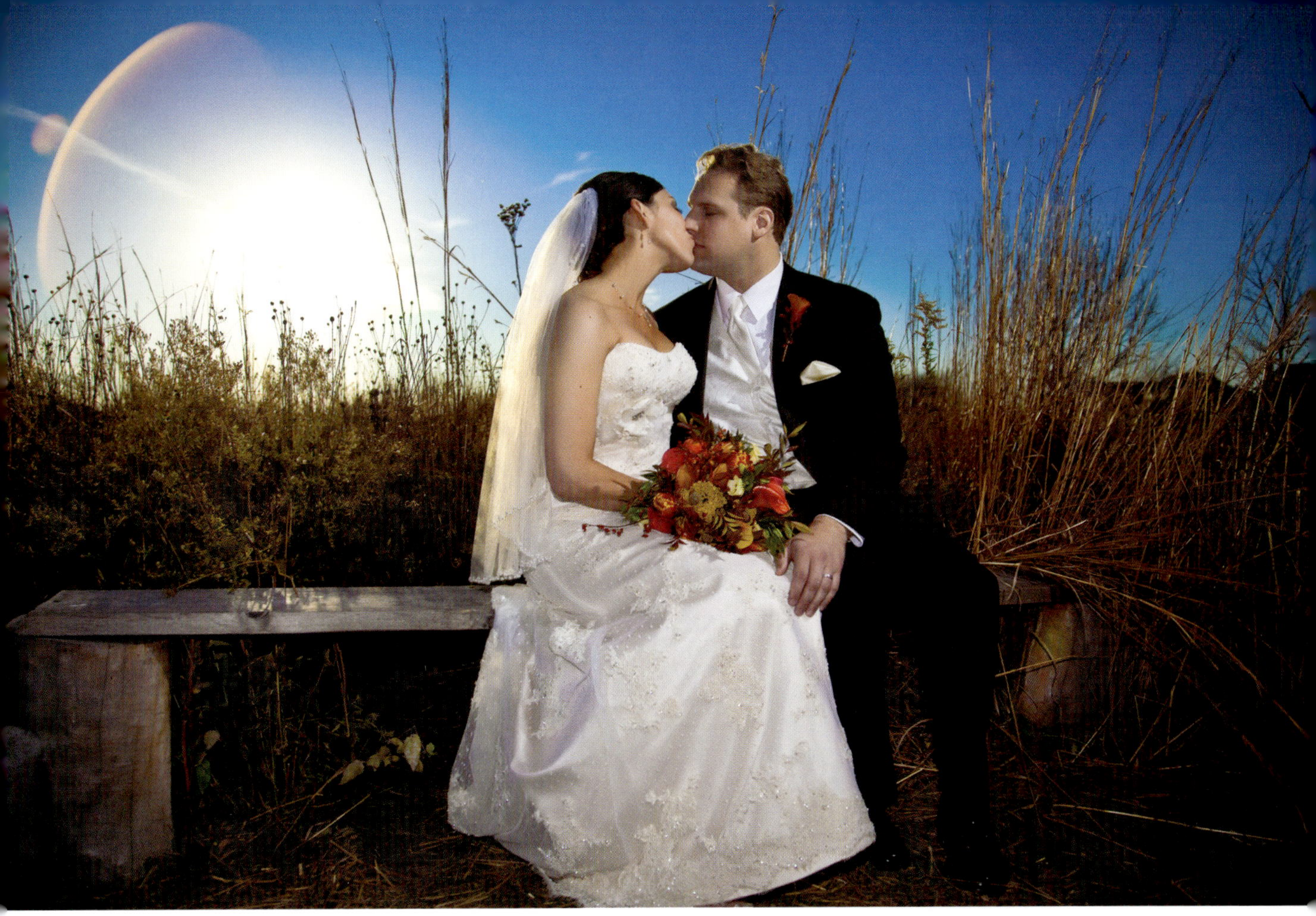

ing in good flare. To me, good flare is a compositional element like a leading line. However, one should be careful to not overuse it or overdo it. I see many outdoor portraits and wedding images in a natural-light, "vintage" style where the flare overpowers the subject and in essence becomes the subject. This may be fine for an "art" piece, but when it's done repetitiously, it becomes stale and cliché. To me, it exposes the photographer as one who does not know how to create light to balance a scene.

Balancing the Scene

Here, I balanced the scene by exposing for the sky then by adding in off-camera flash for dimension and on-camera flash for fill. The result

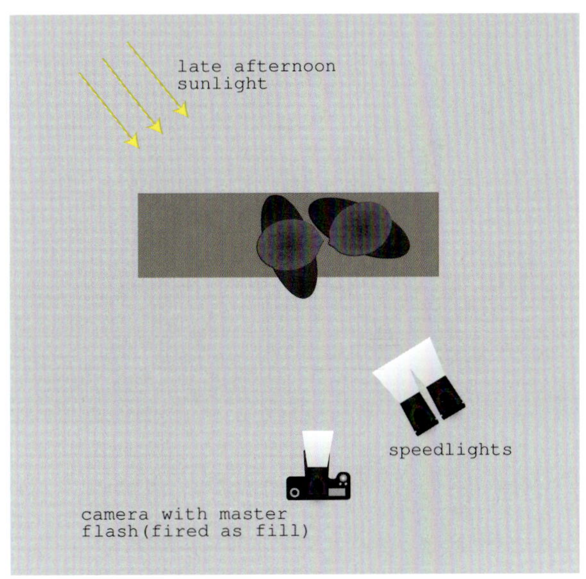

is a nicely balanced, romantic portrait that has a little flare as an artistic touch.

21

Black Swan

Uplight for drama

odel Erin Thomson approached me with the idea of teaming with makeup artist Katrina King and body painter Christy Grace to create a Black Swan look. After shooting "pret-ty" for a while, I decided to take the lighting and overall look edgier. In Erin's own words, she pulls off "creepy and edgy" pretty well, so I pushed the look further in that direction.

Change It Up

Your defined style may be lucrative and give customers what they expect, but how often do you present the unexpected? Or, what would you do for a repeat client who wanted something different? Complacency will not help you to grow. Push yourself to add one more set or one different look to a session—especially once you have the "required" images in the bag. Cut loose and try something new. It doesn't have to be wildly different, just new to you.

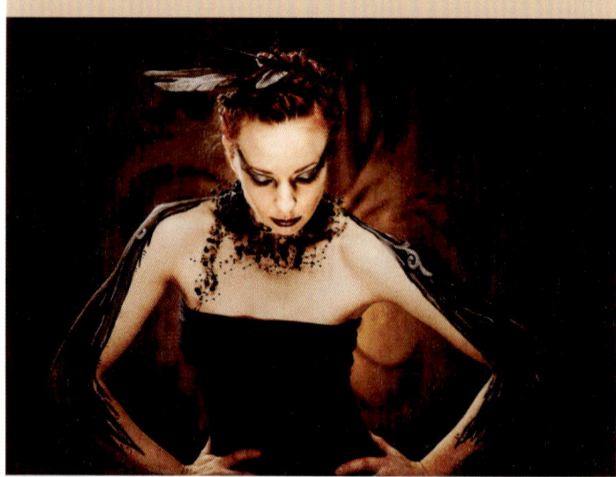

Camera: Canon 5D MKIII with Canon 85mm f/1.8 lens
Exposure: $^1/_{160}$ second, f/4, ISO 100 (manual)
Lighting: Five Canon 580EX II speedlights manually controlled using the RadioPopper JrX system coupled with RadioPopper Cubes. *Main light*: 48-inch Larson Lightbender softbox with speedlight shoe adapter. *Fill light*: 22-inch Kacey Enterprises beauty dish. *Edge lights:* Two 1x4-foot Creative Light softboxes with speedlight speedrings and front egg crates. *Background light:* Bare speedlight.

Uplighting

I teach students that a main light at the proper height puts catchlights at either the 10 or 2 o'clock position in the eyes. "Never shine the main light up at a client," I often say, "as this would give them horror lighting." In this case, though, I wanted a little "horror" lighting.

"After shooting 'pretty' for a while, I decided to take the lighting and the overall look edgier."

I positioned a 48-inch Larson Lightbender softbox in front of Erin, waist high and tilted up at her face. Then, I positioned a beauty dish on a boom above her and tilted down to help soften any shadows cast by the low-angle main light. The lighting ratio was 1.5:1 (main light to fill light). This gave me dramatic lighting on her eyes that still accentuated the angles of her face. The goal was "striking" rather than "creepy." I finished with dual edge lights in 1x4-foot stripboxes. A final bare speedlight on a short light stand was aimed at the background.

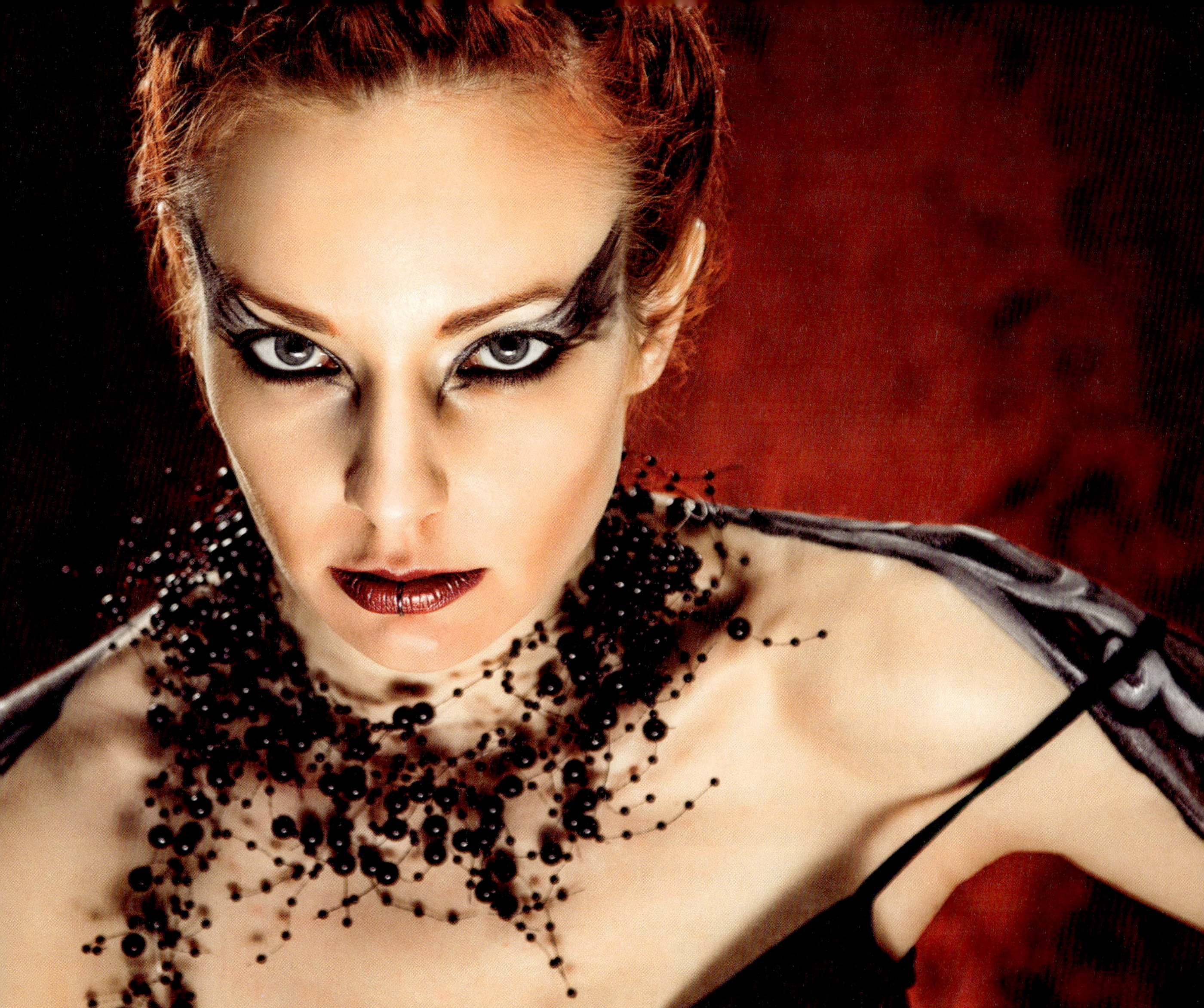

All of the speedlights were set in RadioPopper Cubes with the power controlled using a RadioPopper JrX transmitter at the camera position. The main and fill lights were together in group 1, with the lighting ratio created by having the fill light (the beauty dish) placed about a foot farther from Erin than the main light. The background light was in group 2, while the edge lights were in group 3.

Postproduction

The final image was cropped tightly for impact and finished off in postproduction using Nik's Tonal Contrast filter and Imagenomic's Portraiture filter for skin softening.

22

Raising the Level of Difficulty

Understand what TTL "sees"

When teaching, the number-one request I get is how to shoot outside in the full, harsh sunlight. It's a challenge I welcome, but the level of difficulty amps up when I demonstrate it to other master photographers—as when I visited the studio of Illinois photographer Cindy Romano, who hosted a program for the Professional Photographers Association of Northern Illinois (PPANI).

Hailee's Senior Portraits

Cindy brought in Hailee, a lovely senior portrait model. I noticed her white dress and recognized that this would be an additional challenge for shooting in full sunlight. The key to this vibrant-blue-sky, shallow-depth-of-field portrait style is the high-speed sync (HSS) feature of flash systems. (In Nikon-speak, this is the focal plane [FP] shutter system.)

As I mentioned in the Core Concepts section of this book, the reflective light meter in your digital SLR has one job only: to turn whatever it sees into 18 percent gray (see page 12). If you are in aperture-priority mode, it checks your preset f-stop and then adjusts your shutter speed to an appropriate setting.

In a general scene, this will usually be dead on or pretty close to the appropriate exposure; in extreme lighting situations, it can be skewed.

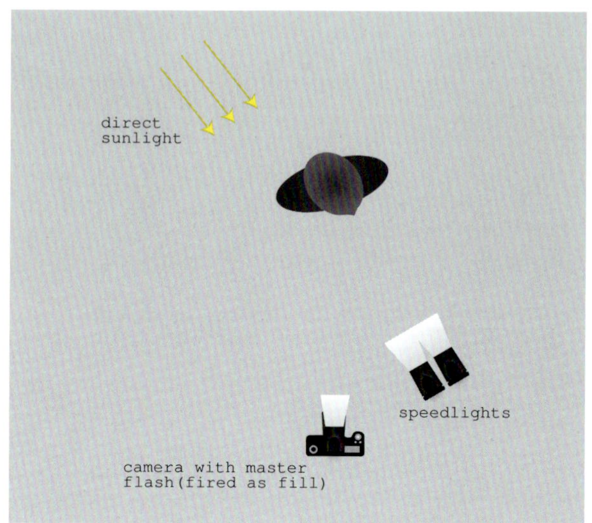

For example, if we are backlighting our subject with the sun, the metering "sees" all of the light in the sky and will underexpose to compensate. A similar thing happens when you photograph a bride (or, in this case, a senior) in a white dress. The TTL "sees" the dress and wants to make it 18 percent gray. Here, we have a bright sky *and* a white dress—double the challenge.

Knowing that the TTL would underexpose for the sky and white dress, I did not need to dial in much exposure compensation to darken the sky; the automatic underexposure would get me pretty close to where I wanted to be. In this case, I used −1/3 EV exposure compensation to darken the ambient light a little more.

The biggest adjustment needed to be to the flash exposure compensation (FEC). This works directly off of the camera's metering system and

Camera: Canon 5D MKIII with Canon 24–105L lens at 47mm
Exposure: 1/2000 second, f/4, ISO 100, −1/3EV exposure compensation (aperture priority)
Lighting: Canon 580EX II speedlight on-camera set to master (fired) with RadioPopper PX transmitter. Two Canon 580EX II speedlights off-camera set to eTTL and slave mode, fired with RadioPopper PX receivers.

will correspondingly choke down the flash in order to accomplish its goal of an "averaged" exposure. In this situation, I started by dialing in +2 EV FEC to open up the light on the subject. After my first exposure, I saw that I needed more power. I cranked the FEC up to +3 stops (the maximum) and got the shot I wanted.

Postproduction

In postproduction, I punched up the vibrancy of the sky using my Gimme Sky Lite Lightroom preset, then popped the detail with Nik's Tonal Contrast filter. I finished it off with a texture screen from my Textureland set, then burned down the edges.

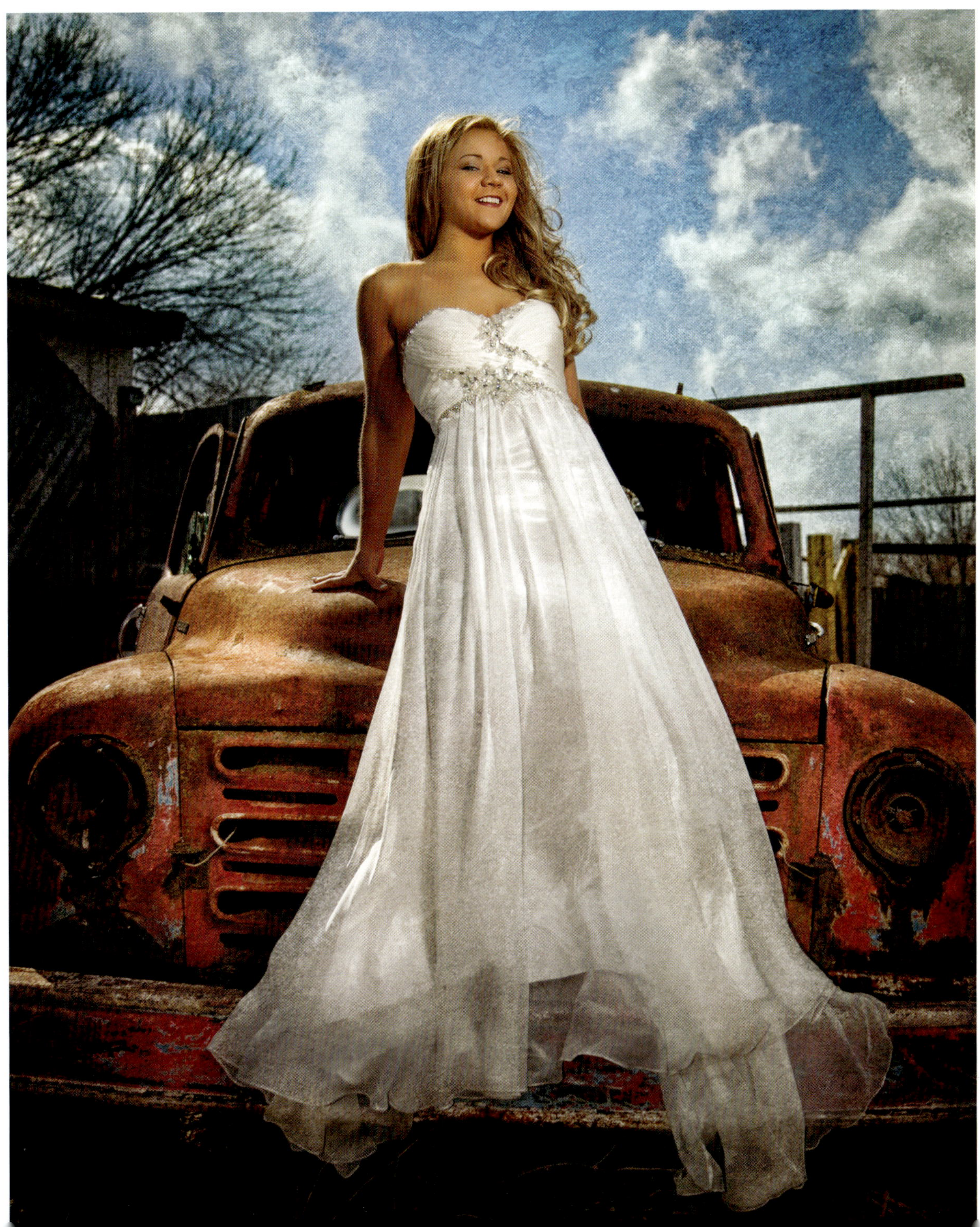

23

Clean and Simple

Speedlights for classic studio portraiture

Many of the images in this book follow a similar mantra: do something different or out of your comfort zone. Heck, for many, the sheer thought of using speedlights for lighting *everything* is already well outside of their comfort zones. Battling the sun, making day look like night, carving light where little or none exists—all of these things are cool and usable concepts, but there is also nothing wrong with creating a simple, classic portrait like the one on the facing page.

Add a Prop

Brendan brought a guitar, so of course I had to rock out a couple of edgy shots.

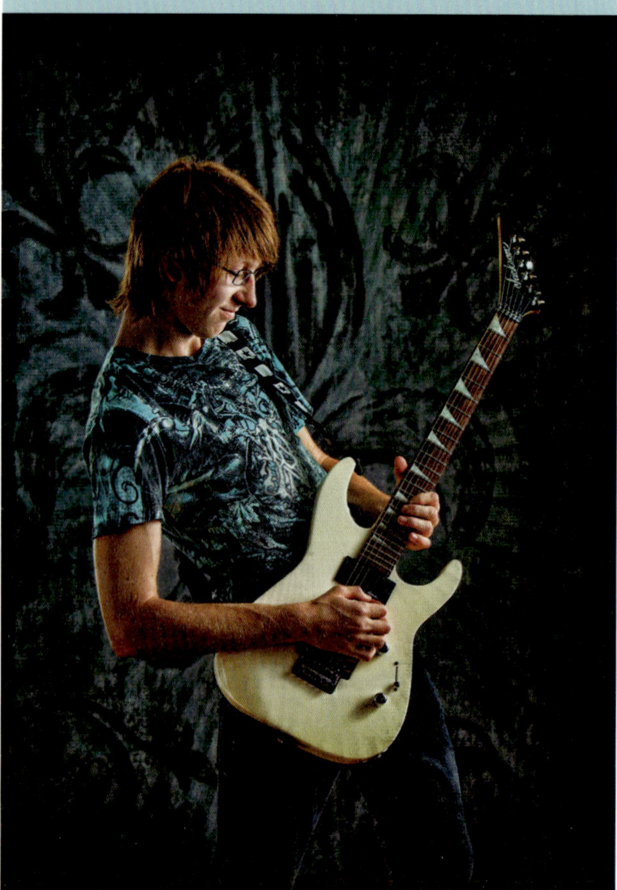

Classic and Cool

To create this image, I used a classic three-light plus reflector setup. The main light was a speedlight in a 3.5x5-foot Larson softbox. I used two edge lights in 1x4-foot Creative Light stripboxes. Finally, a large free-standing silver reflector added some subtle fill from camera right.

A *Little* Rule-Breaking

Maybe what I like about the image is that it actually *does* break some of my normal rules for portraiture. His head is turned slightly away from the main light, making the light a bit broad and actually split down the vertical axis of this face. His head is slightly inclined to the high shoulder. His shoulders are mostly square to the camera. But it all comes together to make a pleasing portrait. The expression is softly neutral, yet there is life there. There is a little light on the studio background, but it is just enough to provide a sense of depth. The wide crop places his face right on a power point, which contributes to the power of the image. It's simple, and it has flaws, but its timelessness and positives far outweigh anything else, making this an infinitely salable, classic portrait.

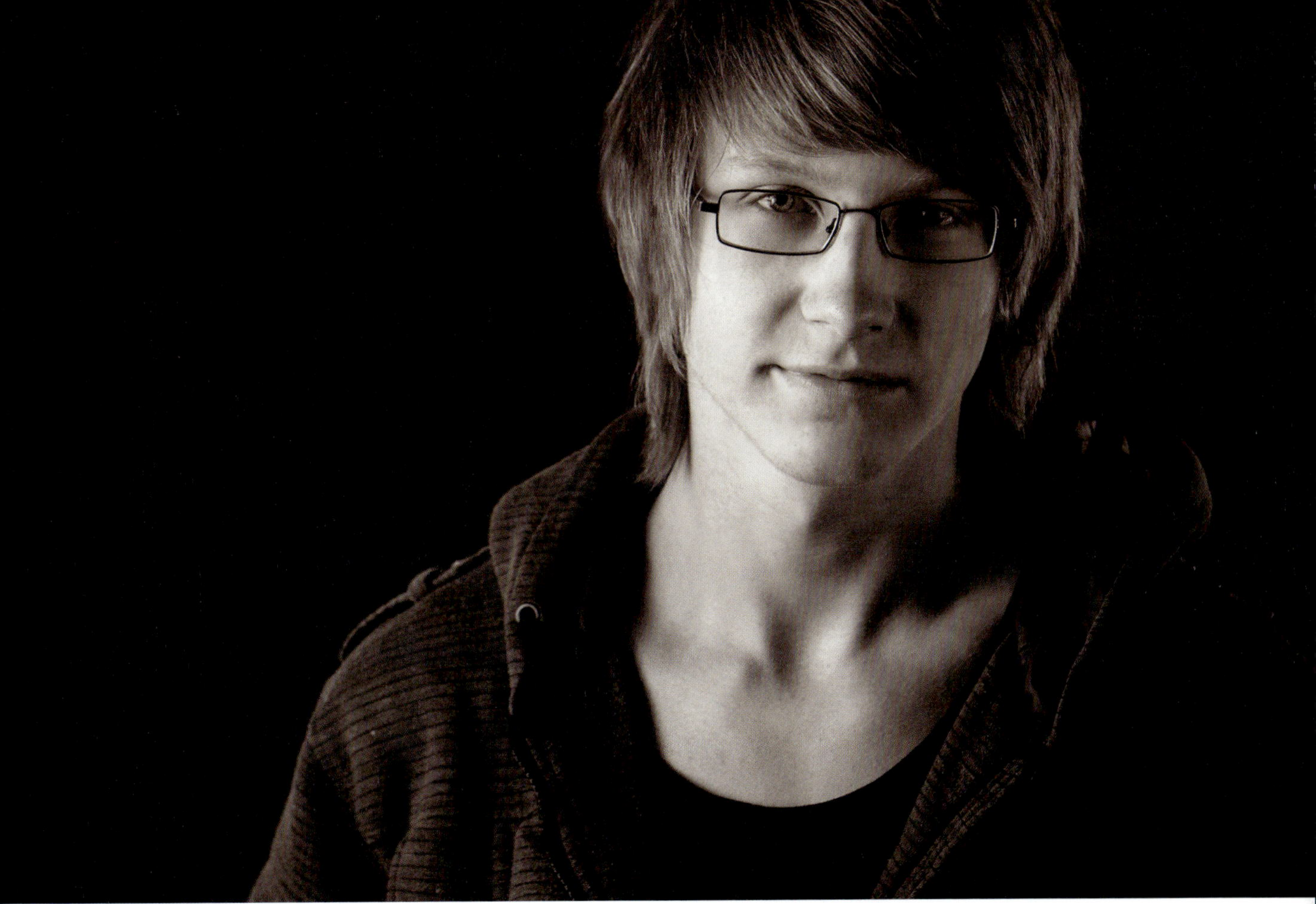

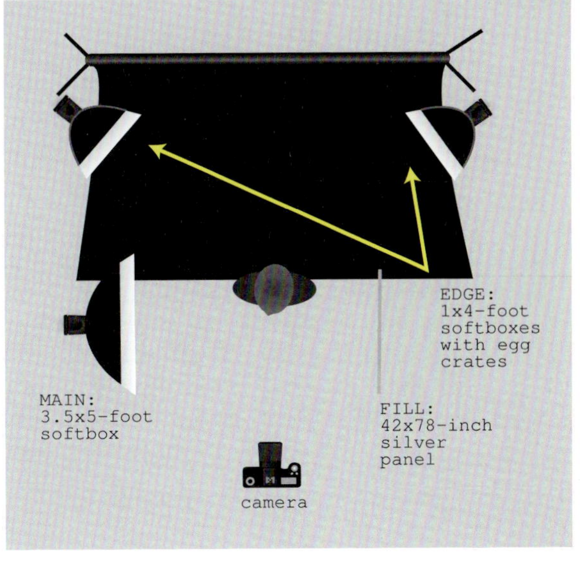

Postproduction

To finish the image in postproduction, I converted the portrait to black & white using my Chocolate Mousse preset in Lightroom. The warm tone this provided contributed to the timeless feel of this image. Some minimal skin softening was done using Imagenomic's Portraiture filter.

Camera: Canon 5D MKIII with Canon 70–200L f/4 IS lens at 150mm

Exposure: $1/160$ second, f/6.3, ISO 200 (manual)

Lighting: Three Canon 580EX II speedlights manually controlled using the RadioPopper JrX system coupled with RadioPopper Cubes. *Main light:* 3.5x5-foot Larson softbox. *Edge lights:* Two 1x4-foot Creative Light softboxes with speedlight speedrings and front egg crates. *Fill light:* Calumet 42x78-inch silver reflective panel (free-standing).

24

Bending the Light

The Lightbender softbox for a beauty portrait

I admit it. I'm a gear-hound. I like to incorporate new tools and new backgrounds to give a boost to my creativity and to help me provide something new and different to my clients. I photographed this senior a day after receiving a new 48-inch Larson Lightbender softbox. In fact, here's another admission: I hadn't even tested it prior to this session. I

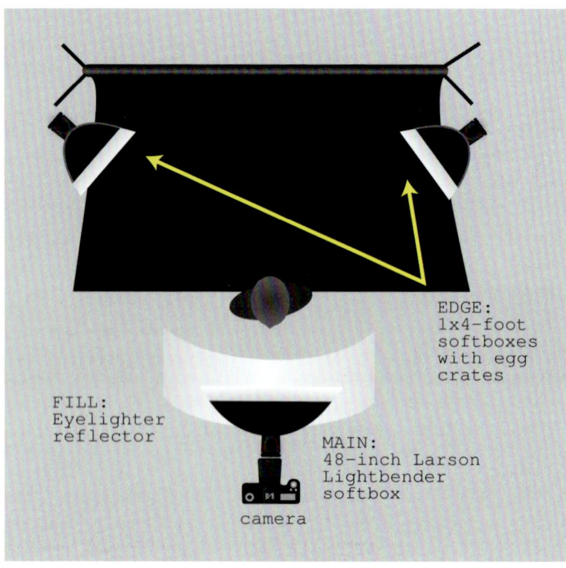

Camera: Canon 5D MKIII with Canon 70–200L f/4 IS lens at 185mm
Exposure: $\frac{1}{160}$ second, f/4.5, ISO 100 (manual)
Lighting: Three Canon 580EX II speedlights manually controlled using the RadioPopper JrX system coupled with RadioPopper Cubes. *Main light:* 48-inch Larson Lightbender softbox. *Edge lights:* Two 1x4-foot Creative Light softboxes with speedlight speedrings and front egg crates. *Fill light:* Larry Peters Eyelighter reflector.

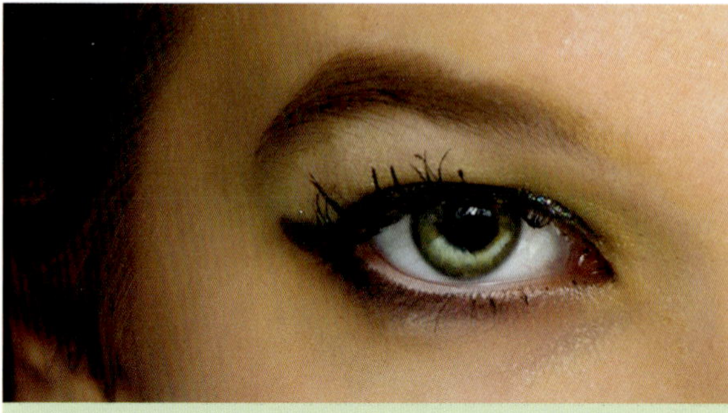

Catchlights

The Eyelighter reflector created curved catchlights in the irises of my subject's eyes. Retouchers often try to add catchlights that look as nice as these, but with this setup the catchlights are already there. Impressive.

definitely recommend that you test out new gear before using it with a client, however—so do as I say, not as I do.

Bend It, Baby

The Lightbender is unusual in that it does not have a flat front like traditional softboxes. Instead, it has a somewhat dramatic curve to the front surface. This curve is meant to create a wrapping effect with the light, one that better mimics the rounded shape of the human face and head. In addition, it creates a "clamshell" effect when coupled with the Eyelighter reflector, a curved reflector created by noted Ohio senior portrait photographer Larry Peters. I used such a clamshell arrangement for creating this portrait.

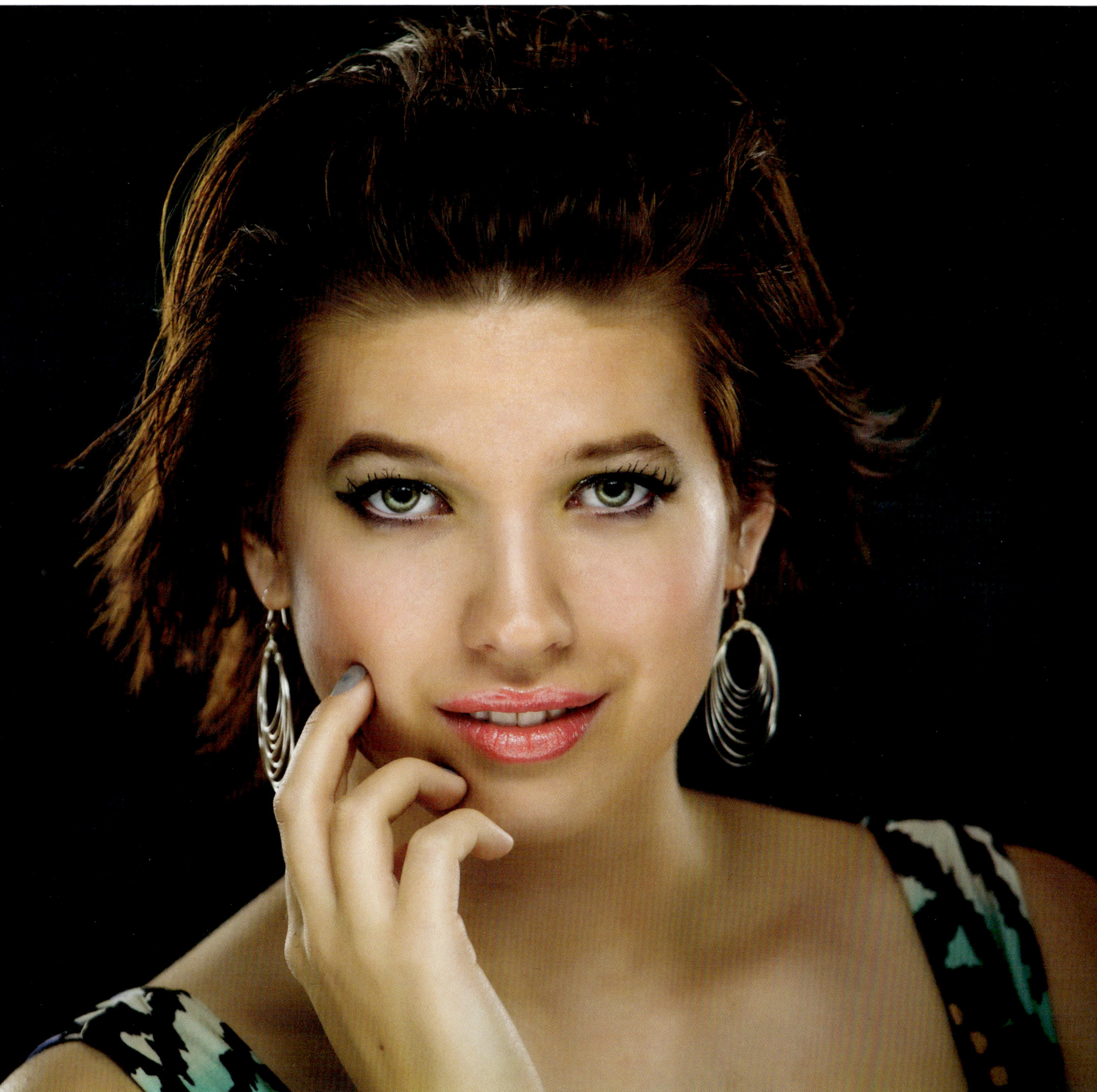

Lighting Setup

The Lightbender softbox was on a boom and oriented to a horizontal axis just above the camera lens, directly in front of the client and tilted down at approximately 45 degrees. The Eyelighter reflector was on a low stand placed opposite the softbox, meaning its curve was aimed up toward the client.

Have Light, Will Travel

Beauty lighting in unusual locations

I often surprise clients with the spots I pick when we go out on location. I rarely pick the obvious, clean and pretty spot—*boring!* Give me decrepit and gritty any day. It's full of character and tends to photograph better.

Barnstorming

Here, the client requested photos outside of an old barn. I created several nice images, but then I started to poke around because I sensed there was more than what met the eye with this place.

I discovered a door into a basement of the barn. Bingo! I found ancient fieldstone walls with light poking through several small eyehole windows. Gritty goodness!

Lighting

I used the directional natural light for my initial "pretty" shots, then decided to get to get a little more dramatic to better match what the space offered. I positioned Kelly in front of and in between the eyehole windows, using them as my edge lights. Then I used one of my go-to location lights, a 20-inch popup Firefly

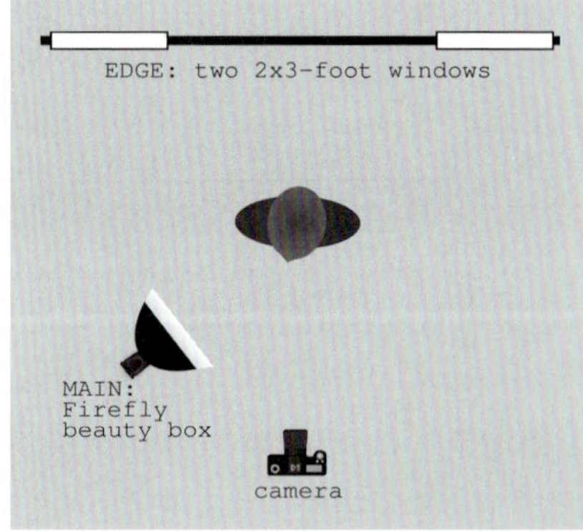

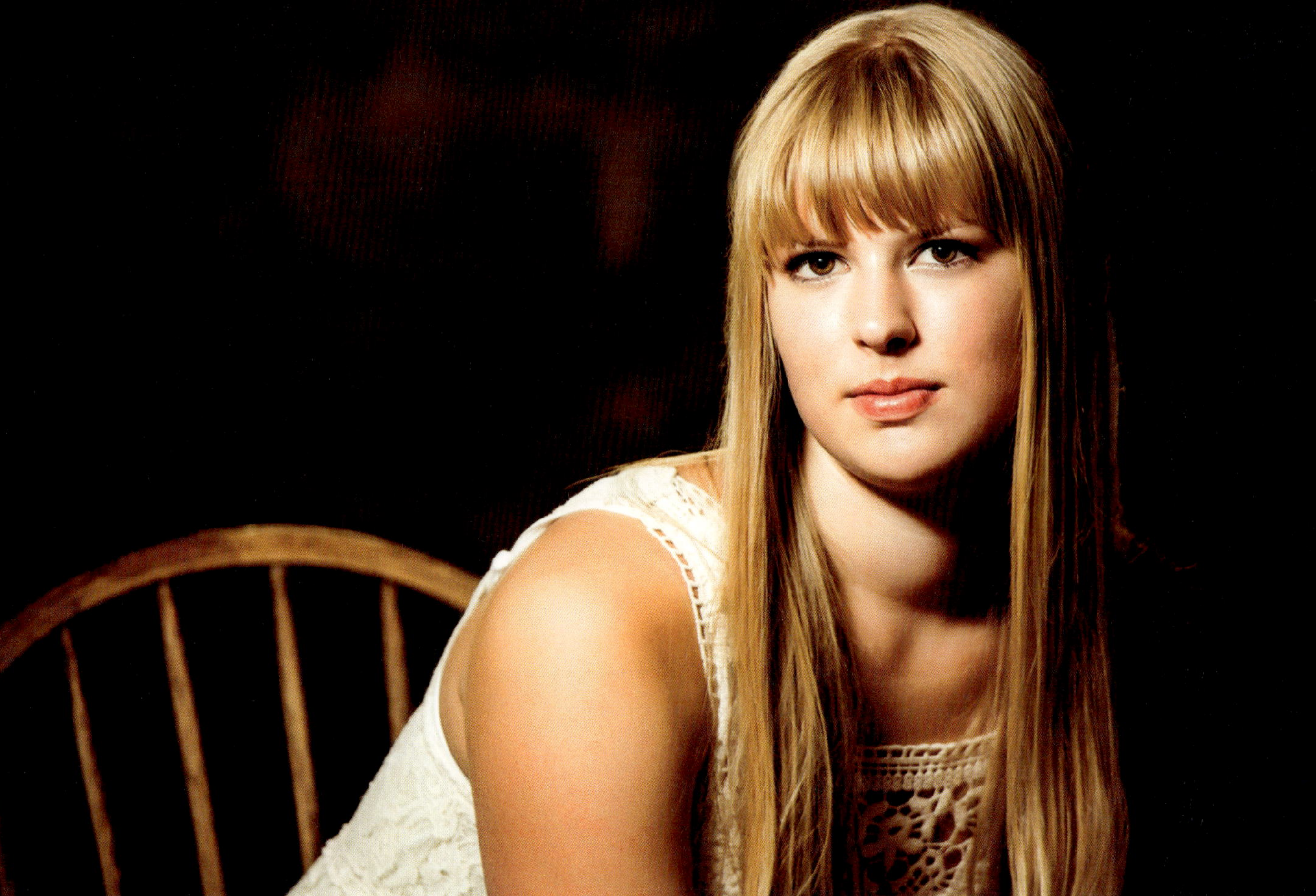

beauty box. This rugged little umbrella-style box provides efficient directional but softened light in a small and very portable package. The

"I used the ambient light from the windows behind her as rim lighting."

Camera: Canon 5D MKIII with Canon 70–200L f/4 IS lens at 93mm
Exposure: $1/80$ second, f/4, ISO 800 (manual)
Lighting: One Canon 580EX II speedlight fired in eTTL using the RadioPopper PX system. JrX system coupled with RadioPopper Cubes. *Main light:* 20-inch Firefly speedlight beauty box. *Edge lights:* Ambient light from two small windows.

light stand connector allows for tipping the box up and down.

Two Looks

For the standing portrait (facing page), I tipped the Firefly down from camera left to create a classic Rembrandt lighting pattern on her face.

For the second look, a seated pose (above), I positioned the Firefly above the lens, angling it down to to create a classic butterfly lighting pattern. Again, I used the ambient light from the windows behind her as rim lighting. I seated her on an old chair we found among the oddities strewn about the barn basement. This image was processed using my Orange Magento Pushup preset in Lightroom.

A Bounce and a Kiss

Bounced flash portraits on location

I do not always use a speedlight as my primary light source. That would be absurd—especially with all of the other beautiful sources of light available wherever we go. Sometimes I blend a speedlight with other light to help even out a scene. It may surprise you to know that I often photograph with ambient light only. *Quelle horreur!*

On the First Bounce

Beautiful sunlight was coming in from windows to camera left. This light alone probably would have sufficed, but I felt I could make the shot better by balancing out the light while maintaining its direction and contrast. To do this, I turned the flash head to the side and aimed it at the junction of the wall and the ceiling.

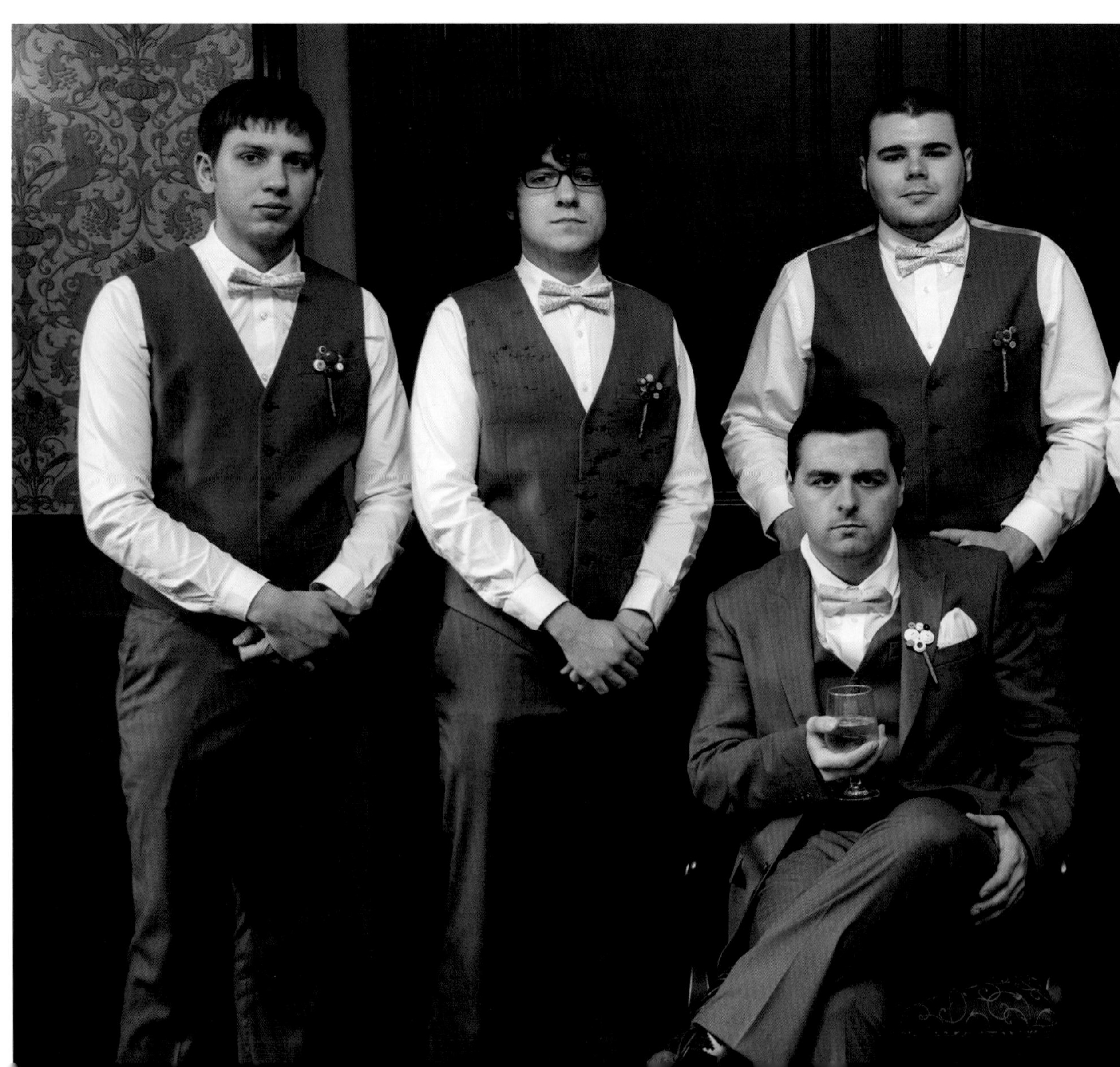

It depends on the height of the ceiling, but for most normal rooms, this technique works well. Also, look for walls and ceilings that are neutral in color (white, gray, off-white); vibrant paint colors can cause horrible color casts.

When bouncing flash, I set my camera's shutter speed, aperture, and ISO based on how much of the ambient light I want in the scene. I set my flash to eTTL and dial the FEC up or down (if needed), depending on how much I want the flash to affect the scene. Here, my base exposure was for the window light as I wanted this to be my primary light. The FEC on my flash was set to +⅔ EV. The flash head was ro-

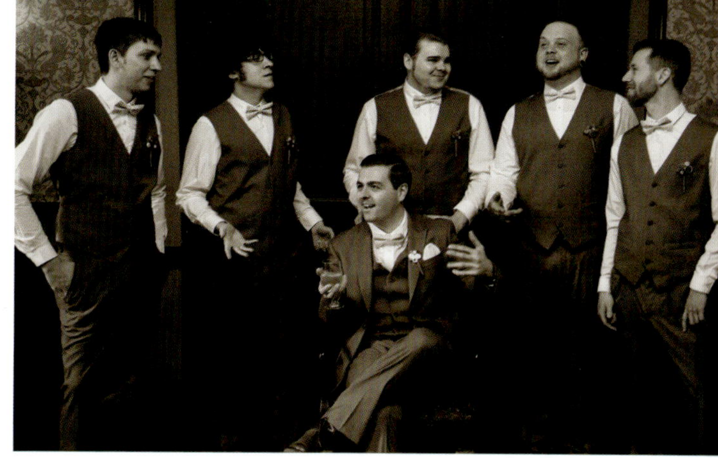

After the stoic main image (left), the groomsman opted for some fake frivolity (above). It was a fun group!

tated up to camera right at the wall and ceiling approximately 10 feet to my right. The resulting exposure has nice, balanced lighting.

Postproduction

I converted the image to a warm-tone black & white using my Chocolate Mousse preset in Lightroom. I felt this monochromatic approach best fit the character of the image.

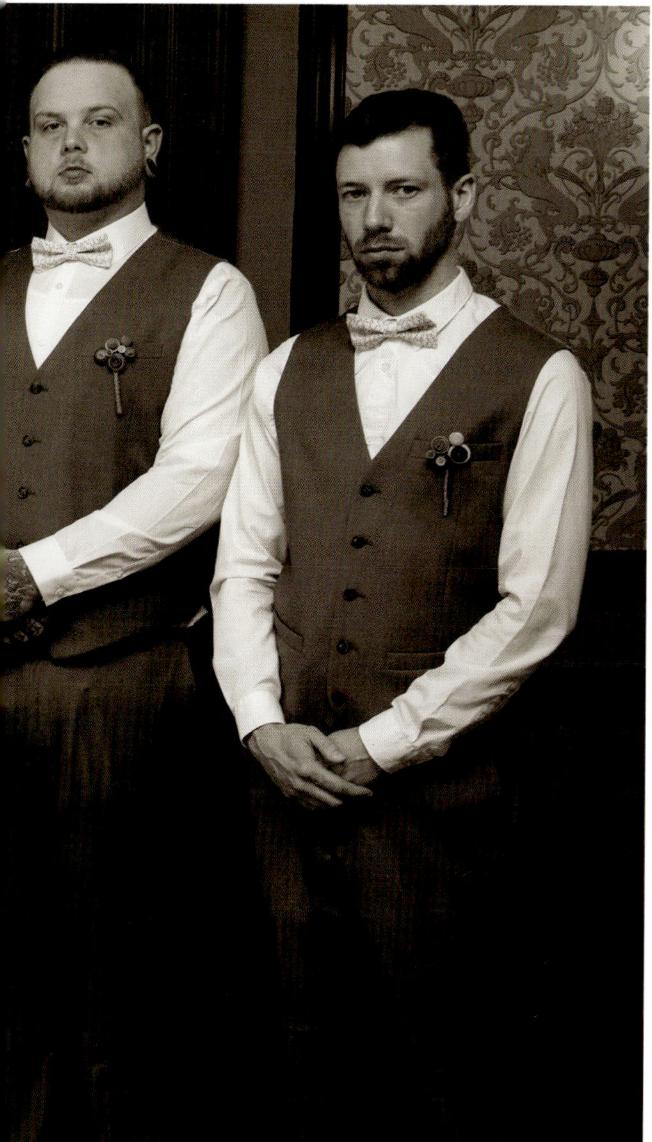

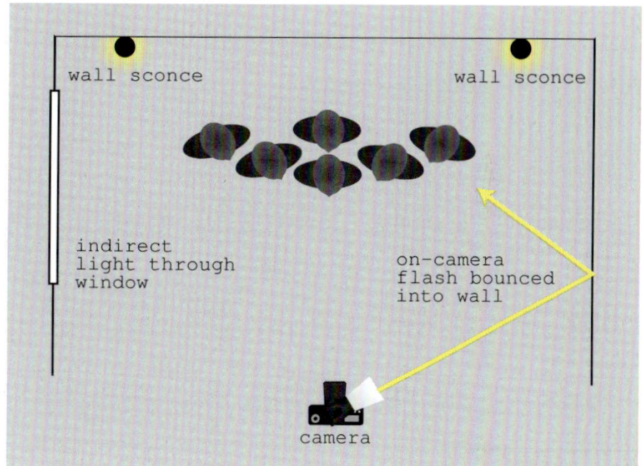

Camera: Canon 5D MKIII with Canon 24–105L f/4 IS lens at 40mm
Exposure: $\frac{1}{125}$ second, f/5.6, ISO 3200 (manual)
Lighting: One on-camera Canon 580EX II speedlight fired in eTTL and bounced for fill. Ambient light from a large bank of windows was the main light.

Getting a Little Punchy

Punch up boring, soft light outside

On this overcast day we had soft, pleasing light, but it was mostly non-directional—and where there *was* direction to the ambient light, it was coming straight down.

A natural-light photographer would have taken the ambient light shot, and would have been happy with it. Indeed, it would have been an "okay" to "good" image. But I do not like to settle for okay.

The problem with the light being too soft and non-directional in this scene is that it lacked any impact whatsoever. Except for Olivia's hair, the whole scene was muted and monochromatic in similar tones of white and gray. The shot needed some punch to match the sassy pose—and the sassy Olivia with her vibrant red hair and cool tattoos. That punch came via the addition of speedlights.

Gang Punch

I placed one set of two ganged speedlights to camera right in order to provide short light on

"Place the off-camera speedlight closer and it will become more dominant in the TTL exposure."

Olivia's face. They were flipped onto the vertical axis using my four-flash bracket in combination with an umbrella adapter. In addition, I set my

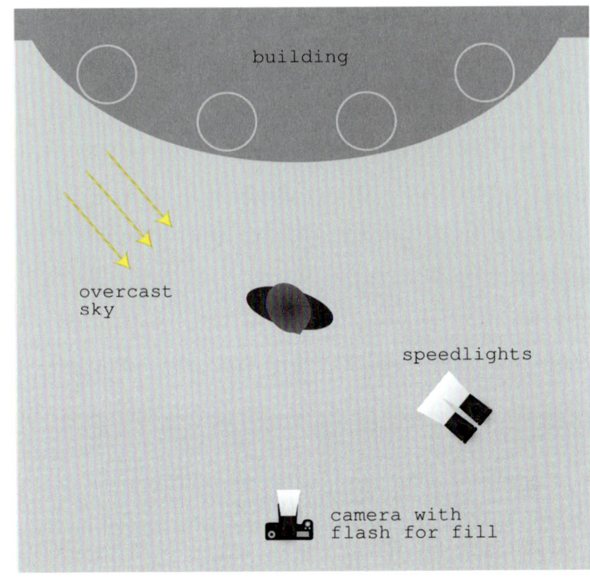

Camera: Canon 5D MKIII with Canon 24–105L f/4 lens at 35mm
Exposure: $^1/_{200}$ second, f/13, ISO 200 (manual)
Lighting: Canon 580EX II speedlight on-camera set to master (fired) with RadioPopper PX transmitter. Two Canon 580EX II speedlights off-camera and rotated to a vertical axis, set to eTTL and slave mode, fired with RadioPopper PX receivers.

on-camera master flash to fire and contribute to the exposure as fill light.

Since the off-camera speedlight setup was closer to Olivia than I was with my on-camera flash, the off-camera speedlight provided a directional main light for the image. It's a simple but effective way to combine off-camera speedlight with on-camera speedlight: place the off-camera speedlight closer and it will become more dominant in the TTL exposure.

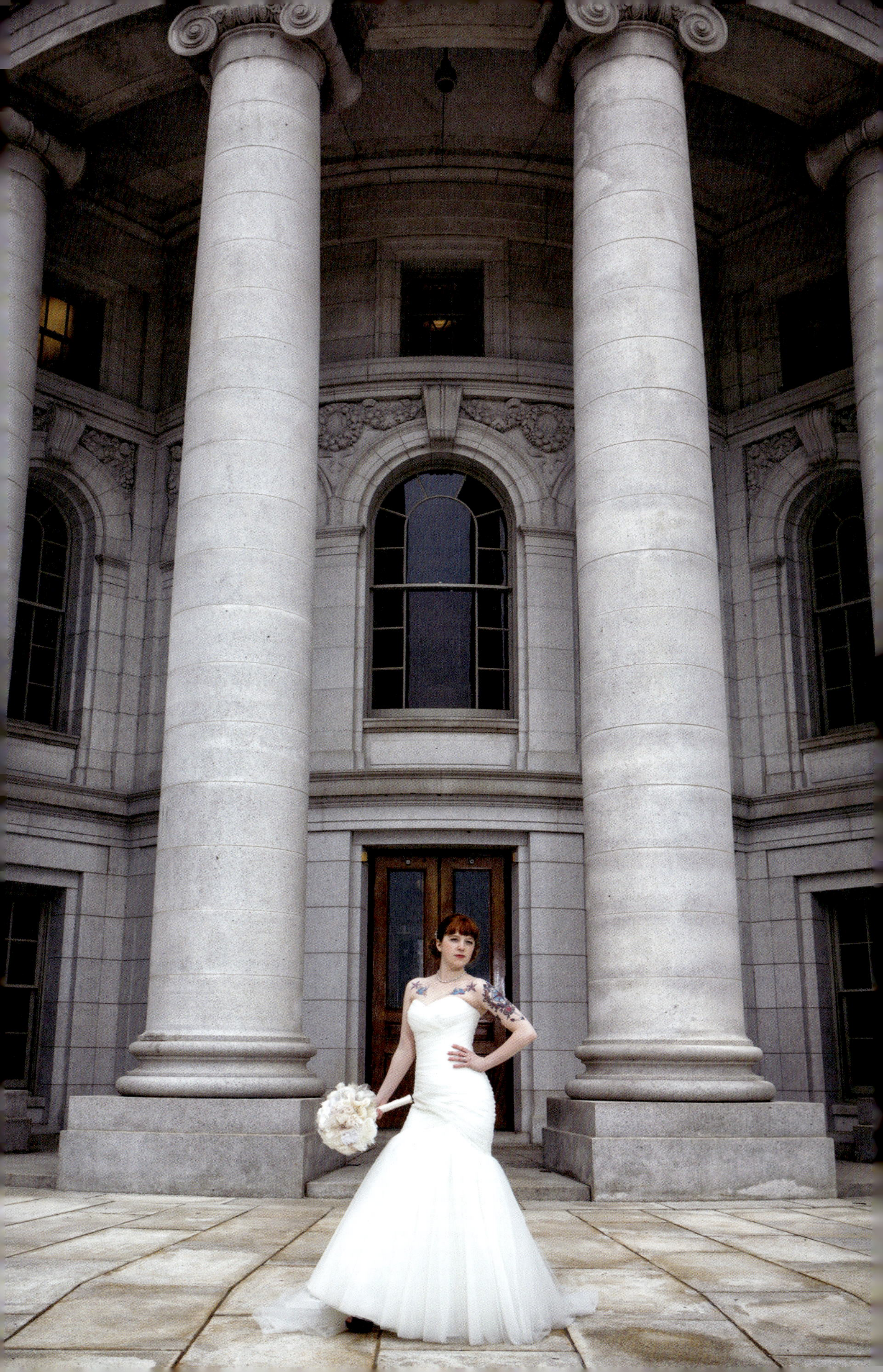

All this additional light from the combination of speedlights helped to subtly pop Olivia out from the background while still maintaining a pleasing monochromatic look on the scene.

I often photograph images like this in aperture-priority mode, setting my aperture to a wider setting (like f/4) in order to achieve a shallow depth of field. In this case, however, I changed it up and went with a manual exposure for two reasons: (1) I wanted more front-to-back sharpness, including sharpness on the columns behind Olivia; and (2) in aperture-priority mode, the camera's built-in meter would have read all of the light tones in the scene and underexposed it. I opted for a manual exposure to prevent this. Sometimes I would welcome that underexposure (for example, when I am trying

to darken a bright sky). In this case, however, I wanted to achieve a more natural appearance to the scene.

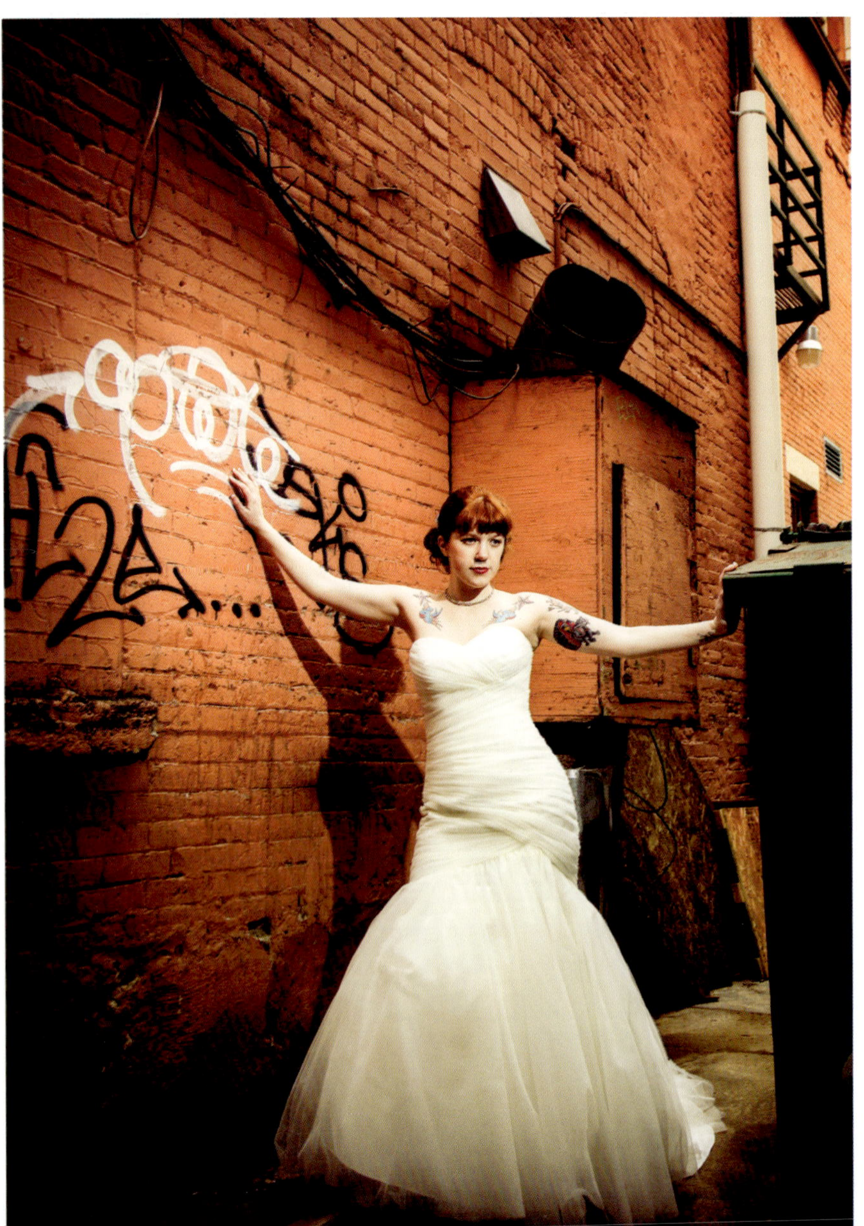

An even punchier shot of Olivia created in a back alley.

I have a *lot* of Canon Speedlites—but, you know, a guy gets the "wandering eye" every once in a awhile. (Of course I mean this *only* in the context of camera gear. Love you, dear! Mwah.)

My eye started to wander about the same time I saw the Canon 580EX II disappearing from inventories as Canon committed to the 600EX-RT. This flash looks cool, but in my mind, it's about five years too late. I wanted the radio transmitter back then—and I found it with the RadioPopper PX system. Now that I own almost as many PX receivers and transmitters as I have Canon flashes, I would need some serious coinage to make the transition to the new 600EX-RT; I'd need at least four, which would ring in at about $2500. Yikes!

> *"I bundled up my PX gear and sent it to RadioPopper for the update, which they handled within a week."*

Still, I could see potential trouble on the horizon as I needed to replace 580EX II units in the future. At about the same time, I received a phone call from Nissin Flash USA asking if I would like to test their flagship Di866 II flash, which coincidently *was just upgraded to work with the RadioPopper PX system.* Say what? Um, yeah. Send me some and let me play!

What You've Been Missin' by Not Going Nissin

In addition to the firmware update Nissin provided for their flashes, which can be installed by just connecting the flash to your computer (are you listening, Canon?), RadioPopper also offered a free firmware update for all of their PX transmitters and receivers. So I bundled up my PX gear and sent it to RadioPopper for the update, which they handled within a week. Then it was time to play.

One of my favorite models, Kj Lyn, contacted me to update her headshots. It timed

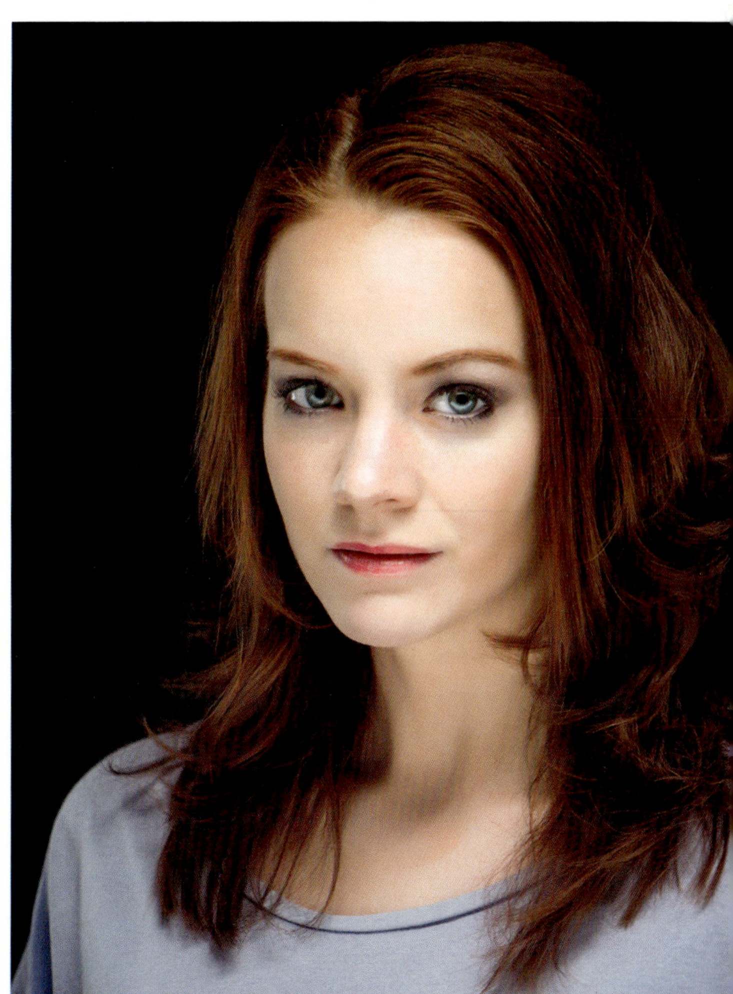

perfectly with the arrival of the Nissin flashes (three of them) and my updated PX gear. I devised test one for the Nissins: TTL portraiture in the studio.

The setup for these shots of Kj included one Nissin Di866 II with a RadioPopper PX receiver (set to group A) as the main light. This flash was fired into a Larson 48 Lightbender on a boom, positioned in line between the camera and my model.

"The flash output was set to TTL, and the ratio compensation (A:B) was set at 4:1 on the master."

Two additional Nissin Di866 II flashes with RadioPopper PX receivers were set to group B to function as my edge lights. These flashes were fired into 1x4-foot Creative Light strip-

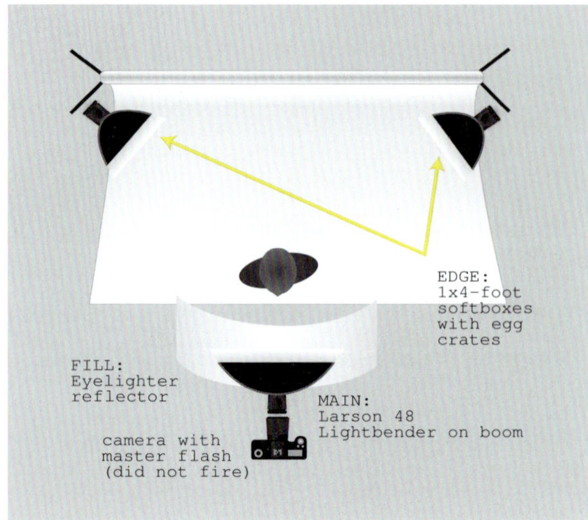

Camera: Canon 5D MKIII with Canon 70–200L f/4 IS lens at 200mm

Exposure: $^1/_{160}$ second, f/5, ISO 200 (manual)

Lighting: Nissin Di866 II with RadioPopper PX receiver (group A) in Larson 48 Lightbender as main light. Two Nissin Di866 II with RadioPopper PX receivers (group B) in 1x4-foot stripboxes with egg crates as edge lights. Larry Peter Eyelighter for fill.

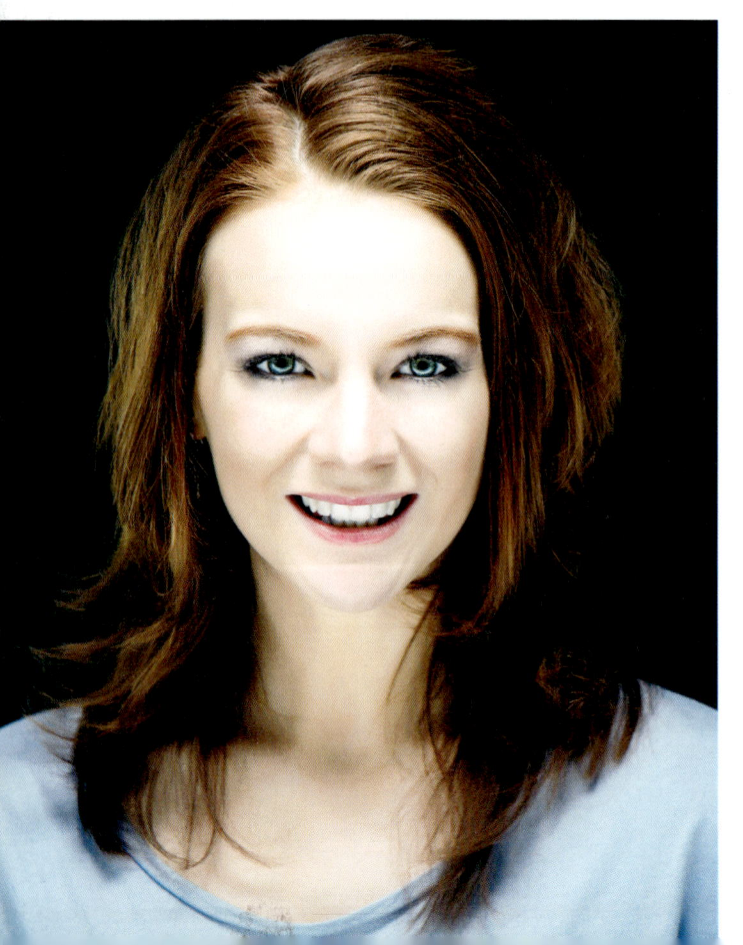

boxes with egg-crate grids. They were positioned to either side and behind Kj.

The flash output was set to TTL, and the ratio compensation (A:B) was set at 4:1 on the master. The flashes were triggered by an on-camera Canon 580EX II flash sct to Master/Do Not Fire with a RadioPopper PX transmitter.

A curved Larry Peter Eyelighter reflector was used below Kj for fill and uplighting.

The final image (facing page) also incorporated a Canon 480EX II with a Strobies grid (group C) as a background light.

The final two images (left and facing page) were processed with my Feeling a Little Blu Photoshop action.

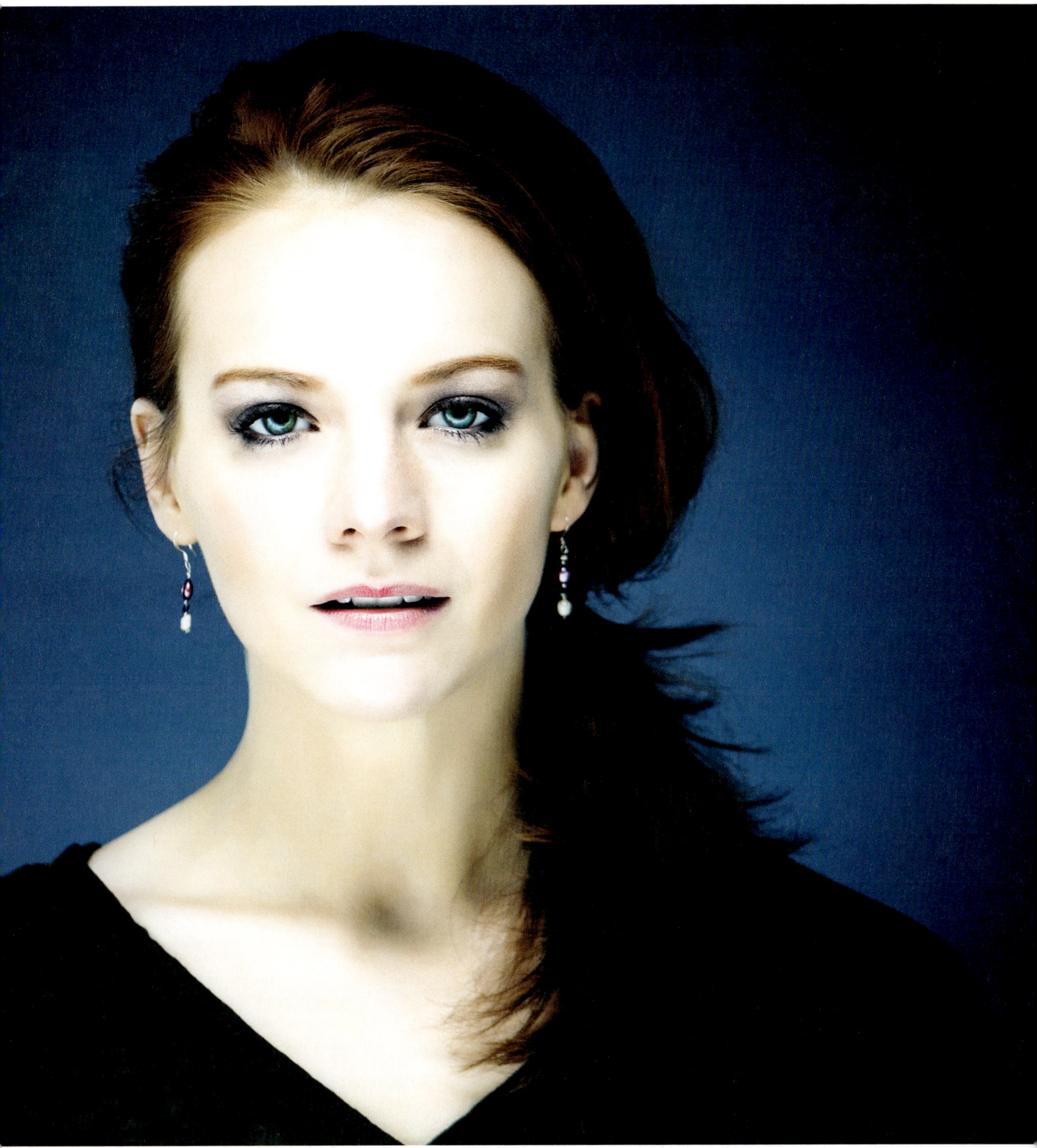

29

Here, Kitty, Kitty

TTL model images outside in the brutal cold

After testing the TTL performance of the Nissin Di866II flashes in the studio, the next step was to take these bad boys outside to see what they could do on location. I contacted one of my favorite models, Erin, to see if she wanted to shoot outside. Of course, being the middle of January in Wisconsin, it was a little chilly. Okay, it was downright cold. But the weather gave Erin an excuse to wear her new furry kitty hat.

On a Mission with the Nissin

We did our session on a gray, overcast, windy, cold day in downtown Madison near the University of Wisconsin campus. I sought out loca-

tions that would not only help to coordinate colors but would also keep us out of the wind as much as possible. A back alley near a parking garage and a narrow entrance into a commercial building served our purposes nicely.

Given the subdued natural light from the overcast sky, I was able to use a new Westcott Apollo stripbox that I had acquired and needed to test. My gear setup was the same for each of the shots shown here.

Shot 1 (below, left) is a tight close-up. As you can see, the TTL flash in the stripbox pro-

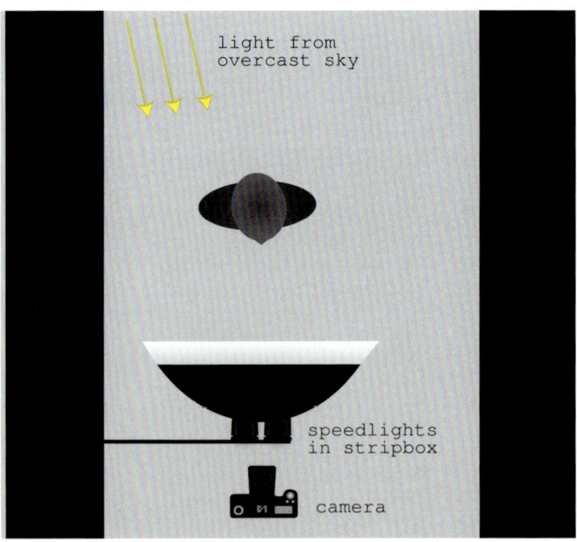

Camera: Canon 5D MKIII with Canon 70–200L f/4 IS lens at 200mm

Exposure: *Shot 1:* $^1/_{100}$ second, f/4, ISO 100, –1EV exposure compensation (aperture priority). *Shot 2:* $^1/_{200}$ second, f/4, ISO 200, –1EV exposure compensation (aperture priority). *Shots 3 and 4:* $^1/_{200}$ second, f/4, ISO 200, –1EV exposure compensation (aperture priority)

Lighting: One Nissin Di866 II on-camera as the master (did not fire). RadioPopper PX transmitter. Two Nissin Di866 II flashes off-camera in a Westcott Apollo stripbox. RadioPopper PX receivers.

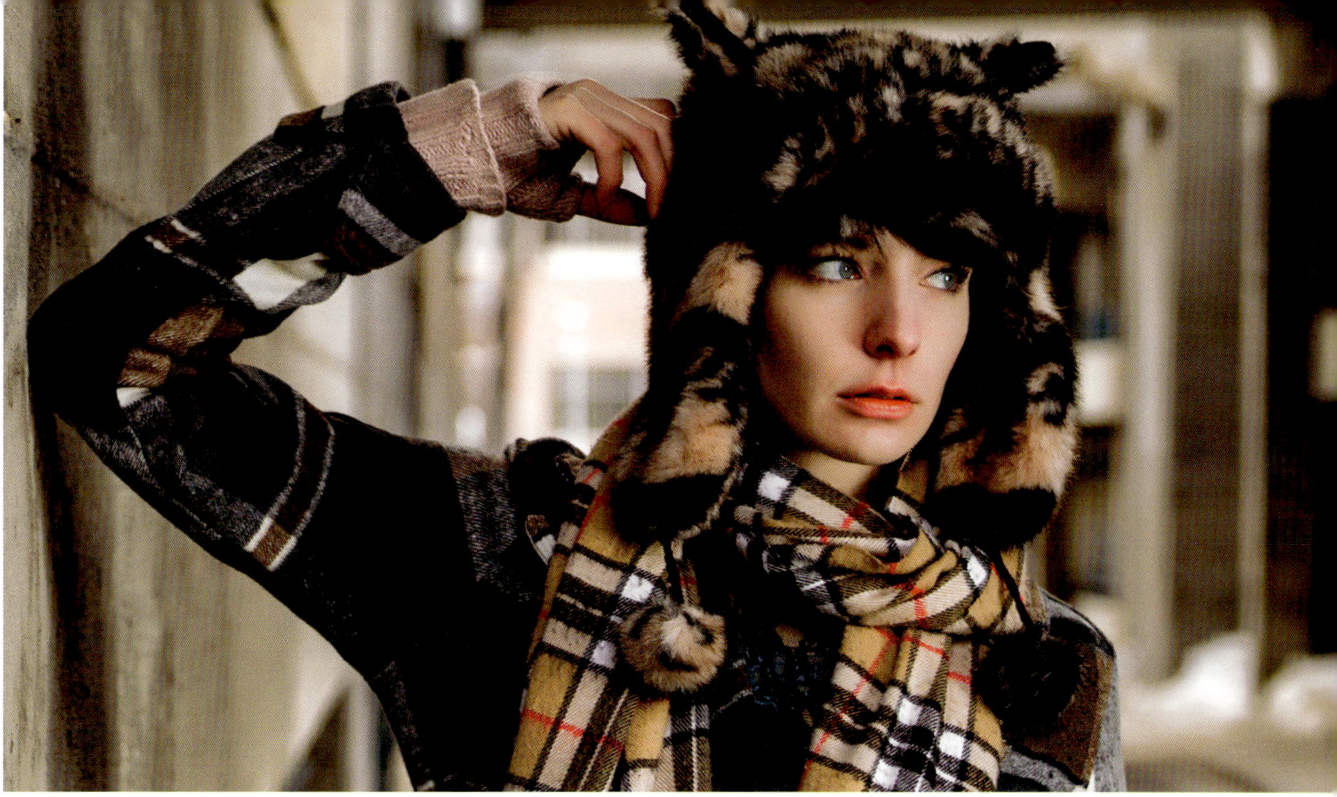

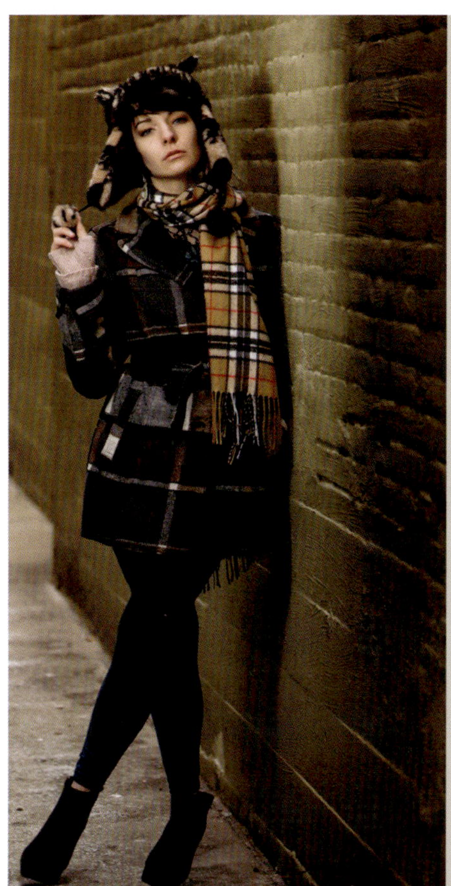

vided a pleasing level of contrast and contouring on Erin's face.

For shot 2 (above), I turned Erin to put her face into a two-thirds view. I also moved the stripbox off to camera right in order to provide proper short lighting on her face. Again, the lighting sculpted her face beautifully with a nice level of contrast.

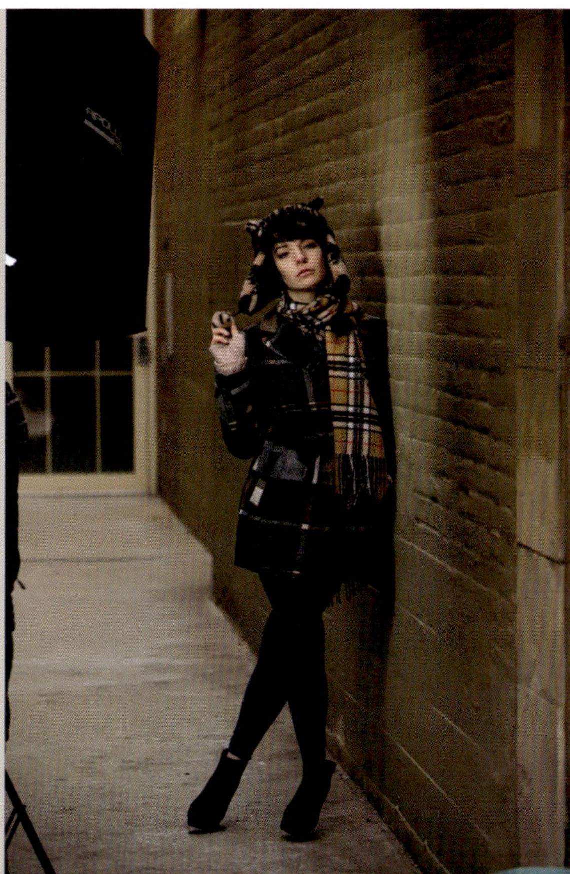

The final two images (shots 3 and 4) show the setup and the final cropped image from the narrow entryway I mentioned earlier. You can see the Westcott stripbox at the left edge of the final frame.

30

Many Ways to Soften

Simple diffusion panels, instant softboxes

I have trained myself to photograph portraits outside in the middle of the day, largely because that is the hand that is dealt to me on most wedding days. The side benefit is that I can use those skills for other types of portraiture, including high-school senior portraits. Summers are short in the upper Midwest, and I don't want to spend every summer evening chasing a senior around with a reflector during "sweet light" time. I would much rather photograph them at 2 or 3 o'clock in the afternoon and have my evenings to relax with my family.

Find the Shade

One obvious technique to use when photographing during the bright, sunny midday is to find locations that are shaded. This will suf-

A second image using the same lighting technique.

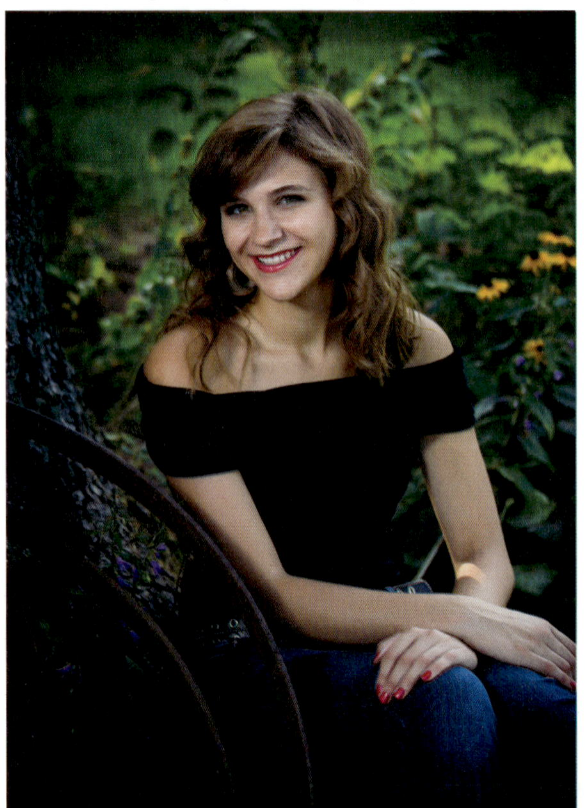

Camera: Canon 5D MKIII with Canon 70–200L lens at 70mm
Exposure: $^1/_{200}$ second, f/4, ISO 200, $-^2/_3$EV exposure compensation (aperture priority)
Lighting: Canon 580EX II speedlight on-camera set to master (fired) with RadioPopper PX transmitter. Two Canon 580EX II speed lights off-camera and rotated to a vertical axis, set to eTTL and slave mode, fired with RadioPopper PX receivers. One Canon 580EX II speedlight off camera (rim light), set to eTTL and slave mode, fired with RadioPopper PX receivers.

fice for some images, but what about locations where there is full or spotty sunlight?

Balancing the Exposure

For the image on the facing page, Emily was seated in the shade, but the grass behind her was brightly lit by the full sun. If I exposed for her, the grass would blow out to nearly white; if I exposed for the background, she would go dark. I needed to add light to balance her exposure with the level of the light on the grass.

"It transformed a small, hard light source into a larger, softer light source that still had snap."

I often use a bare speedlight in this situation, but in this case the mood of the pose and the image called for softer light. I didn't have a softbox or umbrella with me, but I did have a

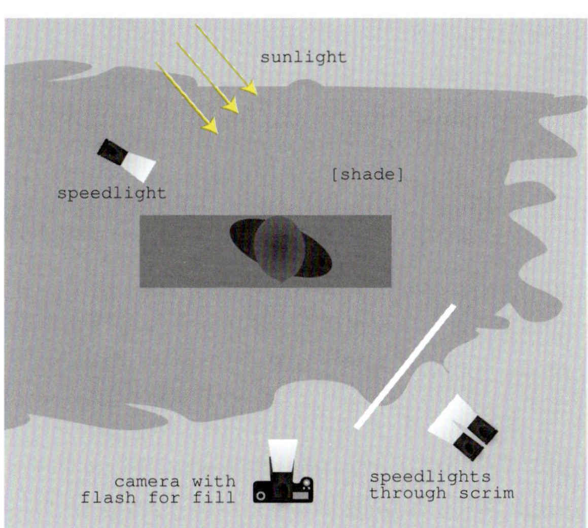

pop-up translucent diffusion panel from Denny Manufacturing. I use this to soften strong overhead sunlight, but it also works as a pseudo-softbox in a pinch. With my assistant holding it about two feet in front of my off-camera speedlights, it scattered the specular light and transformed a small, hard light source into a larger, softer light source that still had snap. Here, the speedlights and the panel were rotated to a vertical axis for even illumination top to bottom.

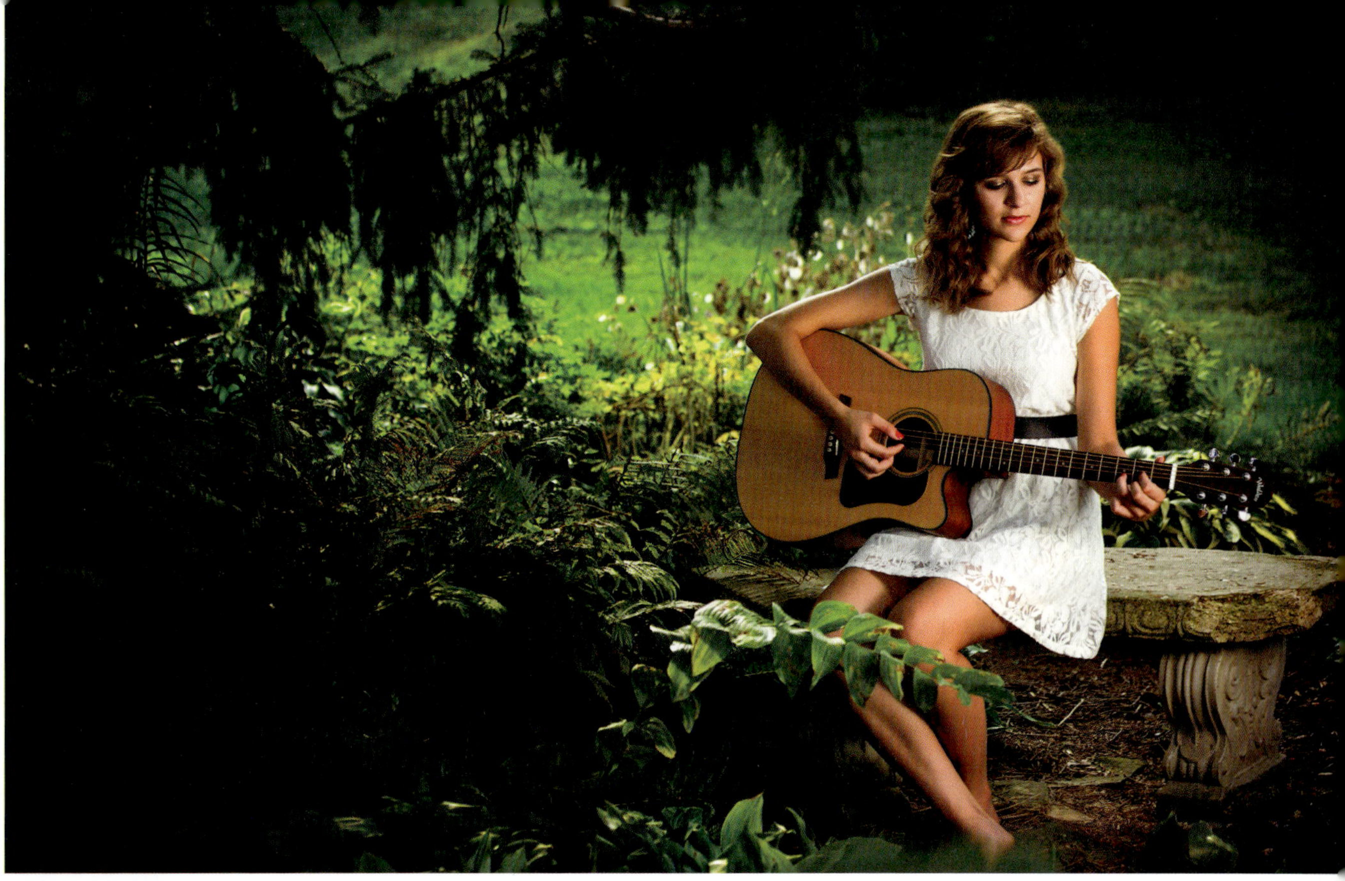

A third speedlight was placed behind Emily and to camera left to create rim lighting.

Finally, my on-camera master flash fired to provide a little fill light. Because I was using a longer lens, the distance from the subject was great enough that my on-camera speedlight did not overpower my off-camera speedlight setup.

Postproduction

To complete the look, I added a slight vignette during postproduction. Darkening the corners and the edges helped bring the viewer's focus in toward the beautifully lit subject.

31

Lighting with an Accent

Your speedlight as an accent light

Throughout my career, I have had a love/hate relationship with overcast days. When I was inexperienced, I loved them because they provided such soft, general light. Every setting looked reasonably good.

As I trained and grew, I recognized the downside to overcast days: low contrast, and downward light that shadows the eye sockets, creating the dreaded raccoon-eye effect. As I advanced further, I found ways to create contrast and properly light faces through additive (speedlights, reflectors) and subtractive (scrims, gobos) lighting.

The final piece of the puzzle for me was to become experienced and confident enough to know when to use creative posing to leverage the existing light and when to create light to enhance a desired pose. This example from an engagement session for Alais and Aaron shows a combination of both techniques (see "Can You Relate?" on the facing page).

Lighting

After I established a pose that made best use of the available light, the final ingredient was a little pop from an off-camera speedlight to camera right and slightly behind them. I added this simply to light her hair and help separate her from the background. It's subtle—like adding a little secret spice to a recipe.

This was my maiden field test for the Canon 600EX-RT system, and I found it to be impressive. Granted, I am more familiar with speedlights than the average photographer, but I found the 600EX-RT to be quite intuitive.

Postproduction

In postproduction, I added some selective darkening, saturation, and contrast in Photoshop to create my trademark "pop" and to better direct the viewer into the image.

Camera: Canon 5D MKIII with Canon 70–200L lens at 70mm
Exposure: $^1/_{250}$ second, f/4.5, ISO 320, $-^2/_3$EV exposure compensation (aperture priority).
Lighting: Canon 600EX-RT speedlight on-camera set to master (did not fire). Canon 600EX-RT speedlight off-camera, set to eTTL and slave mode, fired with built-in radio transmitter system, –1EV flash exposure compensation set at the master flash.

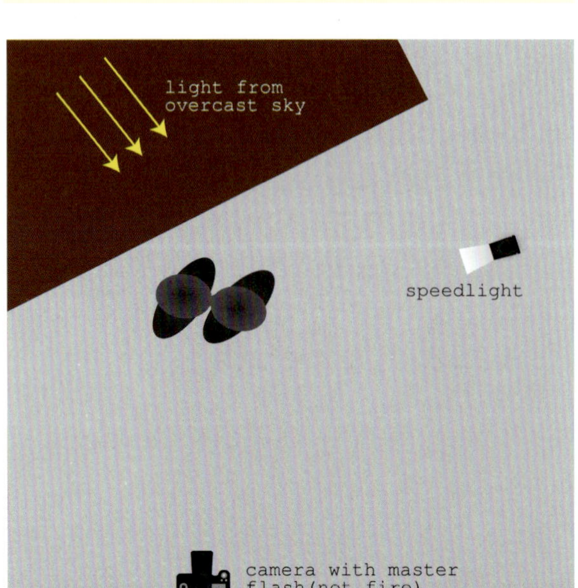

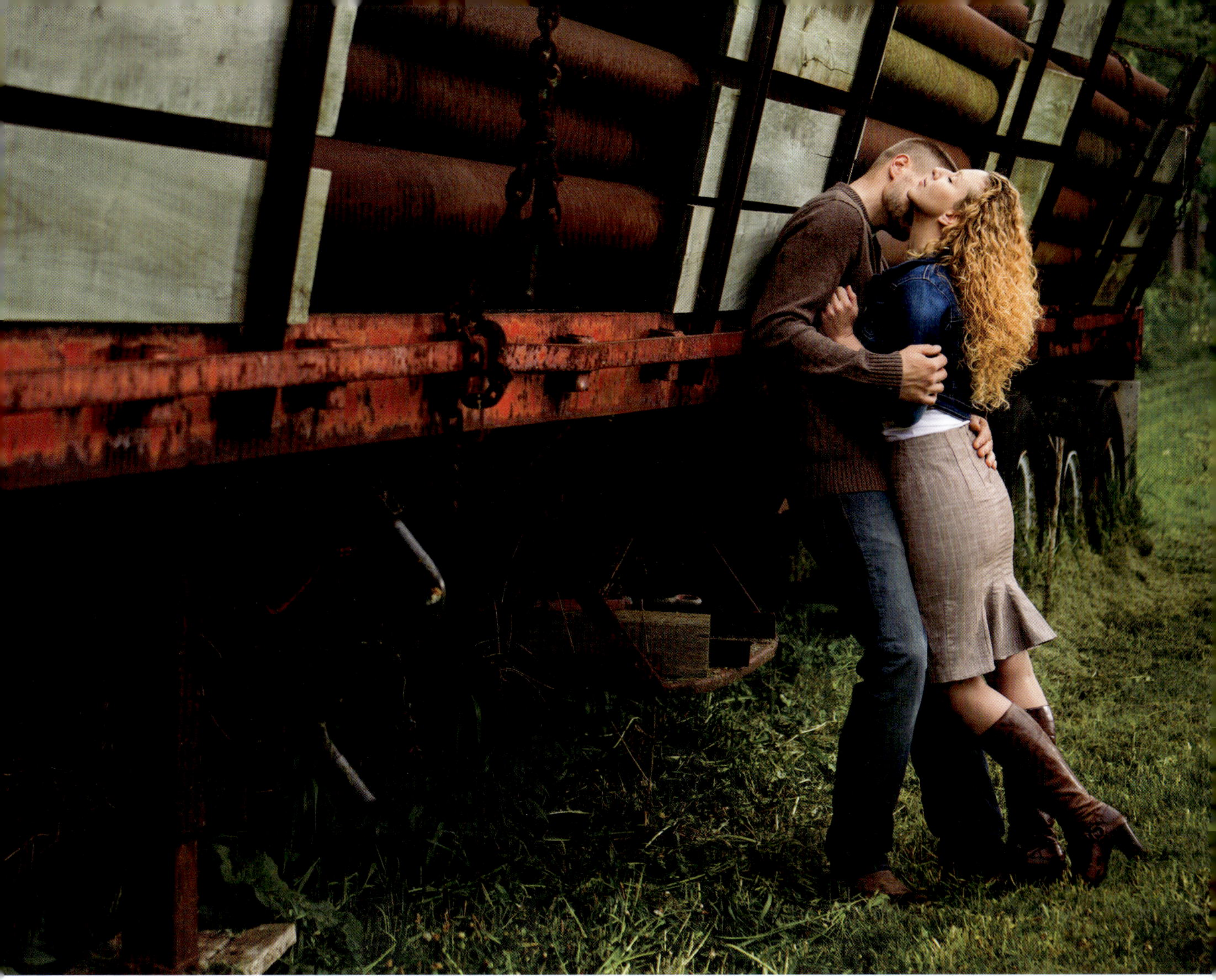

Can You Relate?

I prefer inter-relational posing for a majority of my couples' portraits for engagement sessions and weddings. It's a storytelling approach that lends itself better to more dramatic imagery.

Here, I directed a pose to show passion; Alais and Aaron are disengaged from the viewer and lost in a moment together. It's a pseudo-voyeuristic style that created an image with impact. By tilting Alais' head up to the sky, I also worked her face toward the direction of the ambient light. I didn't have to worry about shadowing on Aaron's eyes, because his head was tipped down and blocked by her head as he kissed Alais on the neck.

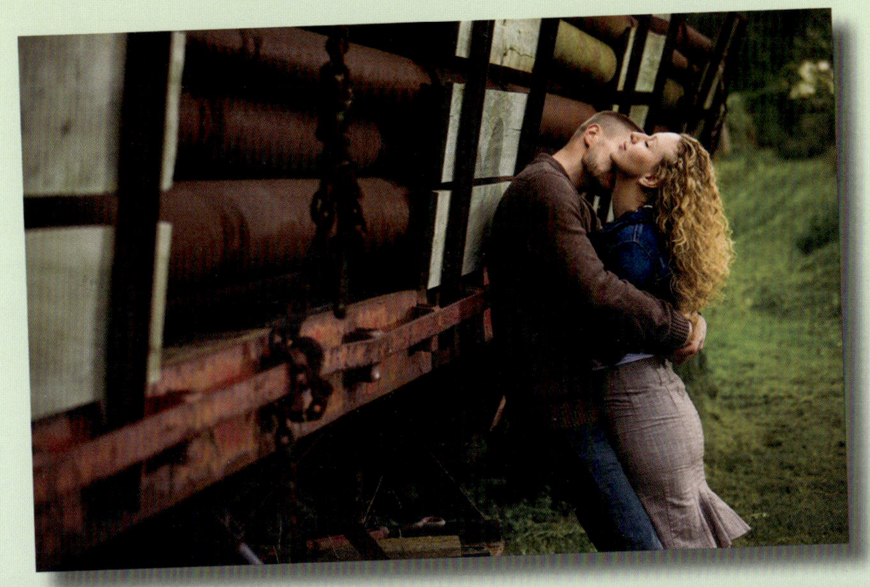

A simple posing variation.

32

Isolating the Subject

Using framing and light to pull attention

We have many tools to guide the viewer to what we want them to see—shallow depth of field (especially with a telephoto lens), framing, composition, and additive/subtractive lighting are a few. In the image on the facing page, I used all of them to pull my subjects out from a potentially busy background.

Background and Composition

I selected this spot for the concrete pillars at the pergola. The rows are set in a gentle curve, making them perfect as a framing device. The narrow frame the pillars created necessitated a tall, narrow composition. I also noticed the

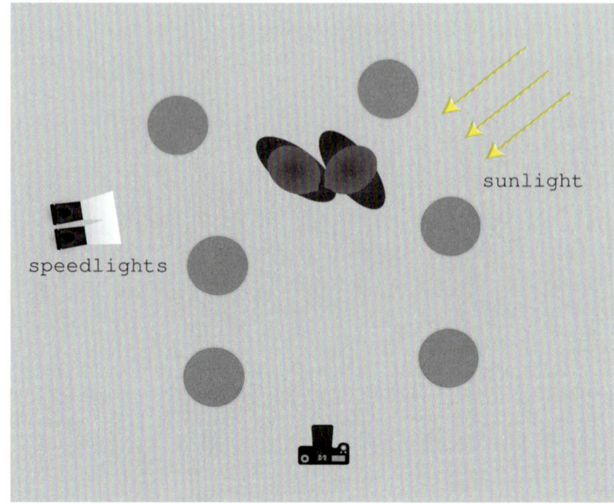

Camera: Canon 5D MKIII with Canon 70–200L lens at 144mm

Exposure: $1/200$ second, f/5, ISO 125, $-2/3$EV exposure compensation (aperture priority).

Lighting: Canon 580EX II speedlight on-camera set to master (did not fire) with RadioPopper PX transmitter. Two Canon 580EX II speedlights off-camera and rotated to a vertical axis, set to eTTL and slave mode, fired with RadioPopper PX receivers.

Another Look

Here's an image from later in the session using my "spiky sun" technique (see section 13).

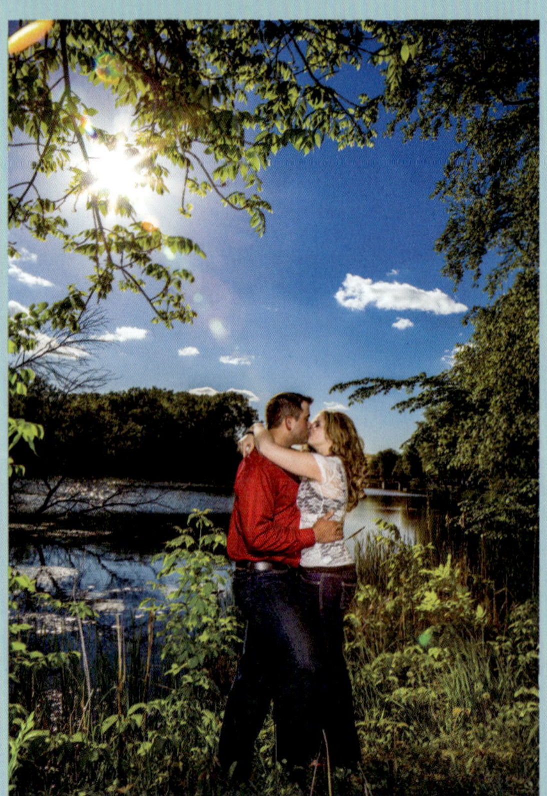

diagonal twisting pattern on the pillars, which inspired my pose for Michael and Chandra.

Lighting and Exposure

I shot at f/5 to keep the couple sharp while also creating rapid fall-off and shallow depth of field with my 70–200mm lens. I "subtracted" from the ambient light by setting $-2/3$EV exposure compensation in aperture-priority mode. The final touch was an off-camera speedlight from camera left, perpendicular to the couple. This helped separate them from the scene.

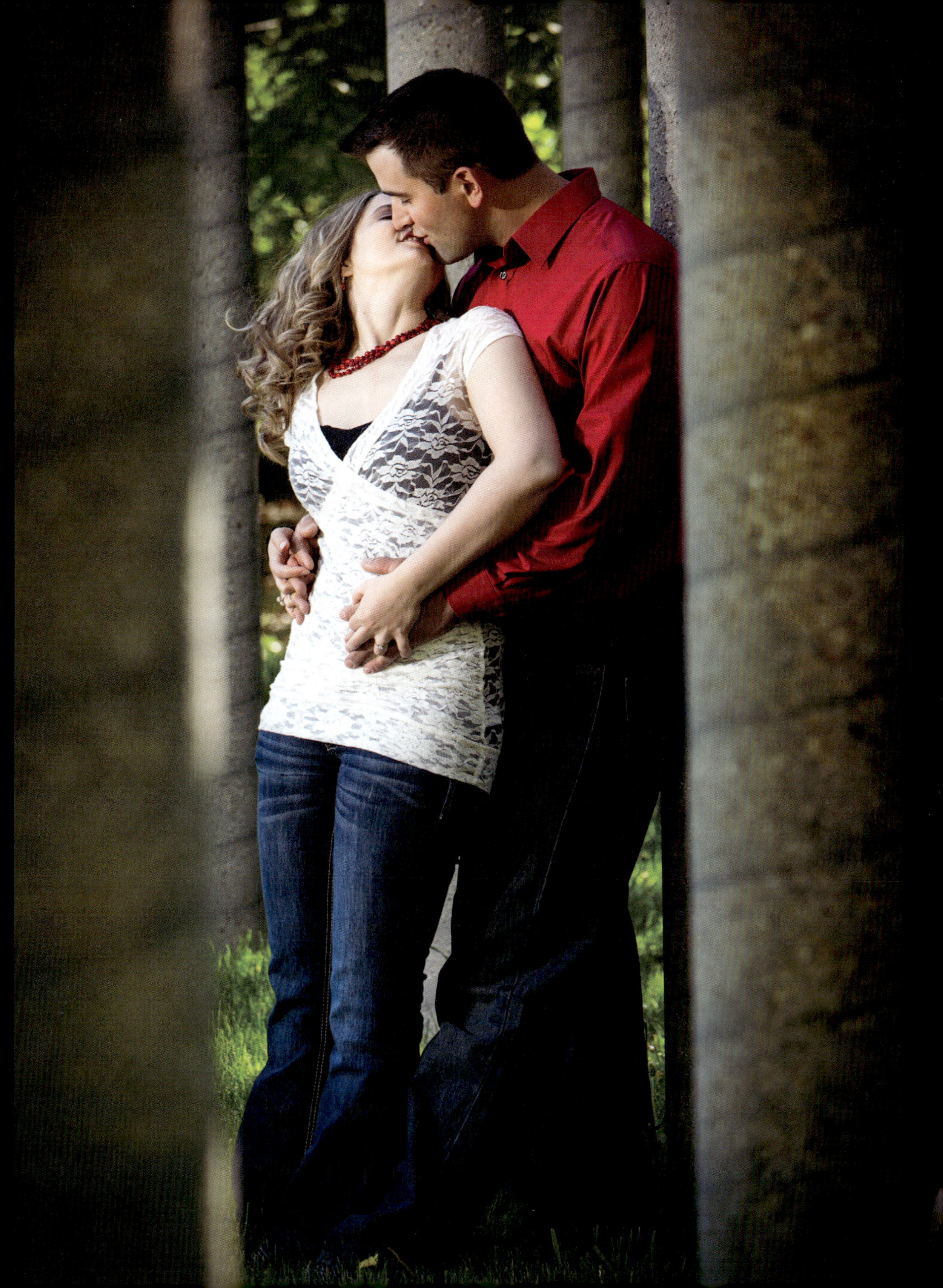

33

Zooming Is Far Out

Extra power and distance from your flash

It is often best to get your speedlight(s) as close as possible to the subject. This makes your lighting more power efficient, which is critical when using the high-speed sync (HSS) feature. But what happens when you physically cannot get your flashes really close? Get them as close as you can, then use the manual zoom feature to tighten your lighting beam to achieve more effective power from your flash and to "throw" the light farther.

An image with the flash heads zoomed to 35mm.

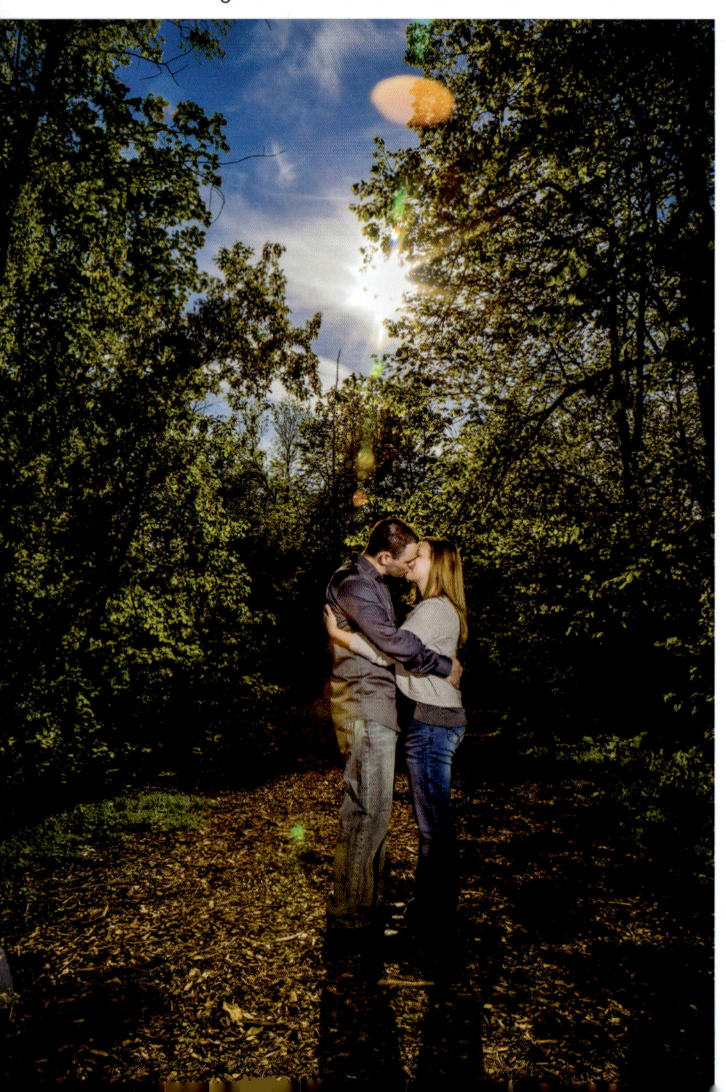

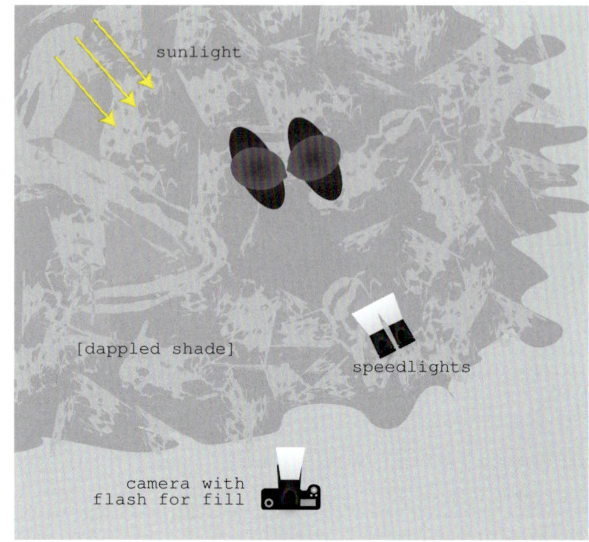

Camera: Canon 5D MKIII with Canon 70–200L lens at 106mm
Exposure: $^1/_{160}$ second, f/5, ISO 160, –1EV exposure compensation (aperture priority).
Lighting: Canon 580EX II speedlight on-camera set to master (fired) with RadioPopper PX transmitter. Two Canon 580EX II speedlights off-camera and rotated to a vertical axis, set to eTTL and slave mode, fired with RadioPopper PX receivers.

Does a Bare Speedlight Fire in the Woods?

The image on the facing page was created in the dappled light of a small forest. In my opinion, dappled light is some of the worst light one can ever face; it leads to a distracting pattern of light and dark on the subject. My technique for dealing with it is not exactly elegant: I use off-camera speedlights to blow through the shadowed part of the dappled light and bring the shadows' EV up to the same level as the brighter parts of the dappled light. This is relatively easy when I can put the speedlights close to the subject.

In this case, however, Ashley and Jeff were on a small wooden bridge over a stream. I couldn't get the flashes close to them without sacrificing my assistant to the stream, so the closest I could place the speedlights was the shore on camera right. To compensate for the distance, I had my assistant manually set the zoom on each speedlight (there were two) to 80mm. This provided me with a narrower beam of light that would travel farther before dissipating. I didn't worry about vignetting because I knew that the beam of light would widen as it traveled. I also fired my master flash to help open up the shadows in the foreground.

The resulting image spotlights my subjects and provides the needed separation from the background. The little bit of dappled light that remains on them serves as an appealing hair light only.

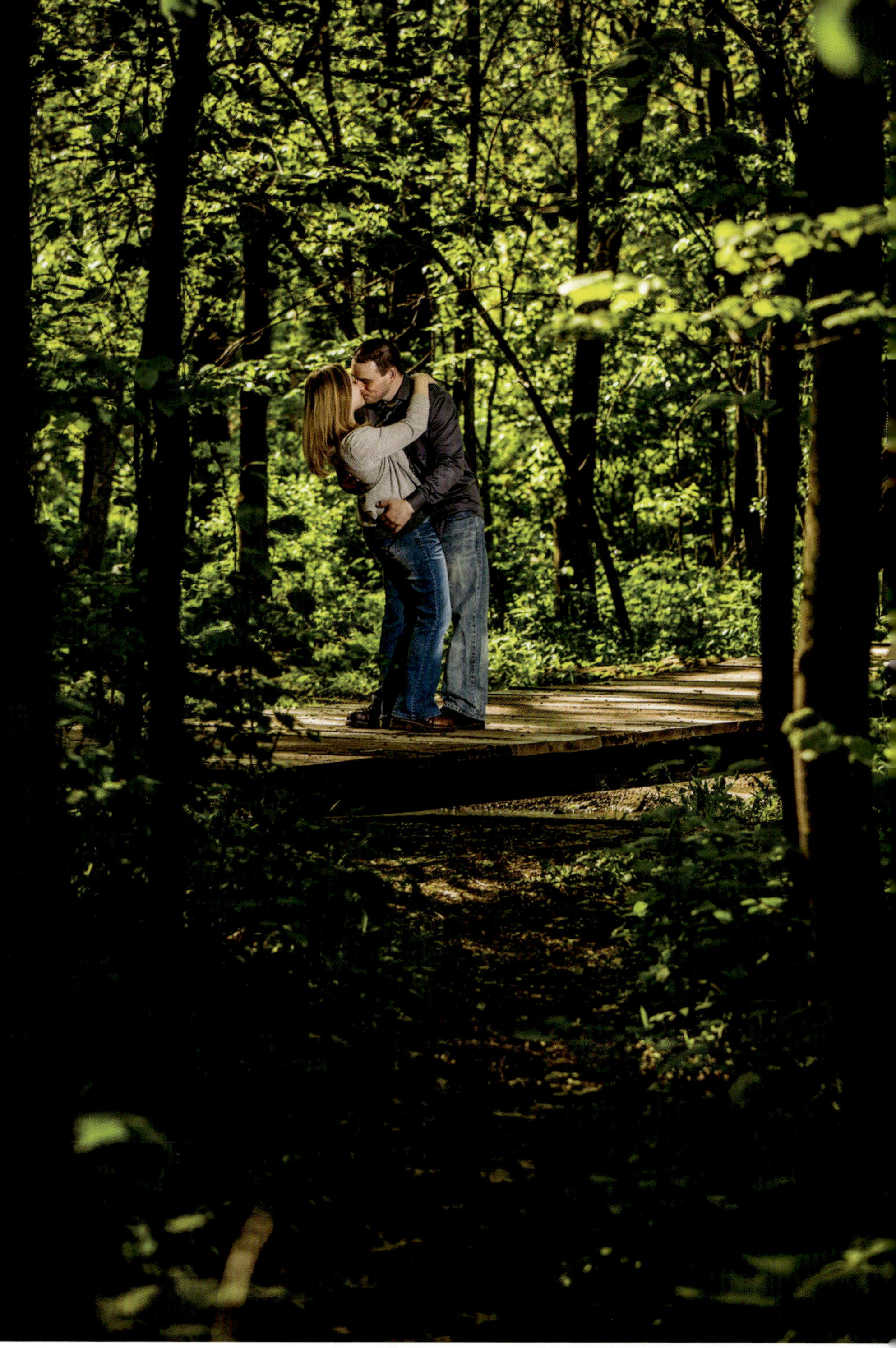

34

A Kiss of Light

Cut the green color cast

Sometimes, the light is soft and beautiful and the setting and pose are almost perfect. All this image needed was a little spark—provided by a speedlight.

Cleaning up with a Speedlight

The primary role of the off-camera speedlight here was to provide a little more direction for contouring on their faces and to add a small catchlight in their eyes. I did not want or need to overpower the beautiful ambient light.

The secondary role was to clean up the green color cast that is often prevalent with ambient light filtered through leaves and bouncing up from the grass. I fired my master flash as fill to help clean up this color cast and to open up the shadows on camera right.

For a subtle effect with the speedlights, I dialed in −1EV flash exposure compensation. I also dialed in −1/3EV exposure compensation (in aperture-priority mode) to counteract the camera's tendency to slightly overexpose based

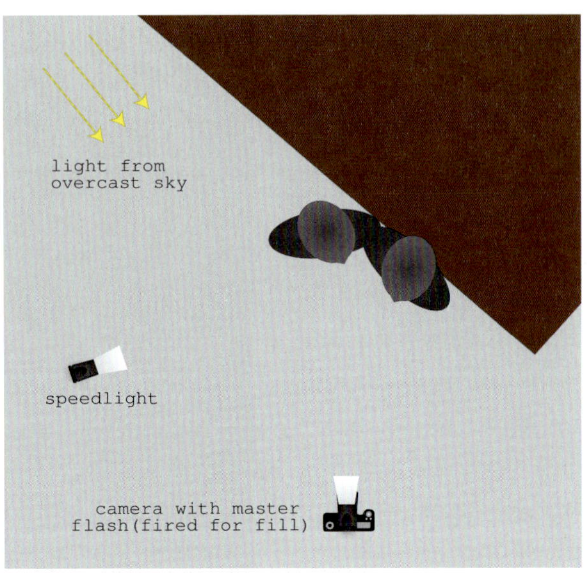

Camera: Canon 5D MKIII with Canon 70–200L lens at 121mm
Exposure: 1/80 second, f/5, ISO 420, −1/3EV exposure compensation (aperture priority)
Lighting: Canon 600EX-RT speedlight on-camera set to master (fired). Canon 600EX-RT speedlight off-camera, set to eTTL and slave mode, fired with built-in radio transmitter system. −1EV flash exposure compensation set at the master flash.

on the darker tones in the subjects' clothing and in the scene.

The ambient light from the overcast day created rim lighting on the couple and kept the overall lighting soft and pleasant.

This was another image from my initial field test of the Canon 600EX-RT flashes. Again, the flashes performed as advertised, communicating eTTL exposure settings via the built-in radio system between the master and slave flashes.

Another Look

Here's another image where flash was used to clean up the color casts and add some direction to the light.

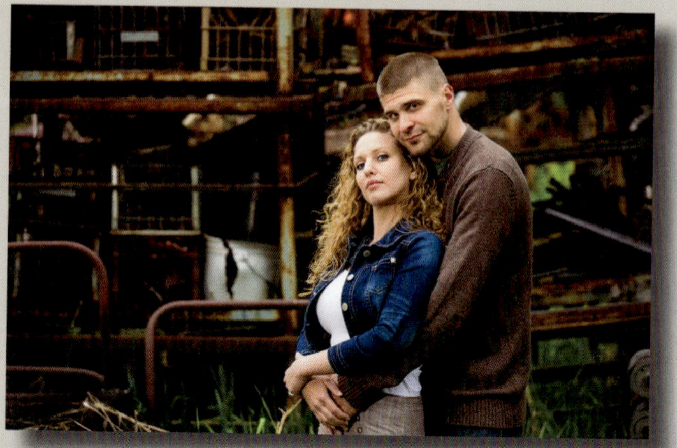

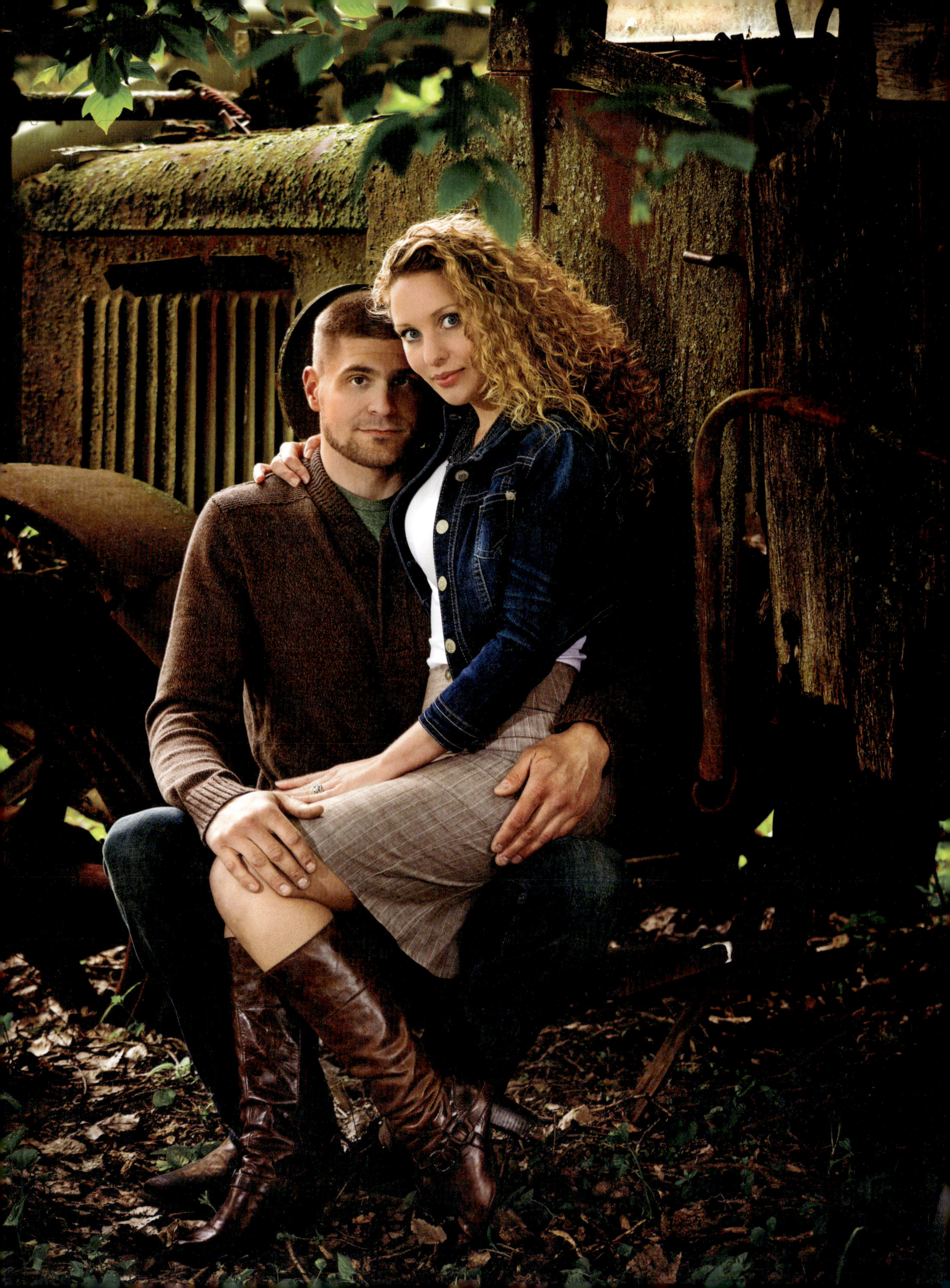

35

Theatrical Performance

Creative light in a historic theater

Hands-on learning workshops have been the rage the past couple of years. For this session, I got the chance to work indoors at the grand Al Ringling (yes, *that* Ringling) Theatre in Baraboo, Wisconsin—the location of the Circus World Museum and the winter home of The Ringling Bros. Circus for 34 years. I was paired

"In reality, this rim light was coming from a speedlight outfitted with a Snootzie . . ."

up with Twig Noir, a model and stylist with a tremendous sense of flair and style. She didn't disappoint with her wardrobe of top hat, striped shirt, petticoats, striped socks, and high black boots. (Why can't every client dress like this?)

Box Seats

I photographed a few spots around the theater, but my eye kept wandering to the ornate box seats. My concept was to use the warmth of the red curtains and gilding throughout the interior of the theater to contrast with the monochromatic look Twig had donned.

Lighting and Exposure

I set my base exposure to record some detail in the theater behind Twig, while keeping it dark enough that it did not compete with her. I included the chandelier to visually account for the

light outlining Twig from behind. In reality, this rim light was coming from a speedlight, outfitted with a Snootzie, placed two balconies over to camera right. The main light was a speedlight in a 20-inch Firefly beauty box raised up and tipped down toward her face. The fill light came from my on-camera flash bouncing off the wall and ceiling above and behind me.

Postproduction

The detail and color were popped in postproduction using a mix of Nik's Tonal Contrast and Topaz Adjust filters.

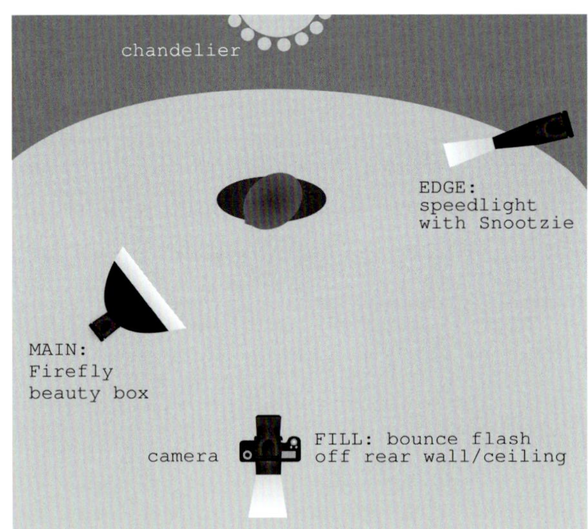

Camera: Canon 5D MKIII with Canon 24–105L f/4 IS lens at 28mm

Exposure: $1/20$ second, f/4, ISO 1600 (manual)

Lighting: Canon 580EX II speedlight on-camera set to master (fired) with RadioPopper PX transmitter. *Main light:* Off-camera Canon 580EX II speedlight with 20-inch Firefly beauty box. Set to eTTL and slave mode (group A), fired with RadioPopper. *Rim light:* Off-camera Canon 580EX II speedlight with Snootzie. Set to eTTL and slave mode (group A), fired with RadioPopper PX receiver.

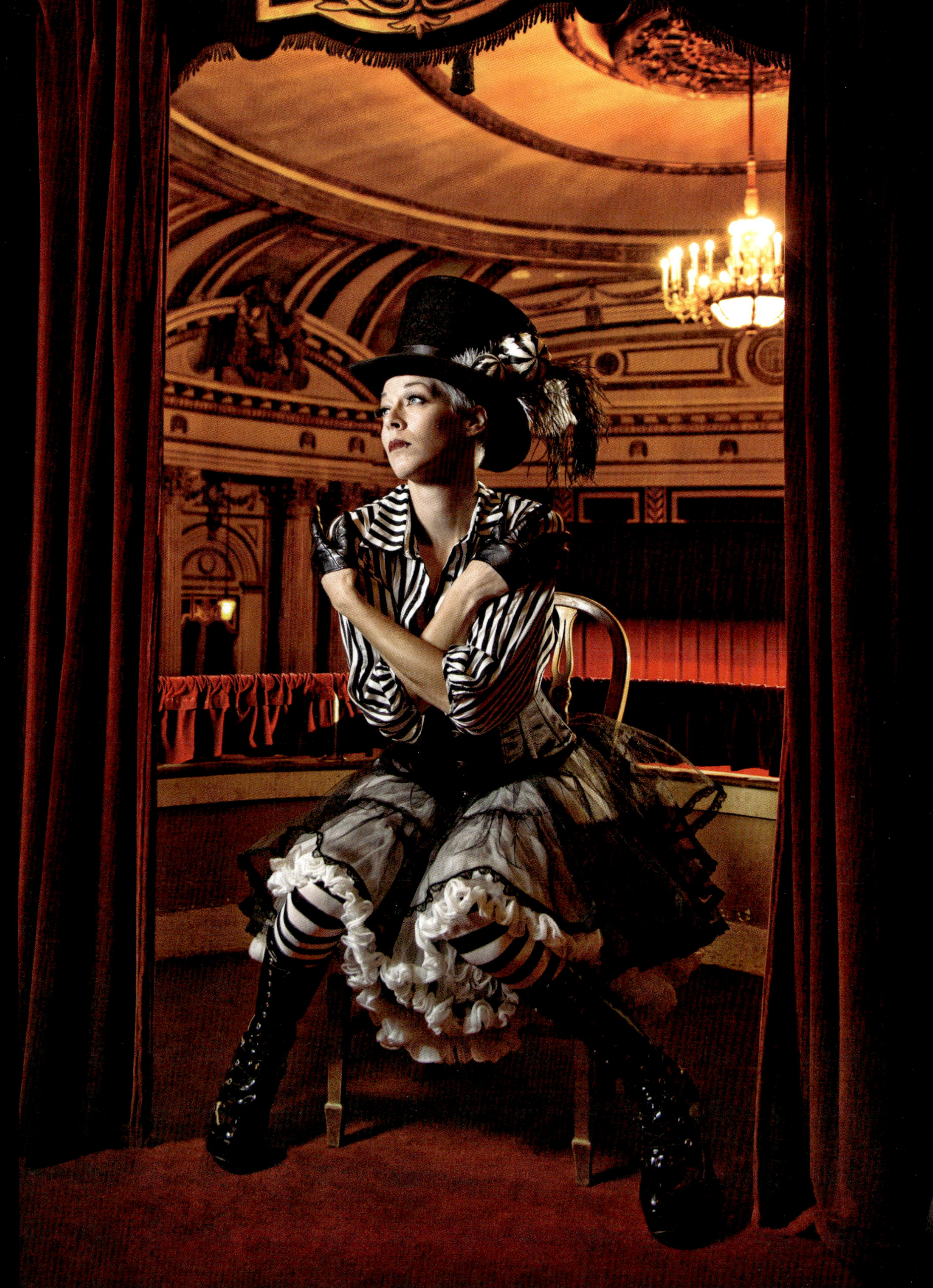

36

Brassy and Sassy

Cool and unusual places for portraiture

Most people would drive by this mural and think, "What a cool mural of Louis Armstrong." I saw it and thought, "What a cool place for a portrait!" The bell of the trumpet made a nice frame, with the flow of the rest of the mural driving the viewer to where I placed Julia, my senior model.

The Title Set the Tone

When I come up with a title for a portrait as I am creating it, I know that I have something special on my hands. In this case, the phrase "brassy and sassy" jumped into my head and guided me the rest of the way. I immediately knew that the pose and the expression needed to be angular and sassy to stand in contrast to the round bell of the trumpet.

Clothing Selection

Julia's blue dress stands in nice contrast to the warm tones that are surrounding her. The color also picks up the blue tones in the dark areas of the painting, as well as the blue flowers sprouting up at the bottom of the frame. It's an interesting play in complementary colors; the color harmony is one factor that helps to pull everything together.

Lighting

The light also needed to be in harmony with the overall concept, so I used a sassy speedlight out-

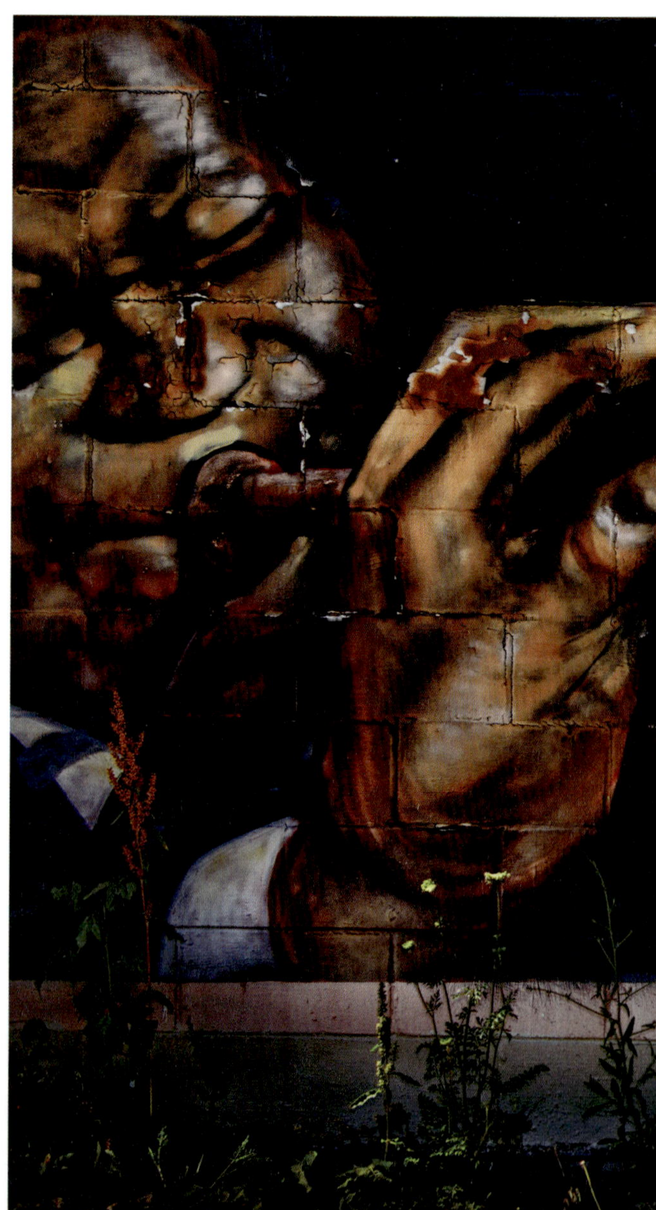

Camera: Canon 5D MKIII with Canon 24–105L f/4 IS lens at 93mm
Exposure: $^{1}/_{640}$ second, f/4, ISO 100, $-^{1}/_{3}$EV exposure compensation (aperture priority)
Lighting: Canon 580EX II speedlight on-camera set to master (did not fire) with RadioPopper PX transmitter. One Canon 580EX II speedlight off-camera outfitted with a Snootzie, set to eTTL and slave mode (group A), fired with RadioPopper PX receiver.

fitted with a Snootzie to put my subject squarely in the spotlight.

The image was created at 10:54AM, so there was a lot of ambient light bouncing around off the parking lot that is situated opposite this mural's location. To compensate, I underexposed the image slightly by dialing in $-\frac{1}{3}$EV exposure compensation in aperture-priority mode.

Postproduction

The final image was selectively darkened to keep the primary focus on Julia.

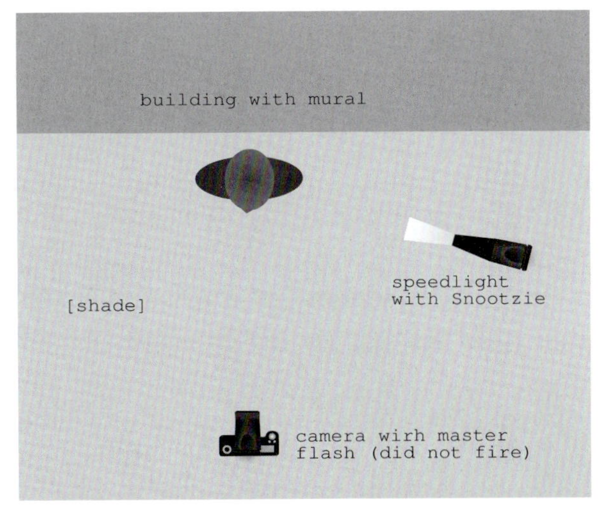

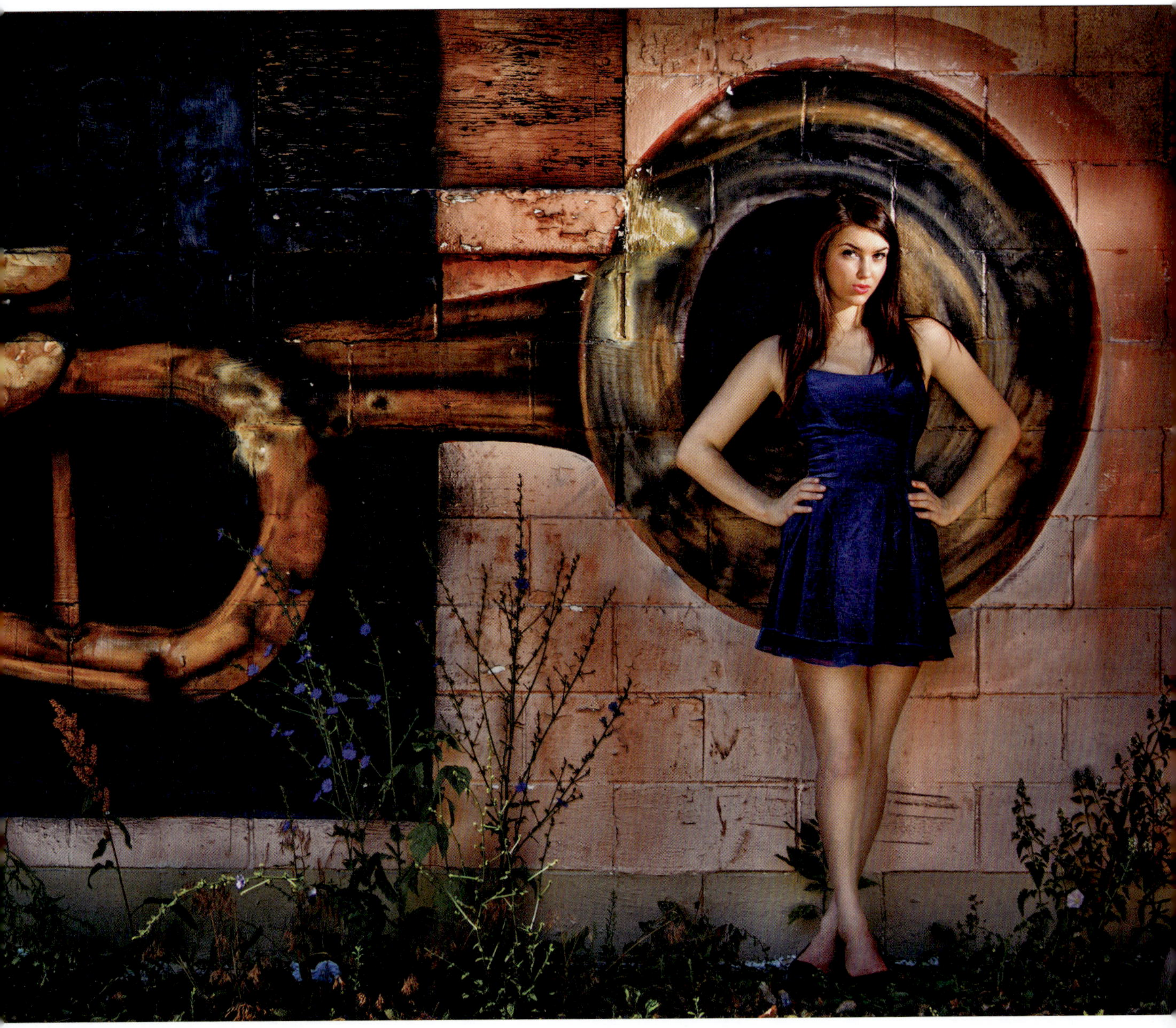

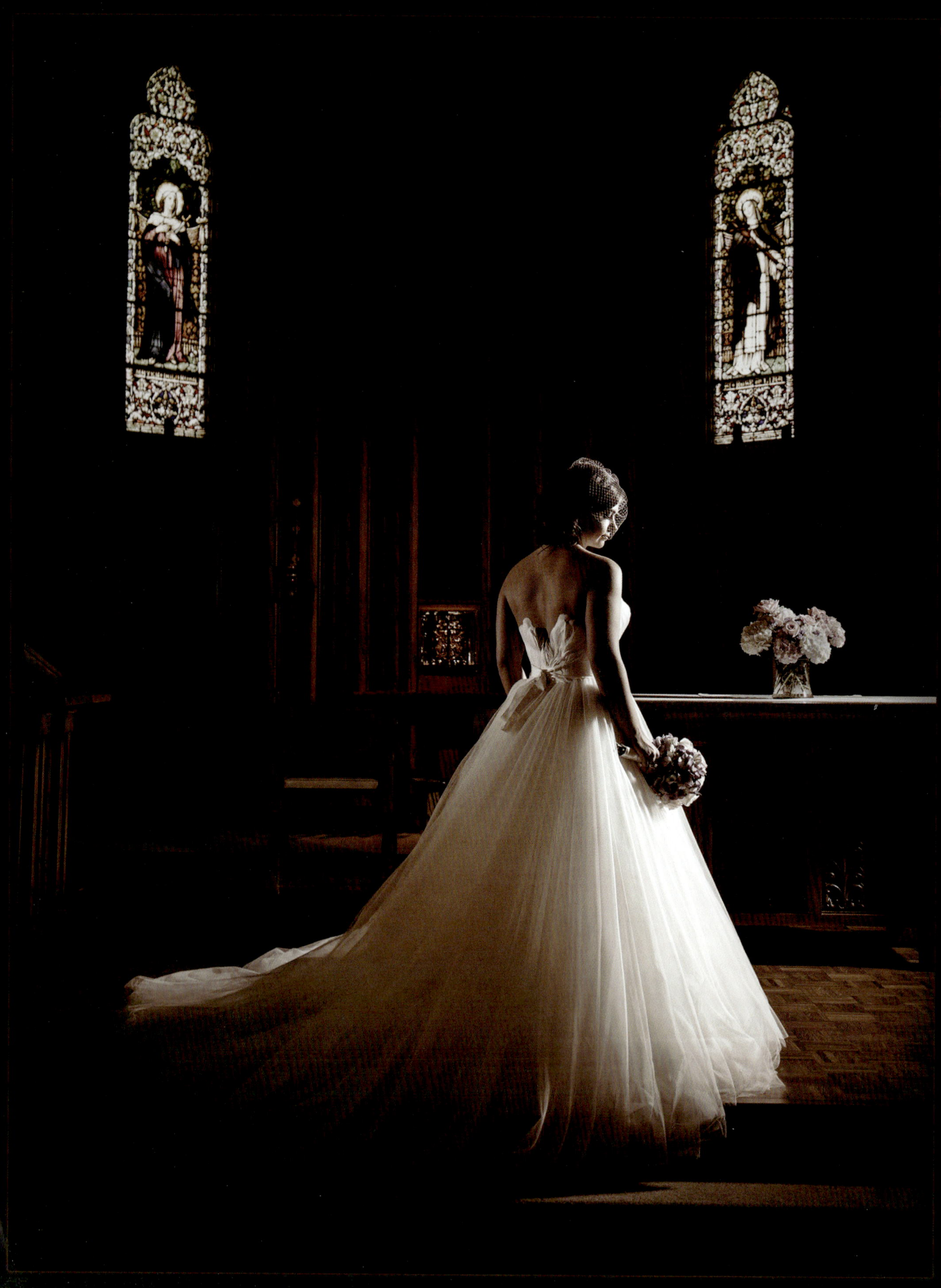

Every bride deserves a beautiful, full-length portrait in her wedding dress. Anastasia's gown was soft with ruffles and feathers; it deserved soft, beautiful light to complement it.

Light Softly in a Church

While I wanted the church to contribute to the setting, I did not want it to overpower the bride. At the same time, I wanted to hold detail in the stained glass windows.

Camera: Canon 5D MKIII with Canon 24–105 f/4 IS lens at 45mm
Exposure: $^1/_{200}$ second, f/5, ISO 1250 (manual)
Lighting: Canon 580EX II speedlight on camera set to master (did not fire) with RadioPopper PX transmitter. *Main light:* Canon 580EX II speedlight off camera with a 20-inch Firefly beauty box, set to eTTL and slave mode (group A) fired with RadioPopper PX receiver. *Rim light:* Canon 580EX II speedlight off camera with a Snootzie, set to eTTL and slave mode (group A), fired with RadioPopper PX receivers.

I wanted her sharp with fairly rapid falloff behind her, so I chose f/5. The corresponding settings to allow me to darken the background yet hold detail were a $^1/_{200}$ second shutter speed at ISO 1250. This also allowed me to hold enough detail in the windows that I could selectively darken them in postproduction without obvious signs of burning. I directed Anastasia into a classic profile pose that contributed to the soft, reflective mood of the image.

"While I wanted the church to contribute to the setting, I did not want it to overpower the bride."

My main light was a speedlight set in a 20-inch Firefly beauty box (group A) up high and tipped down toward Anastasia. For separation I used a speedlight with a Snootzie (group B) to camera left. I set the A:B ratio at 8:1 in order to give dominance to the main light, especially since I was losing a little over 1 stop of light from the diffusion of the softbox.

Postproduction

In postproduction, I converted the image to a desaturated vintage look using my Desaturally Warm Vintage preset in Lightroom. I selectively burned down the windows, edges, and other parts of the background in Photoshop.

Glam Black & White

A high-contrast black & white beauty portrait

Here is a glam look that works well for seniors, brides, models, boudoir—just about any beauty shot. I haven't tried it on a dude yet, but it might look great there, too! It's a great option to work into your sessions as it almost always adds to the sale. And that's a good thing.

Lighting

The lighting setup for this is my mainstay beauty lighting configuration. The main light was a 22-inch beauty dish with a diffusion sock directly in front of and above the subject, just barely out of the shot. This was tipped down approximately 30 degrees. An Eyelighter reflector was below the subject to help soften the shadows under the nose and chin. It also provided a unique catchlight in the bottom half of the subject's iris. Two 1x4-foot stripboxes were used as edge lights on either side.

For these images, I did add one additional speedlight to my normal setup. This was positioned behind the subject to brighten the background.

Overexposing the Beauty

There are two additional secrets to getting this look, beyond the lighting setup. First, I overexpose by $+\frac{2}{3}$ to +1 stop. Next, I apply my BW Glam Platinum preset for Lightroom to push the contrast without blowing out the highlights, giving nice, smooth tone to the skin. I also split-toned the final image to emulate a platinum black & white print. Some dodging may be necessary in the highlight-to-shadow transition areas, but overall this recipe gets the image very close to the final look.

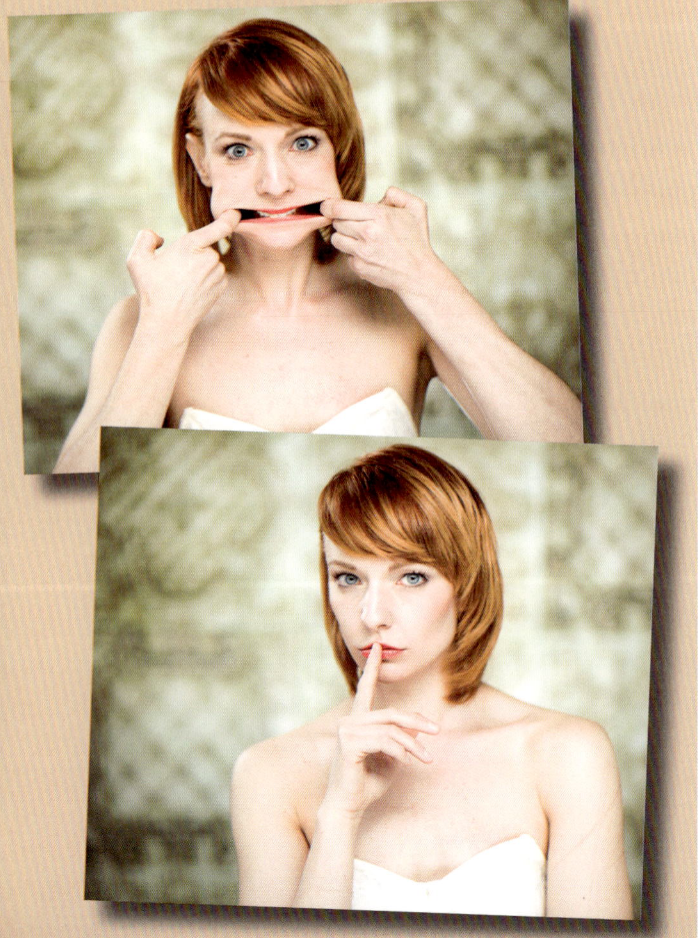

Variations in Color

Some expressive outtakes from the session show the scene and subject in color—and the lighting looks just as good.

Camera: Canon 5D MKIII with Canon 85mm f/1.8 lens

Exposure: $\frac{1}{160}$ second, f/2.8, ISO 125 (manual)

Lighting: Four Canon 580EX II speedlights manually controlled using the RadioPopper JrX system coupled with RadioPopper Cubes. Main light in group 1, background light in group 2, and edge lights in group 3. *Main light:* 22-inch Kacey Enterprises beauty dish with a white diffusion sock. *Fill light:* Eyelighter reflector. *Edge lights:* Two 1x4-foot Creative Light softboxes with speedlight speedrings and egg crates.

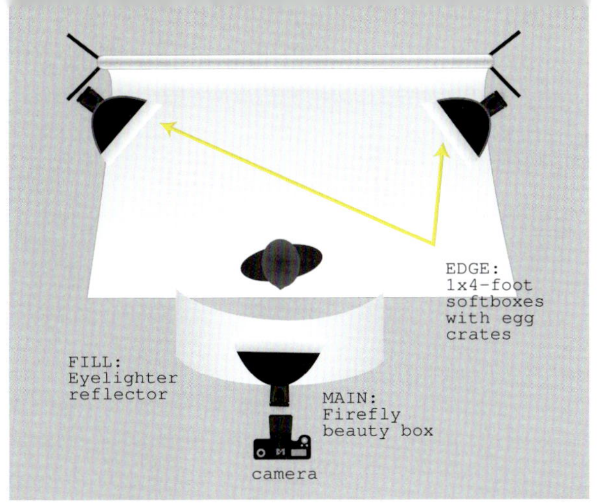

EDGE:
1x4-foot
softboxes
with egg
crates
FILL:
Eyelighter
reflector
MAIN:
Firefly
beauty box
camera

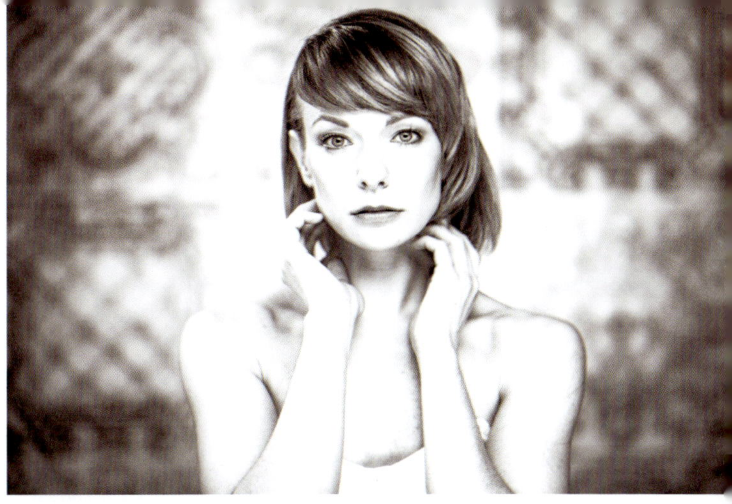

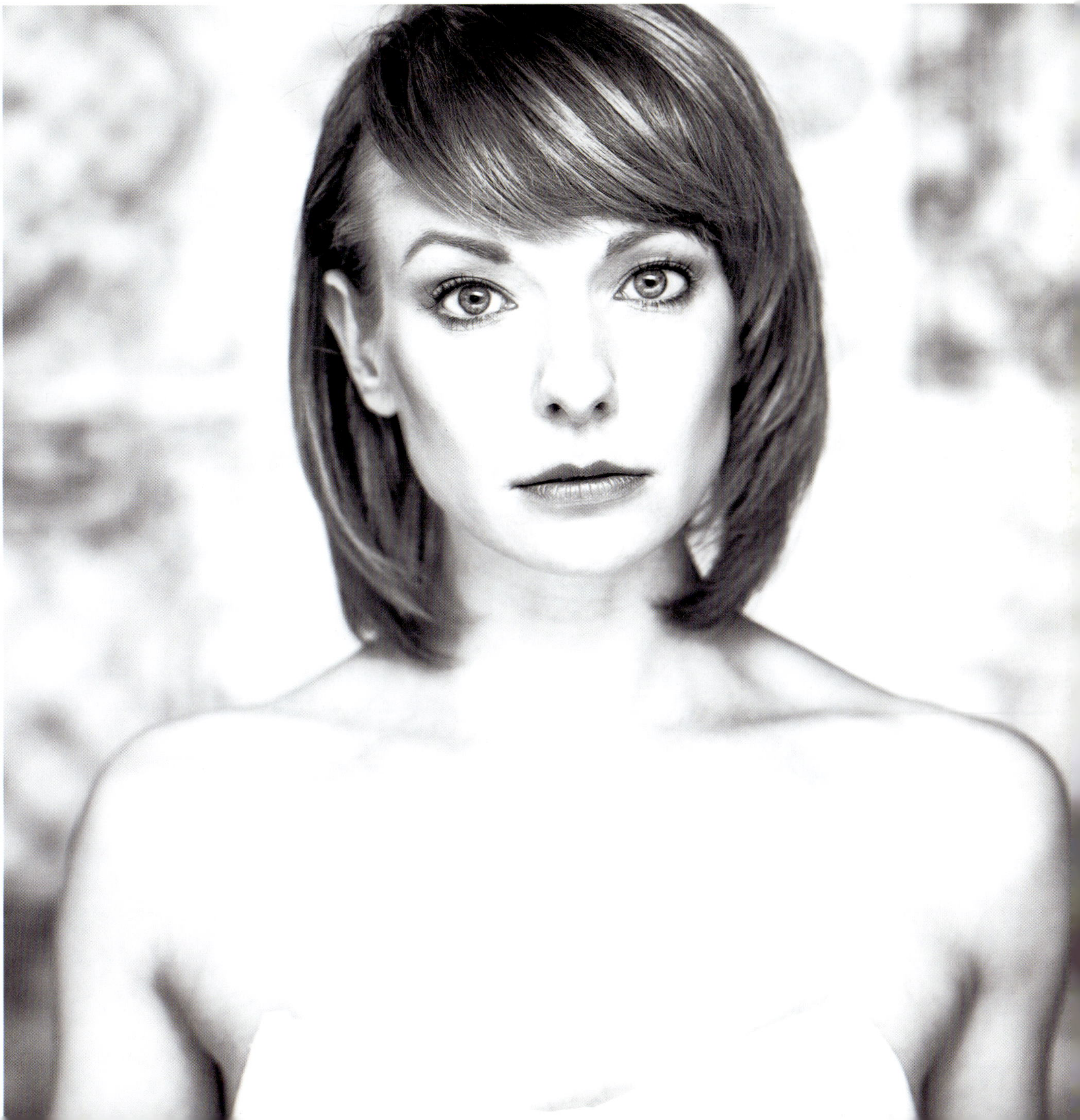

39

Empire of the Sunset

Working with TTL to create a powerful portrait

Clients and photographers are drawn to sunsets like moths to a flame. Sunsets have to be in the top three of "most popular photos" (followed by selfies reflected in a mirror, and whatever you had for lunch). Luke and Kristen had asked if I could possibly get a sunset shot during their wedding reception at Lake Windsor Golf Club. I told them I could—as long as Mother Nature cooperated. Fortunately, she served up a beautiful sunset that evening.

Seeing Sun Spots

This shot had several tricky aspects to it. First, I was photographing directly into the setting sun,

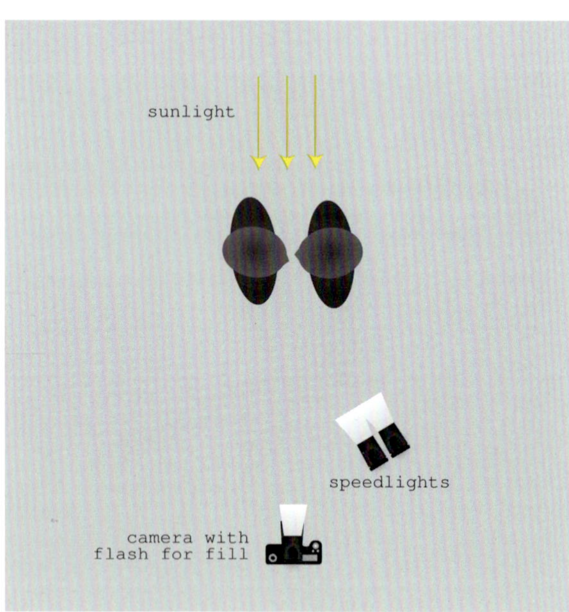

Camera: Canon 5D MKII with Canon 70–200L lens at 200mm
Exposure: 1/8000 second, f/4, ISO 320, –1/3EV exposure compensation (aperture priority)
Lighting: Canon 580EX II speedlight on-camera set to master (fired) with RadioPopper PX transmitter. Canon 580EX II speedlight off-camera set to eTTL and slave mode, fired with RadioPopper PX receiver.

which messes with not only the camera's internal metering and TTL system but also with its focusing. Second, I needed to dial in just the right amount of light to open up detail on the couple without blowing them out or letting them fall into total silhouette (which I also photographed as part of this series). Lastly, I needed to work quickly as the sun was dropping rapidly in the sky.

I opted to work with aperture priority and eTTL flash. This is my "speed" system throughout the day; it enables me to work quickly because I know it so well. It also gives me speed—as in high-speed sync (HSS)—to deal with sunlight.

Because I was shooting directly into the sun, the camera's metering system automatically kicked up to a high shutter speed (in this case, 1/6400 second). This would have underexposed and darkened the sun and sky a bit. However, I opted to darken the sky and sun *further* by dialing in –1/3EV exposure compensation, kicking the shutter speed up to 1/8000 second.

To complete the image, I mixed in both a pair of off-camera speedlights placed to camera right and an on-camera flash for fill light. This helped to open up the shadows on the couple and give us just the right amount of detail. I simply waited until the sun dropped to the position I wanted, then directed my clients to tip their heads together.

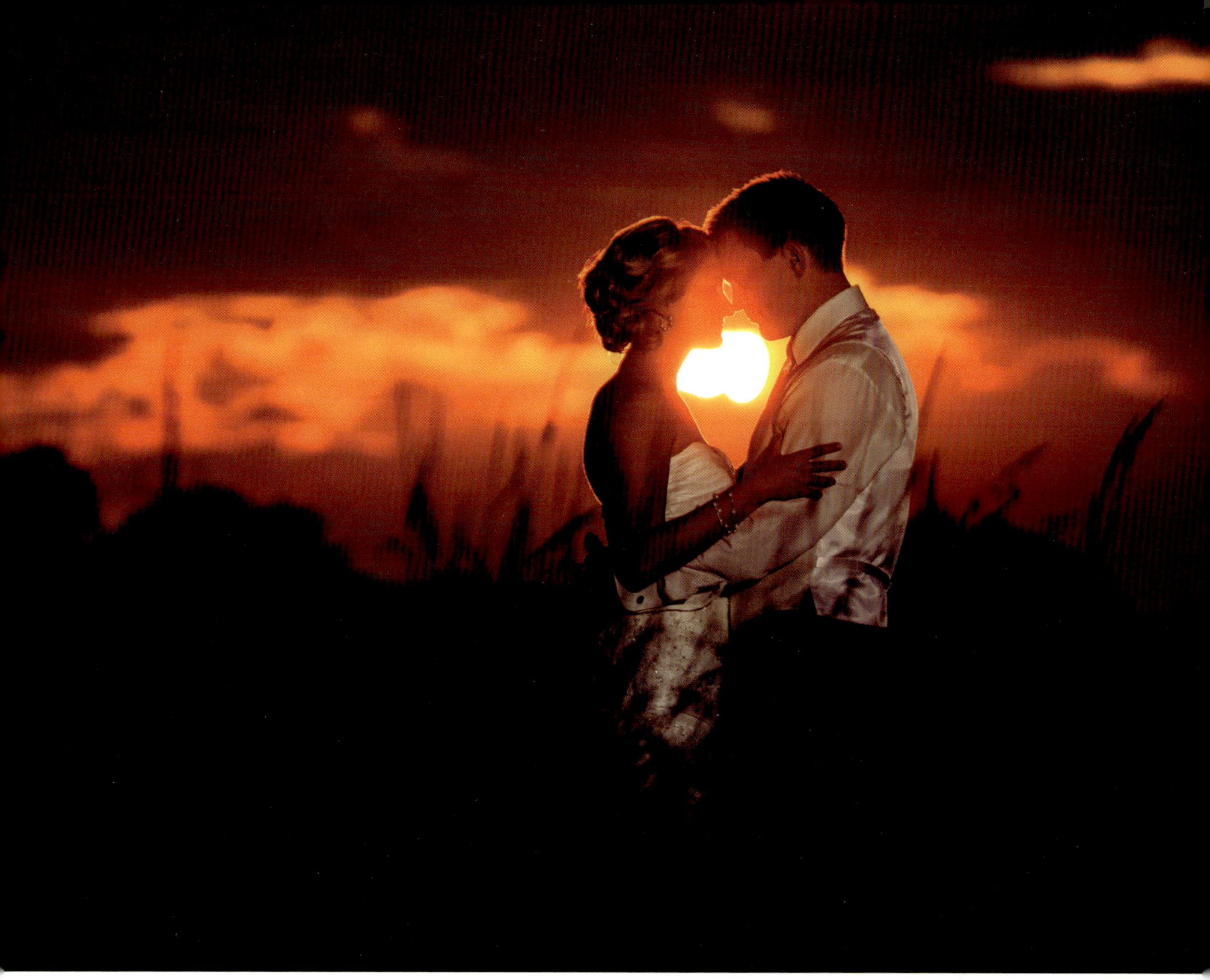

How It Really Looked . . .

These images show how the sunset looked to my eyes at the time when I shot the photograph above. For these images, I just added a bit of fill flash from off-camera to light the subjects appealingly and creatively.

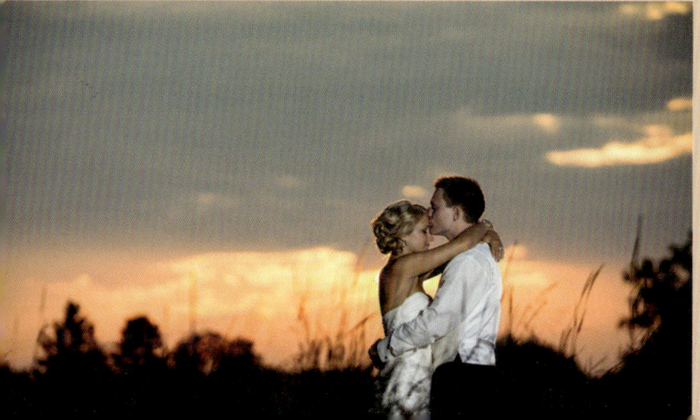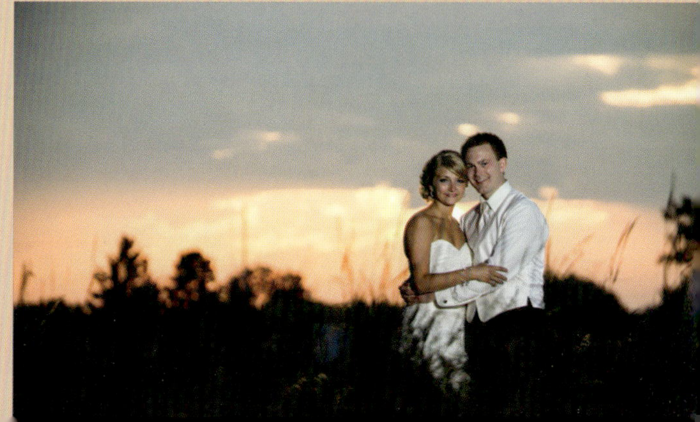

40

Let There Be a Light

Speedlights and a little Photoshop magic

It was a dark, dreary day in the city. Even the alley cats had found something better to do than haunt this particular dank alley. (My apologies to Dashiell Hammett.)

She's Been Framed

I was on a noir kick this day, so when I saw this vintage wall, door, and light combo, I envisioned a scene out of a noir novel. The only problem was that the lamp was missing a bulb; it wasn't lit.

No problem. I decided to light it with a speedlight, then fix it in Photoshop. "Fix it in Photoshop" are four words I typically hate when used together, but in this case there was no other option. I had my assistant hold a speedlight on a stand as high and as laterally as he could to simulate the light from the lamp.

Postproduction

In postproduction, I edited out the light stand and speedlight using content aware fill in Photoshop CS6. I tightened up the edit with the Clone Stamp and Patch tools.

> ***"I had my assistant hold a speedlight on a stand as high and as laterally as he could . . ."***

I then created a path using the Pen tool to outline the shape of the beam of light. I feathered this, and then inverted the selection on a separate layer and filled it with black. I changed the blend mode for this layer to Soft Light, which gave me the shadowed area of the scene.

I went back to my path and selected it again on a new blank layer, which I filled with a golden color to simulate tungsten light. I also set the blend mode of this layer to Soft Light, then added in some monochromatic Gaussian noise. I lowered the opacity on this layer slightly to achieve my desired look.

Lastly, I drew in the light bulb using an oval shape and a brighter shade of my golden color.

Original image showing the lighting setup.

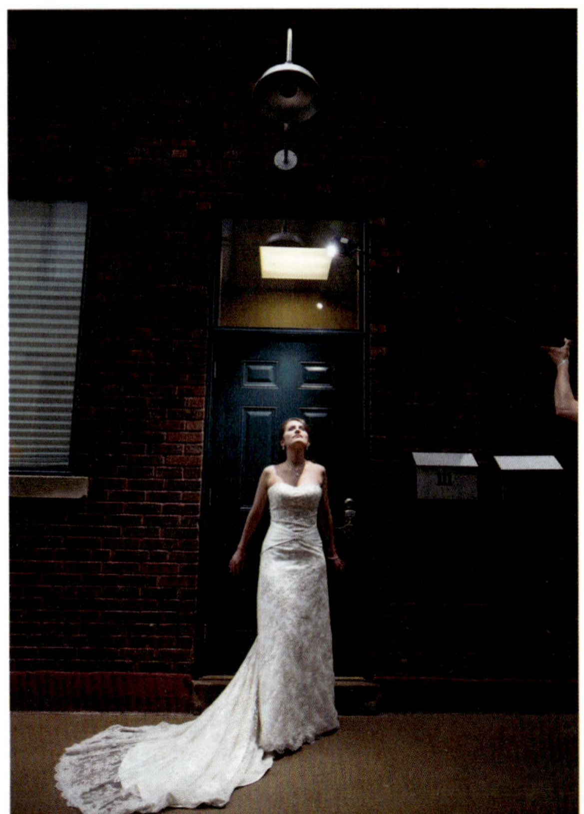

Camera: Canon 5D MKIII with Canon 24–105L lens at 24mm

Exposure: $1/160$ second, f/4, ISO 200, $-1\frac{1}{3}$EV exposure compensation (aperture priority)

Lighting: Canon 580EX II speedlight on-camera set to master (did not fire) with RadioPopper PX transmitter. Canon 580EX II speedlight off-camera set to eTTL and slave mode, fired with RadioPopper PX receiver.

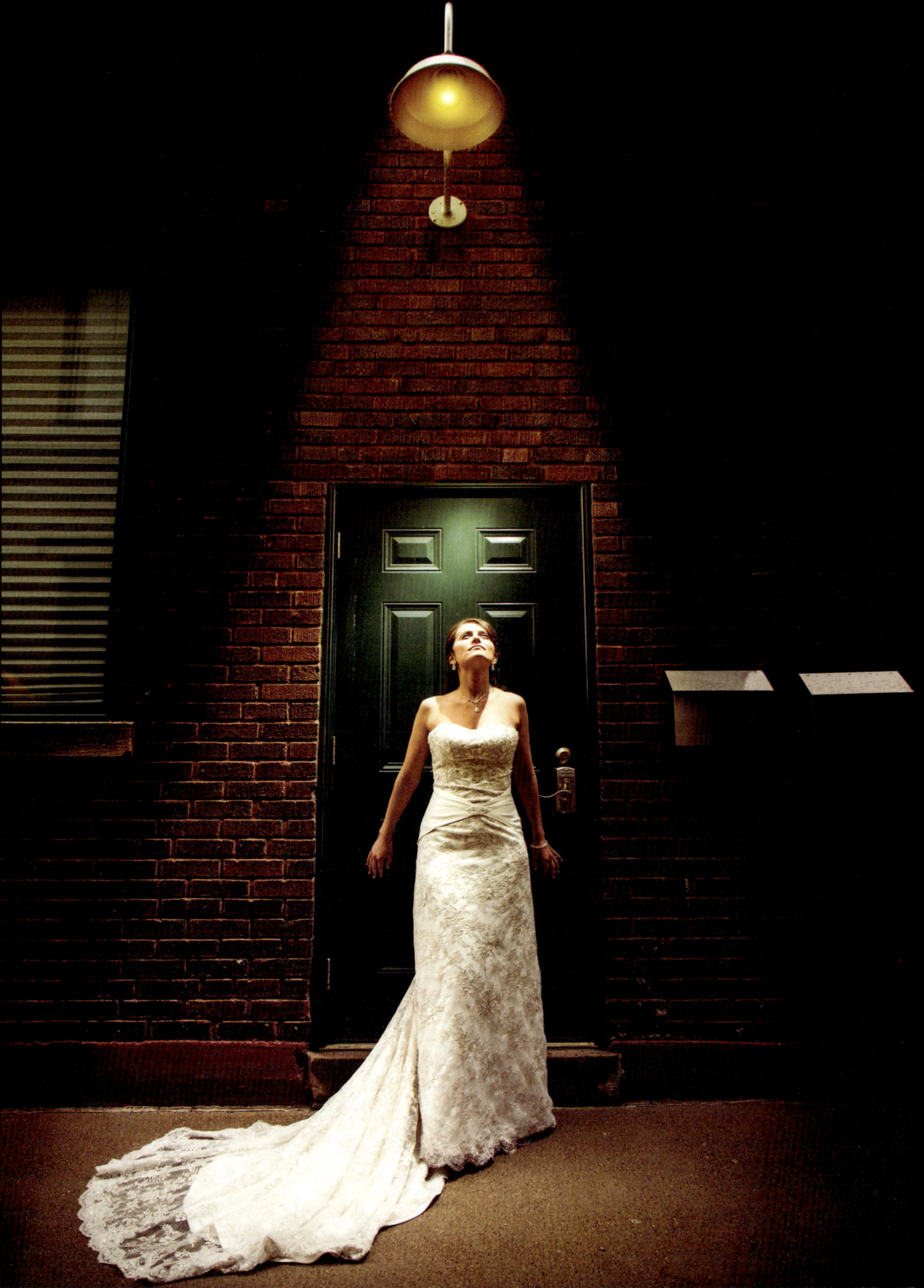

41

Doing Double Duty

Controlling the direction and spread of light

I set up this shot of Lindsay and Noah as part of my instruction for a class at the Mid-American Institute of Professional Photography (MAIPP). I was demonstrating how I pick locations and create light as needed.

Lighting Two Birds with One Flash

I started by positioning Lindsay on the bench and lit her with a double speedlight setup to camera left and a single speedlight with a Snootzie to camera right as a kicker.

This worked fine for individual portraits of Lindsay, but when I added Noah in, he blended into the background; he lacked light on his face. I could have set up a fourth speedlight, but the quicker solution was to take the Snootzie off the edge light and feather it (turn it) so that the light fell on both Noah and Lindsay. This maintained the nice edge light on Lindsay while still

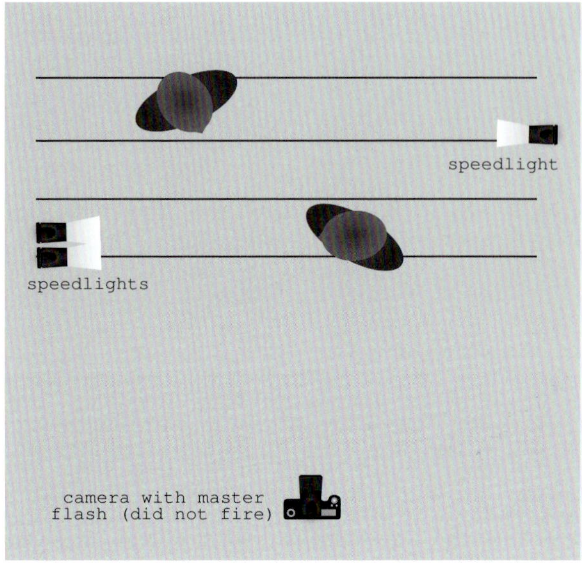

putting some dimension on Noah's face—but not so much that he competes with Lindsay.

The Spread of Light

To master this technique, you must understand the spread of light—how far (side-to-side and

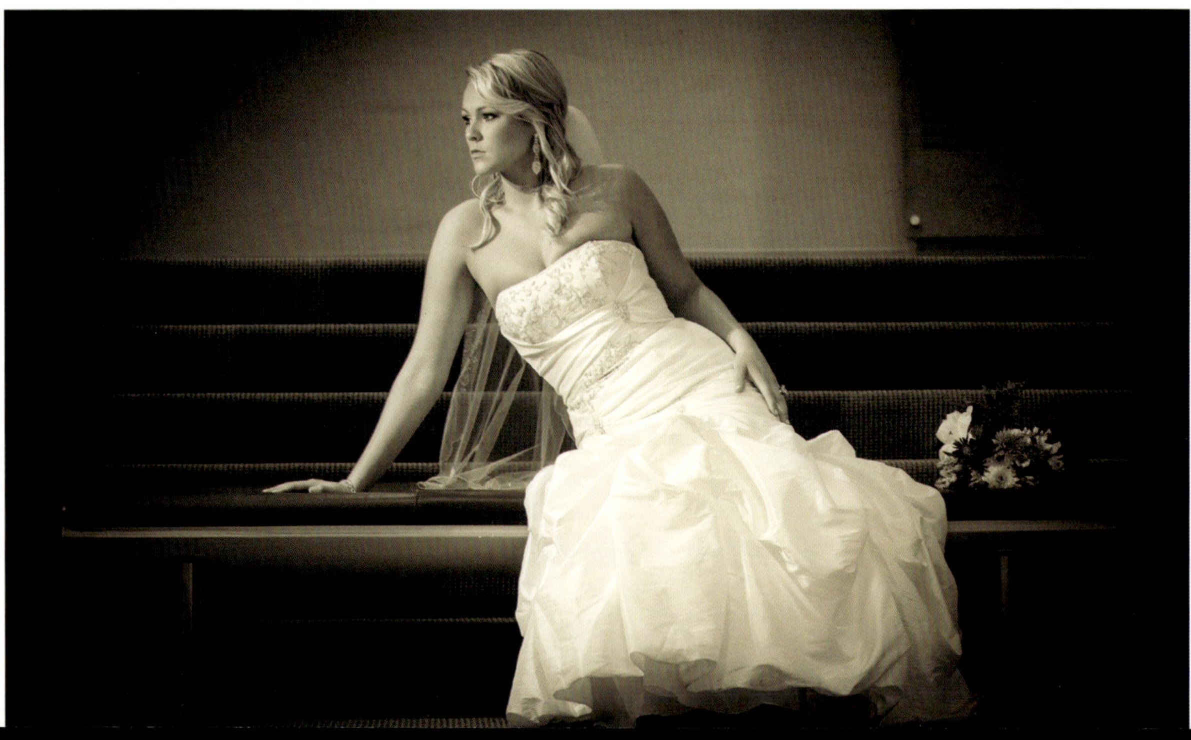

top-to-bottom) the flash's light will spread. Most speedlights default to a 35mm zoom level when used off-camera. You can manually override this setting and widen it to 24mm in the zoom menu. You can widen it further to 17mm using the diffusion panel built into most Nikon and Canon speedlights. This is yet another tool to use in your creative lighting arsenal.

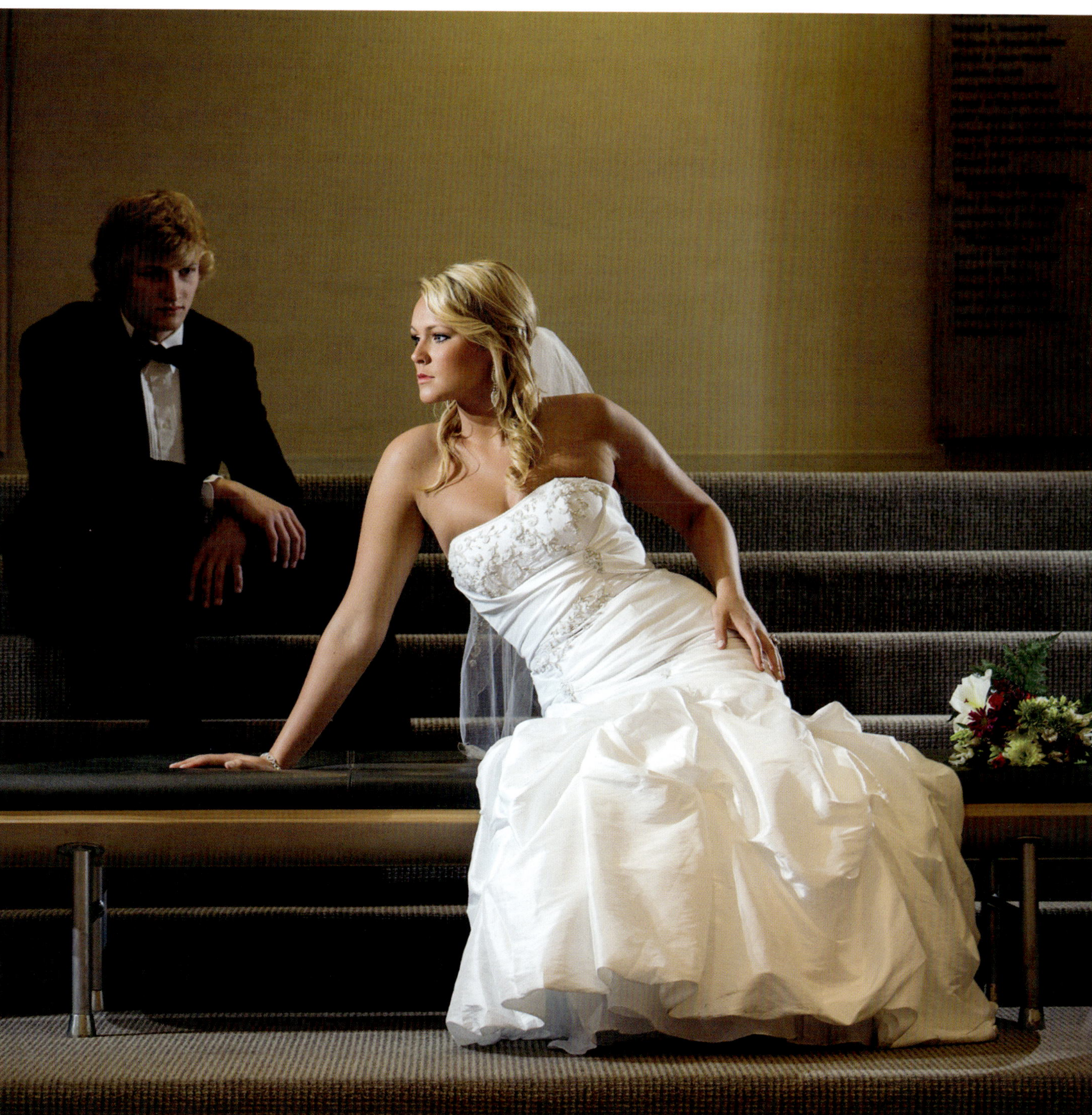

42

Joan of Arch

Lighting a dramatic bridal pose on location

The doorway of the original Parker Pen building in Janesville, Wisconsin (home of the iconic Parker Pen Company) stands in this park as a sculpture. The monument held special meaning for my bride, Catherine, whose grandfather was from the company's founding family.

Light Writing

With strong winds and overcast skies mixing off and on with light rain, I needed my speedlights to carve some light and create contrast in the scene. I placed Catherine in a dynamic pose that showed off her dress and her figure. I then lit her in profile with two speedlights ganged together from camera right. I underexposed the background slightly to darken it and produce better separation.

For this setup, it is important to place the speedlights perpendicular to the subject—think about aligning them with the direction of her face. This ensures that you will properly light her face and the leading edge of her body without splashing too much light onto her back. That would ruin the effect and make the light too flat. A third speedlight was added to help light her veil and the back edge of her dress.

Camera: Canon 5D MKII with Canon 24–105L lens at 28mm

Exposure: 1/400 second, f/4, ISO 100, –1/3EV exposure compensation (aperture priority)

Lighting: Canon 580EX II speedlight on-camera set to master (fired as fill) with RadioPopper PX transmitter. Two Canon 580EX II speedlights off-camera set to eTTL and slave mode, fired with RadioPopper PX receivers. Canon 580EX II speedlight with a Snootzie off-camera set to eTTL and slave mode (group A) fired with RadioPopper PX receiver.

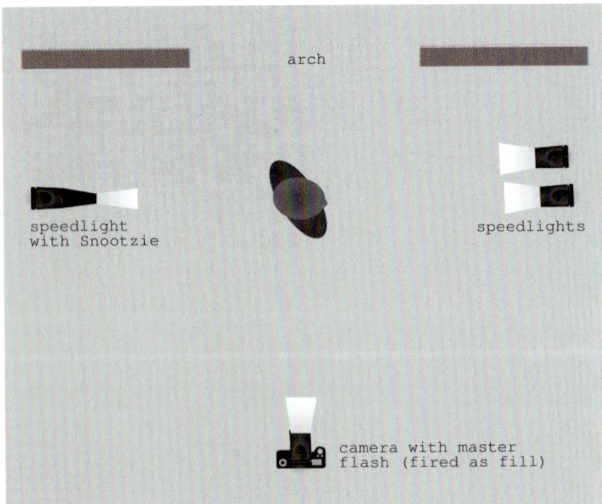

Another Look

I brought in the groom, positioning him in the background for a simple variation.

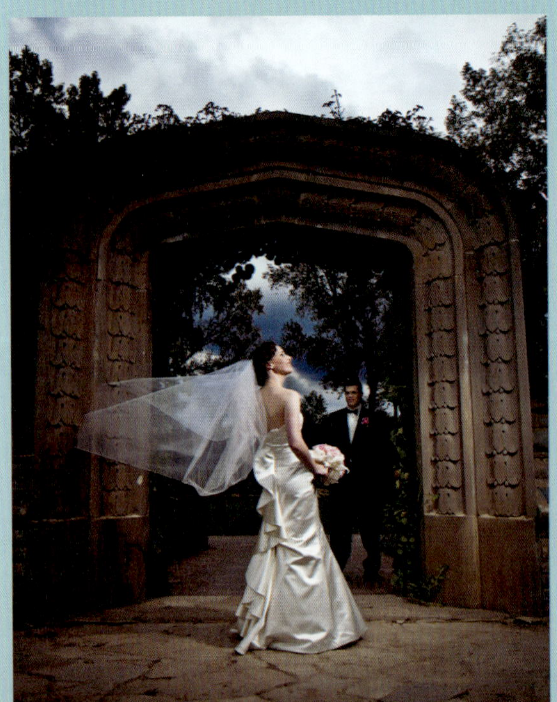

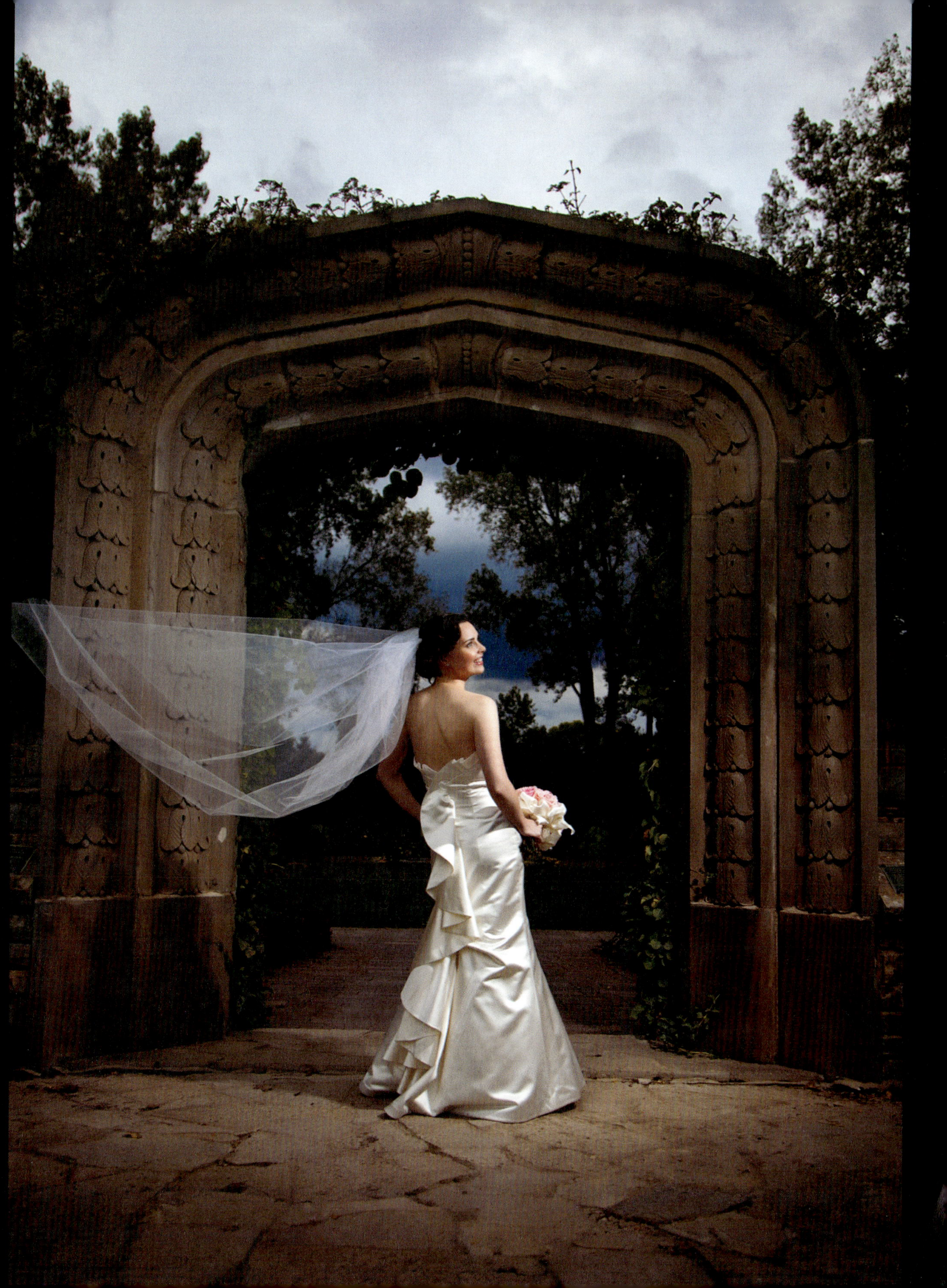

43

Take the Dress for a Walk

The visual contrast of pretty versus gritty

Many girls drop $600 or more on prom dresses they wear once, then sometimes bring to their senior portrait sessions. I like to help them get their money's worth. I start with some pretty studio shots, but I really like to coax them outside—into a field or down a gritty urban alley—and give those dresses a chance to breathe and have fun! I enjoy the visual contrast of pretty versus gritty. It makes a bold statement that resonates with many seniors.

Out Standing in Her Field

I had envisioned Katie in a field of golden hay, but we showed up a day too late. The farmer had cut that field in the morning. We just went with the flow and worked to create something cool anyway. The field became secondary in the setting. Instead, I focused on getting low and using the really cool sky behind her to help isolate and frame my subject.

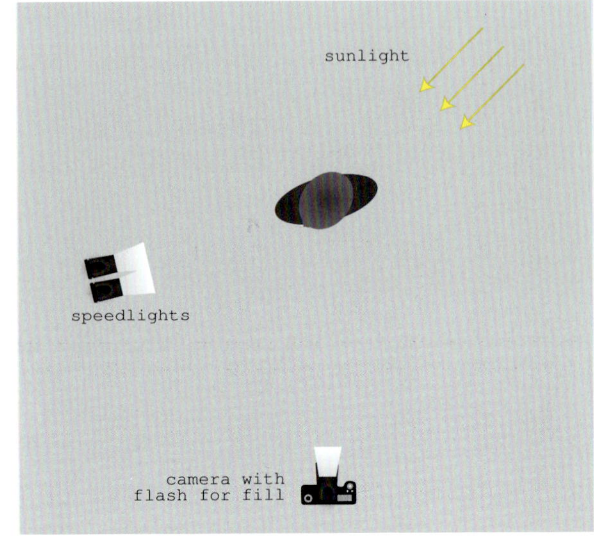

Camera: Canon 5D MKII with Canon 24–105L lens at 24mm

Exposure: $^1\!/_{1600}$ second, f/4, ISO 100 (aperture priority)

Lighting: Canon 580EX II speedlight on-camera set to master (fired) with RadioPopper PX transmitter. Two Canon 580EX II speedlights off-camera set to eTTL and slave mode, fired with RadioPopper PX receivers.

Fun and Funky

I switched to a fisheye lens to make a funkier, fun shot at the same location.

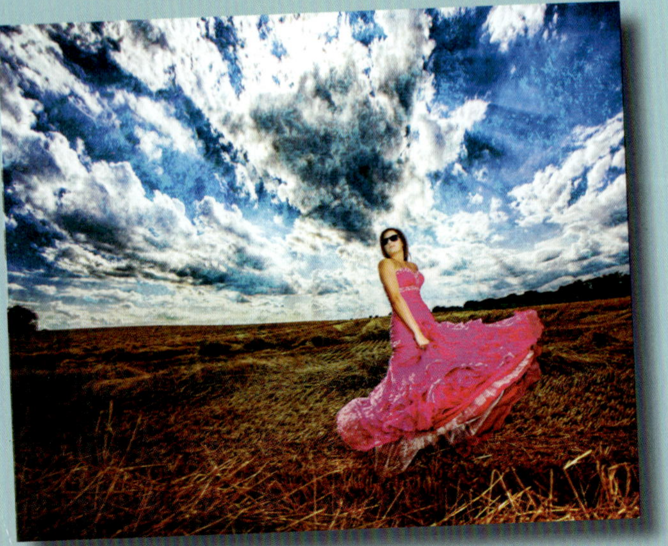

Lighting

The lighting for this portrait included two off-camera speedlights flipped into a vertical orientation. My on-camera master flash fired as fill.

Postproduction

I punched up the texture and color using Nik's Tonal Contrast and Topaz Adjust filters, then applied a texture screen to complete the look. The image was finished with selective dodging and burning.

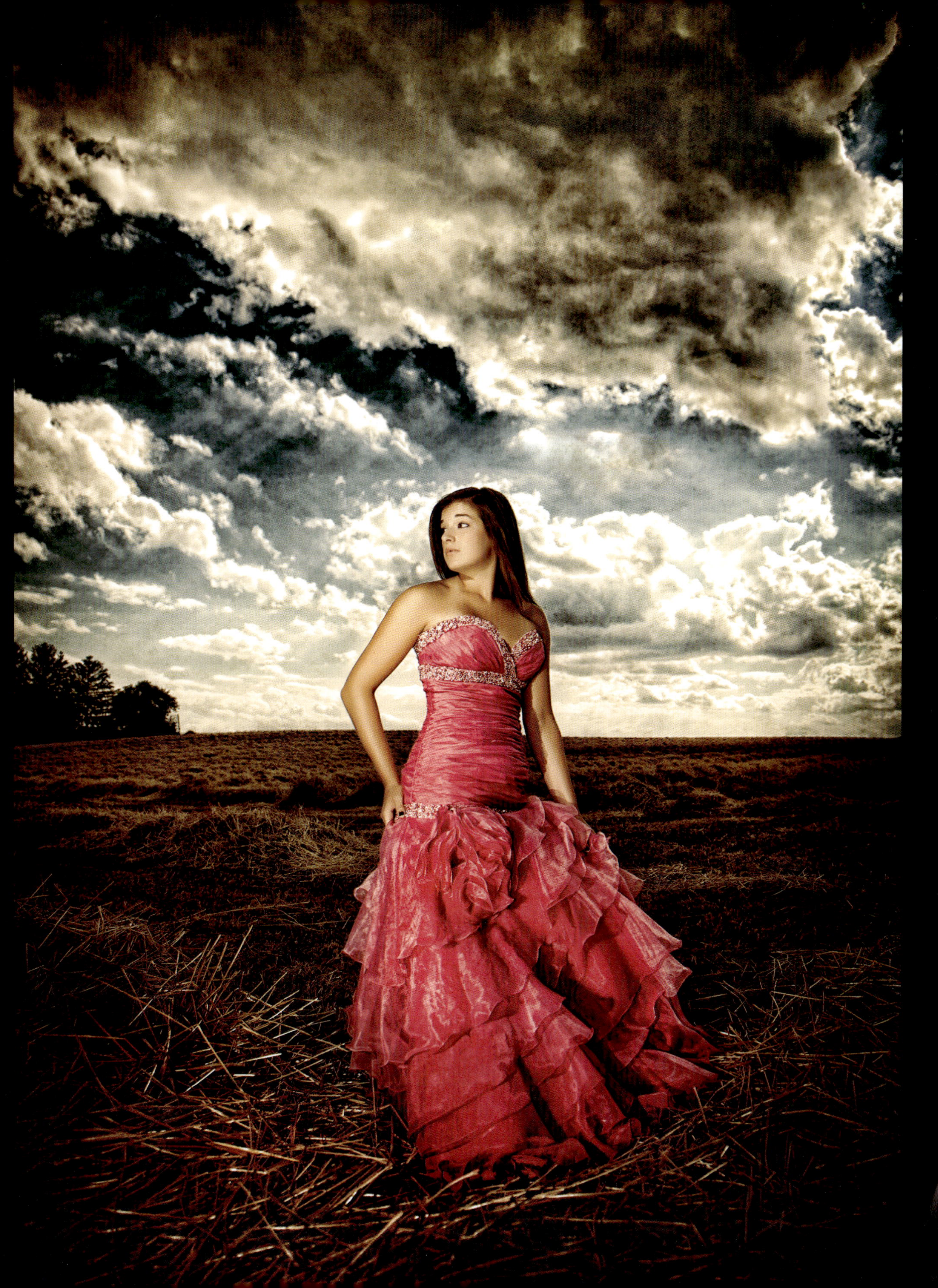

44

Lighting Naturally

Soft speedlight to blend with outdoor light

It's important to master all types of lighting. Many images in this book show the dramatic lighting that is one of my signature styles and works well with speedlights. However, subtle lighting sells well—especially for headshots like the one on the facing page.

Dial It Back

It can be tricky to achieve soft light when you start with the hard light from a speedlight, but if you understand your speedlight (and light in general), you can achieve almost any effect. For the image on the facing page, the sun had ducked behind a cloud, so there was soft, general light in the scene. I did not want much punch from my off-camera speedlights, just a little extra light to open up the shadows on her face, clean up the green color cast from the

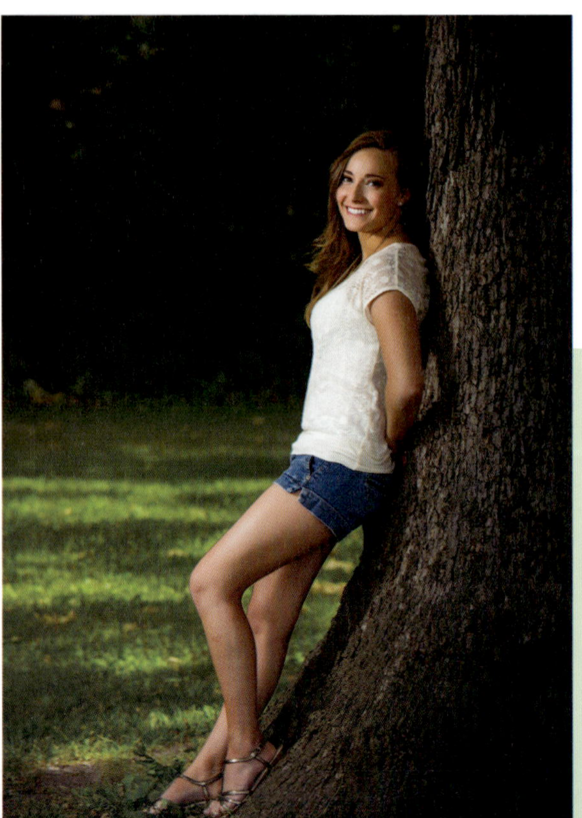

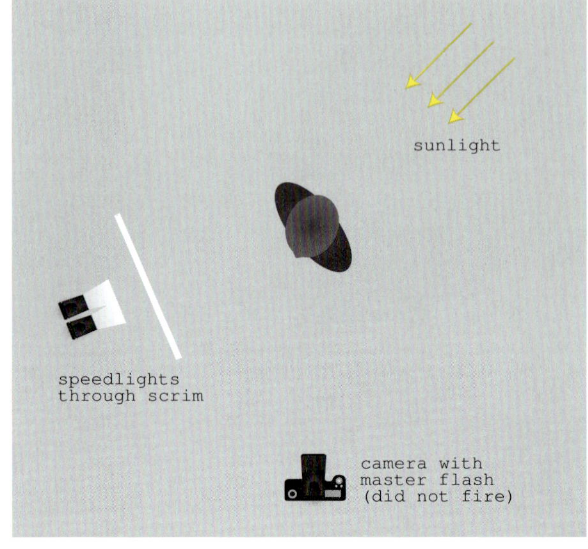

Camera: Canon 5D MKIII with Canon 70–200L lens at 200mm
Exposure: $^{1}/_{200}$ second, f/6.3, ISO 100 (manual)
Lighting: Canon 580EX II speedlight on-camera set to master (did not fire) with RadioPopper PX transmitter. Canon 580EX II speedlight off-camera set to eTTL and slave mode, fired with RadioPopper PX receiver.

foliage, and create nice catchlights. Instead of firing my speedlights at full power, I dialed in –$^{2}/_{3}$EV flash exposure compensation. This cut the speedlights by $^{2}/_{3}$ stop for the subtle light I needed to blend with the existing ambient light.

Too "Flashy"?

Photographers who experiment with speedlights often feel the look is too "flashy." The images here—and, for that matter, in the rest of the book—are my response. You have to learn to control how the speedlight affects the exposure. You can turn the power up and down in manual mode, or adjust the flash exposure compensation in TTL. If the result is too "flashy," make an adjustment. It's not about the *flash*—it's about *you*.

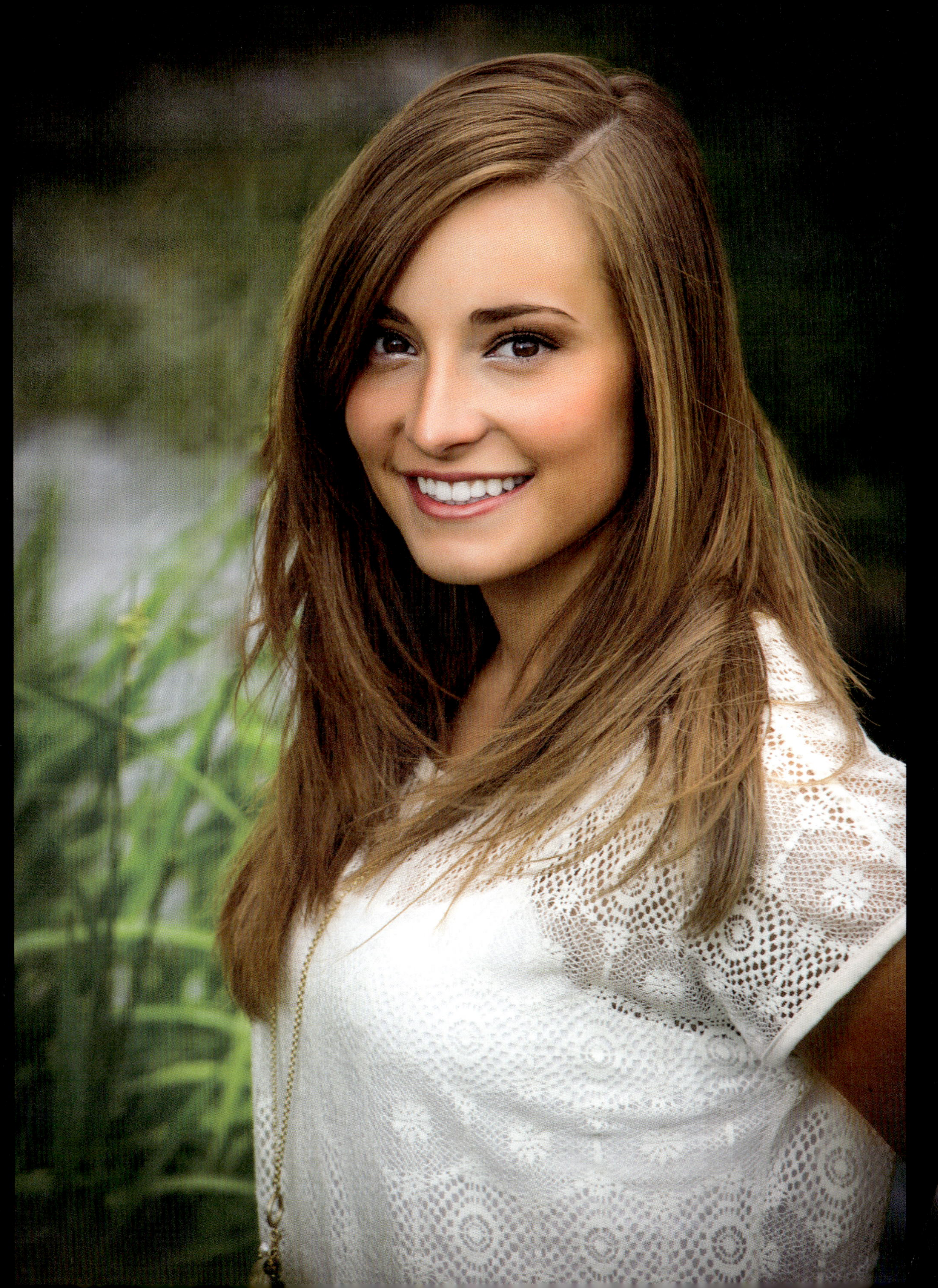

45

Spice It Up with a Little Color

Using colored gels on location

I liked the elements of this scene, but it felt a little too monochromatic. It needed some spice—a punch of color.

Lighting and Exposure

The first bit of color came from the dusk sky behind the windows. I made sure that my base ambient exposure held the tone and detail in that sky. Then I lit my couple via two speedlights ganged together from approximately 80 feet away on a balcony perpendicular to and slightly above them. The last bit of spice came from a third speedlight on the stair behind them. It was fitted with a magenta gel inside a Snootzie. The flash was zoomed to 105mm and pointed straight up at the sculpture above them. The goal was to add in a fun splash of color.

From the technical standpoint, the main lights were set in group A and the colored background light set to group B. A ratio of 2:1

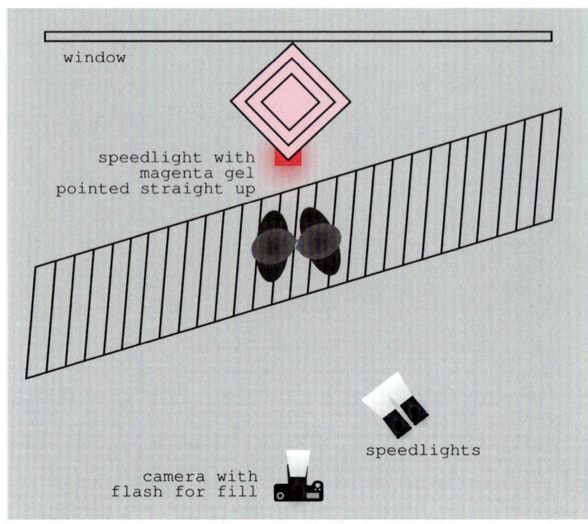

Camera: Canon 5D MKIII with Canon 70–200L lens at 72mm

Exposure: $1/160$ second, f/5.0, ISO 1000, $-1/3$EV exposure compensation (aperture priority)

Lighting: Canon 580EX II speedlight on-camera set to master (fired) with RadioPopper PX transmitter. Two Canon 580EX II speedlights off-camera set to eTTL and slave mode (group A), fired with RadioPopper PX receiver. One Canon 580EX II speedlight with a Snootzie and a magenta gel off-camera set to eTTL and slave mode (group B), fired with RadioPopper PX receiver.

(A:B) was set from my on-camera master flash, which also fired as front fill.

Postproduction

The colors and details were punched up with the Topaz Adjust 5 Spicify plug-in for Lightroom. The effect was minimized on the couple using the "brush out" feature in Adjust 5, which is very handy for Lightroom workflows.

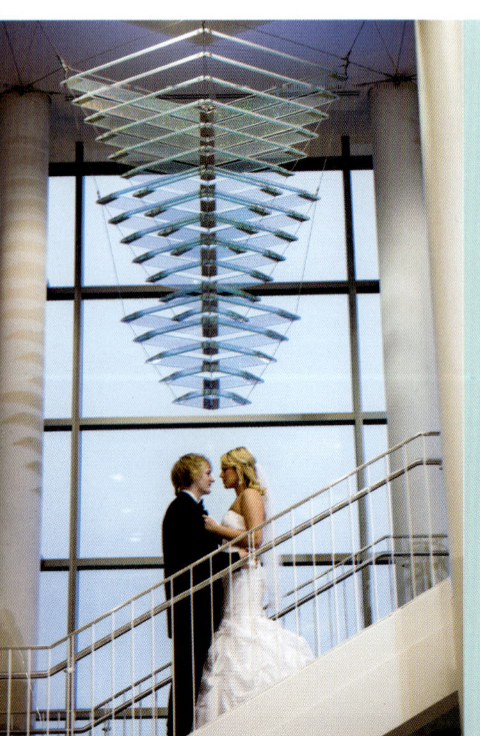

Test Shot

This test shot shows a light check before I added the gelled strobe. Some people may actually prefer this version. I like having both versions available as options.

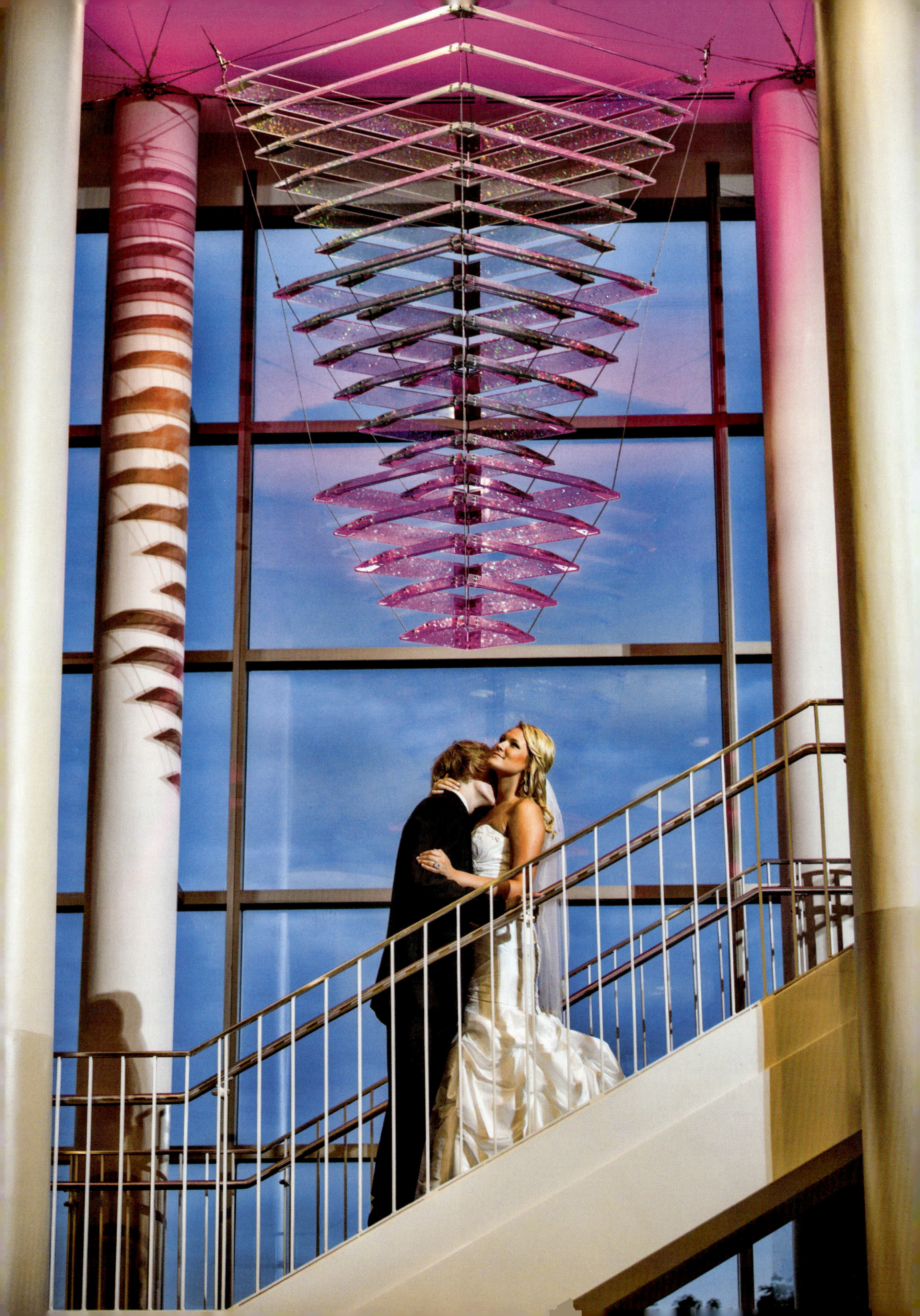

46

Temperature, Temperature

Cool blue tones in tungsten light

One annoyance when working with speed-lights in mixed lighting conditions is dealing with the different color temperatures.

The most common ambient light in buildings is tungsten-based, typically in the 2800–3200K range. This is visually much warmer than daylight-balanced speedlights, generally in the 5500–6000K range. When you mix the two at approximately the same exposure values, you of-

A dramatic shot of Maria before I added the speed-light as an accent light on the background.

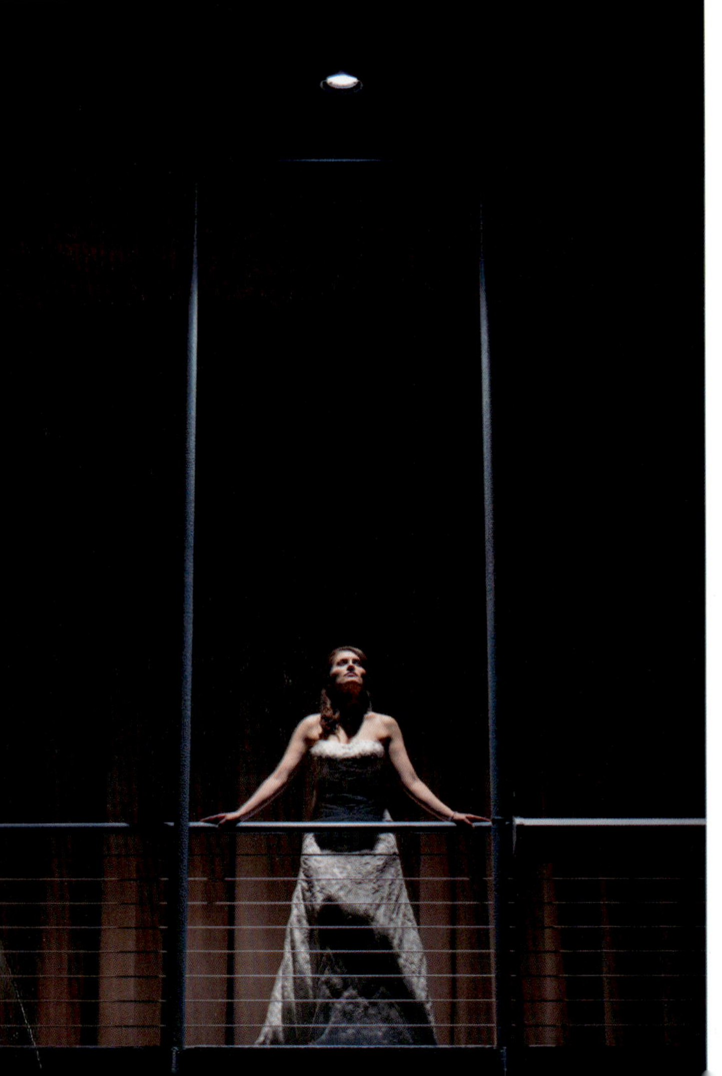

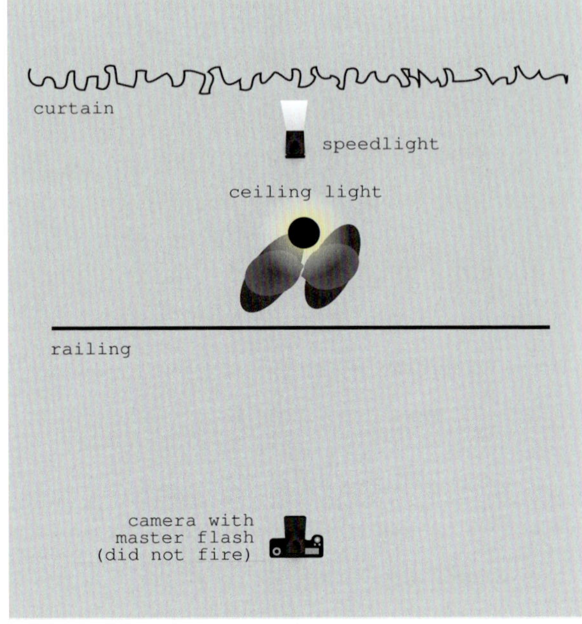

Camera: Canon 5D MKIII with Canon 70–200L lens at 70mm

Exposure: ⅟₈₀ second, f/5, ISO 3200 (manual)

Lighting: Canon 580EX II speedlight on camera set to master (did not fire) with RadioPopper PX transmitter. One Canon 580EX II speed-light with a Snootzie off-camera set to eTTL and slave mode (Group B), –1EV flash exposure compensation, fired with RadioPopper PX receiver.

ten get weird color contaminations; some parts of the skin are cool, others are warm, and some are in between. Yuck.

Color Balance

In these situations, I recommend picking one dominant light source (ambient or flash) and then making sure that your accent lighting is

at least 2 stops differ-
ent from your main
lighting. This helps to
alleviate much of the
color contamination on
the skin. Or, you could
fit your flash with a
CTO/CTS gel so that
it emulates a tungsten
light source.

Color Contrast

For the image to the
right, I used the differ-
ence in color tempera-
tures for accent lighting
that contrasts with my
subjects.

My main light source
was the tungsten can
light above the bride
and groom, so I set my
camera's color balance
to tungsten and exposed
for the ambient light.

I then positioned
an ungelled speedlight
on the floor directly
behind them, pointed
up at the curtain in the
background. Because
the speedlight is a much
cooler light source compared to the warm
coloration of the tungsten ambient light, and
because I had my camera's white balance set to
tungsten, the light from the speedlight recorded
as blue.

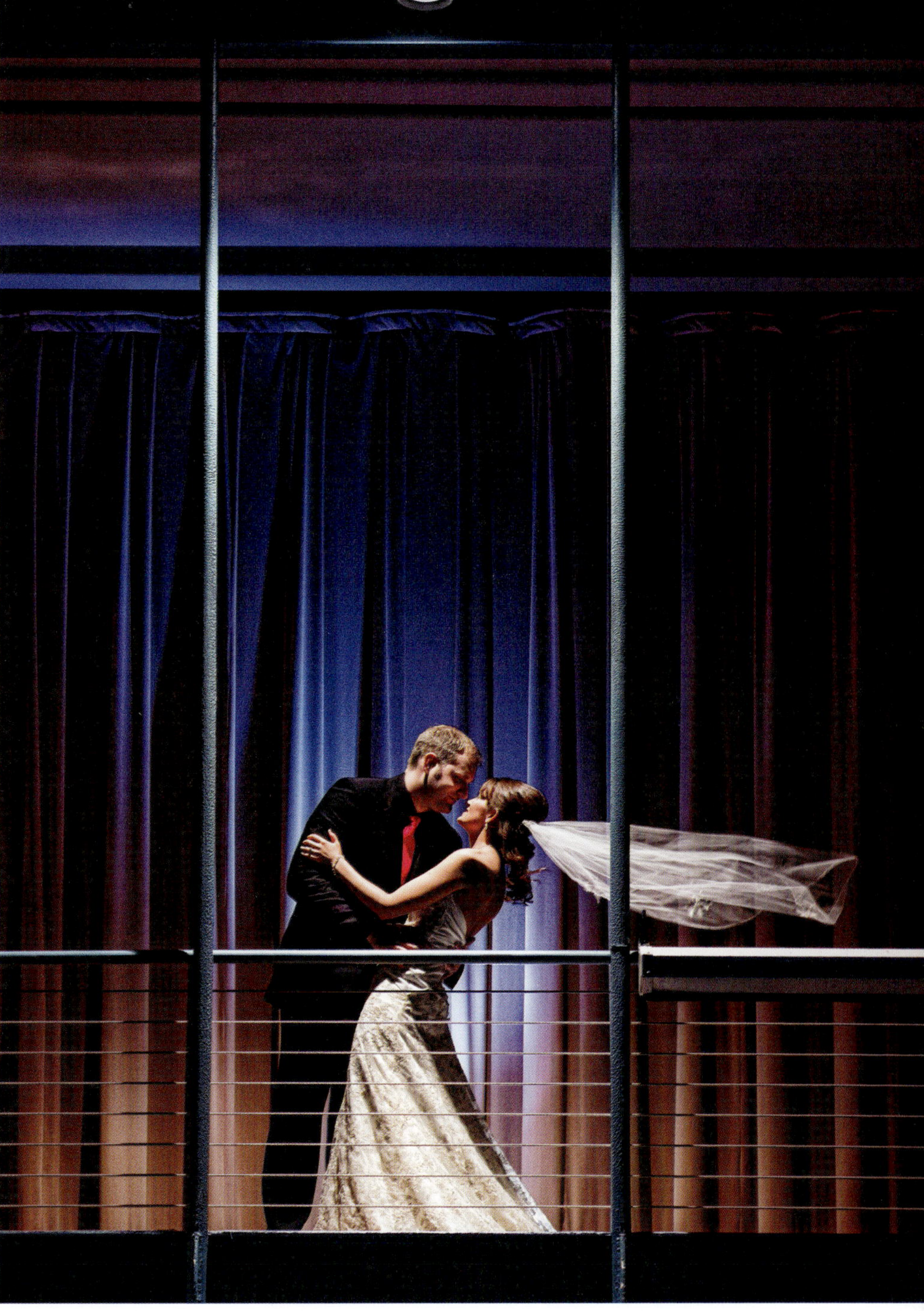

This is a good example of how we can think
about the different colors provided by our
mixed light sources and then use them to our
creative advantage.

 | # Getting Soft on Location

Creating an instant softbox on location

I mostly use bare speedlights on location because I am trying to match the hard ambient light (such as direct sun) or I need as much power as I can get and can't afford to cut it with diffusion. However, there *are* times when I need a quick, soft light source.

A Quick Solution

There are myriad pop-up softboxes and umbrellas out there to choose from, and they all have their pluses and minuses.

My favorite Johnny-on-the-spot softener, however, is a simple pop-up diffusion panel—in fact, we've already seen outdoor applications of this in sections 30 and 44. It's the same as the common oblong pop-up reflector, except the fabric is translucent white. You could call it a scrim or a silk, as it is often used to diffuse strong sunlight hitting the subject. However, I use it most often as a sideless pseudo-softbox.

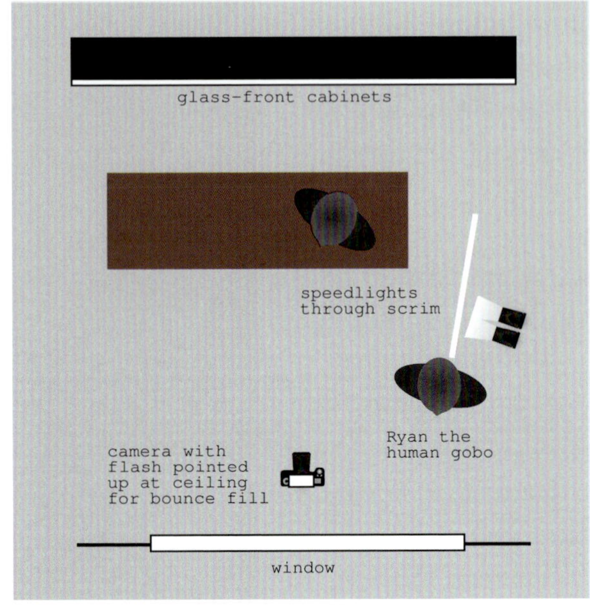

I simply place the panel in between the speedlights and the subject (about two to three feet from my speedlights if possible). Voilà! I have soft lighting from an instant softbox.

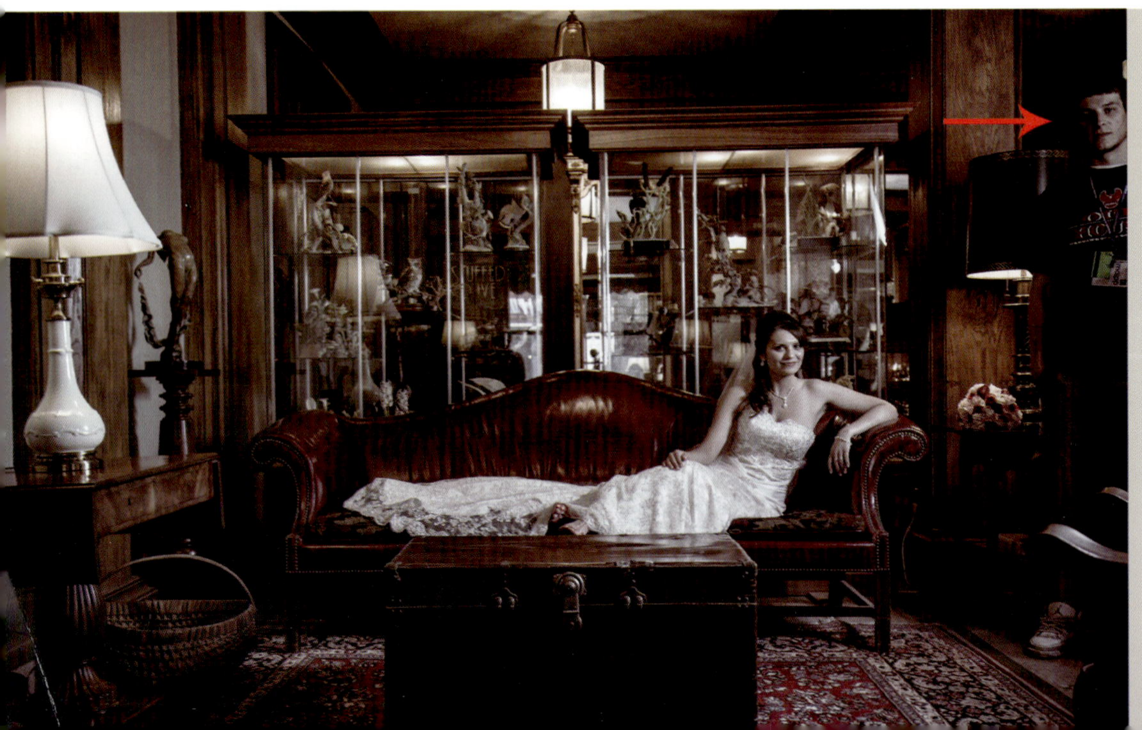

A Human Gobo

I needed a gobo to help block the light from reflecting onto the glass in the background. Fortunately my student, Ryan, fit the bill.

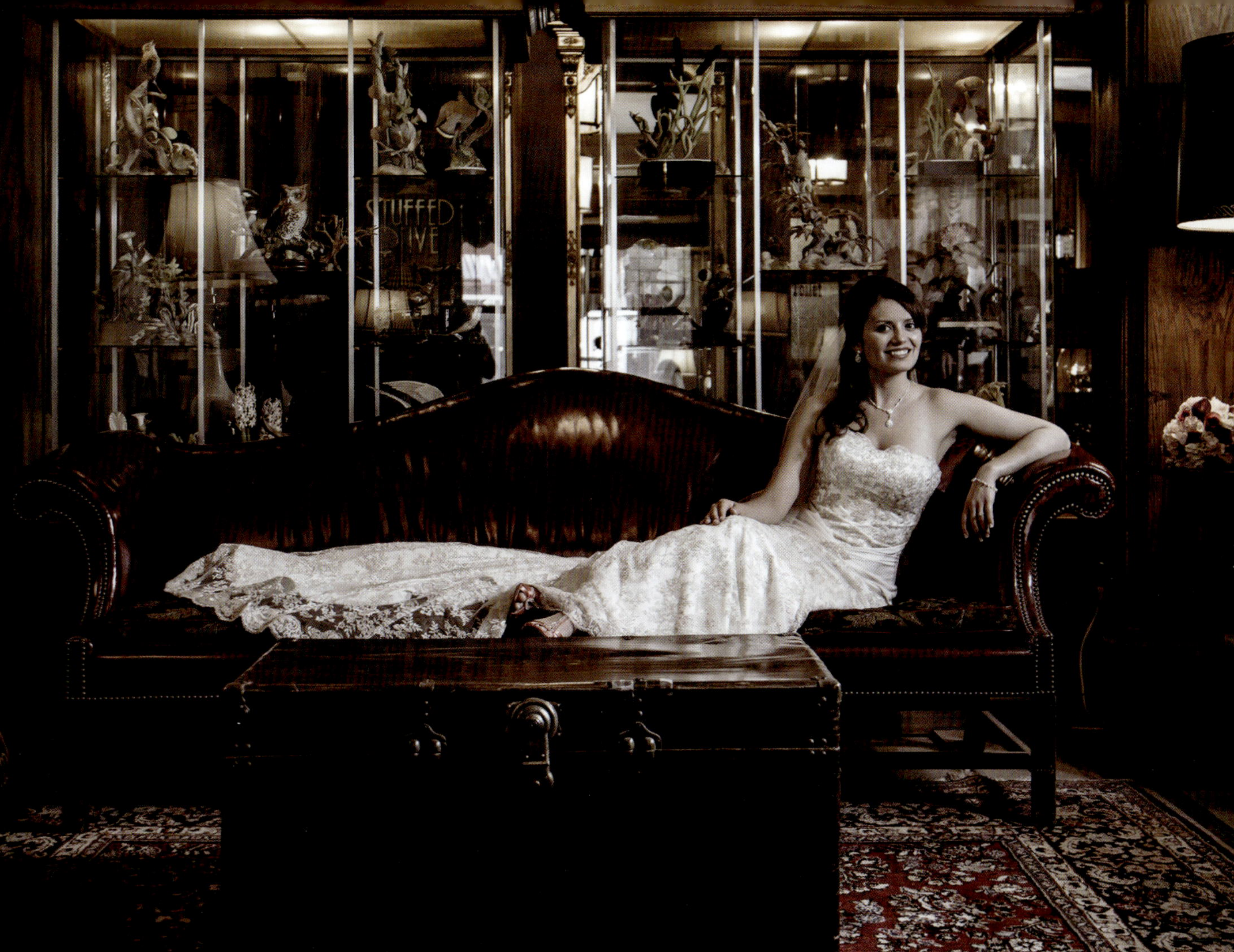

If you look closely you can see people reflected in the glass. This image was created as part of my class at the Mid-American Institute of Professional Photography.

How Do You Solve a Lighting Problem Like Maria?

The diffusion panel provided soft yet directional lighting on Maria, my subject. We had an initial challenge, though. You will notice the glass cabinets behind her. When we originally positioned the speedlights and the diffusion panel to provide pleasing short light on Maria, the reflection of the diffusion panel was caught in the glass. Ugh. So we turned the panel counterclockwise (toward the camera) until the reflection disappeared yet the soft light still was feathered onto Maria. (Note the angle of the panel in the lighting diagram.)

Postproduction

The vintage effect was applied using my Desaturally Warm Vintage preset in Lightroom.

Camera: Canon 5D MKIII with Canon 24–105L lens at 32mm

Exposure: $1/60$ second, f/4, ISO 1000 (manual)

Lighting: Canon 580EX II speedlight on-camera set to master, fired straight up into the ceiling as fill, with RadioPopper PX transmitter. Two Canon 580EX II speedlights off-camera set to eTTL and slave mode, $+2/3$EV flash exposure compensation, fired with RadioPopper PX receiver.

48

Vintage Studio

Studio light modifiers with speedlights

Hopefully, I have shown that speedlights can be used to replace studio strobes in virtually *any* situation. So, naturally, speedlights (even non-Canon and Nikon brands) will work for a classic studio portrait. For the portrait below, I used the Nissin Di866II—a pretty remarkable flash that's a worthy (and affordable) alternative to the Canon 580EX II or Nikon SB900. Since Canon discontinued the 580EX II after the introduction of the 600EX-RT, the Nissin Di866II can serve as a replacement, because it is compatible with the RadioPopper PX system.

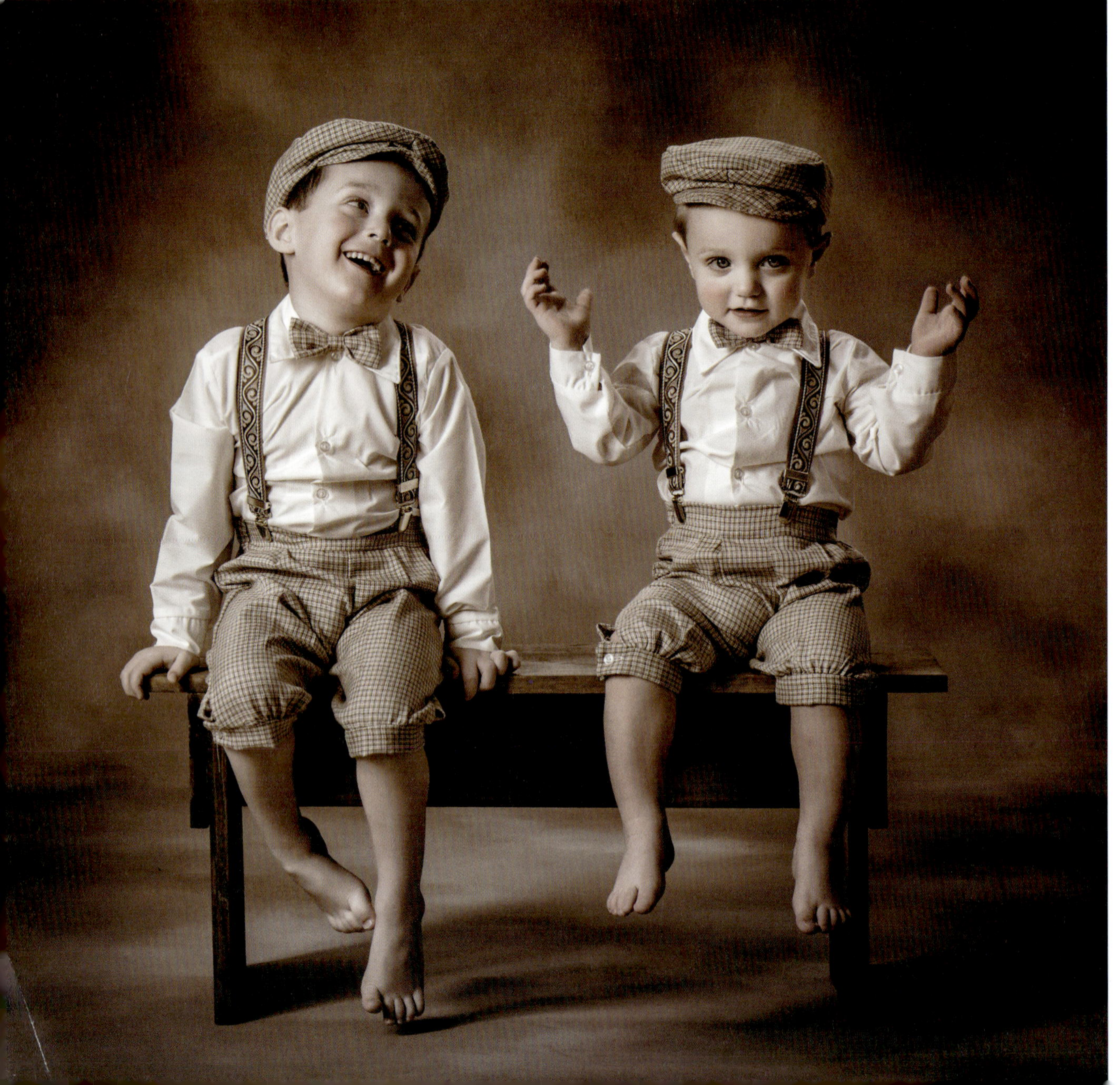

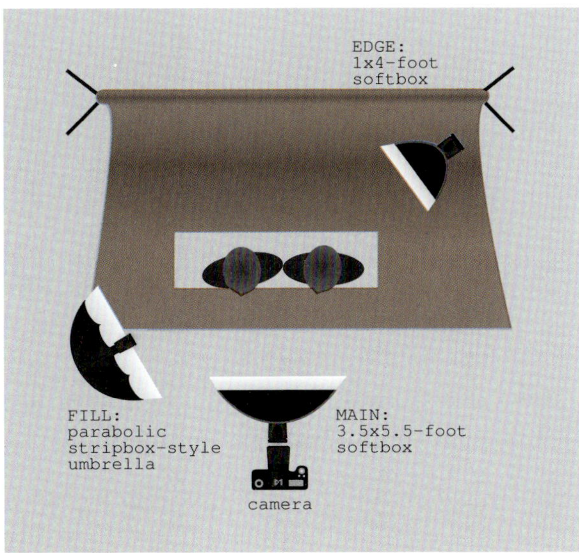

Camera: Canon 5D MKIII with Canon 24–105L lens at 93mm

Exposure: $1/160$ second, f/11, ISO 500 (manual)

Lighting: Three Nissin Di866II flashes. Two set to manual at $1/2$ power as the main and fill lights, and the third set to $1/4$ power as the subtle edge light. All triggered and fired with the RadioPopper JrX system; transmitter in the camera's hotshoe and receivers connected to the flashes' PC connection ports.

Classic Lighting

The lighting setup for this studio portrait was fairly standard. The main light was a unique parabolic stripbox-style umbrella to camera left with the flash set to $1/2$ power on manual. The fill light, directly behind me, was a flash set to $1/2$ power and placed in a Larson 3.5x5.5-foot softbox. Lastly, a 1x4-foot stripbox held a flash to camera right and behind the subjects. That flash was set to $1/4$ power.

Vintage Style

I've photographed both of these boys periodically since they were born, so it was fun to dress them in vintage clothes for a different look. I completed the vintage style in postproduction by using my Desaturally Warm Vintage preset for Lightroom. Additional dodging and burning were completed in Photoshop.

Additional speedlight portraits from the same session.

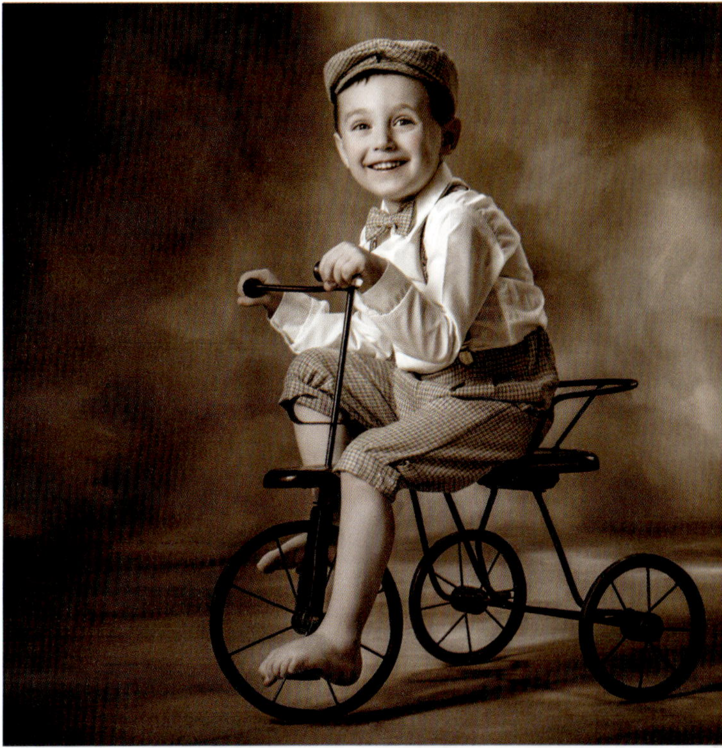

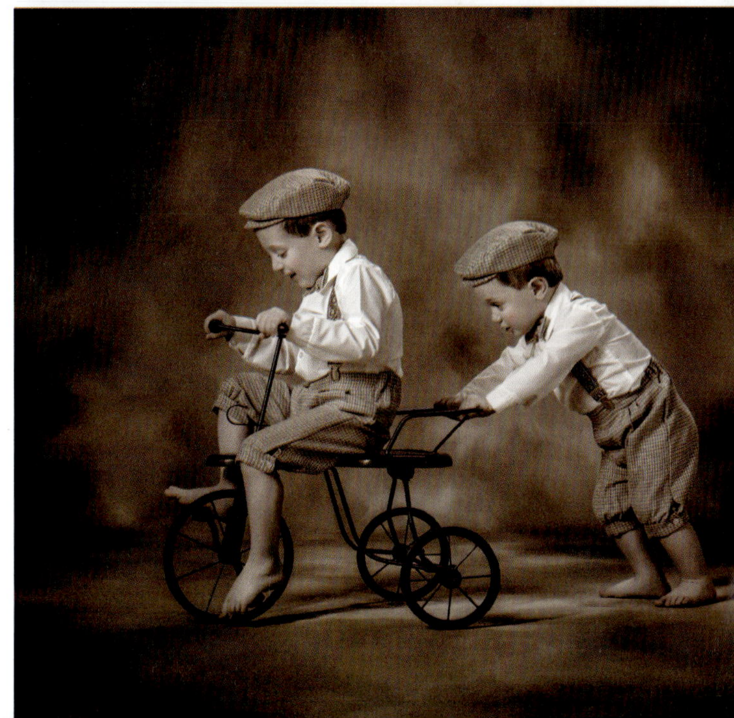

49

Slash of Light

A simple spotlight effect with the Snootzie

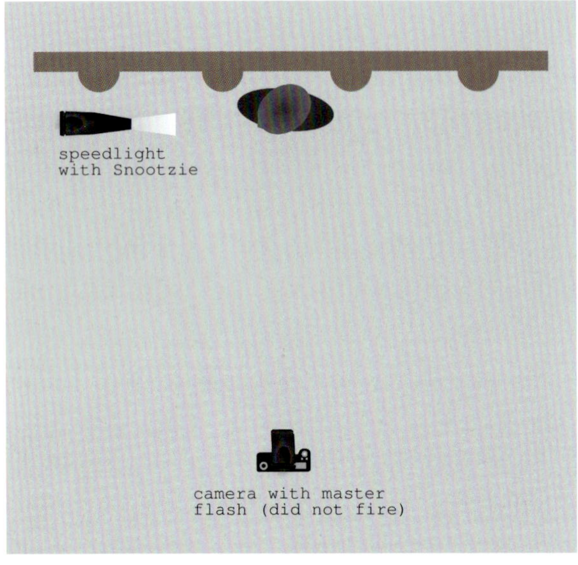

A close-up made in the same location.

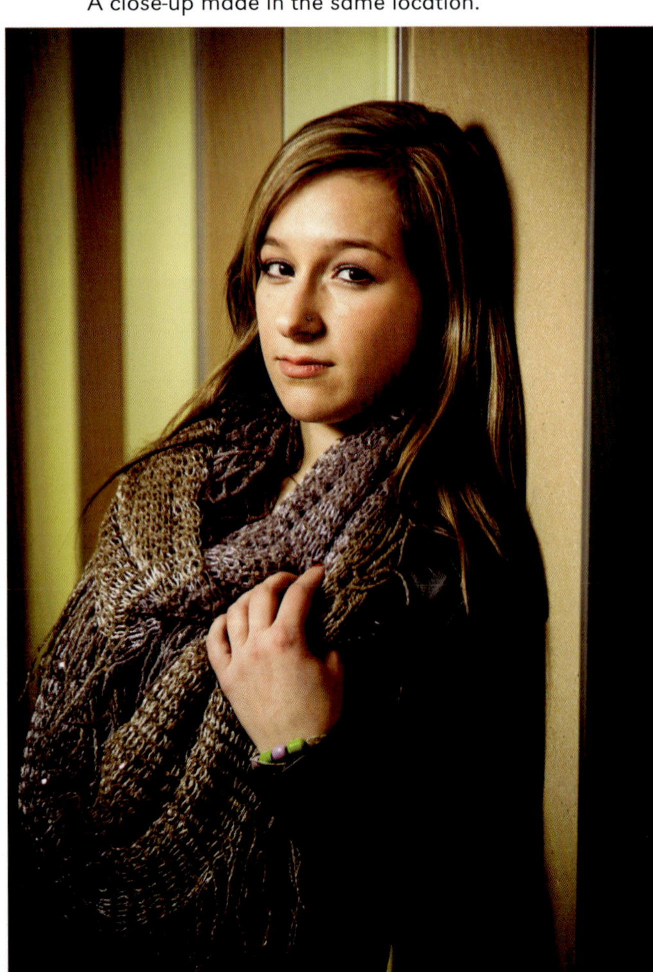

I'm always looking for cool locations, even after a shoot is "technically" over. I was leading a shootout at the Northern Light PPA convention in St. Paul, Minnesota, and we were making our way back to the hotel via the many underground tunnels in the downtown area. I found these interesting vertical lighting fixtures in the tunnel and thought the spot was definitely photo-worthy.

Lighting and Posing

I have a Snootzie and I'm not afraid to use it. I positioned my model, Alex, in between two fixtures and then went for a dramatic lighting approach. I zoomed a single speedlight to 105mm to get a tight, narrow beam. I tight-

Camera: Canon 5D MKIII with Canon 24–105L lens at 45mm
Exposure: $^1/_{160}$ second, f/4.5, ISO 160 (manual)
Lighting: Canon 580EX II speedlight on-camera set to master (did not fire) with RadioPopper PX transmitter. Canon 580EX II speedlight off camera set to eTTL and slave mode, fired with RadioPopper PX receiver.

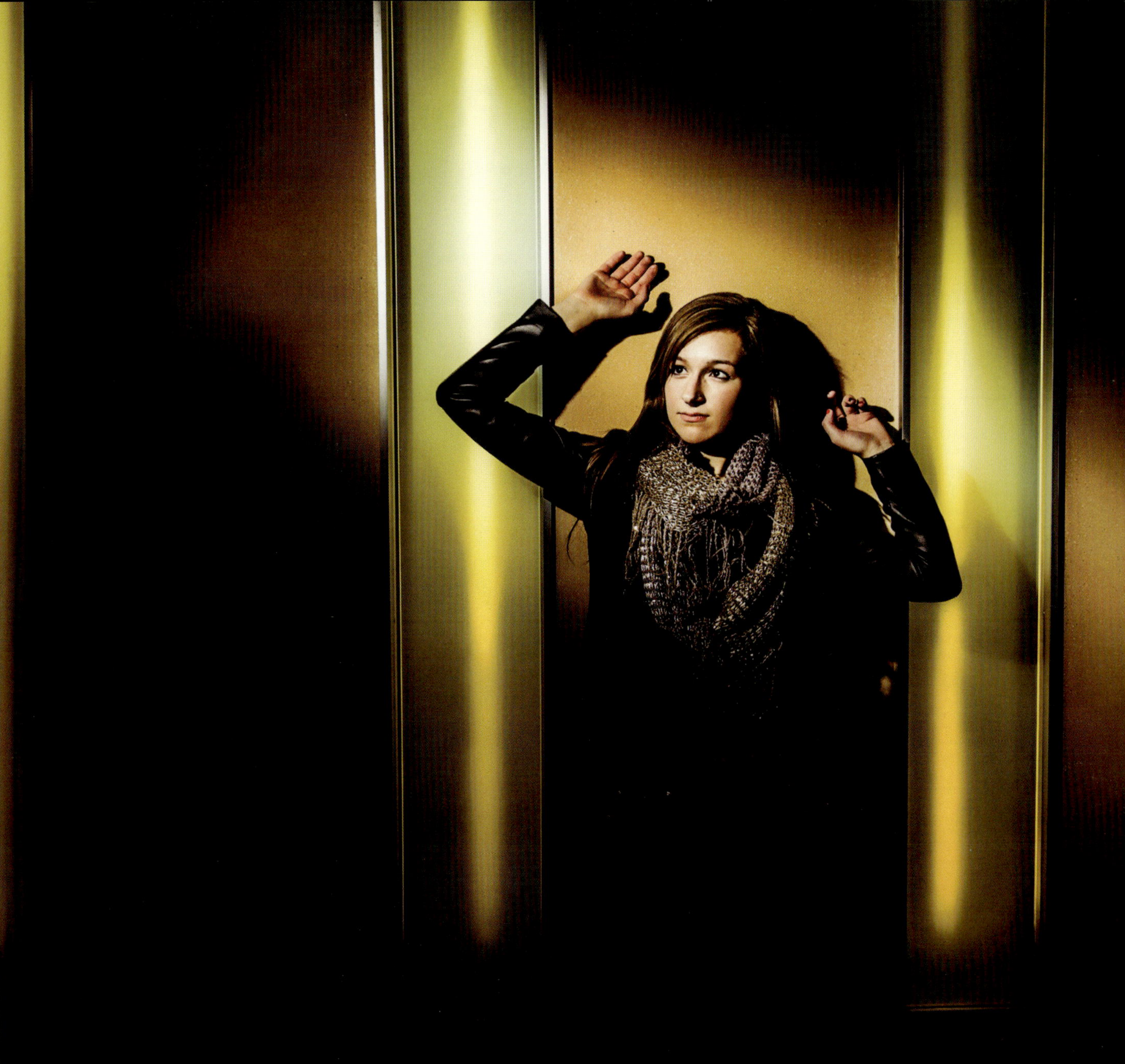

ened the beam further using a Snootzie. I had my assistant hold the light stand up and aimed down at Alex. This combination of a narrowed beam and angle gave me a dynamic slash of light across the scene.

I worked Alex's pose to create matching angles with her arms to complete the look.

Postproduction

I finished the edgy look with my Orange Magento Pushup Lightroom preset, which adds in an orange and magenta splittone, plus a healthy bump up in contrast.

50

Environmental Portraits

Executive portraits, quickly and efficiently

Small, portable speedlight kits are perfect for on-location headshots and executive environmental portraits. Quick to set up and tear down, and easily moved between locations, speedlights can do the job well and efficiently. I use both eTTL and manual flash setups for these portraits.

Consistent Sequences

If I am photographing headshots on location and need the same lighting across all the portraits, I opt for a manual lighting setup using

Classic Looks

Speedlights work well for classic business portraits in the studio and on location.

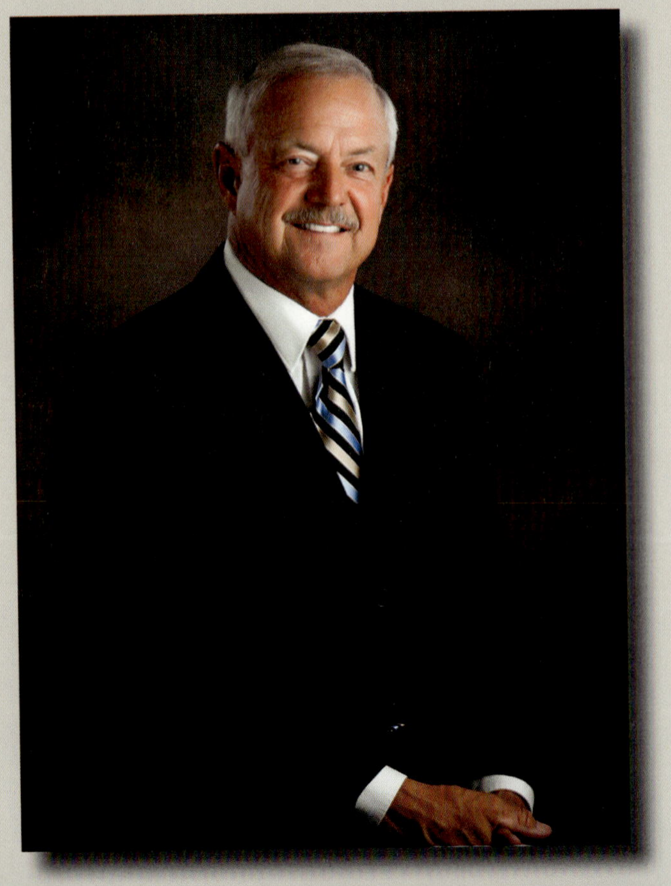

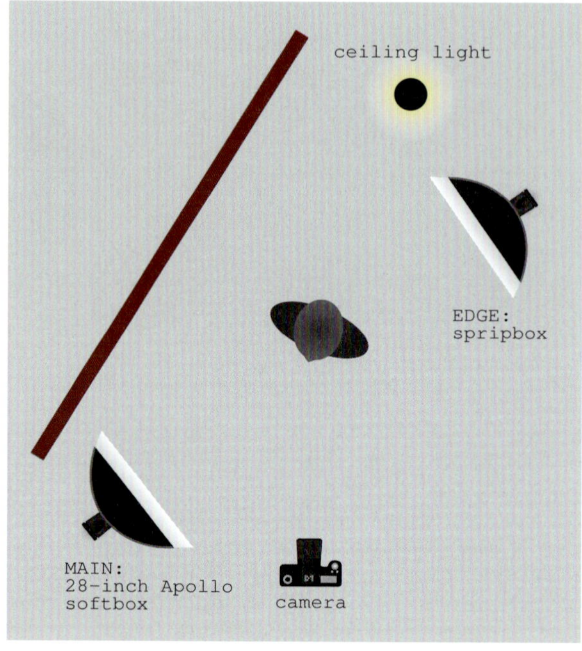

Camera: Canon 5D MKIII with Canon 70–200L lens at 100mm
Exposure: $^1/_{125}$ second, f/4.5, ISO 640 (manual)
Lighting: Two Canon 580EX II speedlights attached to RadioPopper Cubes triggered by Radio-Popper JrX receivers and powered up and down by leveraging the TTL system using a RadioPopper JrX transmitter.

my Canon 580EX IIs with the RadioPopper JrX system. My location kit for these portraits includes three lights: a Westcott Apollo 50-inch umbrella-style softbox as my main light; a Westcott Apollo 28-inch umbrella-style softbox as my fill light at the camera position; and a Westcott stripbox as my edge light.

The main and fill speedlights are set manually on each flash to ensure that I have the same, repeatable output for each portrait. The edge light, however, is attached to a RadioPopper Cube that allows me to remotely dial the power up and down on the edge light. Why? I often photograph forty or more people at a time on location for these business portraits, so I have a wide variety of people in front of my lens. For women with long hair, I dial up the edge light to create a nice highlight on the hair. However, if my next subject is a bald male, I turn down the edge light so I do not get a strong highlight on his head. My main and fill stay the same; my edge light varies by subject.

Environmental Portraits

For environmental portraits such as the one shown to the right, I use this same RadioPopper Cube setup for all of my lights. My primary system for these images includes a Westcott 28-inch Apollo as my main light and a Westcott stripbox as my edge light. Typically, these lights are set 180 degrees across from each other (as shown in the diagram on the facing page). I meter for the ambient light and then set my main and edge lights accordingly to overpower the ambient, removing any color casts that may be caused by tungsten or fluorescent lighting at the workplace.

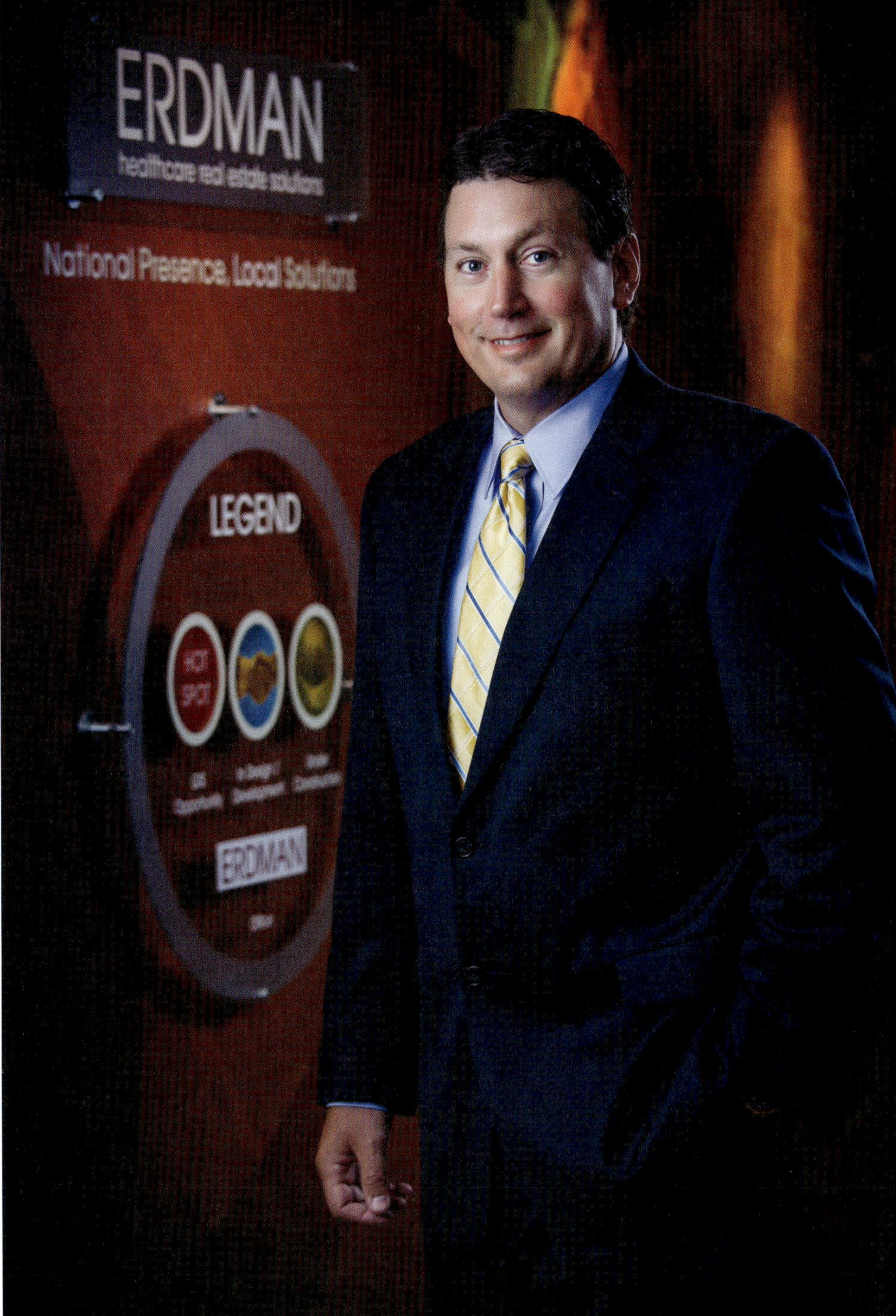

51

In-Depth Lighting

Switch the depth of field with TTL off-camera speedlights

Shallow depth of field is desirable in a lot of outdoor portraiture, but imagery that is sharp front to back can have tremendous impact.

Blending the Light

Straight out of the camera, the image of the bride and groom on the facing page had an

Camera: Canon 5D MKIII with Canon 24–105L lens at 24mm

Exposure: 1/200 second, f/22, ISO 100 (manual)

Lighting: Canon 580EX II speedlight on-camera set to master (fired) with RadioPopper PX transmitter. Two Canon 580EX II speedlights off-camera set to eTTL and slave mode, fired with RadioPopper PX receivers.

almost painterly quality. The framing of the couple against a mountainous cloud cried out for depth.

Since you can see the sun in the shot, you know that the couple had to be lit separately with off-camera lighting (otherwise, with the sun behind them, their faces would have been in shade). The blend, however, is subtle—despite coming from bare speedlights. This is a good

An Alternate Look

An alternate image of the bride alone created with similar lighting as that used in the couple shot.

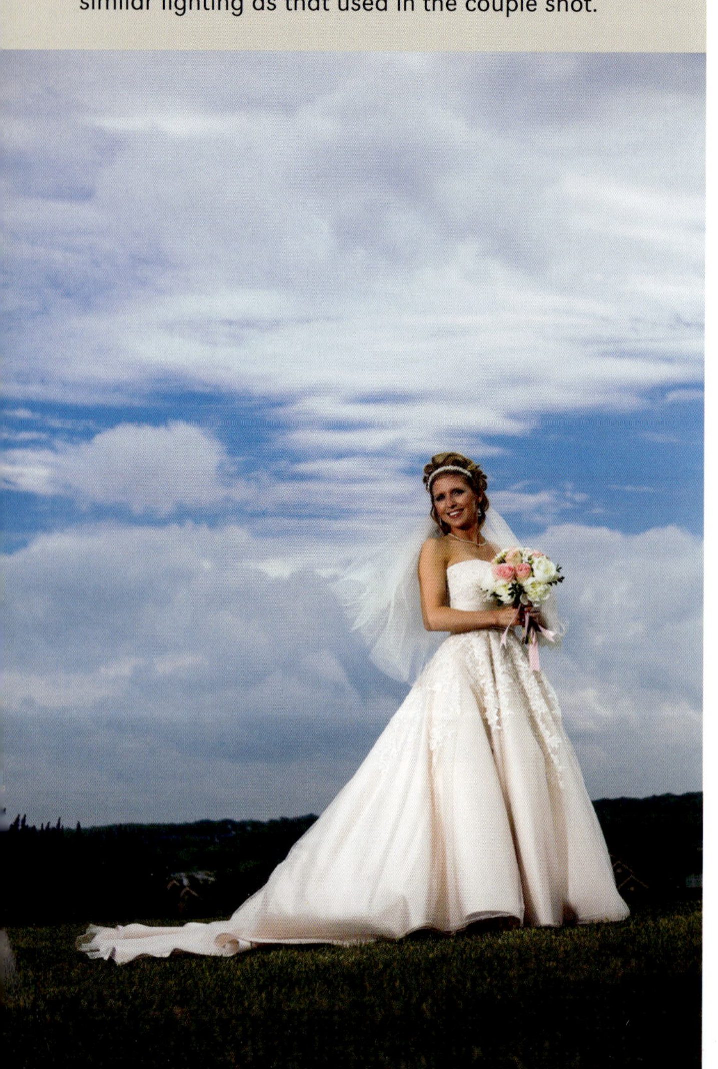

example of matching the lighting quality of the off-camera speedlight with the quality of the ambient light—in this case, full, direct sun. The light from the off-camera flash makes visual sense on the couple because the lighting quality matches the ambient light in the scene.

Two Approaches

There are two ways to light this type of image with speedlights. One is to go 100 percent manual and meter everything.

The other approach is to set your camera manually and let the TTL system handle the flash portion of the exposure. This is my preferred method. I set my camera to its maximum flash-sync speed and the desired f-stop. In this case, that was $\frac{1}{200}$ second and f/22. I then used to the lowest natural ISO setting, ISO 100.

With the addition of two off-camera speedlights plus my on-camera flash as fill, I was able to coax enough light onto the couple to balance the scene and create a memorable image.

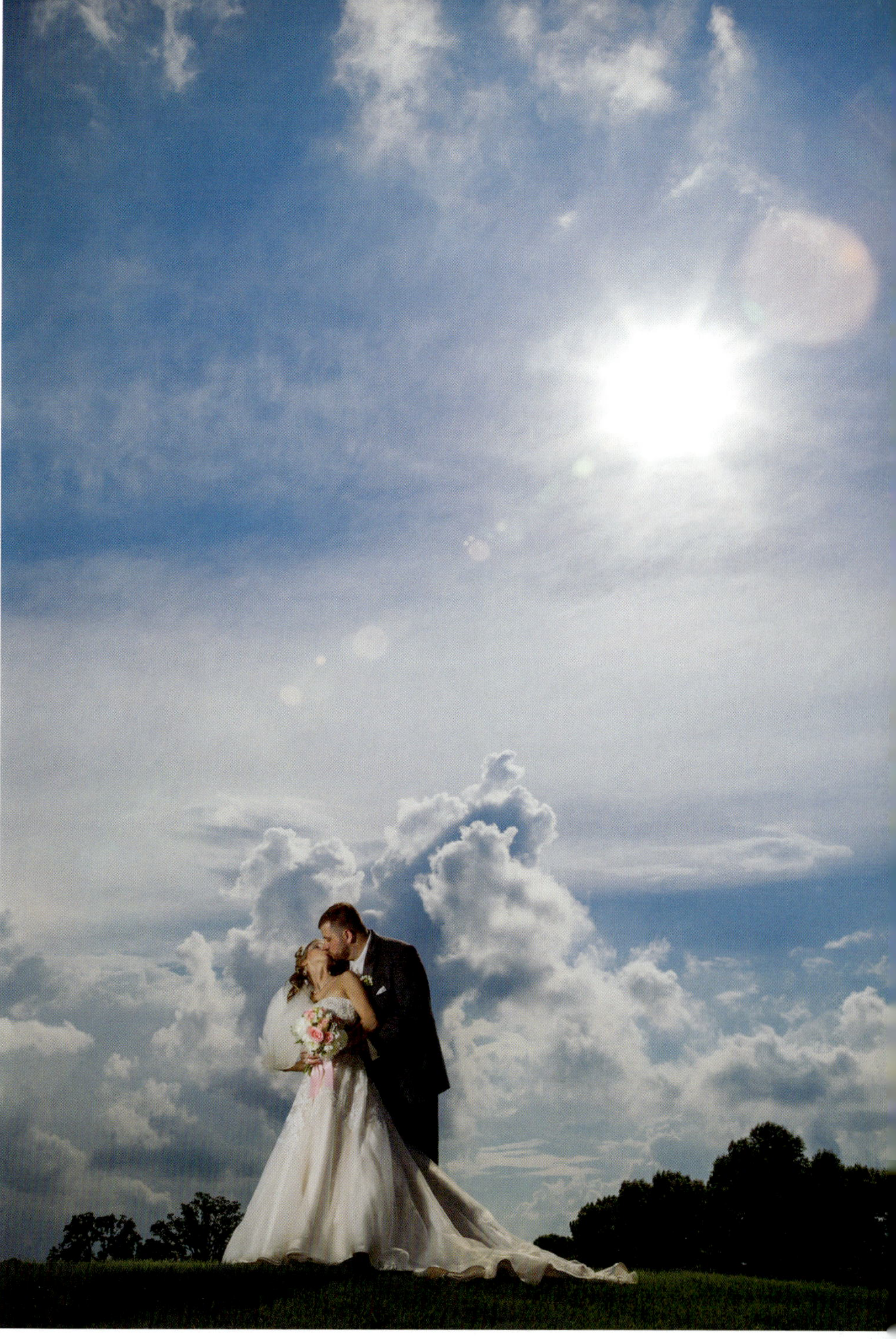

Two More Tips

1. To maximize their power, position the off-camera speedlights as close as you possibly can to the subject(s).
2. Watch the lens flare. I made sure to adjust my composition so the lens flare would not run through my subjects' heads.

52

Spring Out of the Blossoms

Separate subjects from a busy background

In a beautiful setting like this, it is easy to lose your primary subject (the couple) amidst everything going on around them. It is vitally important to use lighting and posing to make them the primary focus, while still encouraging the viewer to enjoy the setting.

Light Is Busting Out All Over

My couple was in the shade and in relatively poor light for portraiture. However, the light on the trees and on the background was soft and beautiful. To create the look I wanted, I needed to create lighting that would:

1. Flatter the couple.
2. Marry appropriately with the existing light.
3. Pop the bride and groom out of the scene.

I chose a double-speedlight combination to camera left as my main light and a single speedlight outfitted with a Snootzie to camera right to provide a subtle edge light from behind the couple. Both were set to group A, and I built my ratio between the two by controlling the distance of each light from the subject. My on-camera master flash fired as fill.

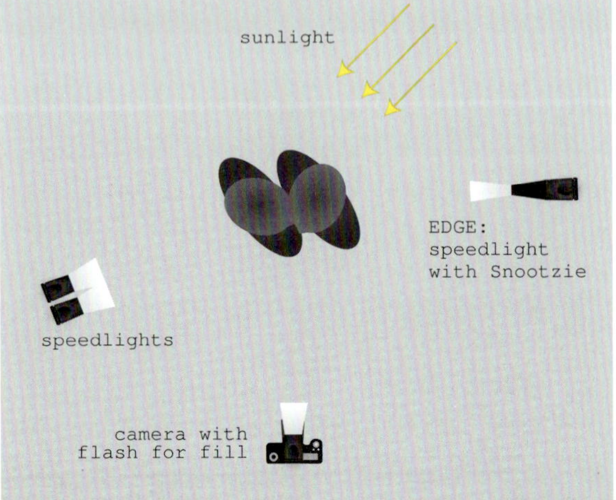

Postproduction

In postproduction, I pulled out detail and popped the saturation using my Topaz Adjust Spicify preset in Lightroom, being careful to

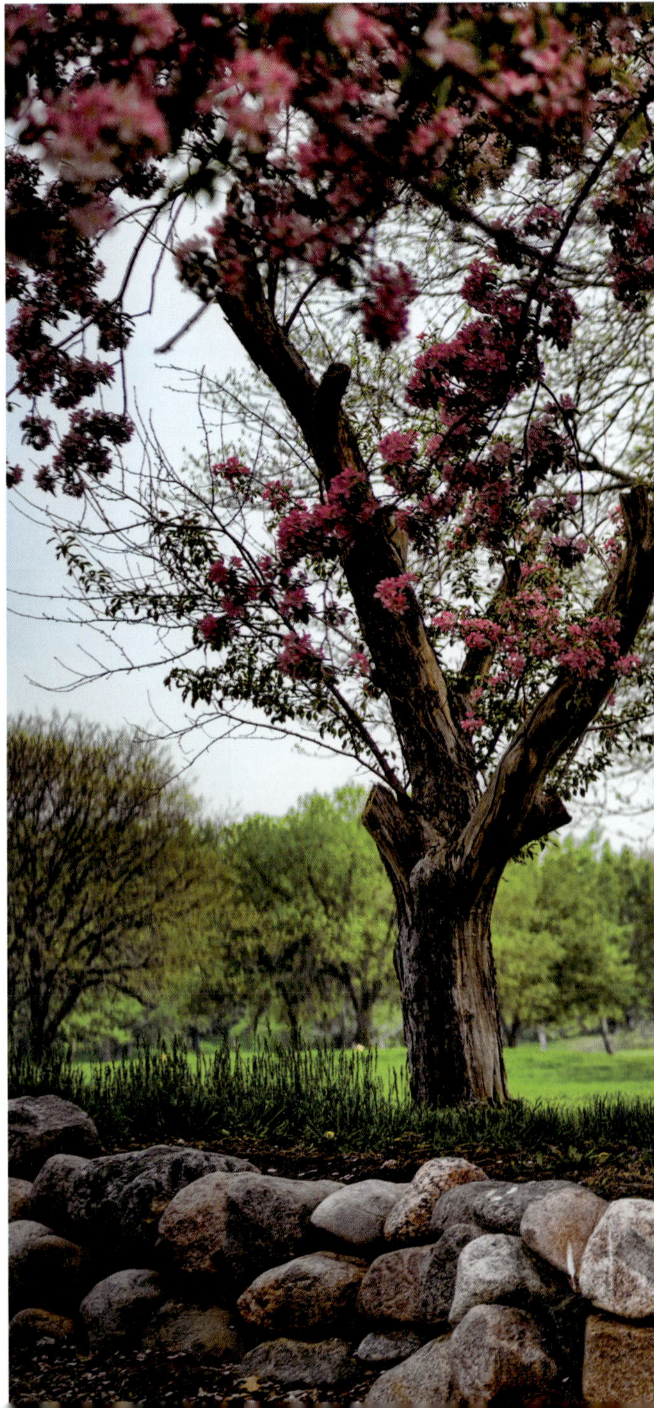

use the "brush out" tool to remove most of the effect from the couple's skin. I also used the handy "burn" tool in Topaz Adjust to burn down the corners and the edges.

It streamlines the workflow when I can accomplish all of this using the same product. I've said it before and I'll say it again, time is money is this business!

<table>
<tr><td>Camera:</td><td>Canon 5D MKIII with Canon 24–105L lens at 85mm</td></tr>
<tr><td>Exposure:</td><td>$1/400$ second, f/4.5, ISO 100, $-1/3$EV exposure compensation (aperture priority)</td></tr>
<tr><td>Lighting:</td><td>Canon 580EX II speedlight on-camera set to master (fired as fill) with RadioPopper PX transmitter. Two Canon 580EX II speedlights ganged together off-camera set to eTTL and slave mode (group A), fired with RadioPopper PX receivers. Canon 580EX II speedlight with a Snootzie off-camera set to eTTL and slave mode (group A) fired with RadioPopper PX receiver.</td></tr>
</table>

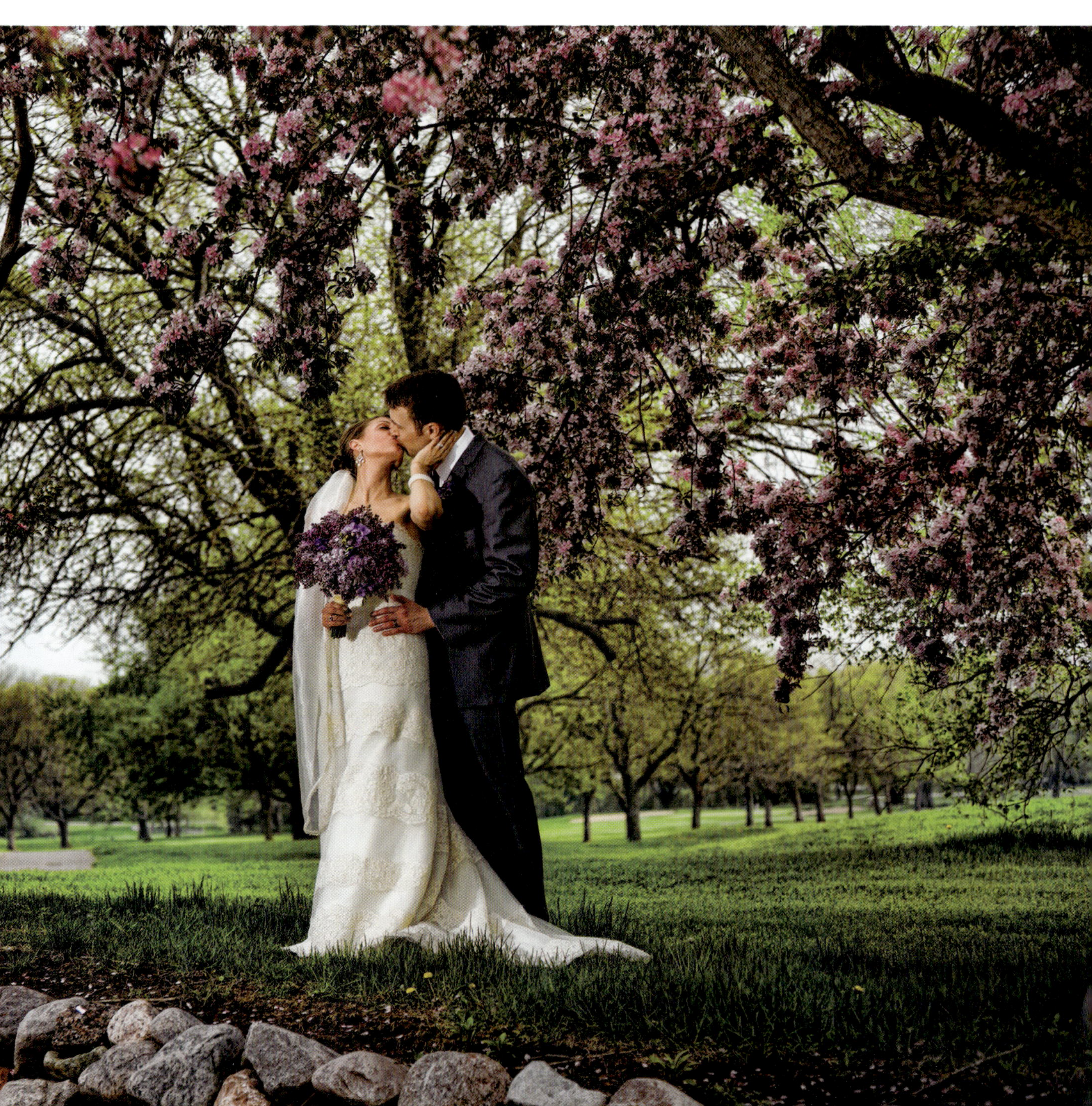

53

Blue Sky at Night

Lighting a nighttime portrait

Street shots at night are a common wedding request and make for great ending shots in your album designs. The challenges are getting them done well while dead tired (because you've been shooting all day) and getting them done quickly (because there tends to be traffic in the street). It's not a situation that is conducive to an elaborate setup to say the least.

Wham Bam, I Gotta Scram

I go back and forth on shooting this on manual mode versus aperture-priority. I shot this particular image on manual after getting a quick meter reading from the dome in the background and then choosing to slightly underexpose it. The lighting on my couple was a simple two-light setup. The main light was on a stand held by my assistant, Krystal (so she could move

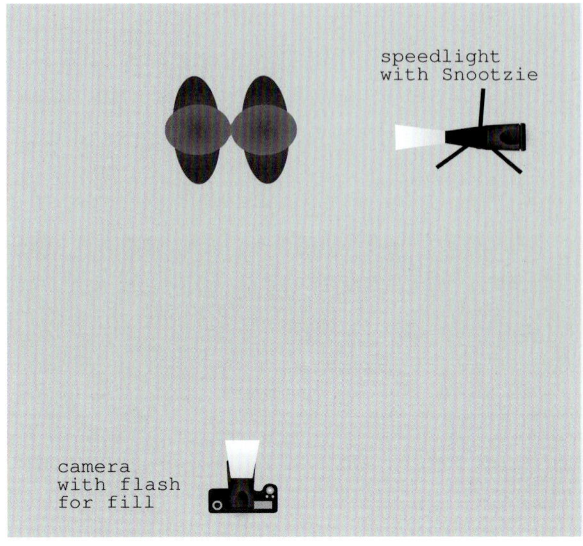

Camera: Canon 5D MKIII with Canon 24–105L lens at 93mm
Exposure: $^1/_{125}$ second, f/4, ISO 1600 (manual)
Lighting: Canon 580EX II speedlight on-camera set to master (fired as fill) with RadioPopper PX transmitter. Canon 580EX II speedlight with a Snootzie off-camera set to eTTL and slave mode (group A), fired with Radio-Popper PX receiver.

quickly to get out of the way of cars). The fill light was from my on-camera flash. Sometimes, I will add a third speedlight behind the bride, but that didn't seem safe in this case—I really didn't want to have a car eat my speedlight.

Ready . . . Action!

I like action in my poses. I see too many couple poses that are static, straight up-and-down—*booooooring*. For these images, I had Alex pick up Olivia. This simple request instantly created a cute love story.

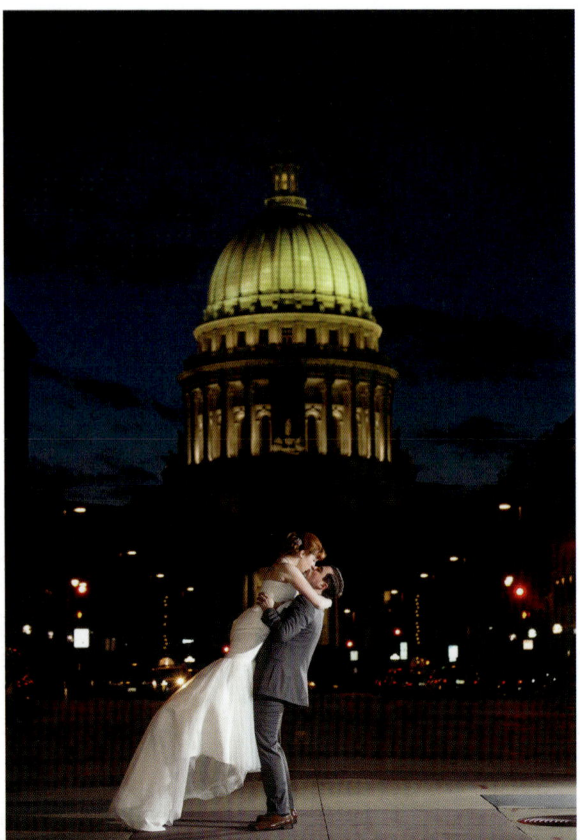

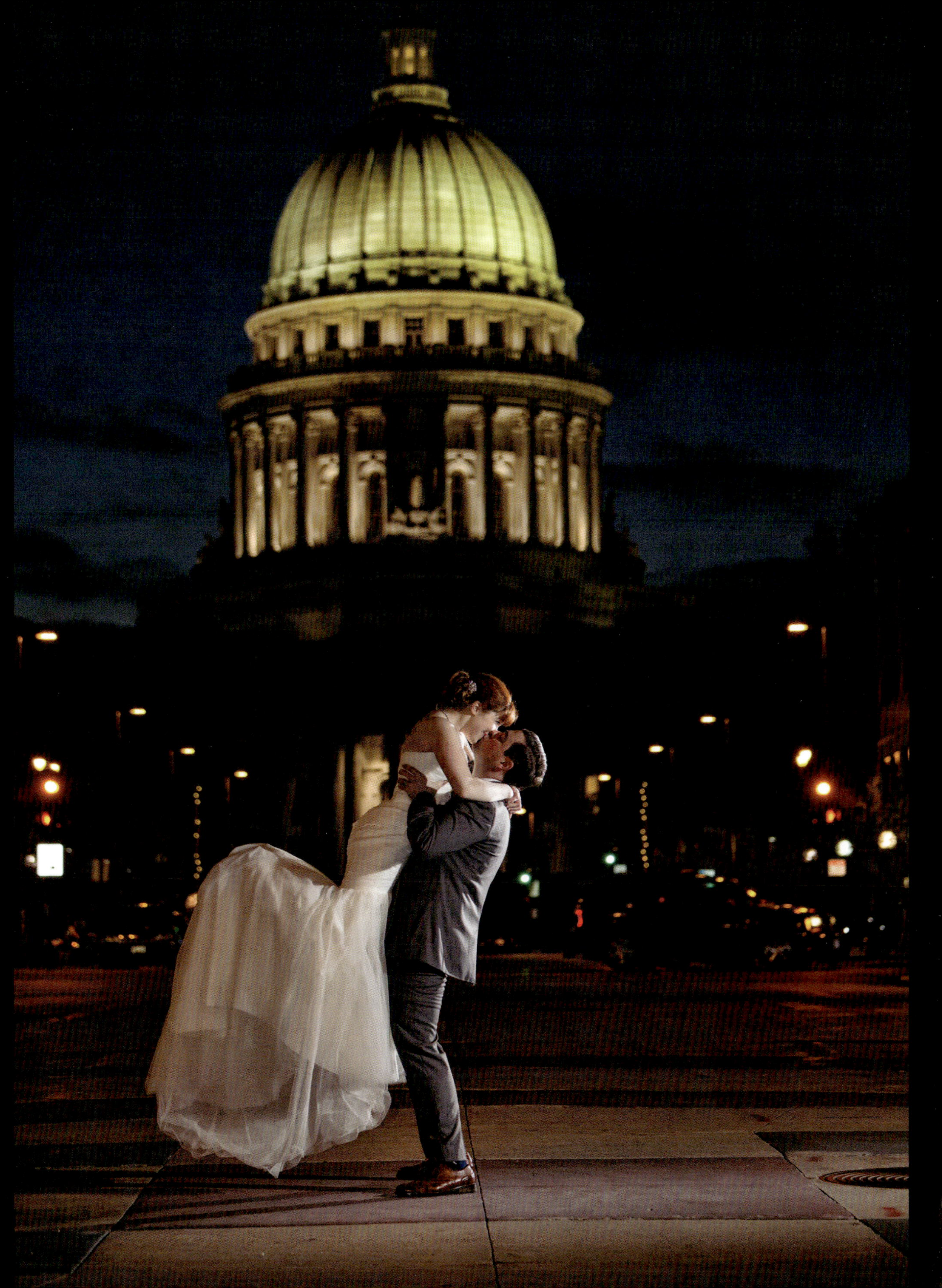

54

Building Family Connections

A new way to create winning family portraits

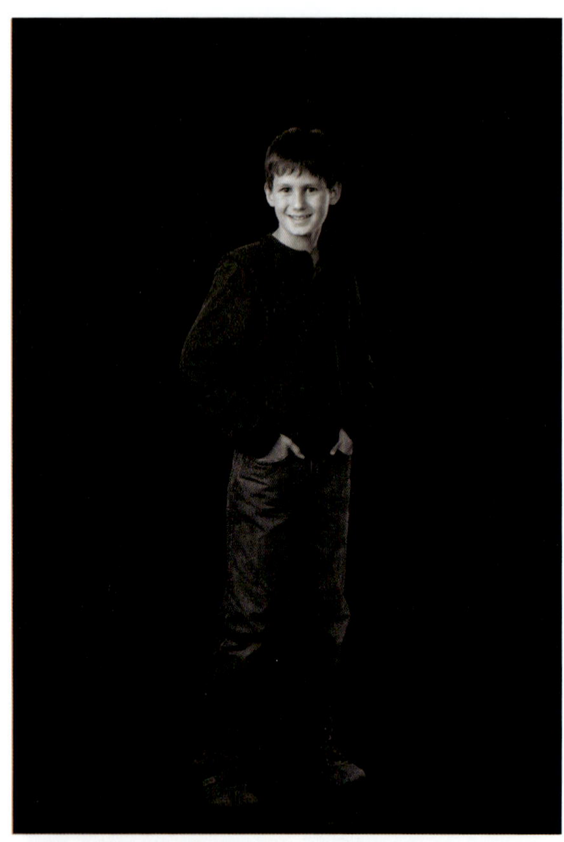

All family portrait photographers have run across the problem where all but one person liked themselves in the portrait, and that one naysayer killed the sale. Frustrating! I've always said, the more people you add to the photo, the more difficult it is to please everyone. I have great respect for successful family photographers!

Frustration Leads to Innovation

There—put *that* on a t-shirt. (In fact, I think I will!) After one such frustrating experience, I decided to find a new way (at least for me) to photograph families. Here's my solution.

I start by photographing each person individually on a black felt background. For this sequence, I used a Larson 3.5x5.5-foot softbox rotated to

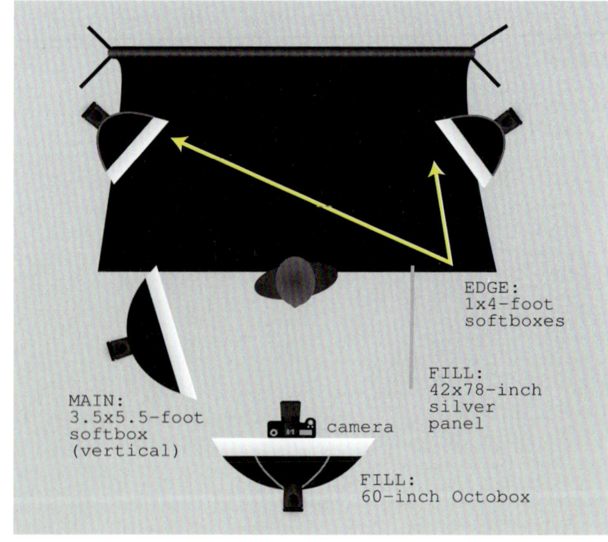

Camera: Canon 5D MKIII with Canon 24–105L lens at 65mm

Exposure: $^{1}/_{160}$ second, f/10, ISO 400 (manual)

Lighting: Four Canon 580EX II speedlights off-camera set in RadioPopper Cubes and controlled manually in three different groups from camera position using the RadioPopper JrX system.

the vertical axis as my main light, a 60-inch octobox as my fill light, and dual 1x4-foot strip-boxes on each side of each subject as my edge lights. The edge lighting is vitally important with a portrait like this. Without it, the subjects would blend in with the background.

My camera was on a camera stand and set to a fixed height and zoom level. I began with the tallest person, the dad, as my first subject to set my framing. Then I worked through each individual with different poses, maintaining the same lighting and settings throughout.

Postproduction

After converting the images to black & white I had each person in this group select their favorite image of themselves. Using their selections, I designed a simple composite.

To do this, I created a 30-inch black canvas in Photoshop. Then, I dragged each person's image onto the black background, keeping them on separate layers. I switched the blending mode of each layer to Lighten.

"The more people you add to the photo, the more difficult it is to please everyone."

From there, it was a simple procedure to apply masking where one person overlapped another. I also painted in shadows as necessary.

It sounds like a lot of work—but, in reality, the entire process generally takes me about ten minutes. Everyone is happy, and I sell a large wall portrait.

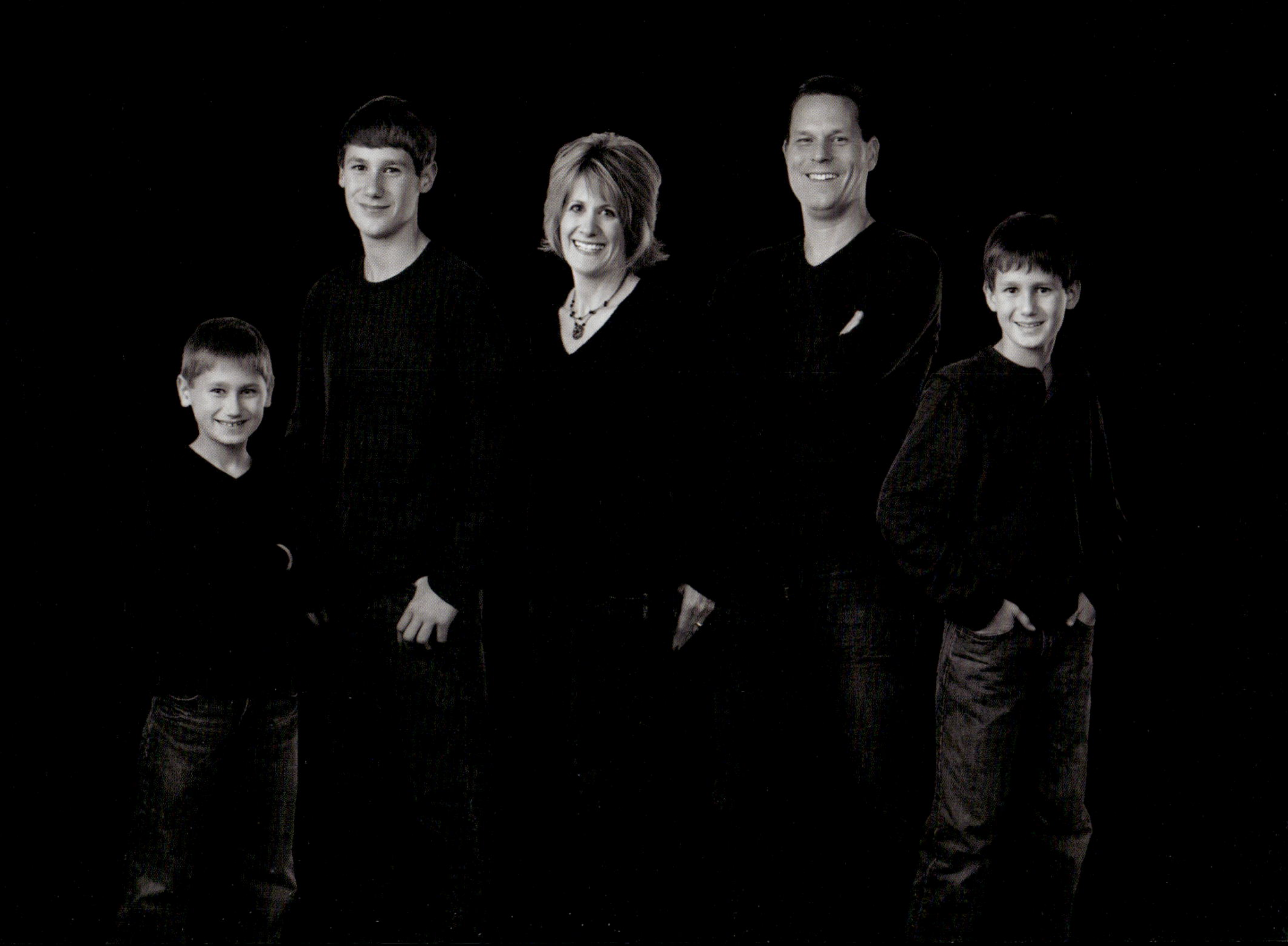

55

Xtreme Portraits for Athletes

Compositing leads to big sales

A growing and lucrative segment of my senior portrait business is tailoring sessions and products to the high-school athlete. As professional photographers facing growing competition, we need to define distinct differences between ourselves and snapshot "artists" who stick a senior in front a tree and snap away with an iPhone. Creative, high-quality portraiture, skilled postproduction techniques, and high-end products (ones that cannot be found at Wal-Mart) are my answers to this challenge.

Composite a Winning Image

These Xtreme Athlete football portraits of Anthony and Lane are the perfect way to get the athletic male seniors to care about their portraits—and, more importantly, to get order sizes headed north into profitability land. They also create strong demand among female athletes.

I initially shot these images on white, but I have since changed to a green-screen process for this type of work.

Background First

I believe it is important to choose the background for the image first and then match your subject's pose and lighting to fit that selection. For these images, I selected backgrounds from Mark Bryant's Streetscape collection (www.streetscapebackgrounds.com).

Camera: Canon 5D MKIII with Canon 24–105L lens at 85mm
Exposure: $^1/_{160}$ second, f/10, ISO 400 (manual)
Lighting: Four Canon 580EX II speedlights off-camera set in RadioPopper Cubes and controlled manually in three different groups from camera position using the RadioPopper JrX system.

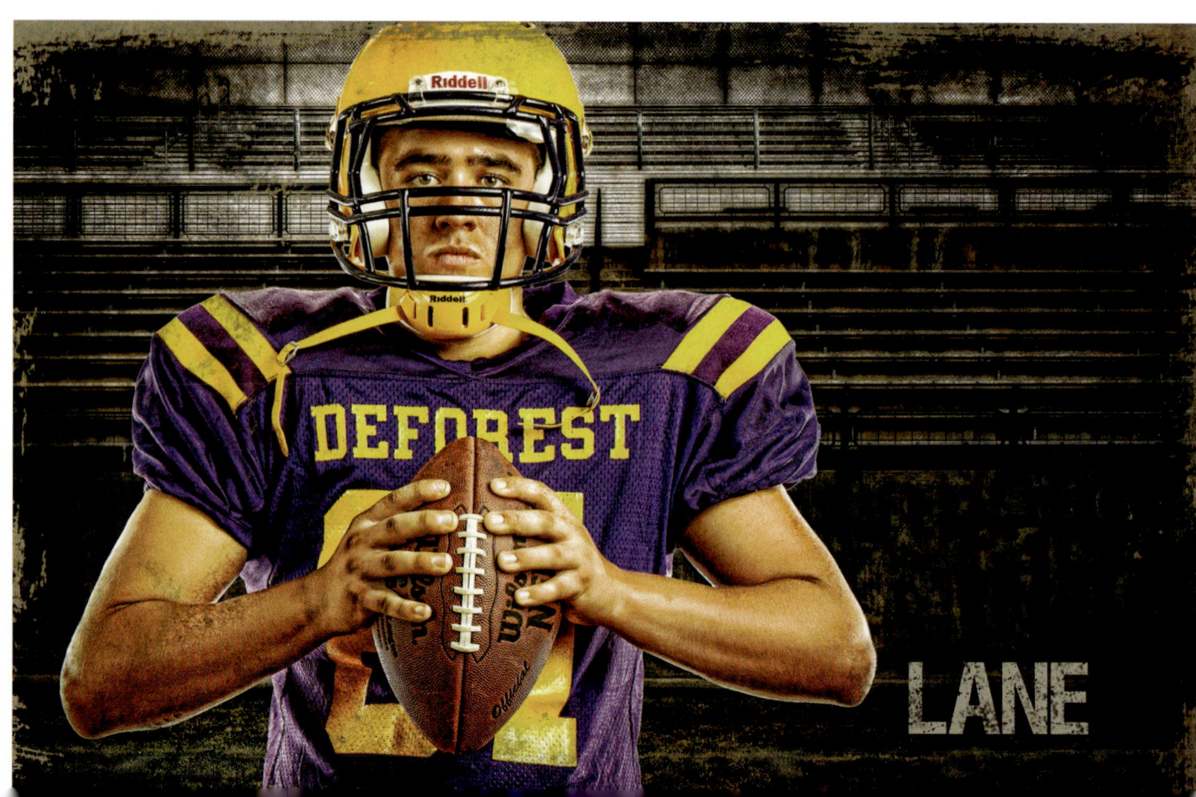

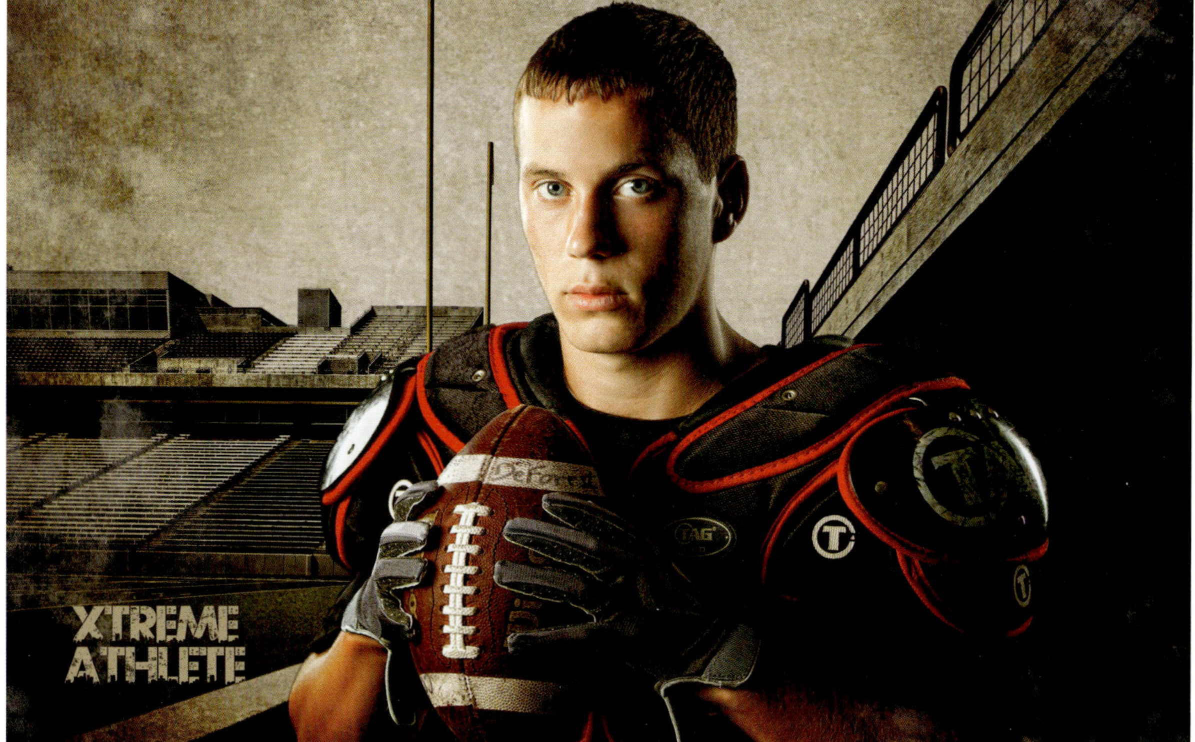

Postproduction

Extracting the subject is relatively easy using Photoshop's Quick Selection tool combined with the Refine Edge settings (Select > Refine Edge). There are also a number of stand-alone extraction programs available. The key is to achieve a clean, smooth extraction.

I open a blank document in Photoshop, drag in the chosen background as the base layer and then drag in the extracted client image onto an overlying layer. Then, I typically add a slight color wash on another layer to help unify the tone and color of the two underlying images. Next, I pump up the edginess by running my Topaz Adjust Lightroom plugin or Nik's Tonal Contrast filter on the composited image.

Often, I also add a texture screen overlay, being careful to mask any unsightly texture from the subject's skin. I also like to use a grunge

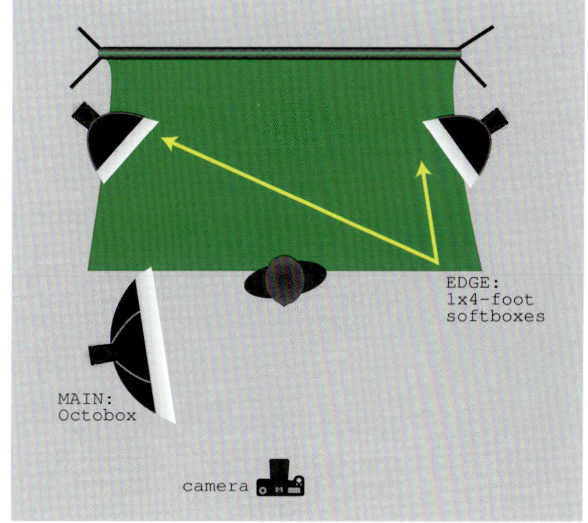

brush to add some interest at the edges of the frame, painting with a tone sampled from the image.

Products

The final composited image is perfect to finish off as a gallery-wrap canvas or a metal print (printed on a panel of aluminum).

Two Tips

1. Dramatic lighting that fits the chosen background is important.
2. Strong edge lighting will help you easily extract the client from the background.

Filling the Blues

More than half the battle outdoors

While I like to carve out dramatic lighting scenarios with my speedlights, sometimes all I need is a little fill to even out the scene. That was exactly the case here. The couple was silhouetted against a late evening sky and I needed to bring up their tonality to help separate them from the background and make them the primary subject of the photo.

I selected blue chairs from the nearby seating area to coordinate with the blue in the sky and to help direct the viewer to the couple.

Triple the Filling

I set up two off-camera speedlights on the dock about eight feet to my right. I also fired my on-camera flash as fill. The three speedlights combined to even out the light on the couple

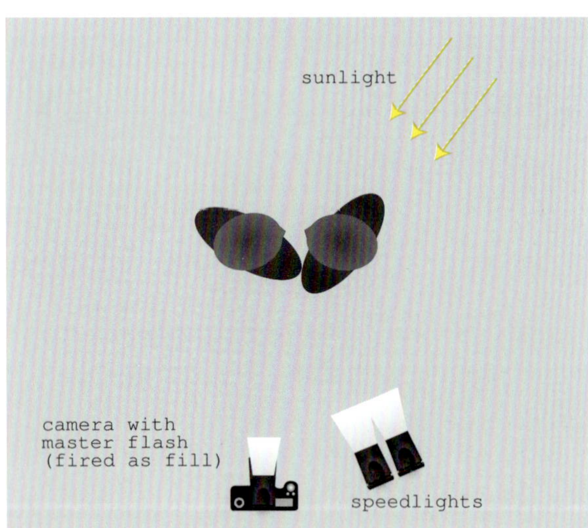

Camera: Canon 5D MKII with Canon 24–105L lens at 32mm

Exposure: $1/200$ second, f/16, ISO 100 (manual)

Lighting: Four Canon 580EX II speedlights off-camera set in RadioPopper Cubes and controlled manually in three different groups from camera position using the RadioPopper JrX system.

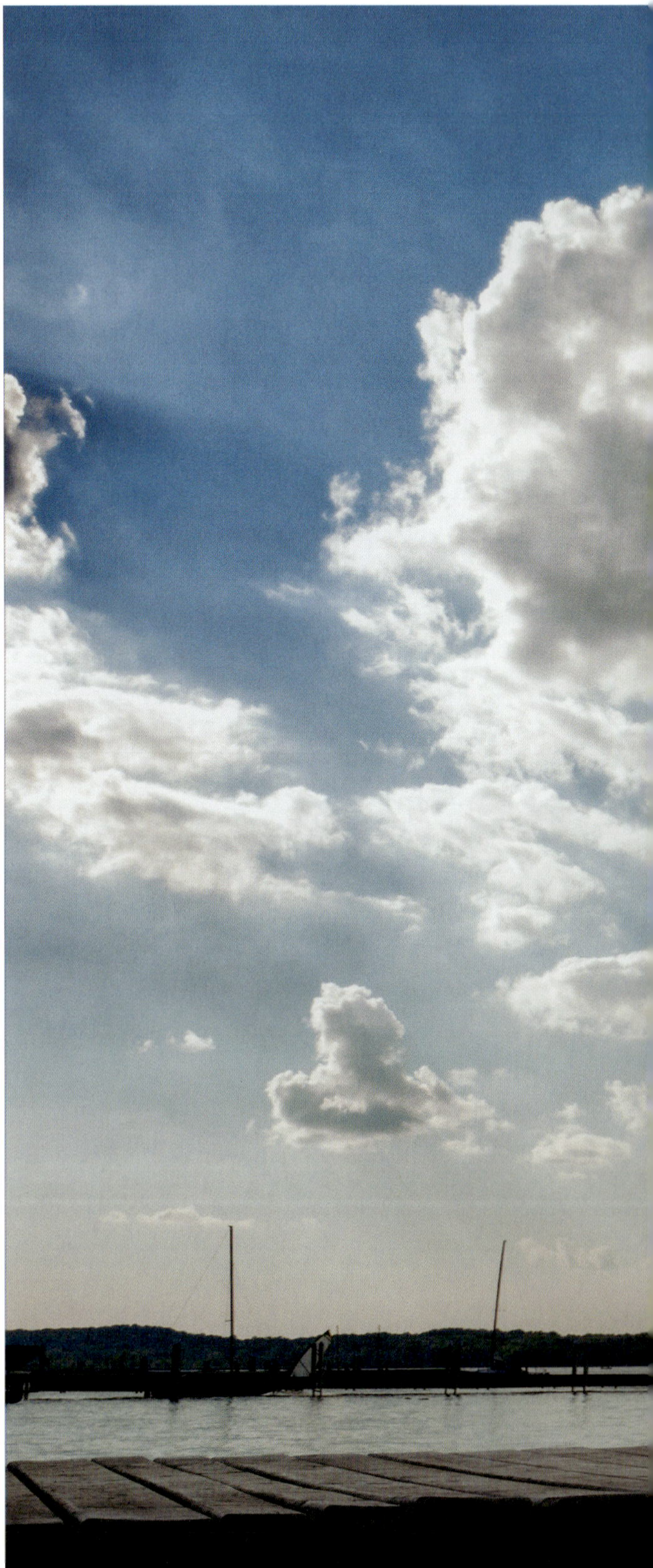

while maintaining the beautiful evening sky behind them.

The setup was nothing overly fancy, but not every image needs to be over-thought and over-produced. Simple is good, and this image has served well to draw couples to my work. I have featured it in my advertising on Wedding Wire and Facebook.

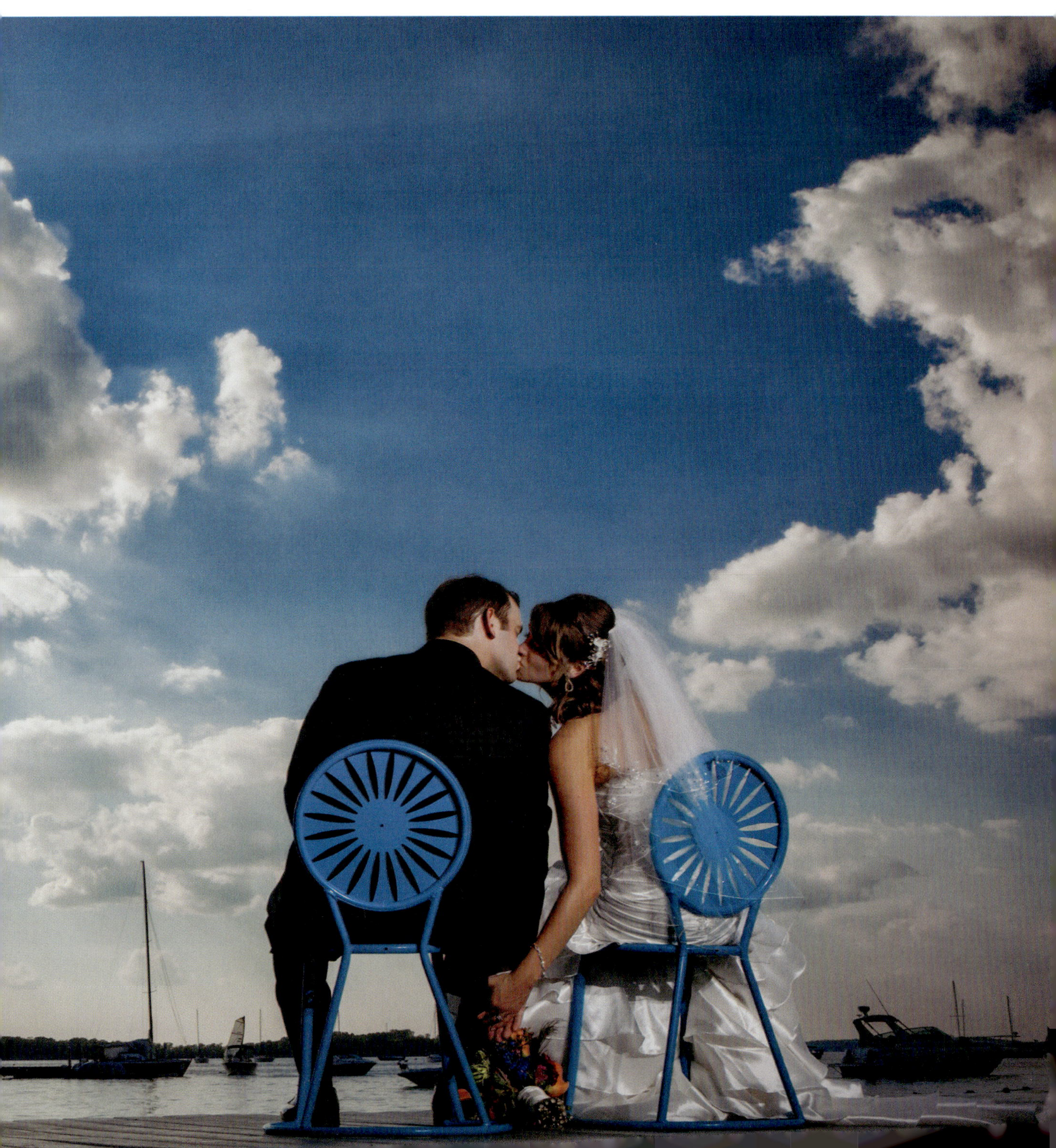

57

TTL Studio Portraits

Know TTL better by using it for everything

s I mentioned in the foreword to this book, I formally made the commitment to become a 99.99 percent speedlight studio in early 2011. At that time, I was already 99.99 percent speedlight for my on-location work. The real test was to commit to speedlights in the studio. This image is from that initial "test," which consisted of shooting an entire studio session using only TTL speedlights—no manual settings allowed.

Looking Up the Drama

The lighting was pretty simple for this image. I had one speedlight in a Creative Light 24-inch square softbox suspended on a boom over Sophie. I was seeking to create a simple, dramatic, almost noir-like portrait. The speedlight was set to eTTL in slave mode and triggered by an

> **"I was seeking to create a simple, dramatic, almost noir-like portrait."**

on-camera master flash, which was set to "not fire." Both flashes were augmented with the RadioPopper PX system to transmit the TTL information between the camera and the lights.

As I worked with TTL flash throughout the session, one nice benefit I discovered was that I could change my f-stop up and down to suit my creative vision and the TTL flashes would

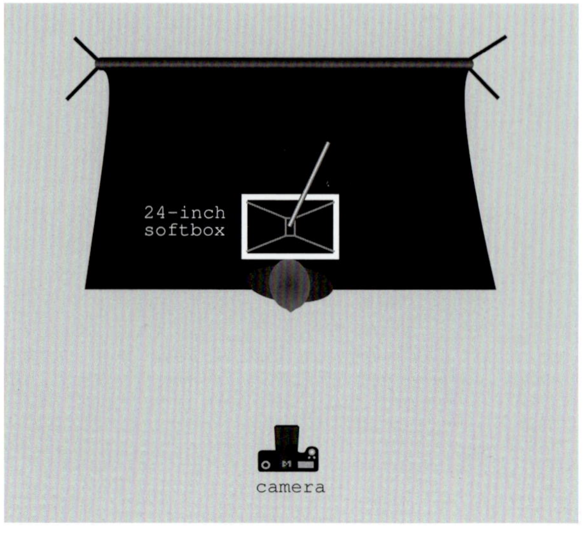

Camera: Canon 5D MKII with Canon 70–200L lens at 73mm
Exposure: $1/160$ second, f/5.6, ISO 250 (manual)
Lighting: One Canon 580EX II speedlight off-camera set to eTTL and slave mode, fired with RadioPopper PX receiver.

respond appropriately. I could shoot one image at f/4 and the next at f/8 without changing anything but my aperture setting. The system adapted on the fly.

Postproduction

The final image was processed in Lightroom using my Golden Crunch preset.

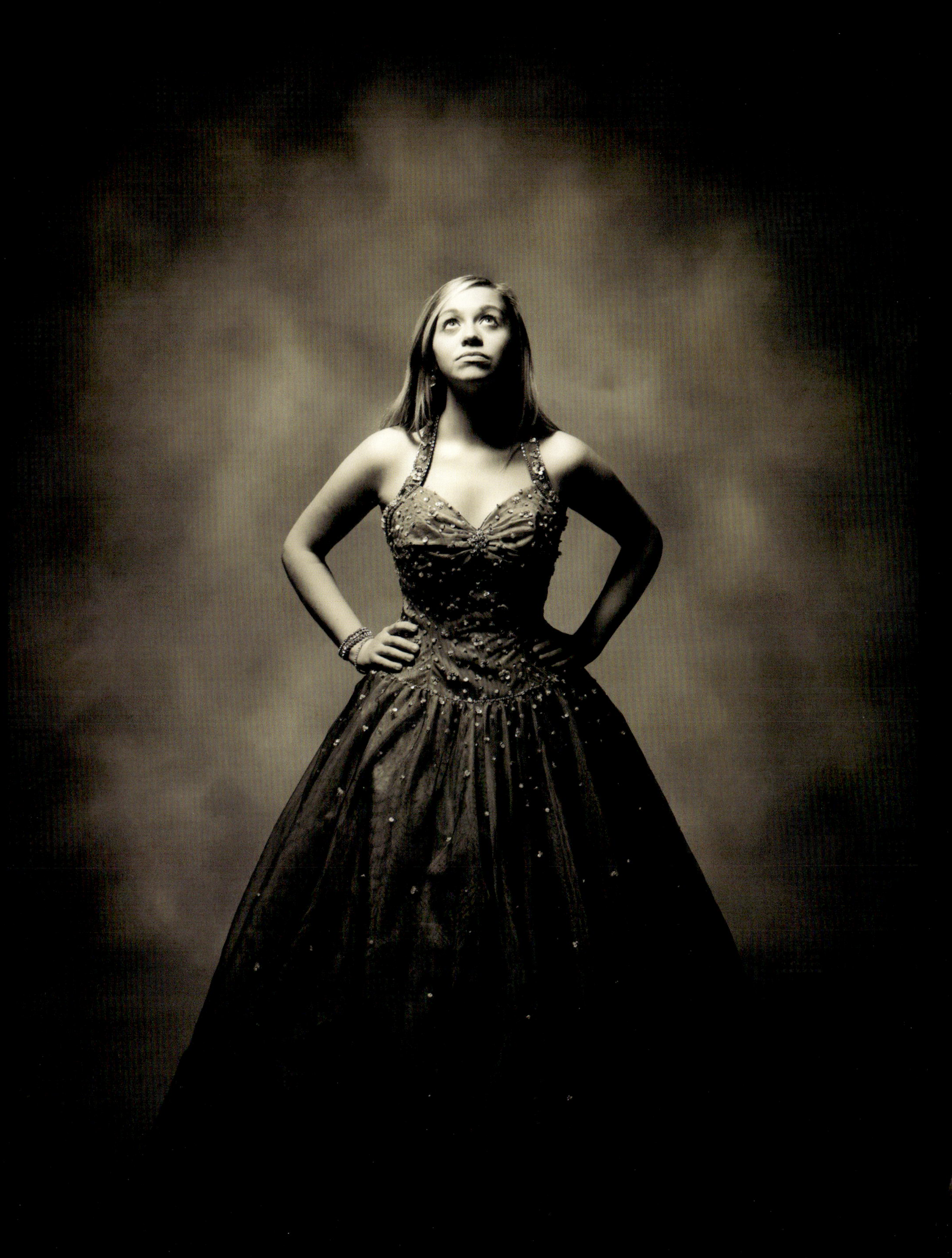

58

Smoking Hot Bass Riff

Creating a cool look for an aging rocker

Taryn has been playing bass in rock bands for over thirty years and wanted some new promo images. This gave me the perfect excuse to do some edgier lighting—and to bust out the fog machine, of course.

Foggy Portrait Break Down

I opted for split lighting, not a common choice for portraiture, to give Taryn's portrait an edge and a sense of mystery. This came from a Larson 48-inch Lightbender to camera right. I used my signature pair of 1x4-foot stripboxes behind and to either side of Taryn, cranking them up a little more than normal to get the strong rim light on her hair, jacket, and bass.

For this variation, I added more fog using a Woody Walters smoke brush, then punched up the color with my Topaz Adjust Lightroom effect.

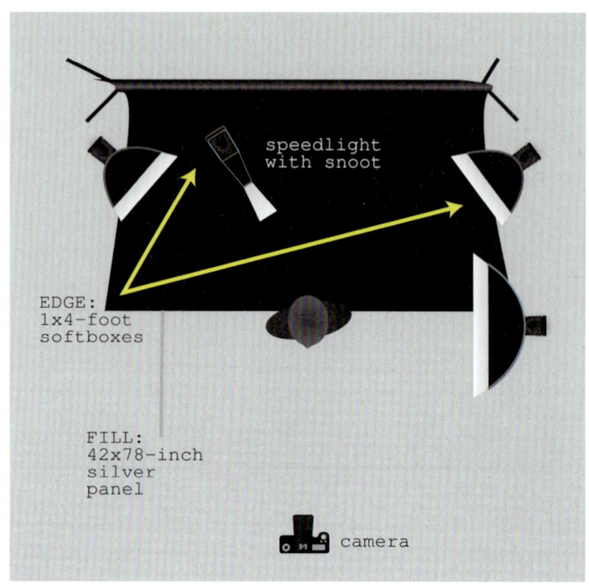

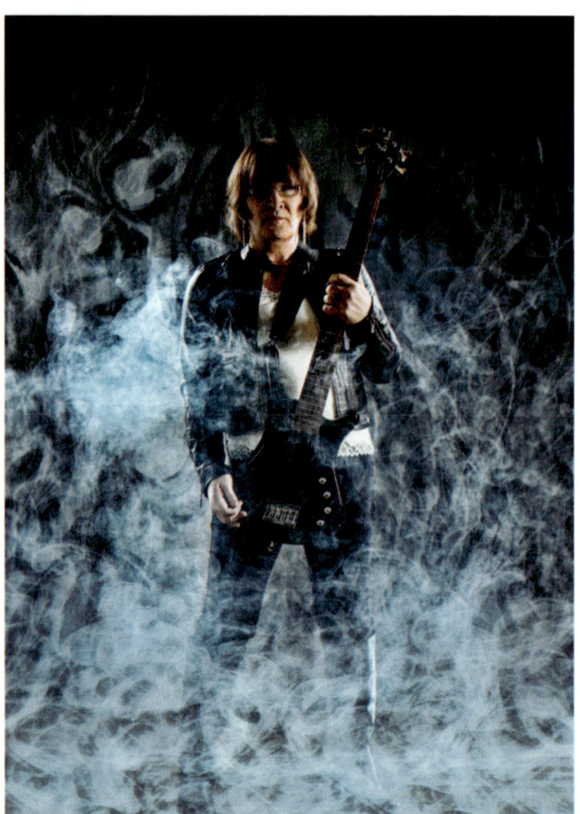

The fog also needed a light from behind to help it stand out, so I added a fourth speedlight on a stand behind Taryn to camera left. I outfitted this with a Strobies snoot to simulate stage lighting coming from behind.

Postproduction

Fog machines can be a little finicky. Most of the fog in this shot is real, but I did use a smoke brush in Photoshop to enhance it as needed. I finished off the image with my Topaz Adjust Psychedelic Lightroom plug-in, which seemed appropriate. It punched up the color and texture and gave the image more depth.

Camera: Canon 5D MKIII with Canon 70–200L lens at 78mm

Exposure: 1/160 second, f/5.6, ISO 250 (manual)

Lighting: Four Canon 580EX II speedlights off-camera set in RadioPopper Cubes and controlled manually in three different groups from camera position using the RadioPopper JrX system.

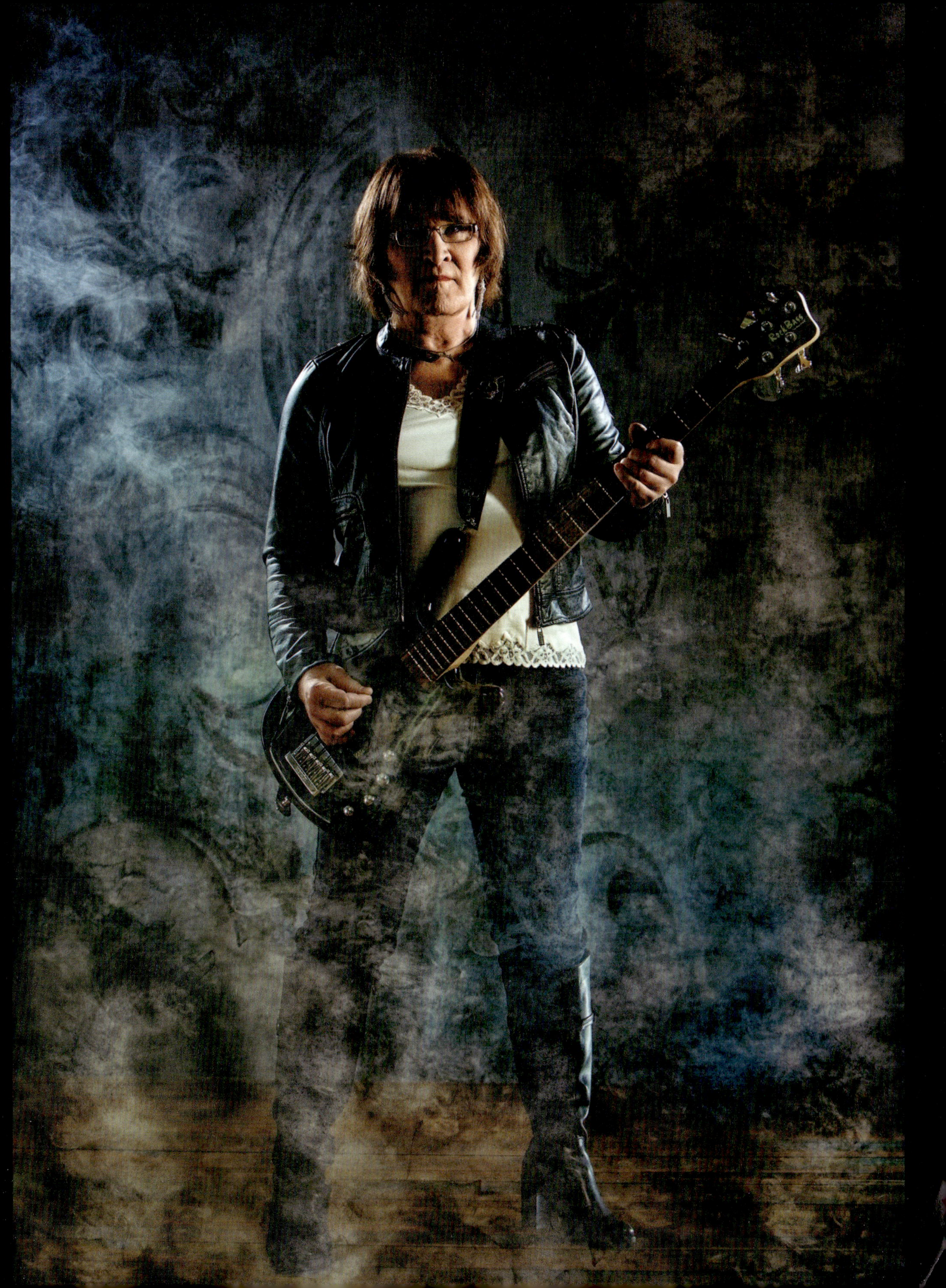

59

Going Commercial, Part 1

Complex lighting for a commercial project

Before I became a photographer, I was an executive at a mid-sized Midwestern ad agency. Those connections bring me a handful of commercial projects each year—such as this one for ARAMARK Refreshment Services.

Energized Lighting

The concept here was "Energized People." I needed to show a range of people in the work-place looking happy, energetic, and productive while drinking coffee (that's the hook). Time was of the essence and the budget wasn't large (what budget is?), so I worked with a friend/model/coordinator to get ten models booked quickly. Then, I located some vacant office space near my studio.

Space was tight, especially for group shots. Fortunately, speedlights don't take up much space; I used up to seven for some of the images. For the image on the facing page, I lit my primary model with four lights. A 50-inch Westcott Apollo to camera right was my main light. A 3.5x5.5-foot Larson softbox to camera left added fill. A Larson 48-inch Lightbender to camera left and above and behind the subject produced edge lighting, as did a Creative Light 1x4-foot stripbox to camera right and behind the subject. A 28-inch Westcott Apollo lit the workers in the back of the image. I blended the flash with the ambient light coming in from two

"It was vital for the speedlights to recycle quickly so I could maintain consistent lighting."

large windows at the back of the office, dropping my shutter speed to allow them to go to "white with detail" (zone 9 in the zone system). All the flashes were set manually and triggered with the RadioPopper JrX system. I wanted a rapid fall-off in depth of field, so I opted to shoot with an 85mm lens set at f/3.2.

Recycle Time

It was vital for the speedlights to recycle quickly so I could maintain consistent lighting as models moved through various looks. My first

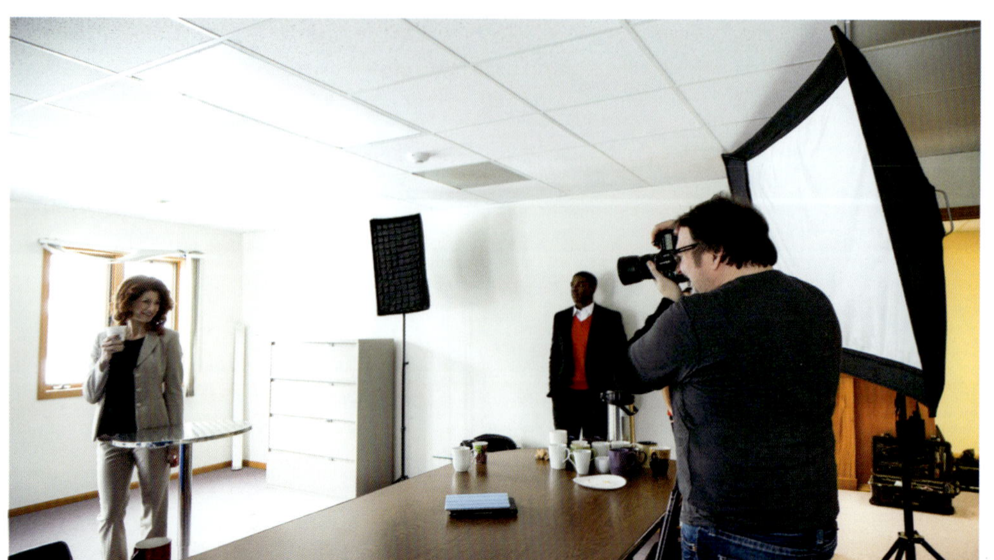

A pullback from one of the individual model photos during the session.

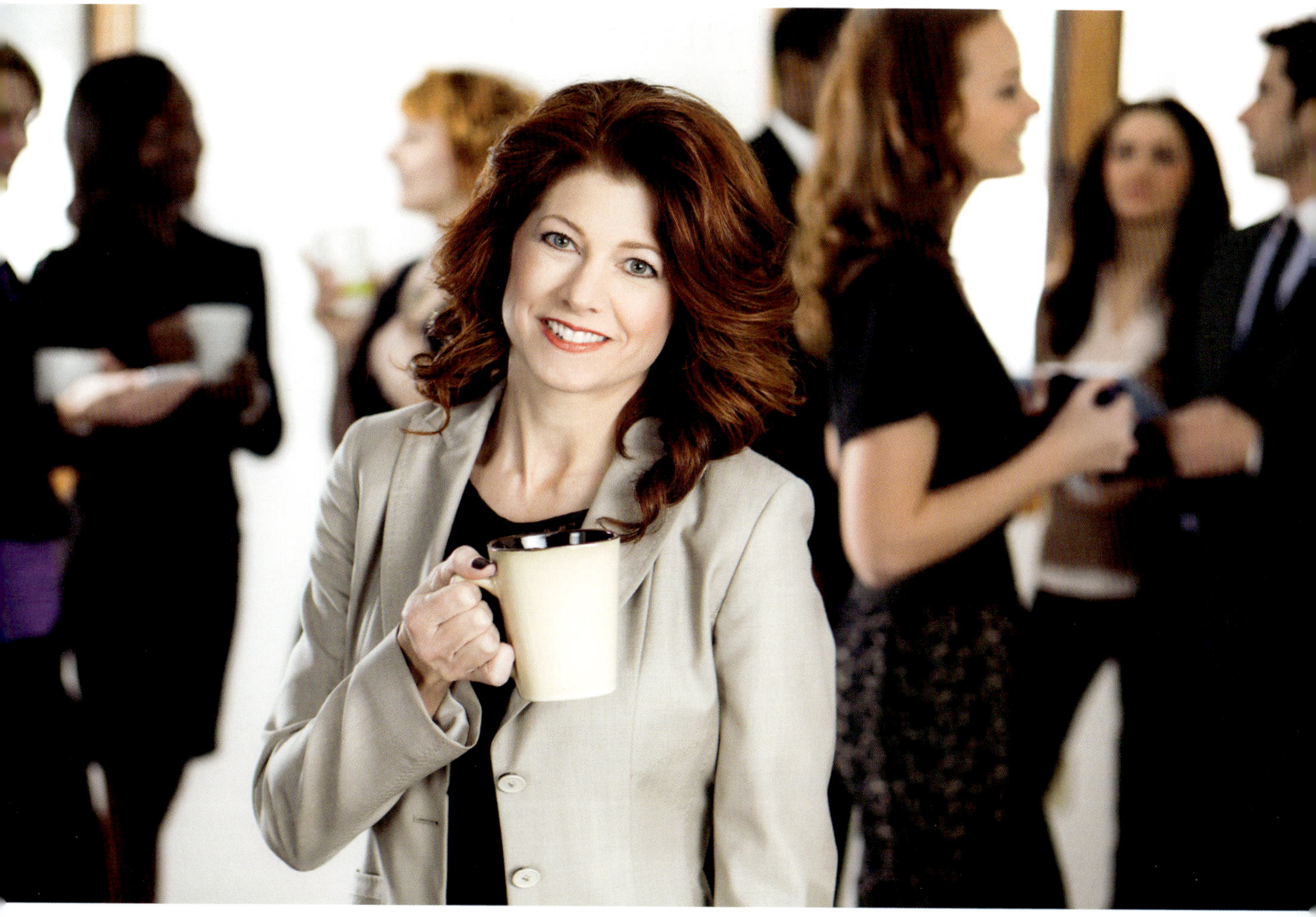

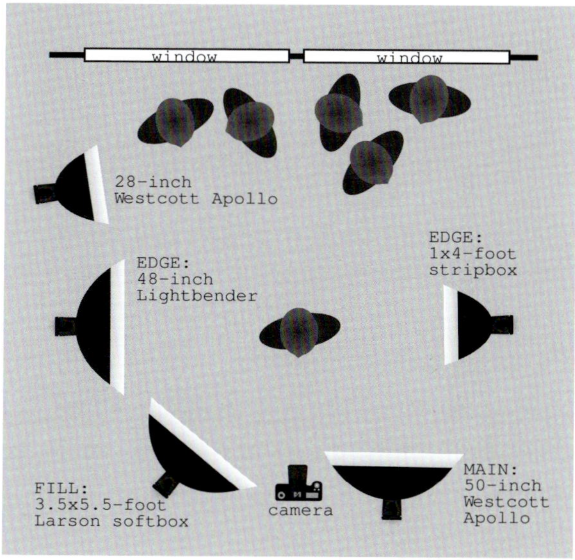

decision was to set all the speedlights to half the maximum power (many accent lights were set lower than this) to help with recycle time. In addition, each speedlight had an accessory battery power pack. My main and fill lights had the Nissin PS 300 power pack (which has since been replaced by the PS 8). These gave me recycle times of 1 second or less. The remaining speedlights had Canon CPE-4 battery packs or the generic equivalent from Pixel (the TD-381). I own several of these and have found them to be on par with the name-brand version.

Camera: Canon 5D MKIII, Canon 85mm f/1.8 lens
Exposure: $1/125$ second, f/3.2, ISO 500 (manual)
Lighting: Five to seven Canon 580EX II speedlights off-camera set manually from $1/8$ to $1/2$ power, triggered with the RadioPopper JrX system.

60

Going Commercial, Part 2

Green screening for maximum flexibility

After shooting on location for most of the day, we quickly packed up and reset back at the studio for some green-screen images.

Versatility

I had suggested green-screen images to the client because our goal was to build a library of photography that could be used for catalogs, sales sheets, and other marketing materials in the future. In essence, we were producing our own custom stock library. The green screen would allow us to drop in different backgrounds. Need to show someone working at a car dealership? Drop in that background.

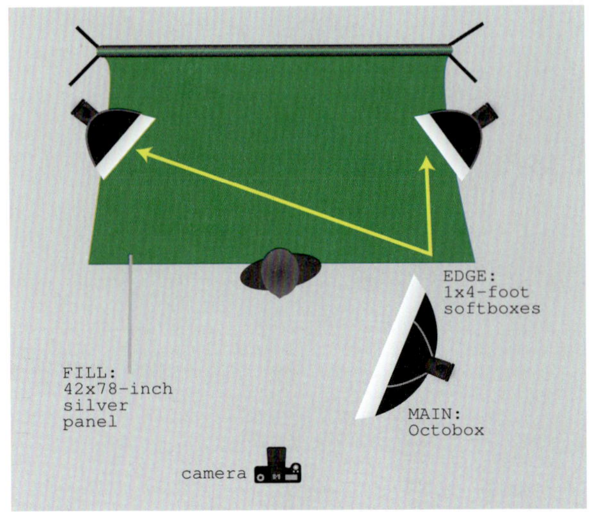

Kill the Spill

When using a green screen, it is important to limit or eliminate spill from the green background. This can cause weird green color casts on your subject. To do this, make sure that you pull your subject off of the background; keep at least a 6-foot separation between him and the background. Also, be sure to use edge lighting to help define the perimeter of your subject.

Targeting a sales sheet to a hotel chain? Drop in a hotel lobby or commons area.

Postproduction

Green screens can be removed rather simply using Photoshop, or a number of plug-ins or other software such as Topaz ReMask.

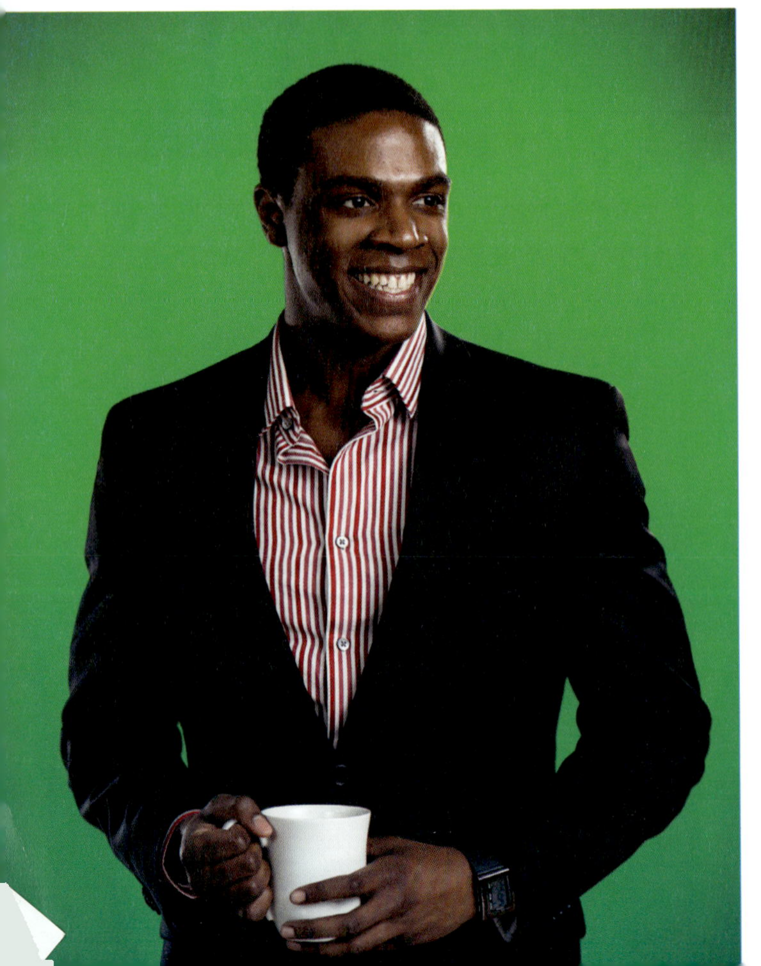

Camera: Canon 5D MKIII, Canon 85mm f/1.8 lens
Exposure: $1/160$ second, f/4, ISO 100 (manual)
Lighting: Canon 580EX II speedlights off-camera controlled and triggered with the RadioPopper JrX system using Radio-Popper Cubes.

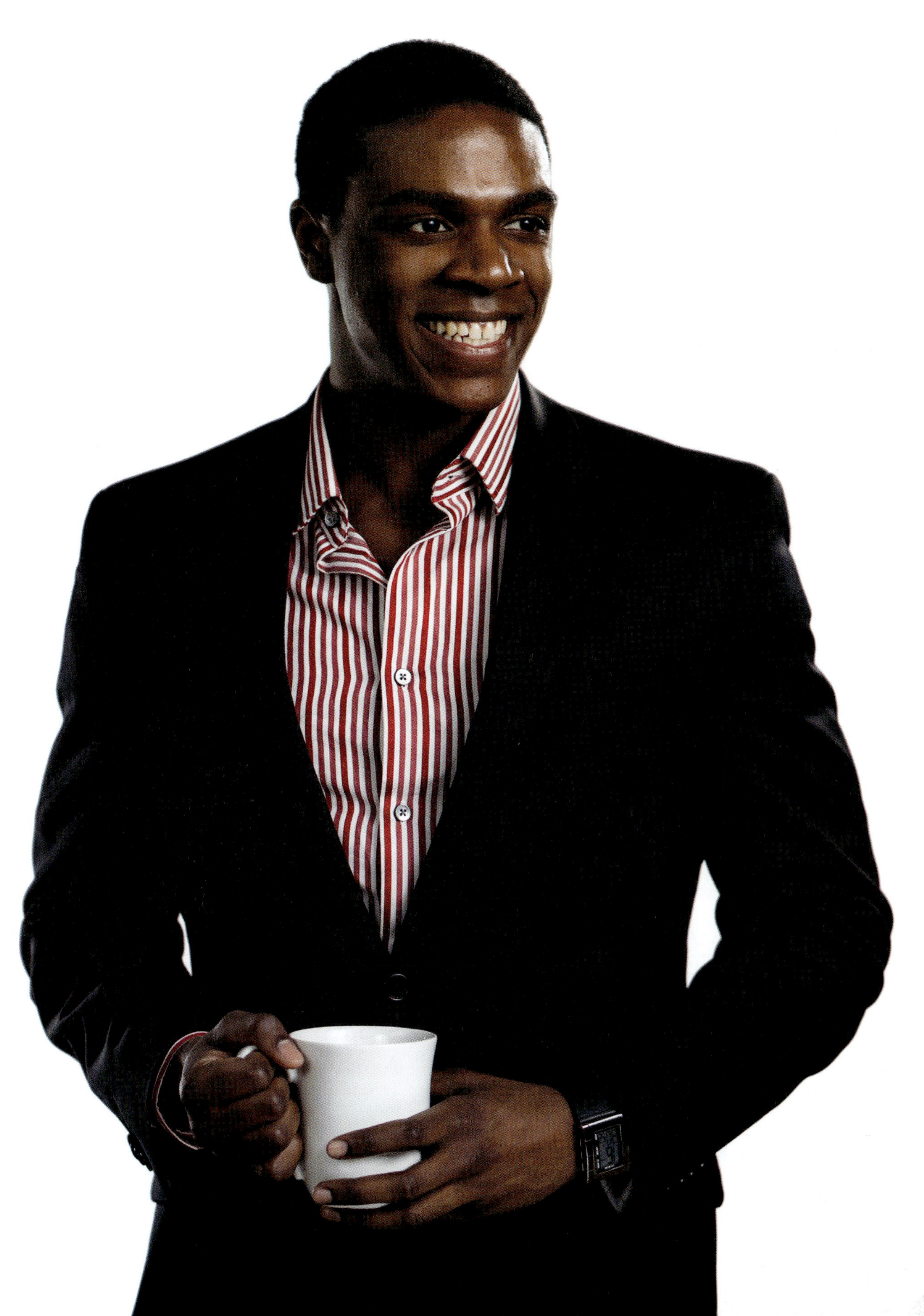

Conclusion

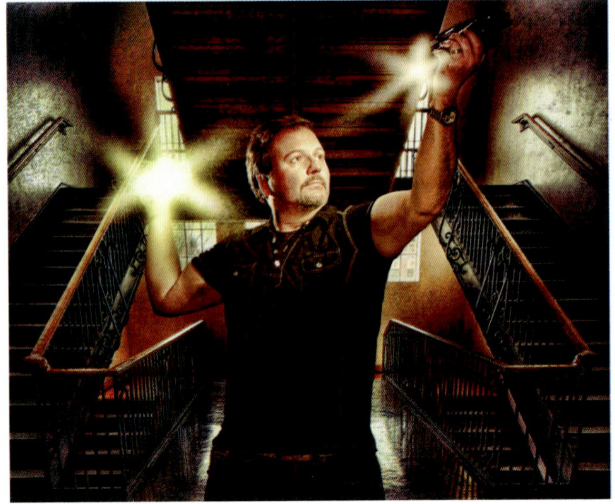

I hope that I have inspired you to use your speedlight flashes in new and creative ways. And, I have hopefully dispelled the myth that a speedlight flash is not an "appropriate" tool to use to light a portrait. It's a quality light source like anything else in your arsenal; understand how it works and how to use it properly and you can use a speedlight to light virtually any type of portrait. Follow the guidelines I set down in this book and soon you, too, could become a Flash Fu master!

Acknowledgments

I dedicate this book to my lovely wife, Lisa, and my wonderful children, Brianna and Patrick. Thank you for being so supportive as I chase down the winding path of this crazy but rewarding career. A special shout out goes to my wonderful assistants and lighting monkeys over the past few years who help me create what I want and take direction flawlessly: Krystal Lamberty, Olivia Linden, Rachel Waldmer, Callie Strouf, Allison Halkey, and Brianna Mowbray.

Sponsors

Special thanks to my sponsors: American Color Imaging (www.acilab.com) and Nissin Flashes USA (www.nissindigital.com).

References

Cameras

Canon | www.canonusa.com
Nikon | www.nikon.com

Lenses

Canon | www.canonusa.com
Sigma | www.sigmaphoto.com

Light Modifiers

Calumet | www.calumetphoto.com
Creative Light | www.creativelight.com
Denny Manufacturing | www.dennymfg.com
Firefly | www.aurora-store.com
Kacey Enterprises | www.kaceyenterprises.com
Larson | www.larson-ent.com
Larry Peters Eyelighter | www.theeyelighter.com
Larry Peters Lightbender | www.larson-ent.com
Photek | www.photekusa.com
RPS Lighting | www.rpsstudiolighting.com
Snootzie | www.michaelmowbray.com
Strobies | www.interfitphotographic.com
Westcott | www.fjwestcott.com

Organizations

Fuji Masterpiece Awards | www.fujifilmusa.com
Kodak Gallery Awards | www.kodak.com
Mid-American Institute of
   Professional Photographers
   (MAIPP) | www.maipp.com
Professional Photographers Association
   (PPA) | www.ppa.com

Software

Adobe® Photoshop® | www.adobe.com
Adobe® Lightroom® | www.adobe.com
Imagenomic | www.imagenomic.com
Preset-O-Rama Collection
   | www.michaelmowbray.com
Nik Color Efex Pro | www.niksoftware.com
Streetscape Backgrounds
   | www.streescapebackgrounds.com
Textureland Texture Screens
   | www.michaelmowbray.com
Topaz Adjust | www.topazlabs.com
Topaz ReMask | www.topazlabs.com
Woody Walters Digital Photo Candy
   | www.woodywaltersdigitalphotocandy.com

Speedlights

Canon | www.canonusa.com
Nikon | www.nikon.com
Nissin | www.nissindigital.com
Quantum | www.qtm.com

Speedlight Communication

Canon | www.canonusa.com
Nikon | www.nikon.com
Paul Buff | www.paulcbuff.com
RadioPopper | www.radiopopper.com
PocketWizard | www.pocketwizard.com

Index

A

Accent light, 22, 26, 29, 96, 126–27, 153. *See also* Edge light *and* Hair light
Adobe Lightroom, 34, 49, 51, 55, 68, 69, 77, 79, 83, 85, 109, 111, 124, 129, 131, 133, 138, 145, 148, 150 *See also* Postproduction
Adobe Photoshop, 41, 49, 69, 90, 96, 109, 114, 131, 143, 145, 150, 154. *See also* Postproduction.
AlienBees, 27, 40, 61
Ambient light, 13–18, 29, 32, 41, 43, 50, 63, 67, 68, 76, 83, 84–85, 86, 98, 102, 107, 122, 124, 126–27, 128, 135, 137
Aperture. *See* Depth of field
Aperture-priority mode, 70, 76, 78, 98, 102, 107, 112

B

Background, 12, 14–15, 26, 28, 32, 36, 43, 47, 48–49, 60, 63, 65, 71, 74–75, 78, 80, 88, 90, 94, 96, 98, 101, 109, 110, 116, 118, 124, 126–28, 138, 140, 142–46, 154
Background light, 26, 74, 75, 90, 100, 124
Backlight, 13, 34, 72, 76
Bare speedlight, 14, 23–24, 44, 74, 94, 100–101, 128, 136
Beauty dish, 26, 27, 38–39, 74–75, 110
Beauty lighting, 27, 38–39, 56, 82 83, 110–11
Benefits of speedlights, 9
Bokeh, 15, 29
Boom, 74, 81, 90, 148
Bounce flash, 29, 38, 84–85
Business portraits, 134–35
Butterfly lighting, 83

C

Calumet, 61, 79
Canon camera, 9, 32, 35, 38, 41, 43–154
Canon flash, 9, 10, 15–21, 26–29, 32–38, 39, 43, 44, 46–86, 89–154
Canon flash controller, 20–22, 96, 102

Canon power pack, 27
Catchlights, 38–39, 74, 90, 102, 110, 122
Chromakey, 144–45, 154–55
Clamshell lighting, 80–81
Color cast, 14, 85, 102–3, 122, 126–27, 135, 154
Commercial portraits, 152–55
Contrast, 26, 35, 36, 43, 45, 46, 49, 51, 55, 61, 75, 77, 84, 93, 96, 104, 110, 118, 145. *See also* Light ratio
Creative Light, 26, 27, 38, 61, 74, 78, 79, 80, 90, 110, 148, 152
CTO. *See* Gel, color

D

Dappled light, 100–101
Denny Manufacturing, 95
Depth of field, 15, 17–19, 28, 51, 58, 63, 71, 76, 78, 88, 98, 136, 150, 152
Diffuser cap, 29
Diffusion, 24, 26, 27, 29, 35, 38, 56, 94, 95, 109, 110, 117, 128–29
Distance of light to subject, 20, 22, 23–26, 95, 100–101, 113
Double speedlights. *See* Gangs

E

Edge light, 13, 22, 26–29, 39, 45, 55, 63, 74–75, 78, 82, 90, 110, 116, 118, 131, 134–35, 138, 143, 145, 152, 154 *See also* Accent light *and* Hair light
Egg-crate grid. *See* Grid
Exposure compensation, 12, 16–18, 50, 71, 76, 98, 102, 107, 112. *See also* Flash exposure compensation
Exposure metering, 12–17
Exposure mode, 16, 19
Exposure value (EV), 14, 16-18, 76, 77, 85, 98, 101, 102, 112, 122, 126

F

Fill light, 14–15, 22, 26–29, 36, 39, 48–50, 54, 65, 73–75, 78, 86, 95, 102, 104, 113, 114, 120, 124, 131, 134–35, 137, 138, 140, 143, 146–47, 152, 153

Firefly, 82–83, 104–5, 108–9
Flare, 34, 45, 73, 137
Flash communication, 20–22 *See also* RadioPopper *and* PocketWizard adjustment from camera, 20–22 groups. *See* Group, flash infrared, 20 radio, 20–21
Flash exposure compensation (FEC), 16, 18, 71, 76, 77, 96, 102, 122, 129
Flash output, 16
Flash-sync speed, 15, 17, 18–19 *See also* High-speed flash sync

G

Gangs, 16, 18, 42–43, 50–51, 54–55, 58–59, 64–65, 68–73, 76–77, 83, 86–87, 94–95, 98–101, 112–13, 116–25, 128–29, 136–39, 146–47
Gel, color, 124–27
Green screen, 144–45, 154–55
Grid, 27, 38, 61, 74, 79, 80, 90, 110
Group, flash, 22, 26–27, 34, 35, 45, 75, 90, 104, 106, 109, 110, 117, 118, 124, 126, 139, 140, 142, 144, 146, 150

H

Hair light, 26, 27, 39, 60–61, 101
Hard light, 23–25
High-speed flash sync (HSS/FP), 15, 18–19, 36, 51, 52, 58, 68, 76, 100, 112

I

Imagenomic, 75–79
Indoor portraits, location, 32–34, 82–85, 104–5, 108–9, 116–17, 124–29, 132–35, 152–53
ISO setting, 16, 17, 43, 63, 85, 109, 137

K

Kacey Enterprises, 27, 38, 74, 110

L

Larson, 26, 27, 61, 74, 78, 79, 80, 90, 131, 142, 150, 152
Lens flare. *See* Flare

Lens selection, 29, 46, 48–49, 50, 58–59, 63, 95, 98, 152
Lighting kits, 26–29
Light ratio, 26, 34, 45, 54, 63, 74, 75, 90, 109, 124, 138
Lightroom. *See* Adobe Lightroom
Light stand, 34, 36, 43, 44, 46, 54, 67, 70–71, 74, 81, 83, 114, 133, 140, 150
Location portraits. *See* Indoor portraits *and* Outdoor portraits
Lumedyne, 40

M
Main light, 22, 26–29, 34, 38, 45, 54–55, 60, 61, 63, 74–75, 78, 86, 104, 109, 110, 124, 127, 131, 134–35, 138, 140, 143, 152, 153
Manual mode, 16, 19, 88, 137, 140
Metering, 12–17, 21, 22, 71, 88, 112, 135, 137, 140

N
Nik Color Efex Pro, 36, 43, 45
Nikon, 9, 10, 15, 18, 20–22, 76, 89, 117, 130
Night portraits, 62–63, 114–15, 126–27, 140–41. *See also* Sunset
Nissin, 9, 19, 26–28, 89–91, 92–93, 130–31, 153

O
Octobox, 23, 26, 27, 61, 143
Off-camera flash, 13, 18, 20, 21, 28, 29, 34, 36, 40, 41, 43, 50, 53, 58, 63, 65, 68, 70–71, 73, 86, 95, 96, 98, 102, 112, 113, 117, 120, 122, 136, 137, 146
On-camera flash, 16, 18, 28–29, 36, 40, 49, 50, 54, 58, 65, 73, 86, 90, 95, 104, 113, 120, 124, 137, 138, 140, 146, 148
Outdoor portraits, 35–37, 40–55, 58–59, 62–73, 76–77, 86–88, 92–103, 106–7, 112–15, 118–23, 136–41, 146–47
Output, flash. *See* Power, flash
Overcast days, 14, 34, 35, 36, 43, 46, 50, 86, 92, 96, 102, 118

P
Parabolic, 26, 131
Paul C. Buff, 41

Photek, 26
Photoshop. *See* Adobe Photoshop
PocketWizard, 21
Posing, 24, 35, 36, 42, 46, 48, 50, 53, 54, 61, 63, 65, 72, 82–83, 86, 94, 96, 98, 102, 106, 109, 118, 127, 132–33, 138, 140, 143, 144
Postproduction, 19, 34, 36, 41, 43, 45, 46, 47, 49, 55, 67, 68, 75, 77, 79, 85, 95, 96, 104, 107, 109, 110, 114, 120, 124, 129, 131, 138–39, 143, 144–45, 148, 150, 154 *See also* Adobe Lightroom *and* Adobe Photoshop
Power, flash, 16, 18, 19, 22, 26–29, 39, 40–41, 43, 56, 58, 75, 77, 95, 90, 100, 122, 128, 131, 135, 137, 153
Power pack, 26–28, 40, 153

Q
Quality of light, 23–25
Quantum, 40–41

R
Raccoon-eye effect, 35, 96
RadioPopper, 19, 20–22
Rain, 32–34, 42–43, 46-47, 118–19
Ratio. *See* Light ratio
Recycle time, 26–28, 152–53
Reflector, 14, 35, 38–39, 60–61, 78–79, 80–81, 90, 94, 96, 110, 128
Rembrandt lighting, 82–83

S
Scrim, 96, 128
Senior portraits, 28–29, 60–61, 76–77, 80–81, 94–95, 106-7, 110, 120–21, 144–45
Separation, 39, 43, 45, 60, 63, 101, 109, 118
Shade, 28, 44, 65, 68, 94, 114, 136, 138
Shutter curtains, 18
Shutter-priority mode, 16
Silk. *See* Scrim
Sigma, 59
Snoot, 34, 45, 53, 104, 107, 109, 116, 124, 132–33, 138, 150
Snootzie, 34, 45, 53, 104, 107, 109, 116, 124, 132–33, 138
Softbox, 20, 21, 24, 27–29, 56, 60, 74, 78, 80–81, 94–95, 109, 128, 131, 134, 142, 148, 152. *See also* Octobox

and Stripbox
Soft light, 23–25
Speedring, 26, 38, 61, 74, 79, 80, 110
Spiky sun technique, 13, 15, 19, 58–59, 98
Spill, 154
Split lighting, 78–79
Spread of light. *See* Zoom, flash
Stripbox, 27, 60–61, 74, 78, 90, 92–93, 110, 131, 134–35, 143, 150, 152
Strobies, 90, 150
Studio portraits, 38–39, 56–57, 60–61, 74–75, 78–81, 89–91, 110–11, 130–31, 142–45, 148–51, 154–55
Subtractive lighting, 16, 96, 98
Sunlight, 9, 13–15, 17, 19–20, 23, 28, 35–37, 41, 44–45, 48–49, 52–55, 58–59, 64–65, 68–73, 76, 78, 84, 94–95, 98, 112–13, 122, 123, 128, 136–37
Sunset, 41, 62–63, 70–71, 112–13

T
TTL, 12–17, 19–21, 28, 29, 34, 39, 43, 45, 51, 62, 71, 76, 85, 86, 90, 92, 102, 112, 122, 134, 137, 148
Tungsten, 114–15, 126–27, 135

U
Umbrella, 24, 26, 27, 56, 83, 86, 94, 128, 131, 134

V
Vignette, 71, 95

W
Wedding photography, 9, 29, 32, 35, 40–55, 62–69, 72–73, 94–95, 108–9, 112–13, 140–41, 146–47
Westcott, 24, 26, 27, 28, 56, 57, 92, 93, 134–35, 152
White balance, 126–67
Window light, 28, 32, 34, 82–83, 84–85, 109, 124, 152

X
X-sync speed. *See* Flash-sync speed

Z
Zoom, flash, 100–101, 116–17, 124, 132